B O O K S
Day by Day

ANNIVERSARIES, ANECDOTES, AND ACTIVITIES

SUSAN OHANIAN

HEINEMANN
Portsmouth, NH

Heinemann

A division of Reed Elsevier Inc.

361 Hanover Street

Portsmouth, NH 03801–3912

www.heinemann.com

Offices and agents throughout the world

Library of Congress Cataloging-in-Publication Data

Ohanian, Susan.

  Books day by day : anniversaries, anecdotes, and activities / Susan Ohanian.

    p. cm.

  Includes index.

  ISBN 0-325-00331-9

  1. Literature—Study and teaching (Elementary)—Activity programs. 2. Children—Books and reading. 3. Anniversaries. I. Title

  LB1575 .O43 2001

  372.4—dc21   2001039314

Editor: Lois Bridges

Production: Vicki Kasabian

Cover design: Jenny Jensen Greenleaf

Manufacturing: Louise Richardson

Printed in the United States of America on acid-free paper

05 04 03 02 01 ML 1 2 3 4 5

For Gloria Pipkin and the magic of discovering an e-mail soul sister

CONTENTS

Introduction . . . . *vii*

JANUARY *1*

FEBRUARY *22*

MARCH *42*

APRIL *67*

MAY *91*

JUNE *116*

JULY *136*

AUGUST *156*

SEPTEMBER *179*

OCTOBER *203*

NOVEMBER *225*

DECEMBER *249*

Subject Index *273*

Author Index *275*

❶NTRODUCTION

With this book at your elbow, any school day can include a brief literary celebration. Each entry, whether historical or contemporary, sophisticated or silly, provides a moment or two of literate illumination. Some entries feature books children are likely to read; others are about literary figures largely unread by children but who are nonetheless an interesting part of our artistic landscape. Recurring themes are the power of art, the importance of beautiful books in the lives of children, and the value drawing has as part of literary and artistic development.

Following many of the entries are reading and writing tips, word games, etymological discussions, spelling hints, and suggestions for close observation, research, and rewriting. Special emphasis is given to the pleasure a writer takes in reading.

Each entry is brief—no author or illustrator or event is given enough space. But teachers and children take celebrations where they can; brief is better than none at all. The books recommended for further reading are not intended to be definitive, and they are by no means a necessary part of the suggested celebration. They are books I happen to have in my collection. A particular title is meant to prod you to find if not that book, then another book. Remember: librarians and libraries are your best resource. Some recommended books are out of print, but most libraries are stuffed with books no longer available for purchase. I commend to you the seldom-used and wonderful resource of interlibrary loan, which makes the world your oyster.

The most important thread running through this book is that different people love different books. Everything from comic books to Shakespeare is honored, but the message comes through that more writers and illustrators have fond memories of Peter Rabbit and *Mad* magazine than they do of *Silas Marner* or even Shakespeare. Garrison Keillor reminds us that we may go through life without using mathematics, but if we learn how to tell a joke, the skill will serve us all our life.

Carl Sandburg once said, "Ordering a man to write a poem is like commanding a pregnant woman to give birth to a red-headed child. You can't do it—it's an act of God." This is why I offer the activities as possibilities. For me, "Have the student do thus-and-so" is an abomination, not to mention an impossibility. Instead, I offer this book as an invitation and suggest you use it as such with your students.

In accepting the 1993 Newbery Medal for *The Giver,* Lois Lowry reminded us that "each time a child opens a book, he pushes open the gate that separates him from Elsewhere. It gives him choices. It gives him freedom." I hope this book offers plenty of choices.

JANUARY

I'm the most terrific liar you ever saw in your life.

J. D. Salinger,
The Catcher in the Rye

BIRTHDAY

1919 J. D. Salinger is born, in New York City. His most famous work is *The Catcher in the Rye*, published in 1951. About the time *The Catcher in the Rye* is published, Salinger moves to rural Cornish, New Hampshire, where he has lived in near seclusion ever since. In the late 1970s he tells a *Boston Globe* reporter, "I love to write, but I write for myself and I want to be left absolutely alone to do it." *The Catcher in the Rye* is credited with having inspired the young adult novel genre and continues to sell about half a million copies a year. Humorist Dave Barry remembers reading it in junior high, recalling it is "the first real book that spoke to me."

EVENT

1660 Samuel Pepys, an English clerk in the navy office, begins the diary that has been called the greatest diary in the English language. Writing in code so that no one else can read it, Pepys chronicles events in and around London for nine years, until failing eyesight forces him to stop.

▶ **WORD FUN** Secret codes fascinate children (and quite a few adults). Write a sentence in simple alphabetic substitution code on the board, challenging students to solve it. Then talk about how what they know about how language works helped them solve it.

JANUARY

Science fiction is modern fairy tales.

Isaac Asimov

BIRTHDAYS

1906 Simms Campbell is born, in St. Louis, Missouri. He is the first African-American cartoonist to publish work regularly in general circulation magazines. Campbell works as a railroad dining car waiter, drawing cartoons of passengers. After studying at the Art Institute in Chicago, he moves to New York City, working in advertising. He becomes *Esquire* magazine's foremost cartoonist.

▶ **ART TIP** Invite students to bring in a favorite cartoon—so they can compare different methods for portraying people. Invite students to try imitating a style they like.

1920 Isaac Asimov is born, in Petrovichi, Russia. When he is three, his family moves to Brooklyn, New York. Often called the most prolific American writer, Isaac writes and edits nearly 500 books. In 1984, when interviewed by *Life* magazine after he had written 289 books, Isaac says, "If my doctor told me I had only six minutes to live, I wouldn't brood. I'd type a little faster." His trilogy, *Foundation*, *Foundation and Empire*, and *Second Foundation*, is considered the cornerstone of science fiction.

1932 Jean Little is born, in Taiwan, with scarred corneas that severely impair her vision. Jean lives in Canada, writes with a voice-activated computer, and travels with her Seeing Eye dog, Zephyr.

▶ **WRITING TIP** Jean offers this advice to children who like to write. "The single most important thing that I have done to help myself become an able writer is to read."

3

If more of us valued food and cheer and song above hoarded gold, it would be a merrier world.

J. R. R. Tolkien,
The Hobbit

BIRTHDAY

1892 J(ohn) R(onald) R(euel) Tolkien is born, in Bloemfrontein, South Africa. Three years later, his family moves to England. Before becoming a professor at Oxford University, he works for two years as a staff writer on the *Oxford English Dictionary*. *The Hobbit* grows out of stories Tolkien tells his children, and in 1938, it is named best book published for children. *The Lord of the Rings* appears seventeen years later.

▶ **READING REFLECTION** When a friend "confesses" that she doesn't care for *The Hobbit*, Harper & Row editor Ursula Nordstrom admits, "It is one of the several books I have tried my best to read but I simply could never get in to it and I have had to hide my shame, but now I can admit it in view of the fact that I will have your distinguished company." This is an important realization for students: different people love different books. You don't have to like them all.

EVENT

2000 The last "Peanuts" daily comic strip appears in 2,600 newspapers, reaching an estimated 355 million readers in 75 countries. In announcing his retirement, Charles Schulz draws Snoopy sitting on top of his doghouse reading a letter in his typewriter. The letter begins:

> I have been fortunate to draw Charlie Brown and his friends for almost 50 years. It has been the fulfillment of my childhood ambition. . . .

Many newspapers run the farewell strip on their front page. Schulz's contract stipulates that no one else will ever draw the strip.

▶ **ART TIP** Although adults like to encourage children to "be creative," a number of children's book illustrators admit to an obsession with copying cartoon characters in general and Snoopy in particular in their youth.

4

Oh, Grandmother, what a terribly big mouth you have!

The Brothers Grimm,
Little Red Riding Hood

BIRTHDAYS

1785 Jacob Ludwig Carl Grimm is born, near Frankfurt, Germany. With his brother Wilhelm Carl, he collects and edits what we now know as *Grimm's Fairy Tales*. Jacob is also a noted grammarian and philologist. Charles Dickens recalls "falling in love" with Little Red Riding Hood. Indian-born writer Ved Mehta, who becomes a staff writer at *The New Yorker* at age twenty-six, says, "The first book I ever read by myself was a fairy tale that had a girl named Susan in it. I remember nothing more about it except that I found the sound of the name 'Susan' thrilling and exciting."

1809 Louis Braille is born, in Coupvray, near Paris, France. He is blinded at age three by an accident while playing with his father's tools. When he is fifteen, Louis devises a system that allows blind people to read by touch. This system is based on a code using six dots.

▶ **WORD FUN** Students can try constructing an alphabet using six dots and then compare theirs with Louis's code. They can see the code on the Internet: *http://disserv3.stu.umn.edu/AltForm/brail-guide.html*

1813 Isaac Pitman is born, in Trowbridge, England. An elementary teacher and then head of his own private school, Sir Isaac establishes the Phonetic Institute to encourage the use of a shorthand system, based on sounds, that he invents. He is also an advocate of spelling reform.

▶ **SPELLING TIP** Invite students to make a list of words whose spelling does not seem logical.

1933 Phyllis Naylor is born, in Anderson, Indiana. She has received many awards, including the Edgar Allan Poe Award from the Mystery Writers of America for *Night Cry*. Her novel *Shiloh*, which is the story of a boy's attempt to save an abused dog and his discovery that sometimes life is not fair, wins the 1992 Newbery Medal.

JANUARY

5

> . . . a small red fox with chicken pox. . . .
>
> Lynne Cherry,
> *Who's Sick Today*

BIRTHDAYS

1944 Betsy Maestro is born, in Crippen, New York. With Guilio Maestro she writes numerous nonfiction picture books, including *A More Perfect Union: The Story of Our Constitution* and *Riddle City, USA!*

▶ **READING/WRITING CONNECTION** *Riddle City, USA* will inspire students to try writing their own geographic riddles.

1952 Lynne Cherry is born, in Philadelphia. One of the most traumatic events of her childhood is seeing the woods where she spends every waking hour bulldozed. When Lynne writes *The Great Kapock Tree*, publishers see it as too risky, "too issue oriented." When finally published, the book becomes a best seller, inspiring a whole genre of children's books.

▶ **WORD FUN** Lynne's *Who's Sick Today?* contains fun rhymes to answer the question of the title, including, "a snake with an ache" and "a small red fox with chicken pox." Challenge students to team up to write a book of animals and ailments that rhyme.

EVENTS

1821 Lord Byron writes in his journal, "Rose late—dull and drooping—the weather dripping and dense."

▶ **WRITING TIP** Challenge students to describe their mood in a metaphor or an alliterative sentence.

1856 Henry David Thoreau writes in his journal that the snowflakes are "glorious spangles, the sweeping of heaven's floor."

1870 Louisa May Alcott notes that fame has its price. She gets letters from fans asking for advice, letters from children begging to meet her. Nosy reporters told by a plainly dressed servant that "Miss Alcott is not home" don't realize that the servant is Louisa May herself.

JANUARY

6

> His heart will get heavy when his songs are all gone.
>
> Carl Sandberg,
> *Rootabaga Stories*

BIRTHDAYS

1854 Sherlock Holmes is born, in Yorkshire, England. This premier detective solves his first case at age twenty, while he's a student at Oxford University. In 1881, he moves to London's 221B Baker Street, sharing his quarters with Dr. John Watson.

1878 Carl Sandburg, the son of Swedish immigrants, is born, in Galesburg, Illinois. This boy, who starts work at age eleven as a barbershop porter, gains fame as a poet and the Pulitzer Prize–winning biographer of Abraham Lincoln. When Carl is asked about this biography, he says, "It's a book about a man whose father could not sign his name, written by a man whose father could not sign his." Carl writes *Rootabaga Stories* for his three daughters, creating fairy tales about the small towns and farmlands of Midwestern America in the early twentieth century, tales employing playful language and peopled with corn fairies wearing overalls instead of princesses in gossamer gowns.

▶ **READ MORE** There are a number of delightful editions of Sandburg's tales for children. In addition to the complete *Rootabaga Stories*, illustrated by Michael

Hague, try *The Huckabuck Family and How They Raised Popcorn in Nebraska and Quit and Came Back*, illustrated by David Small, and *The Wedding Procession of the Rag Doll, the Broom Handle, and Who Was in It*, illustrated by Harriet Pincus. Istvan Banyai offers jazzed-up illustrations to a selection of Sandburg poems published for the first time in 1999, *Poems for Children: Nowhere Near Old Enough to Vote*.

EVENT

1903 President Theodore Roosevelt writes to his son Kermit who is away at school, "Tom Quartz is certainly the cunningest kitten I have ever seen."

▶ **ALL ABOUT NAMES** Pet names can be a provocative topic. Popular author-illustrator Kevin Henkes's cat is named E. B., after E. B. White. Ask children what author(s) they might name pets for.

▶ **READ MORE** There are many fine volumes of cat poems. Try *Cat Up a Tree*, by Anne Isaacs, for humor and mystery and even philosophy in an inventive series of odes and items on cats.

JANUARY

Dear Farmer Brown,
The Barn is very cold at night. We'd like some electric blankets.
Sincerely,
The Cows

Doreen Cronin,
Click, Clack, Moo

BIRTHDAY

1912 Charles Addams is born, in Westfield, New Jersey. In 1932 Charles sells his first cartoon to the newly established *The New Yorker* for $7.50; soon he becomes a staff cartoonist. Charles creates the Addams Family, about which movies and TV shows have been made. One of his books, the *Charles Addams Mother Goose*, offers a ghoulish interpretation of these famous rhymes.

▶ **READING/WRITING CONNECTION** Children of all ages enjoy rewriting favorite Mother Goose rhymes from different points of view. *Whatever Happened to Humpty Dumpty?*, by David Greenberg, provides funny sequels. Jack Spratt and his wife licked the platter clean? "How disgusting can you git?! . . . They licked the doorknobs, licked the chairs . . ." and so on.

EVENTS

1714 A patent is issued for the first typewriter, designed by English inventor Henry Mill.

▶ **READ MORE** In *Click, Clack, Moo: Cows That Type*, attorney Doreen Cronin tells a rollicking tale about what happens when Farmer Brown's typing cows turn his farm upside down. Besides writing picture books, Doreen collects antique typewriters.

1896 Fanny Farmer publishes her first cookbook.

▶ **READ MORE** Many children love reading recipes, and cookbooks are a good lure for so-called reluctant readers. After they read a few, they may want to compile one for the favorite foods of their classmates. *Two for Stew*, by Laura Numeroff and Barney Saltzberg, offers a wacky restaurant romp. In *Eat Your Words*, Charlotte Foltz offers the derivation and description of baked Alaska, hush puppies, coconuts, and lots more. Alexandra Day's *Frank and Ernest* gives children a look at the secret language of diners, where customers get all kinds of belly furniture. The subtitle of *Fannie in the Kitchen*, by Deborah Hopkinson, tells what this charming picture book is about: *The Whole Story from Soup to Nuts of How Fannie Farmer Invented Recipes with Precise Measurements*.

1984 Trina Schart Hyman is notified that her *Little Red Riding Hood* has received the Caldecott Honor Award. All the characters in the book are drawn from the artist's own life. Little Red Riding Hood is Trina herself, and the wolf is based on her beloved pet dog.

JANUARY

Of course, he was far from perfect yet. At dinner his father told him not to slurp his soup. His mother told him to quit eating so fast. And his sister told him to put his feet on his own side of the table. Milo couldn't stand it. "I bet you'd love me if I turned perfect," he said.

Stephen Manes,
Be a Perfect Person in Just Three Days!

BIRTHDAYS

1919 Lee Ames is born, in New York City. He produces the Draw 50 series, which include simple directions for drawing aircraft, animals, boats, athletes, monsters, animals, and cartoons.

▶ **READ/DRAW MORE** Invite students to find a how-to drawing book, such as *Ed Emberley's Drawing Book: Make a World*, which contains directions for drawing 400 different things—from wheelbarrows to witches.

1945 Nancy Bond is born, in Bethesda, Maryland. Her fascination for Welsh culture while attending library school in Wales is revealed in her first book, *A String in the Harp*, a Newbery Honor Book.

1949 Stephen Manes is born in Pittsburgh, Pennsylvania. He is the author of a number of comic novels, including *Chicken Trek; It's New! It's Improved! It's Terrible!; Be a Perfect Person in Just Three Days!;* and *Make Four Million Dollar\$ by Next Thursday!* Manes fans will recall that this last book is mentioned in his best-selling *Be a Perfect Person in Just Three Days!* "Originally, it was just a joke," Manes says. "But over the years, at my lectures and writing workshops, so many kids kept urging me to write it that finally I broke down and did. This is one book that truly came into being 'by popular demand.'"

▶ **WRITING TIP** Invite students to list what they'd have to do to become perfect.

▶ **READ MORE** *In Lima Beans Would Be Illegal*, compiled by Robert Bender, kids offer their ideas on what it would take to make a perfect world.

EVENTS

1863 Five years before writing *Little Women*, Louisa May Alcott writes in her diary, "Five hundred miles from home, alone among strangers, doing painful duties all day long, & leading a life of constant excitement." Louisa is working as a volunteer nurse in Washington, D.C., where more than 250,000 Civil War soldiers are camped.

1938 E. B. White writes to James Thurber, "The woods, after a snowstorm, were lovelier than any cathedral."

▶ **READING/WRITING CONNECTION** In *Snowflake Bentley*, Jacqueline Briggs Martin and Mary Azarian offer a spectacular story about another man who appreciates snow. In *Winter Eyes*, Douglas Florian uses three strong images to describe icicles: "winter's fingers," "winter's arrows," and "dragon's teeth." Douglas also offers two list poems that offer great possibilities for classroom writing: "What I Love About Winter" and "What I Hate About Winter."

JANUARY

. . . blessed be thy advice . . .

I Samuel 25:33

BIRTHDAY

1886 Walter Brooks is born, in Rome, New York. He writes the very popular *Freddy, the Pig* series, which includes Freddy's adventures on the farm, with a baseball team from Mars, in Florida, as a pilot, and as a politician. After reading Sherlock Holmes, Freddy becomes a supersleuth.

▶ **READING REFLECTION** Invite students to share information about a mysteries series they like. They shouldn't tell the plot of any one book but should tell what various books in the series have in common.

EVENTS

1956 The first "Dear Abby" advice column appears in the newspaper. Known as Popo to family and friends, Pauline Esther Friedman and her identical twin sister Esther Pauline (Fifi), who writes under the name Ann Landers, both become celebrated advice columnists. When asked how she got the name Abby, she explains, "Abigail was a prophetess in the Old Testament Book of Samuel, and it was said of her, 'Blessed are thou, and blessed is thy advice, O Abigail.'"

▶ **WRITING TIP** Advice letters provide a good format for young writers. Make the person with the problem anonymous or use a character from literature.

1972 Nonny Hogrogian learns that *One Fine Day*, a cumulative story based on an Armenian folktale, has received the Caldecott Medal. Nonny's husband, writer David Kheridian, says that watching her work he is struck "by the mystery of art and its strange, unknowable processes."

(This is a good story
To read to your folks
When they won't buy
You something you
want.)

Shel Silverstein,
"Little Abigail and the Beautiful
Pony"

BIRTHDAYS

1929 Remy Charlip is born, in Brooklyn, New York. His books include jokes, nonsense rhymes and word play, a jump-rope rhyme, plays, and poems. One of his most popular books, *Fortunately*, is built on a humorous fortunately/unfortunately dramatic structure.

▶ **READING/WRITING CONNECTION** Reread *Fortunately* and invite students to create a series of similar statements about life in your classroom.

1947 Lloyd Bloom is born, in New York City. A popular illustrator, he illustrates books by Patricia MacLachlan, Mavis Jukes, Tony Johnston, and Jill Paton Walsh, among others.

▶ **ART TIP** Invite students to discuss what makes Lloyd's work distinctive and recognizable and very different from, say, the work of Tomie DePaola.

EVENTS

1840 In Britain, the first 112,000 letters carrying the new one-penny postage stamp are delivered. In the 1990s the U. S. Postal Service handles 163,482 first-class letters every minute.

▶ **READ MORE** Gail Gibbons's *The Post Office Book: Mail and How It Works* is straightforward and informative. *Hail to Mail,* by Samuel Marshak, illustrated by Vladimir Radunsky, is a wonderful and wacky paean to mail and the people who deliver it: from New York City to Boise, Idaho, to Switzerland to the shores of Brazil, a succession of unflagging mailmen try to deliver a letter.

1985 This marks the 112th week Shel Silverstein's *A Light in the Attic* is on the *New York Times* adult bestseller list. Everyone has their favorite among the verbal antics—everything from the fate of the child who memorizes the dictionary to what happens to Mary Hume, the girl who is never quite satisfied, when she gets to heaven. Plus the poem about Abigail, which kids can read to their parents when they won't buy them what they want. Maybe they'll want to memorize it.

▶ **READING TIP** Hold a classroom celebration, with each student reading—or reciting—a favorite Silverstein poem.

JANUARY

The real point is this:
We don't know where
to go because we don't
know what we are. . . .
We can read, and with a
little practice, we'll be
able to write, too. I
mean to do both. I
think we can learn to do
anything we want. But
where do we do it?
Where does a group of
civilized rats fit in?

Robert C. O'Brien,
*Mrs. Frisby and the Rats of
NIMH*

BIRTHDAYS

1918 Robert C. O'Brien is born, in Brooklyn, New York. Mystery surrounds this author. Although he says that the telephone call telling him he's won the Newbery Medal is the best phone call he has ever received, O'Brien does not deliver his own Newbery Medal acceptance speech for *Mrs. Frisby and the Rats of NIMH* but asks his editor to give it. Robert C. O'Brien is a pen name for Robert Leslie Conly. For twenty-two years he is an editor for *National Geographic Magazine*. His daughter Jane Leslie Conly, also a writer and a Newbery recipient, writes two sequels to *Mrs. Frisby*.

1931 Mary Rodgers is born, in New York City. When she writes *Freaky Friday*, she works on it each day between two and five A.M. The rest of the time she's busy taking care of five children. Her book has a great beginning: "You're not going to believe me, nobody in their right minds could possibly believe me, but it's true, really it is! When I woke up this morning, I found I'd turned into my mother."

▶ **WRITING TIP** Invite students to write what happens when they wake up and find they've turned into their teacher!

EVENTS

1930 Eighteen-year-old cartoonist Syd Hoff sells his first drawing to *The New Yorker*. Although he's a high school dropout, he studies at the National Academy of Design in New York City.

1962 C. S. Lewis writes to a fan, thanking her for her letter and adding, "Everyone is pleased, you know, to be appreciated, even elderly authors!"

JANUARY

My, what big eyes you
have, Grandmother!

Charles Perrault,
"Little Red Riding Hood"

BIRTHDAYS

1628 Charles Perrault is born, in France. His famous collection of fairy tales includes, "The Sleeping Beauty," "Cinderella," "Tom Thumb," "Bluebeard," "Puss in Boots," among others.

▶ **READING REFLECTION** Invite students to compare the way Perrault's version of "Little Red Riding Hood" ends with the way the Grimm version ends. They may be surprised.

1876 Jack London, novelist, is born John Griffith Chaney, in San Francisco. His father deserts his mother before he is born, and she marries John London, a Civil War veteran. Jack leaves school after the eighth grade, but he is an avid reader and finds a friend to guide his reading in Ina Coolbrith at the Oakland Public Library. At age fifteen, Jack leaves home to become a sailor. Later, Jack returns to high school and graduates. Jack's many pursuits include work as a fisherman, laborer, factory worker, oyster pirate, railroad hobo, gold prospector, and journalist. In an introductory note to his illustrations for *White Fang*, Ed Young says that this book stands out for him not only because of his fond memories of the story, but because of his love of nature and of canines in particular. "Mr. London had an uncanny understanding of nature, and was able to draw parallels between the raising of human children and the raising of animals in the world of man."

1908 Clement Hurd is born, in New York City. The illustrator of more than seventy books, he is best known for his illustrations to Margaret Wise Brown's *Goodnight Moon*. He also illustrates about fifty books written by his wife, Edith Thacher Hurd.

Mr. and Mrs. Brown first met Paddington on a railway platform. In fact, that was how he came to have such an unusual name for a bear, for Paddington was the name of the station.

Michael Bond,
A Bear Called Paddington

BIRTHDAY

1926 Michael Bond, author of the *Paddington* bear series, is born, in Berkshire, England. On his way home from work, Michael misses his bus, and he goes into a department store to get out of the rain. There, he notices one last bear on the shelf—and he buys it for his wife for Christmas. (In the books, the English-speaking bear found at the railroad station comes from Darkest Peru.) Michael says that it is easy to get Paddington into trouble; the difficulty comes in getting him out in a way that is "morally justifiable." He says the nicest compliment he has ever received came from a child who wrote him that she likes his books because they "make pictures in my head."

▶ **ALL ABOUT NAMES** Invite students to conduct research: what do people name their stuffed bears? They can interview people about how they decide on bear names.

EVENT

1990 "The Simpsons" TV show, which debuts on this date, also has some interesting "name" data. When cartoonist Matt Groening is asked to create a cartoon for television, he creates a family with characters' names after his own family, his mother and father Homer and Marge and his sisters Lisa and Maggie. He names Bart for himself, an anagram for "brat."

Eagles do not talk very much. And all they answered in their husky voices was, "You may be sure that we will do our best—for John Dolittle."

Hugh Lofting,
The Story of Doctor Dolittle

BIRTHDAYS

1874 Thornton Burgess is born on Cape Cod—in Sandwich, Massachusetts. While his five-year-old son is visiting relatives in another state, Thornton starts sending him the stories he writes about Peter Rabbit, Jerry Muskrat, Sammy Jay, and Mr. Black Snake. For forty-four years after, he writes a new children's story every day (except Sunday) for the *Associated News* and the New York *Herald Tribune* syndicates. More than 15,000 stories, they fill one hundred volumes and then some. Newbery Medalist Paula Fox recalls reading the "wonderful animal stories" when they ran in the newspaper as a serial.

1886 Hugh Lofting is born, in Maidenhead, England. Later he attends the Massachusetts Institute of Technology. During World War I, while serving in the British army in Flanders and France, he mails illustrated story-letters about an animal doctor to his children. *The Story of Doctor Dolittle* is a hit, and a second book, *The Voyages of Doctor Dolittle*, wins the Newbery Medal.

JANUARY

15

I have a dream that one day this nation will rise up and live out the true meaning of its creed— 'We hold these truths to be self-evident that all men are created equal.' I have a dream. . . .

Martin Luther King Jr.

BIRTHDAYS

1929 Martin Luther King Jr., civil rights leader and Nobel peace prize winner, is born in Atlanta, Georgia. In 1983, the third Monday in January is designated as a legal holiday to celebrate his birthday.

▶ **READ MORE** A sumptuously illustrated edition of King's own words, *I Have a Dream,* by Martin Luther King Jr.; *My Dream of Martin Luther King,* by Faith Ringgold; and *A Picture Book of Martin Luther King Jr.,* by David Adler, are among many volumes available.

1931 Robert Silverberg is born, in New York City. He begins writing science fiction while attending Columbia University and is well established in the field by the time he graduates.

▶ **READING TIP** Celebrate the day as Science Fiction Day. Robert Heinlein is credited as the first American children's science fiction writer; Madeleine L'Engle's *A Wrinkle in Time*, rejected by many publishers, is regarded as the apex of the genre.

EVENT

1759 The British Museum opens its doors for the first time. It serves both as the national museum and the national library for the United Kingdom. The museum gets its start following the death of British medical doctor and naturalist Sir Hans Sloane, who bequeaths his personal collection of books, manuscripts, coins, medals, and antiquities.

JANUARY

16

Happy Valley. What a laugh. They should have called it Pathetic Molehill.

Robert Lipsyte, *Summer Rules*

BIRTHDAYS

1874 Robert Service is born, in Preston, England, the first of ten children. When he is fourteen he leaves school to take a job in a shipping office. In 1896, he lands in Montreal with five dollars in his pocket. He writes poems set in Canada's Klondike, where he works during the gold strike. Here is the first recorded poem written by Robert, a blessing he gives at a family dinner celebrating his sixth birthday:

> God bless the cakes and bless the jam
> Bless the cheese and the cold boiled ham
> Bless the scones Aunt Jeannie makes
> And save us all from belly-aches. Amen.

▶ **READ MORE** Ted Harrison's illustrations for *The Creation of Sam McGee* give unexpectedly brilliant colors to the frozen region depicted in the poem.

1938 Robert Lipsyte is born, in New York City. Robert isn't a sports fan as a child, but after graduating from the Columbia School of Journalism he gets a job as copy boy at the sports desk of the *New York Times*. He becomes a prize-winning sports columnist and also writes prize-winning books for middle grades/young adult readers.

▶ **WRITING TIP** Middle grades writers can practice one Lipsyte technique. Ask them to find the name of a product, toy, sports team, suburban housing development, organization—something that is hyped by PR or advertising. Then they can try out Lipsyte's structure: _____ (name of product). What a laugh. They should have called it _____.

1947 Katy Hall McMullen is born, in St. Louis, Missouri. Katy reads her way through the Children's Room shelves at the public library. *Dr. Doolittle* books and Mary Norton's *The Borrowers* emerge as favorites. Other favorites include comic books and *Mad* magazine. When she becomes a fourth-grade teacher, Katy reads to her students every day after lunch. Reading to students convinces Katy she would like to write, so she gives up her job and moves to New York "where I'd heard that writers lived." Katy works in publishing during the day and writes at night. She writes the *Dragon Slayers' Academy* series, and writing as Katy Hall, she collaborates with Lisa Eisenberg on riddle books: *Creepy Riddles, Bunny Riddles, Sheepish Riddles, Chickie Riddles, Batty Riddles, Grizzly Riddles, Snakey Riddles*, and more.

▶ **READING/WRITING CONNECTION** This riddle, from *Kitty Riddles*, demonstrates the language structure imbedded in good riddles:

What kind of kitty has eight legs?
An octo-puss!

Invite students to create a list of words with other numerical prefixes (quatrain, quarto, quarter horse, quarterback, for example) and then see if the list offers any riddle possibilities.

EVENTS

1787 Thomas Jefferson writes to Col. Edward Carrington: "Were it left to me to decide whether we should have a government without newspapers, or newspapers without a government, I should not hesitate a moment to prefer the latter."

1885 Wilson Alwyn Bentley, of Jericho, Vermont, makes a successful photomicrograph of a snowflake. Eight years earlier, when Wilson was fifteen, his mother had given him a microscope and he began making precise drawings.

▶ **READ MORE** Jacqueline Briggs Martin tells Wilson's story in *Snowflake Bentley*, a book for which Mary Azarian's illustrations win the Caldecott Medal. Mary lives about an hour's drive from Bentley's home.

JANUARY

BIRTHDAYS

1706 Benjamin Franklin is born, in Boston. From his reading as a boy, Benjamin gets the idea for thirteen rules of good behavior. He grows up to be a printer, author, publisher, philosopher, scientist, diplomat, philanthropist, and signer of both the Declaration of Independence and the U. S. Constitution. Benjamin is also fond of using pseudonyms: Proteus Echo, Esq., Richard Saunders (Poor Richard), Philomath, Father Abraham, Anthony Afterwit, The Busybody, and Mrs. Silence Dogood.

1. Don't eat or drink too much.
2. Don't joke or talk too much.
3. Keep your things neat.
4. Do what you set out to do.
5. Don't spend too much money.
6. Don't waste time.
7. Be sincere.
8. Be fair.
9. Don't go to extremes.
10. Keep clean.
11. Keep calm.
12. Don't fool around with the girls.
13. Don't show off.

Benjamin Franklin

▶ **READ MORE** James Cross Giblin's *The Amazing Life of Benjamin Franklin*, illustrated by Michael Dooling, is a sophisticated picture book, packed with information as well as being a strong narrative. Michael's endnotes document the special efforts taken to place the man in his times. Michael enlisted friends and neighbors as models, and he also donned different costumes for his own appearances in the book.

▶ **READING/WRITING CONNECTION** Ask students to come up with some rules for classroom behavior. Once they compile a list, they can compare it with Benjamin's. *The Secret Knowledge of Grown-Ups* will encourage children with a subversive bent of mind to consider Benjamin's rules from another viewpoint. In the book, David Wisniewski offers the real reasons grown-ups tell kids to behave certain ways.

1925 Robert Cormier is born, in Leominster, Massachusetts. He features his hometown in several of his young adult books, renaming it Monument. Among his favorite pieces of writing are *The Adventures of Tom Sawyer*, *The Catcher in the Rye*, and "Marriage Lines," by Ogden Nash.

▶ **READING TIP** Welcome this reminder that Ogden Nash is well worth reading. His word play is a provocative big step up from riddle books.

1938 Mystery writer John Bellairs is born, in Marshall, Michigan. He later uses Marshall as the setting for his first mystery series, where strange things occur in enormous old houses. He later moves to Massachusetts and becomes a Red Sox fan. John Bellairs says he loves ghost stories, coffins, Latin, cathedrals, darkness, England, cobalt blue, Christmas, Italian food, the moon, secret passages, wizards like Gandalf, and those Boston Red Sox.

▶ **WRITING TIP** Asking students to list the things they love can result in a great classroom poster, one that grows over time. A good publishing medium is to list loved things on a piece of adding machine running down the hall. Children can keep adding to the list. An adult version is Barbara Ann Kipfer's best-selling *14,000 Things to Be Happy About*. Challenge students to come up with 14,001 things.

1953 Janet Stevens is born, in Dallas, Texas. Janet says she has been drawing for as long as she can remember. "In school I drew pictures for my book reports, on math assignments, on anything I could find." In her children's books Janet likes to exaggerate the characters' personalities. She also includes furniture from her own home in her drawings. Janet creates the illustrations for *Cook-a-Doodle-Doo!* on paper made by hand from unbleached flour, flowers, baking powder, salt, sugar, eggshells, and a dish towel. Since the text, written with her sister Susan Stevens Crummel, is a funny account of cooking strawberry shortcake, the ingredients in the paper seem especially fitting.

Event

1903 Beatrix Potter writes a friend about how hard it is to find the right model. "I am trying to make a squirrel book at present. I have not a very pretty little model; I bought two but they weren't a pair, and fought so frightfully that I had to get rid of the handsomer—and most savage one—the other squirrel is rather a nice little animal, but half of one ear has been bitten off, which spoils his appearance!"

▶ **WRITING/DRAWING TIP** Invite students to use an animal as a model for a drawing. Ask them to write a paragraph about the experience.

JANUARY

18

Drinking your milk and talking at the same time may result in your having to be patted on the back and dried for quite a long time afterwards.

A. A. Milne,
Winnie-the-Pooh

Birthdays

1779 Peter Mark Roget, English physician and compiler of the best-known book of synonyms, is born. *Roget's Thesaurus*, first published in 1852, features a remarkable system of words organized under a series of ideas: strength, beauty, friendship, and so on. It is the same kind of system used today with computer retrieval data bases.

▶ **WRITING TIP** Ask students to come up with between five and ten words they use a lot. Then they can form teams, trying to come up with as many synonyms as they can for one word from this list. Then tell them that Roget also lists antonyms!

1882 A. A. Milne is born, in London, England. He will be remembered forever for Pooh, the "hummy sort of bear" who gains enormous fame in *Winnie-the-Pooh* and *The House at Pooh Corner*. Pooh is based on a stuffed toy belonging to Milne's son Christopher, as are the other animals in the stories. Ernest Shepard creates illustrations for the books by using the toys as models.

▶ **WRITING TIP** Invite students to bring a toy to school—and then ask them to write at least three paragraphs about it. (These vague directions allow students to write either fiction or nonfiction, depending on their preference.) Then they can illustrate their writing with drawings based on the model.

▶ **READING TIP** Put individual poems from *Now We Are Six* and *When We Were Very Young* in a box. Every half hour, stop classwork and invite two students to pick a poem from the box and read it aloud.

1884 Arthur Ransome is born, in England. The twelve books in his Swallows and Amazons series are based on his childhood summer holidays in England's Lake District. Arthur thinks the best part of childhood is holidays. In his books children do as they please on holidays.

▶ **WRITING/DRAWING TIP** Invite students to design a perfect holiday. Put all their names in a box. Then they can draw names and write a postcard to a friend describing this great holiday. This leaves room for those who like to draw to design the postcard as well as the holiday.

▶ **THINK ABOUT IT** Try a classroom holiday variation. What will they choose to do in a half-day classroom holiday?

1934 Raymond Briggs is born, in Wimbledon, South London. Raymond knows from age eleven that he wants to be a newspaper reporter and a cartoonist. His parents are not pleased when, at age fifteen, he decides to leave school and attend art school. For his book *Father Christmas* Raymond draws on the experience of his father, who had to go out in the snow every day, including Christmas, delivering milk. Raymond writes some of his books, such as *When the Wind Blows*, the story of a quiet, retired couple facing atomic war, as vehicles for social commentary, using cartoonlike formats and visual humor to offset often harsh messages. His most popular books, those in the Snowman series, contain no hint of social criticism but follow the adventures of a snowman that comes to life.

▶ **THINK ABOUT IT** Do students think books should be "happy," or is it important for some to take on tough topics like war, poverty, racism?

EVENTS

1912 "Great God! This is an awful place," writes Captain Robert F. Scott in his journal at the South Pole. He had set out for the Pole two years before and has just found out that Norwegian Roald Amundsen had gotten there first.

1999 Dorothy Hinshaw Patent's one hundredth book, *Fire: Friend or Foe*, is celebrated at the Missoula, Montana, public library. Dorothy, who has a Ph.D. in zoology, began her career writing science and nature books for children twenty-five years earlier when she and her husband and two children moved to Missoula from North Carolina. In 1973 she published *Weasels, Otters, Skunks, and Their Family*, and from then on she has averaged four books a year, on topics ranging from Alex the parrot to wild horses to rain forest frogs and forest fires. Dorothy firmly believes that children are eager to be challenged by new ideas, and she never writes down to them.

Last Full Week ### EVENT

Annually for the last full week in January, in Williamsport, Maryland, it's Celebrity Read a Book Week. Celebrities read to children, and people donate new books to the public library.

▶ **READING TIP** Invite children to read a story to someone elderly. Establishing a read-aloud relationship with a seniors center has many benefits.

19

During the whole of a dull, dark, and soundless day in the autumn of the year. . . .

Edgar Allan Poe, "The Fall of the House of Usher"

BIRTHDAYS

1809 Edgar Allan Poe, poet and America's first writer of horror stories, is born, in Boston. He is the second of three children. After his father disappears and his mother dies when Edgar is two years old, Mrs. Frances Allan of Richmond, Virginia, takes Edgar to live with her family. Edgar is credited with inventing the mystery story (stories like "The Murders in the Rue Morgue" and "The Purloined Letter"). But he is best remembered for such horror stories as "The Fall of the House of Usher," "The Pit and the Pendulum," and "The Tell-Tale Heart." In Edgar's honor, the Edgar, a small bust in his likeness, is given by the Mystery Writers of America every year to the best writers of detective stories in several categories. And the love of horror stories continues. Today, R. L. Stine's novels, the descendants of Poe's horror stories, are big sellers.

1885 Effie Lee Newsome is born, in Philadelphia. She may be the first American poet who writes primarily for children. Her poems celebrate trees, flowers, spiders, ladybugs, snow, and other aspects of the natural world.

▶ **READING/WRITING CONNECTION** Challenge students to make a list of words they might include if they were going to write a poem about spiders or ladybugs. Then they can collect spider poems and see if their words appear in these poems. Then they can write their own poems.

EVENT

1937 The eighteen-year-old British ballerina known as Margot Fonteyn makes her debut, in *Giselle*, at Sadler's Wells Theater, in London. Fonteyn's birth name is Peggy Hookham.

▶ **ALL ABOUT NAMES** Invite students to speculate about why Peggy may have changed her name.

20

It was an exciting moment when the cub met her first elephant, an anxious one too, for poor Elsa had no mother to warn her against these animals who regard lions as the only enemies of their young. . . .

Joy Adamson, *Born Free*

BIRTHDAYS

1910 Joy Adamson is born in Austria. After earning a college degree in music, Joy goes to East Africa for a visit—and stays there for the rest of her life. She marries a Kenyan game warden. Joy's stories of raising Elsa, an infant lion cub, without taming or domesticating her and then releasing her to the wild becomes a popular book and movie.

1937 Mary Anderson is born, in New York City. Her mysteries have titles like *The Hairy Beast in the Woods, The Leipzig Vampire,* and *Terror Under the Tent.*

▶ **READING/WRITING CONNECTION** Ask students to make a list of books they are reading. What do these titles reveal (or fail to reveal) about the books' contents?

1959 Keiko Narahashi is born, in Tokyo; she moves to the United States when she is six. When she starts school, she doesn't know a word of English. Her teacher started teaching her English by pointing to crayons and naming the colors. Keiki loves art because the "language" is the same for everyone. For a while, she draws only horses. Today, Keiko says she gets her ideas from everyday things, and sometimes her children appear in her books.

▶ **ART TIP** "If you love to draw, draw a lot of what you love to draw. Look hard at things that fascinate you and don't pay too much attention to advice about drawing, especially from grown-ups like me."

EVENT

1825 Noah Webster finishes his *American Dictionary of the English Language*. It includes definitions for 70,000 words, 12,000 of which have not appeared in any previous dictionary. Today, experts estimate that the English language includes 4,000,000 words. No dictionary can list the whole language. Using 1755 as its starting point, *Webster's Third New International Dictionary* has 450,000 words.

▶ **RESEARCH TIP** Invite students to see whether they can stump the dictionary. Can they find English words that are not in it? Ask students to consider the most likely places to look for new words.

JANUARY

21

Snow, snow, snow, oh dismal.

Fanny Longfellow

BIRTHDAY

1957 Bob Weber, Jr., is born, in Baltimore, Maryland. He wants to be a veterinarian when he grows up but creates "Slylock Fox and Comics for Kids," one of the most popular children's strips in the world instead. Distributed by King Features Syndicate, it appears in more than 350 newspapers worldwide. The strip includes mysteries, visual puzzles, how-to-draw lessons, gags, and information on nature, pet care, safety, history, geography, conservation, and the environment. The ringleader of all the fun is Slylock Fox, a bright-red woodland Sherlock Holmes who solves problems through logic and reasoning.

EVENTS

1832 Fourteen-year-old Fanny Longfellow writes a letter to her famous father Henry Wadsworth Longfellow, complaining, "Snow, snow, snow, oh dismal."

▶ **READING/WRITING CONNECTION** Invite students to find winter words in their reading, in the newspaper, and elsewhere. They can post them on a wall. A long piece of adding machine tape works well. If the rule is established that only new words can be posted, then everybody will need to read all the words before each new posting (and competition becomes fierce to find new words, driving students to search out new resources). Once they have a large collection of words, they can use these words to write winter stories and poems. Or winter tall tales.

1902 Beatrix Potter adds a postscript to a letter to her publisher: "I do not know if it is worth mentioning—But Dr. Conan Doyle had a copy [of *The Tale of Peter Rabbit*] for his children and he has a good opinion of the story and words."

JANUARY

22

If the mountain won't come to Mahomet, Mahomet must go to the mountain.

Francis Bacon, "On Boldness"

BIRTHDAYS

1561 Francis Bacon is born, in London. A statesman, philosopher, and essayist, some of his quips are repeated to this day as proverbs. Today's term *crocodile tears* stems from Bacon's remark, "It is the wisdom of the crocodiles, that shed tears when they would devour."

▶ **READ MORE** Betty Fraser's *First Things First* presents familiar proverbs in an everyday situation in which a young child would use them. Jim Anton's *Wise & Wacky Proverbs* provides information showing whether sayings like "blind as a bat" are true or not.

1930 Blair Lent is born, near Boston, Massachusetts, and grows up there. He works as a creative designer in an advertising firm by day and then works at his real passion—writing and illustrating picture books—at night. His illustrations for *The Funny Little Woman* win the Caldecott Medal. Blair says, "Books were important to me as a child, and it is for that little boy that I am working. I can never know other children's thoughts as well as I can remember my own."

1930 Brian Wildsmith is born, in a village in Yorkshire, England, which Brian remembers as a gray and black world of mist and fog. He remembers arriving at the Slade School of Fine Art, in London, where sunshine fills his world with brilliant color. On lunchtime breaks from classes Brian studies paintings of Giotto, Michelangelo, Rembrandt, and Goya in nearby art museums. Although Brian admits to few hates, he does hate it when the sun isn't shining. Since 1971, he and his family have lived in southern France, where the sun almost always shines.

1946 Rafe Martin is born, in Rochester, New York. Rafe says, "Though I grew up in New York City, as a child I still managed to spend a lot of time in treetops." Rafe remembers his mother reading fairy tales and Aesop fables aloud. "One of our favorites was 'The Tortoise and the Hare.' 'Slow and steady wins the race,' she would say, 'slow and steady.' As I didn't write my first book until I was thirty-five, I clearly took that story's theme to heart." Two of Rafe's favorite books are *King Arthur and the Knights of the Round Table* and *Robin Hood*. A special favorite is Rudyard Kipling's *The Jungle Book*.

▶ **READ MORE** Rafe's *The Rough-Face Girl* is an Algonquin Cinderella story. Readers may want to compare it with a Zuni tale, *The Turkey Girl*, by Penny Pollard, illustrated by Ed Young. Students can learn more about Rafe and his work in *A Storyteller's Story*, a volume in the Meet the Author series, published by Richard Owen.

EVENTS

1999 Today is the deadline for entries in the HarperCollins oxymoron contest.

▶ **WRITING TIP** Hold your own class oxymoron event. Jon Agee's *Who Ordered the Jumbo Shrimp?* is a good source for finding oxymorons, expressions that combine contradictory or incongruous words (such as jumbo shrimp). Jon's book contains more than sixty oxymorons, and his accompanying illustrations provide a wonderfully humorous interpretation of what these expressions might mean.

2000 Today is Answer Your Cat's Question Day. Stop what you are doing and take a look at your cat. You will see that your cat is looking at you with a serious question in mind.

▶ **READING TIP** Invite students to find a cat poem in the library. Then they can read it to two friends.

JANUARY

23

. . . to write about the great passions that little hearts can have.

Katharine Holabird

BIRTHDAYS

1737 John Hancock is born. The first signer of the Declaration of Independence, he writes his name big "so no Britisher would have to use his spectacles to read it." His name has become a part of our language. We say, "Put your John Hancock on that!" to mean any handwritten signature. We now commemorate January 23 as National Handwriting Day.

▶ **WRITING TIP** Penmanship is something about which lots of people have opinions. Invite students to interview three adults, asking whether they have a penmanship story to share. They might ask, Is the computer making penmanship obsolete?

1948 Katharine Holabird is born, in Cambridge, Massachusetts. She grows up in Chicago where Holabirds have been architects for three generations. "We lived in a tall wooden house, a San Francisco steamboat captain's fantasy that survived the Chicago fire and looked like something Hansel and Gretel might have found in the woods, though it was squeezed between a seedy hotel and a dark rooming house." Katherine says everyone is the family is an artist of one kind or another. "Our father loved painting, and once he took us all down to the basement, gave us paints and brushes, and let us 'decorate' everything in sight." Katherine says that growing up she was a "mad collector of anything wild and usual"—a baby skunk, a rescued owl, a raccoon, and even a crocodile. Katherine says her picture book heroine *Angelina Ballerina* is inspired by her daughter's balletomania. "I knew that I wanted to write about the great passions that little hearts can have."

JANUARY 24

In an old house in Paris that was covered with vines

lived twelve little girls in two straight lines.

Ludwig Bemelmans,
Madeline

BIRTHDAY

1949 Michael Pellowski is born, in New Brunswick, New Jersey. He writes *Amazing But True Sports Stories.*

▶ **WRITING TIP** Invite students to interview adults, asking for "the most amazing sports story" they know. They can compile an anthology of the results.

EVENTS

1911 Captain Robert Scott and his team make plans for staying one year in the Antarctic. Each member of the team is allowed twelve pounds of possessions. A typical kit includes extra socks, extra woolen mitts, a blank notebook, a pencil, and one small book.

▶ **READING/WRITING CONNECTION** Why do students think the adventurers take a blank notebook? If they were going to be gone for one year, what one book would students take?

1915 After he stumbles and drops a tray filled with breakfast meals, sixteen-year-old Ludwig Bemelmans is fired from his job at a hotel in New York City. After this disaster the young immigrant who later writes and illustrates *Madeline* spends a week visiting the aquarium, the zoo, and the Metropolitan Museum of Art. As he wanders around the city, Ludwig makes sketches of what he sees.

JANUARY 25

The woods are lovely dark and deep,

But I have promises to keep. . . .

Robert Frost,
"Stopping by Woods on a Snowy Evening"

BIRTHDAYS

1759 Robert Burns is born, in Alloway, Scotland. He is the oldest of seven children. His father is a poor tenant farmer but hires a tutor to make sure his children are well read.

1882 Virginia Woolf, English novelist and diarist, is born. (James Marshall's famous hippos in the George and Martha series are named for the lead characters in Edward Albee's famous play *Who's Afraid of Virginia Woolf?*)

1935 Roy Gerrard is born, in Atherton, Lancashire, England. He says his boyhood reading of Kipling, Conan Doyle, Walter Scott, and the Arthurian legends influences the books he creates. An art teacher, his picture book illustrations win many international awards. Roy says his paintings "express a sense of whimsy which owes much to Lewis Carroll and Edward Lear." He tells the stories in light verse. *Rosie and the Rustlers* begins

> Where the mountains meet the prairie,
> where the men are wild and hairy
> There's a little ranch where Rosie Jones is boss.
> It's a place that's neat and cozy, and the boys employed by Rosie
> Work extremely hard, to stop her getting cross.

Roy's other books are period pieces, set in such varied locales as Victorian England, the Middle Ages, Elizabethan England, ancient Egypt.

1939 Jean Ferris is born, in Fort Leavenworth, Kansas. Jean says, "I'm fascinated by teenage years. There's so much going on, so many emotional changes, decisions for the future, social problems." She says in her work she tries to give young people "hope for the future and some guideposts for achieving a satisfying life, even when circumstances seem bleak and/or dismaying."

1954 Nicki Weiss is born, in New York City. When she is seventeen, she lives with a French family and learns the language. A year later, she lives on a reservation with a Sioux family, learning to bead and to speak a little Lakota. She has worked as a textile designer on fabric for shirts, a nursery school teacher, and as a helper in a bakery. She is also an animal rights activist. Nikki writes and illustrates her own books on themes important to primary graders.

EVENT

1896 At age twenty-one, Robert Frost, a hopeful poet, expresses his discouragement in a letter to Susan Hayes Ward, a literary editor who has encouraged him. "Perhaps you had better not wait any longer. I have done my level best in the time that has elapsed since you last heard from me, to make good my promise as a poet. But I fear I am not a poet. . . ." Fortunately, Robert continues to work hard on his poetry. On November 16, 1916, he is elected to membership in the National Institute of Arts and Letters—for his poetry. On May 11, 1924, he is awarded the Pulitzer Prize in poetry. On June 2, 1931, he wins another Pulitzer Prize.

JANUARY

26

She came into the room and sat down.

Charles Mikolaycak

BIRTHDAYS

1831 Mary Mapes Dodge, author of *Hans Brinker, or the Silver Skates*, is born, in New York City. She is the first editor of *St. Nicholas* magazine, the most famous children's magazine of the late nineteenth and early twentieth century. Among the eminent writers published in the magazine are Twain, Longfellow, Whittier, Emerson, and Thoreau. Asked to name his favorite book, Charles Schulz, creator of the "Peanuts" cartoon strip, says, "*Hans Brinker, or the Silver Skates.*"

1929 Jules Feiffer, cartoonist and children's author, is born, in New York City. He remembers drawing Popeye when he is four. The squint-eyed, bulging-forearmed sailor is also four; he started appearing in the newspapers the same year Jules is born. Later, the adventure comic strips transport Jules out of the Bronx to desert islands "where a young man with his wits about him might well find buried treasure." After paying tribute to all the comics he loves, Jules points out that we live "in a time when mature people are embarrassed to read *Spider-Man* in public but feel no such qualms about *Entertainment Weekly* or the *New York Post.*" Jules's *The Man in the Ceiling* is about a little boy who dreams of being a cartoonist.

1937 Charles Mikolaycak, illustrator and graphic designer, is born. He makes dramatic use of negative spaces in many of his books. He says when he teaches aspiring illustrators, he asks them to illustrate this sentence: "She came into the room and sat down." Charles points out that the illustrator has all kinds of choices to make: Will it be a distant view of the woman or a close-up? What will she look like? What will the room look like? Where is this room? In a house? In a castle? Or in a railroad station?

▶ **READING/WRITING CONNECTION** One way for students to see choice in action is to look at several renditions of the same subject: For example, James Marshall's *Cinderella* is very different from Walt Disney's, and both are very different from Marcia Brown's. Ask students *how* they are different.

1956 Ashley Wolff is born, in Boston. In an illustrator's note to Carol Ryrie Brink's *Goody O'Grumpity*, Ashley explains that in order to figure out how to portray Goody O'Grumpity baking a cake, she traveled to the Plimoth Plantation to do research. Not only does she illustrate the cooking process, from churning the milk to slicing the cake, at the end of the book Ashley provides a seventeenth-century recipe for spice cake.

EVENT

1784 Benjamin Franklin writes a letter to his daughter noting his disappointment over the choice of the eagle as the symbol of America. "I wish the bald eagle had not been chosen as the representative of our country; he is a bird of bad moral character; like those among men who live by Sharping and Robbing, he is generally poor, and often very lousy. The turkey is a much more respectable Bird, and withal a true original Native of America."

▶ **THINK ABOUT IT** Invite students to think about choosing an animal that symbolizes your class.

JANUARY

27

"What is the use of a book," thought Alice, "without pictures or conversations?"

Lewis Carroll,
Alice's Adventures in Wonderland

BIRTHDAYS

1832 Charles L. Dodgson, the English author and mathematician better known as Lewis Carroll, is born, in Daresbury, England. In 1862 he gives a handwritten story, *Alice's Adventures Under Ground,* as a Christmas gift to a child friend, Alice Liddell. Three years later, in 1865, the manuscript is published as *Alice's Adventures in Wonderland*, with illustrations by Sir John Tenniel. Author Joyce Carol Oates says, "Lewis Carroll's *Alice in Wonderland and Through the Looking-Glass* with its fluid blend of dreamlike narrative and surreal fantasy, and its courageous, curious girl heroine, has probably been the book that most influenced my imaginative life." Prize-winning poet Richard Wilbur says when he was growing up, he reread the Alice books every year.

▶ **WORD FUN** In 1879, Lewis Carroll invents a new word game. He calls it doublets; today we refer to it as Word Ladders. For directions, see March 29.

1928 Harry Allard is born, in Evanston, Illinois. He writes the popular Miss Nelson series and The Stupids series. The books in both series are illustrated by James Marshall. Harry is Jim Marshall's French teacher as well as his collaborator.

▶ **THINK ABOUT IT** Ask students to come up with an idea for a book on which they might collaborate with their teacher.

1939 Julius Lester is born, in St. Louis, Missouri. He is raised in Kansas City and Nashville. Although he is the son of a Methodist minister, some of his books reflect his conversion to Judaism. Julius's first book for children, *To Be a Slave* (1968), earns a Newbery Honor. Later books include retellings of African-American folktales. Julius says his library, holding between 5,000 and 10,000 books, is the center of his house and his life.

JANUARY

28

When you're making things, time goes fast.

Vera B. Williams,
Scooter

BIRTHDAYS

1927 Vera B. Williams is born, in Hollywood, California. After graduating from the High School of Music and Art, in New York City, Vera attends the Black Mountain School, in North Carolina, a school where learning is considered a community activity. *A Chair for My Mother* and *"More, More, More," Said the Baby* are Caldecott Honor books. Williams says she wrote *A Chair for My Mother* to acknowledge that people who work very hard to put food on the table for their families also need roses. Williams recalls staying up all night painting roses for the back of the book jacket, roses for her mother.

▶ **WRITING TIP** Invite students to consider a special piece of furniture in their house, something with a story.

1932 Ann Jonas is born. She grows up in Long Island, New York. While studying art at Cooper Union, she meets her husband Donald Crews. Her books demonstrate a dramatic sense of design and often contain a visual game.

29

I drew on the sly in all my classes by hiding a tablet in my desk and sneaking a drawing into it now and then. . . . I also drew in my books, on the margins of the pages, which was graphic evidence that I had spent very little time reading the text.

Bill Peet,
Bill Peet: An Autobiography

BIRTHDAYS

1915 Bill Peet is born, in Grandview, Indiana. He graduates from the John Herron Art Institute, in Indianapolis. Bill loves animal stories, and his favorites are those by Ernest Thompson Seton, a naturalist who illustrates his own books. In *Bill Peet: An Autobiography*, Bill recalls that throughout his childhood drawing is his hobby. He turns his hobby into a profession, working for twenty-seven years as an illustrator for the Walt Disney studios. Bill gets his start in creating stories for children by telling his two sons bedtime stories.

▶ **READING TIP** Invite students to find a book of favorite animal stories to share with the class.

1930 Christopher Collier is born, in New York City. A high school teacher and history professor, Christopher collaborates with his brother James Lincoln on the Newbery Honor book *My Brother Sam Is Dead*, a gripping story of the American Revolution. Christopher says he does the historical research, finding the factual story. Then he and James make up some fictional characters, and James writes the true story around these fictional characters. Christopher says "for fun" he lives in a house that was built in 1790, and that he cuts a lot of firewood to keep the house's five fireplaces going.

1930 Sylvia Cassedy is born, in Brooklyn, New York. A second-grade teacher as well as a writing teacher of primary and secondary students, Sylvia's novels show the importance of children's make-believe worlds. Two of her collections, *Roomrimes: Poems* and *Zoomrimes: Poems About Things That Go*, present a poem for every letter of the alphabet. These are the titles of some of her room poems: "Attic," "Basement," "Closet," "Den," "Elevator," "Fire Escape," "Greenhouse."

▶ **WRITING TIP** The alphabet is a wonderful way to imagine as well as organize. Invite students to try making alphabetic lists. For starters, they can list things in the classroom alphabetically . . . and then see what happens from there.

1943 Rosemary Wells is born, in New York City. She says the characters in her books, Max and his older sister Ruby, are inspired by her two daughters. In their adventures, Ruby, who is sure she knows what is best for the younger Max, tries to control him. But Max always has other ideas. *Shy Charles,* again featuring a character based on one of her own children, wins the Boston Globe–Horn Book Award. Rosemary says she makes her characters animals because she finds them easier to draw than children. Whatever animal she's drawing, she makes sure the story touches the heart. In creating a story, she says, "Once the words are right, the pictures take on a life of their own. Then I will sit down with my inks, and glasses fit for a jeweler, and try to put the proverbial thousand words that are not in the text into the face of one worried raccoon."

EVENTS

1998 Carl Gorman, a Navajo artist and one of the "codetalkers" during World War II, dies. Gorman and twenty-eight other Navajo volunteers turned their native language into a secret code that Japanese code-crackers were never able to break. Navajo is a complex language without an alphabet. In 1942, other than Navajos, only thirty people in the world had any knowledge of the language.

▶ **READ MORE** Encourage students to explore codes. *Secret Codes for Kids,* by Robert Allen, and *The Usborne Book of Secret Codes,* by Eileen O'Brien, are places to start.

1999 Today's the deadline for a HarperCollins contest inspired by *Meet My Staff,* by Patricia Marx and Roz Chast. In the book, Walter has an illustrious staff to take care of all the icky details of his life so that he has more time for fun.

▶ **WRITING TIP** Invite students to list at least five icky details in their life and to come up with a job title and description for the person they will hire to rid them of these icky details. They can write memos or newspaper ads announcing the jobs.

JANUARY

The Goops they lick their fingers,

And the Goops they lick their knives. . . .

Gelett Burgess,
The Goops

BIRTHDAYS

1866 Gelett Burgess is born, in Boston. A master of nonsense verse, Gelett invents silly characters called the Goops. His "Purple Cow" is probably the most quoted verse of the first half of the twentieth century:

> I never saw a purple cow
> I never hope to see one. . . .

Gelett grows so tired of people quoting his quatrain at him that he writes a sequel:

> Ah, yes, I Wrote the 'Purple Cow'—
> I'm Sorry, now, I wrote it!
> But I can Tell you Anyhow,
> I'll Kill you if you Quote it.

1924 Lloyd Alexander is born, in Philadelphia. He decides at age fifteen that he wants to be a writer. His parents tell him he should consider doing something useful. Lloyd writes for adults for seventeen years before he produces his first book for children. *The Black Cauldron* is a Newbery Honor book, and *The High King* wins the Newbery Medal. In accepting the Newbery Medal for *The High King,* Lloyd admits, "Coming to the last page of *The High King* was a sad moment for me, a feeling more akin to loss than liberation; as if something one had loved deeply for a long time had suddenly gone away."

▶ **WRITING TIP 1** Lloyd says that "'write what you know' is sound advice. But we also need to understand that we know many things, more than we suppose. Our work lies in discovering what they are, in discovering what matters to us."

▶ **WRITING TIP 2** Asked how many times he revises before bringing a manuscript to the publisher. Lloyd replies, "I revise a lot. Some pages I've rewritten twenty times, some books [have been] rewritten three times."

1931 Allan Eckert is born, in Buffalo, New York. After leaving college Allen works as a postman, private detective, fireman, cook, trapper, commercial artist, and police reporter before he settles on being a writer. *Incident at Hawk's Hill,* a Newbery Honor book, is based on a real event: a young Canadian boy, lost in the wilds, is adopted by a female badger.

1957 Polly Horvath is born, in Kalamazoo, Michigan. Her favorite book growing up is *Half Magic,* by Edward Eager, and she begins sending her own manuscripts off to publishers when she is nine years old. Polly says that although she doesn't get anything published, she receives nice, encouraging letters from editors at almost every publishing house in New York. At age eighteen, Polly gives up writing to study at the Canadian College of Dance, in Toronto, and the Martha Graham School of Contemporary Dance, in New York City. But she returns to writing, and *The Trolls* is the result.

▶ **READING TIP** Polly notes that most of her fan mail is from adults. "And why not? When I was a child my mother used to tell us anybody can read anything. . . . I didn't like *Charlotte's Web* when I was a kid but I adore it as an adult. This idea of reading in your age slot is bunk. Read what you like."

EVENTS

1847 Yerba Buena is renamed San Francisco.

1851 The Library of Congress, the national library of the United States, buys Thomas Jefferson's book collection of 6,500 volumes for $23,950. By 1987, the Library of Congress contains 532 miles of bookshelves holding over 85 million items. Students can visit the Library online to see just what an exciting place it is: *http://lcweb.loc.gov*

1936 New owners of the Boston Braves ask newspapermen to pick a new nickname. They pick "the Bees." When it hasn't caught on by 1940, this nickname is dropped.

▶ **ALL ABOUT NAMES** Invite students to take a look at team nicknames they know and to offer opinions about why this one fizzled.

JANUARY

31

The role of the artist is that of the shaman, penetrating surface reality to perceive a universal truth, drawing out the essence of an idea.

Gerald McDermott,
Caldecott acceptance speech

BIRTHDAYS

1872 Pearl Zane Grey is born in Zanesville, Ohio, a town founded by his mother's ancestors. Growing up, he likes fishing, baseball, and writing. Zane's baseball ability earns him a scholarship to the University of Pennsylvania's Dental Department. Although he earns his dentist's degree, when he leaves college, Zane plays amateur baseball and then gains fame for his books about the western frontier. Frank McCourt, whose childhood memoir is *Angela's Ashes,* recalls reading "dozens and dozens of cowboy books," including Zane Grey's *Riders of the Purple Sage.*

1941 Gerald McDermott is born, in Detroit, Michigan. When he is four he begins taking classes at the Detroit Institute of Art. While studying at the Pratt Institute he produces a series of animated films on mythology. His first book, *Anansi the Spider,* is adapted from one of his films and is a Caldecott Honor book. His second book, *Arrow to the Sun*, wins the Caldecott Medal.

1950 Denise Fleming is born, in Toledo, Ohio. In third grade she is chosen to participate in classes at the Toledo Museum of Art, and one of her paintings is chosen to be the cover of a teachers' magazine. Now, she likes to make her own paper. "Paper-making for me is cathartic. Part of its appeal is that it's very physical—toting buckets of water, beating large quantities of pulp, hand-mixing huge vats of color. . . It is wet, messy, and wonderful."

EVENT

1990 An atlas sells for $1,925,000 at Sotheby's, New York City. It is a version of Ptolemy's *Cosmographia* dating from 1492.

▶ **RESEARCH TIP** Invite students to find an interesting fact in an atlas and share it with the class.

FEBRUARY

Knock knock.
Who's there?
Accordion!
Accordion who?
Accordion to the weather bureau, February is short but stormy.

FEBRUARY

1

Well, son, I'll tell you:

Life for me ain't been
no crystal stair.

It's had tacks in it.

And splinters. . . .

Langston Hughes,
"Mother to Son"

BIRTHDAYS

1902 James Langston Hughes is born, in Joplin, Missouri, an only child. As a young boy, Langston lives with his grandmother in Kansas. He sees reading as his way to escape loneliness. Besides reading, he also writes, and his first poems appear in print when he is in high school. After a year at Columbia University, Langston joins the crew of the S. S. *Malone,* which visits more than thrity ports in Africa. One of the most original and versatile of African-American writers, Langston is particularly influenced by the poetry of Paul Laurence Dunbar and Carl Sandburg. He is known as the poet laureate of Harlem.

1910 Ursula Nordstrom is born, in New York City. Beginning her career at Harper & Row as a clerk in the college textbook department, five years later she becomes an assistant in the children's book department. In 1940 she becomes director of Harper's department of books for boys and girls and gains fame as a brilliant editor and the single most creative force for innovation in children's book publishing in the United States. She likes to say that she champions "good books for bad children," and the authors and illustrators she works with include Margaret Wise Brown, E. B. White, Garth Williams, Ruth Krauss, Crockett Johnson, Charlotte Zolotow, Maurice Sendak, Mary Stolz, Tomi Ungerer, Louise Fitzhugh, Else Holmelund Minarik, Mary Rodgers, Karla Kuskin, Russell Hoban, John Steptoe, and Shel Silverstein.

1941 Jerry Spinelli is born, in Norristown, Pennsylvania. One morning in 1979, this father of six children gets up and discovers a pile of bones instead of the fried chicken he'd planned to pack in his lunch bag. He usually writes during his lunch break, and since he is still angry about the bare chicken bones, that day he writes about them. In a sudden inspiration, he decides to write the story from the point of view of the kid who ate the chicken. This is the genesis of his first book, *Space Station Seventh Grade.* (Jerry says the culprit who ate his chicken still hasn't confessed.)

▶ **WRITING TIP** Invite students to think of an incident in which they disagreed with somebody—and to write about that incident from the other person's point of view. One way to get started is to try writing a letter to themselves from that other person.

EVENTS

1709 Alexander Selkirk, a Scottish sailor stranded on Mas a Tierra Island, four hundred miles west of Valparaiso, Chile, for nearly five years, is rescued on this day. A shoemaker's son who had run away to sea, Alexander had quarreled with the captain and been put ashore. He reports that at first he was pestered by rats, which gnawed at his feet when he tried to sleep. Fortunately, there were cats on the island. He befriended them and they ate the rats.

▶ **READ MORE** Daniel Defoe based *Robinson Crusoe* on Selkirk's adventures.

1854 Clara Barton becomes a clerk in the U. S. Patent Office. She is paid ten cents for every one hundred words she writes. Her pay ranges from $71 to $83 a month.

▶ **WRITING TIP** Students enjoy the novelty of keeping track of how many words they write in a day. At Clara's rate, how much would they make in a month?

1940 Captain Marvel makes his first appearance, in *Whiz Comics No. 2.*

► **READING TIP** Invite students to bring in their favorite comics for a comic-sharing festival.

1999 When Mary Azarian's phone rings before 8 A.M., she is annoyed to have her reading time interrupted. Informed that *Snowflake Bentley* has won the Caldecott Medal, Mary replies that such a joke is in poor taste. When she calls her oldest son, he says, "Well, don't get excited, Mom, they'll probably call back and tell you they miscounted." It isn't a joke and they didn't miscount. Mary, a longtime resident of Vermont, has received the premier award for children's book illustration—for a book about a man who photographed snowflakes in Jericho, Vermont. In Mary's words, "By many people's standards, Bentley would be considered a failure. And yet, in the most important aspects, his life was a roaring success. He found as much joy in a snowstorm at age seventy as he did at age ten."

FEBRUARY

If I were in charge of
the world

A chocolate sundae
with whipped cream
and nuts

would be a vegetable.

Judith Viorst,
"If I Were in Charge of
the World"

BIRTHDAY

1931 Judith Viorst is born, in Newark, New Jersey. A successful magazine columnist, when she begins writing books for children, she writes about events in the lives of her own children—and even uses their real names, Anthony, Nicholas, and Alexander. Judith is famous for the titles of her books as well as for their content. Who can resist a book with the title *Sad Underwear*?

► **READING/WRITING CONNECTION** Invite students to read Judith Viorst's poem "If I Were in Charge of the World," asking them to invent their own "in charge" statements. Point out that some of her statements are positive, others negative. Which do they think are more powerful, rules to get rid of or rules to invent?

EVENTS

Annually Today is Groundhog Day, when according to a popular U. S. tradition the groundhog comes out of his hole after a long winter sleep to look for his shadow. If the day is cloudy and he doesn't see it, the groundhog takes it as a sign of spring and stays above ground. If he sees his shadow, this is an omen of six more weeks of bad weather, and he returns to his hole. Groundhog Day is associated with Candlemas Day, when, according to an old English song:

> If Candlemas be fair and bright,
> Come, Winter, have another fight;
> If Candlemas brings clouds and rain,
> Go Winter, and come not again.

► **RESEARCH TIP** Invite students to research weather superstitions. They can go to the library, search the Internet, or interview oldsters they know for anecdotes about weather lore. *Weather Proverbs: How 600 Proverbs, Sayings, and Poems Accurately Explain Our Weather,* by George D. Freier, contains interesting lore ("Wet May, dry July"; "As high as the weeds grow, so will be the bane of snow.")

1863 Samuel Clemens becomes Mark Twain when he sends a report to a Virginia City, Nevada, newspaper using the new name. The term comes from Clemens's days working on riverboats on the Mississippi River. "Mark twain" is the river call for a water depth of two fathoms.

► **ALL ABOUT NAMES** Challenge students to think of a term from the working lives of someone they know that might be used as a pseudonym. For example, do doctors, bankers, auto mechanics, carpenters, figure skaters, basketball players, and so on have special words that might make interesting pen names?

1909 President Teddy Roosevelt is never too busy to find time for the birds. Nearing the end of his second term in office, President Roosevelt makes a list of the kinds of birds he has seen in and around Washington. The list contains the name of ninety-three varieties. Roosevelt notes he has seen fifty-seven of them on the White House grounds. He has found nine kinds nesting on the White House grounds: red-headed woodpeckers, flickers, orchard orioles, purple grackles, redstarts, catbirds, tufted titmice, wood thrushes, and robins.

▶ **WRITING TIP** Invite students to keep a "listing" kind of notebook for two or three weeks. They can choose the subject: birds, out-of-state license plates, people wearing hats, whatever. Remind them that they should describe the item and the time that they note its sighting.

▶ **READ MORE** *The King of the Birds*, written and illustrated by Helen Ward, is not to be missed. It is an enthralling visual delight. Birds representing species from all over the world get together to decide who should be the king. Questions arise: should it be the bird with the biggest beak? the largest feet? A key at the back brings encyclopedic identification to the tale.

FEBRUARY

Ben stretched out in the shade of a bush and rested his massive head on extended forepaws. Mark sat down cross-legged beside him, idly scratching his ears as he stared dreamily off to sea.

Walter Morey,
Gentle Ben

BIRTHDAYS

1902 Walter Morey is born, in Hoquiam, Washington. In his youth he lives in various locales in the Northwest, depending on his father's construction jobs. Walter doesn't learn to read until he is fourteen. He credits his job as a projectionist in a movie theater—watching movies over and over—with showing him what makes a good story. Although he had written stories for adults, he doesn't try one for children until, at his wife's urging, he writes *Gentle Ben*. Here is a year 2000 review on *Amazon.com* from a young reader: "*Gentle Ben* is probably the best book I have ever read. At first I didn't even want to read it, but my mom made me. Since then I have read it five times and plan on reading it a lot more in the future."

▶ **READING/WRITING CONNECTION** Invite students to read reviews of their favorite books posted at online booksellers. Then they can write their own reviews for these sites.

1927 Joan Lowery Nixon is born, in Los Angeles, California. She studies journalism at the University of Southern California. Four-time winner of the Edgar Allan Poe Best Juvenile Mystery Award, given by the Mystery Writers of America, Joan is the author of more than a hundred books, including tall-tale picture books, the rip-snortin' Claude series, the Orphan Train Adventures series, and the Colonial Williamsburg series. Before she becomes a full-time writer Joan teaches kindergarten and first grade in Los Angeles. Her favorite bookstore is Murder by the Book, in Houston.

▶ **READING REFLECTION** Invite students to take a look at Joan's book titles in the library. Can they separate the books for teenage readers from the books for young readers just by the titles? Ask them to discuss these decisions. What does a book's title reveal about its contents? Do predictions about a book's content from the title always work? Invite students to create a poster of "tricky titles."

EVENT

1850 Nathaniel Hawthorne finishes *The Scarlet Letter* and reads the last part to his wife. In Nathaniel's words, "It broke her heart . . . and sent her to bed with a grievous headache, which I look upon as a triumphant success."

▶ **READING REFLECTION** What do students think about books that break the reader's heart? How about books that win prizes? Are there more happy ones or more sad ones? Do books get sadder as kids get older? Encourage students to reinforce their opinions by citing specific book titles.

FEBRUARY

4

"You've got to be able to make those daring leaps or you're nowhere," said Muskrat.

Russell Hoban,
The Mouse and His Child

BIRTHDAY

1925 Russell Hoban is born, in Lansdale, Pennsylvania. His father gives his three children nickels for clever remarks and for excellent drawings. Russell says everybody takes it for granted that he will be a great artist when he grows up. Russell draws illustrations for *Time, Sports Illustrated,* and *The Saturday Evening Post,* but other people illustrate the children's books he writes. Russell collaborates with his illustrator-wife Lillian Hoban on many projects. The Frances stories, written by Russell and illustrated by Lillian, grow out of their experiences with their own four children. A new edition of the not-to-be-missed *The Mouse and His Child* is reillustrated by David Small.

▶ **WRITING TIP** Russell's *Egg Thoughts* gives his impressions of various types of eggs. "Soft-Boiled" begins:

I do not like the way you slide.
I do not like your soft inside.

Invite students to follow Russell's pattern, writing rhyming couplets about a food they do not like. Remind them to address the food directly.

FEBRUARY

5

Do not put your face in your food, snort, or smack your lips while eating. . . .

Do not lick your greasy fingers or wipe them on your coat.

Patricia Lauber,
What You Never Knew About Fingers, Forks, and Chopsticks

BIRTHDAYS

1924 Patricia Lauber is born, in New York City. She writes detail-filled nonfiction books, examining everything from dinosaurs to the geologic formations on distant planets. Patricia's topics in the Let's-Read-And-Find-Out Science series for beginning readers range from garbage to earthworms to Amelia Earhart. For older readers, her titles also cover a wide range: *The News About Dinosaurs, Snakes Are Hunters, Tales Mummies Tell, Too Much Garbage, Your Body and How It Works.* And that's just a few.

▶ **WRITING TIP** Patricia says she gets her best ideas by looking at things: "I like to stand and stare at things." She also reads a lot and travels extensively to provide the detailed information her readers have come to expect. She found these exhortations about eating in a medieval book of etiquette. This is a fun pattern for young writers to follow. Invite them to compile a "do not" book about cafeteria etiquette, playground etiquette, classroom etiquette, and so on. Pointing out the pattern will help students structure their rules: each sentence should start with *Do not* and should contain two verb phrases connected by *or.*

1956 David Wiesner is born, in Bridgewater, New Jersey. As a boy David practices drawing by watching artist Jon Gnagy's television show and completing the accompanying workbooks. David's high school art teacher encourages him to practice with a variety of media, including comic books and film. While attending the Rhode Island School of Design, he does the art for a cover of *Cricket.* Years later, an invitation to draw frogs for another *Cricket* cover gives David the idea for *Tuesday,* a nine-word book that is awarded the Caldecott Medal.

There is far more of imagination and enthusiasm in the making of a good dictionary than in the average novel.

Eric Partridge

BIRTHDAY

1894 Eric Honeywood Partridge is born, on a farm in Waimata Valley, New Zealand. His family moves to Brisbane, Australia, in 1907. By the time he is thirteen Eric has written a novel and several short stories. In 1937, *A Dictionary of Slang and Unconventional English* is published. Partridge stands with the unique few who have written a dictionary by themselves. No one else in the twentieth century managed such a feat. The *Oxford English Dictionary*, a group effort, cites his work 770 times.

▶ **WORD FUN** Dictionaries are something everybody takes for granted. Challenge students to write definitions for five things in their desk. They can compare their definitions with those in a classroom dictionary. Then they can estimate the number of words in that classroom dictionary and figure out how long it would take them to write a dictionary.

EVENT

1995 Sharon Creech receives a phone call from the American Library Association telling her that *Walk Two Moons* has received the Newbery Medal. Sharon says that the idea for the book came from a message she found in a fortune cookie: "Don't judge a man until you've walked two moons in his moccasins." Sharon thinks that Salamanca and her mother are very much like herself and her own daughter. In all her books the characters are combinations of people she knows.

Once upon a time, sixty years ago, a little girl lived in the Big Woods of Wisconsin, in a little gray house made of logs.

Laura Ingalls Wilder,
Little House in the Big Woods

BIRTHDAYS

1812 Charles Dickens is born, in Portsmouth, England. Charles says that "papa, potatoes, poultry, prunes, and prism are all very good words for the lips." He also notes, "No man is useless in this world, who lightens the burdens of someone else." Isaac Asimov says his favorite book is Dickens's *Pickwick Papers*, which he has read "at least twenty-five times."

▶ **READING REFLECTION** Invite students to interview three adults, asking them their favorite childhood book. Invite student teams to come up with questionnaires asking the same question of students in other classes. They can decide if they want to break the question down into parts: favorite preschool book, favorite book someone read aloud, favorite book they read themselves.

1837 James Murray is born, in Harwick, Scotland. Because of his family's poverty, James has to leave school at fourteen, but he has already proven himself well able to educate himself. By the time he is fifteen, James knows French, Italian, German, Latin, and Greek. He is the single individual most associated with the creation of the *Oxford English Dictionary*.

▶ **READ MORE** A fun read for teachers: *The Professor and the Madman: A Tale of Murder, Insanity, and the Making of the Oxford English Dictionary*, by Simon Winchester.

1867 Laura Ingalls Wilder is born, near Pepin, Wisconsin. Her family then moves to the area near Independence, Kansas. At age sixty-five, Laura publishes her first book, *Little House in the Big Woods*, describing Ingalls family life in Wisconsin. *Little House on the Prairie* describes the family's life in Kansas. Other books describe other places where they live. Five of Laura's books are Newbery Honor books. By the 1990s her books have sold more than forty million copies. Laura's editor at Harper & Row, Ursula Nordstrom, comments on her work, "None of the manuscripts ever needed any editing. Not any. They were read and then copy-edited and sent to the printer."

1908 Fred Gipson is born, in Mason, Texas. He grows up on the Texas frontier listening to his father's stories. *Old Yeller*, a Newbery Honor book, features fourteen-year-old Travis Coates, who is trying to take care of his family in his father's absence and grows to love an ugly stray dog.

1954 Shonto Begay is born, in Shonto, Arizona, a Navajo reservation in the northeast corner of the state, the fifth of sixteen children born to a Navajo medicine man. Shonto comes from a family who live without electricity, running water, and television; they are a family who give him a strong sense of the importance of stories. He illustrates Caron Lee Cohen's *The Mud Pony: A Traditional Skidee Pawnee Tale*.

EVENTS

1879 The Philological Society and Oxford University Press sign a contract to produce what becomes known as the *Oxford English Dictionary*. Editors are now working on the first complete revision in its history, at a cost of about fifty-five million dollars. Part of this effort includes publishing the OED online, incorporating at least a thousand new and revised entries every quarter. John Simpson, chief editor, says, "There is no longer one English—there are many Englishes. Words are flooding into the language from all corners of the world." He asks for reader contributions at <http://oed.com>. The site also includes the OED newsletter, with interesting articles on how they track down derivations of new words such as *nachos*.

1938 Donald Duck cartoons are so popular in theaters and as a Sunday comic strip that a daily newspaper comic strip is launched on this day.

FEBRUARY

8

I felt—or rather fancied I felt—the machine sinking down to the lowest beds of the sea. Dreadful nightmares beset me; I saw in these mysterious asylums a world of unknown animals, amongst which this submarine boat seemed to be of the same kind, living, moving, and formidable as they.

Jules Verne,
*Twenty Thousand Leagues
Beneath the Sea*

BIRTHDAYS

1828 Jules Verne is born, in France. Trained as a lawyer, Jules writes librettos for operettas. In 1863, he starts writing novels that show his intense interest in science. In Verne's pages the reader finds geography, geology, physics, biology. By today's standards many of Verne's facts are wrong, but nonetheless these facts continue to make the stories seem very real.

1934 Anne Rockwell is born, in Memphis, Tennessee. She studies art at the Sculpture Center, in New York City, and at the Pratt Institute, in Brooklyn. She creates popular books about transportation—boats, cars, trucks, trains, and planes. She also writes fairy-tale collections.

▶ **READING REFLECTION** Nonfiction often doesn't get the same attention as fiction. Invite students to create a bulletin board of book reviews and posters about favorite nonfiction titles and/or authors.

▶ **WRITING TIP** Ask student teams to choose a topic they don't know much about—and to find out as much as they can. Create a Facts Bulletin Board; hold a Facts Festival where students present their favorite facts verbally and/or visually.

9

mudluscious
in just-spring

e. e. cummings

BIRTHDAYS

1927 Dick Gackenbach is born. In *Harry and the Terrible Whatzit* Dick invents the word *vomitrocious*. Dick is a commercial artist with the J. C. Penney Company, and as a hobby he collects books, including volumes by Frank Baum, Maurice Sendak, Shel Silverstein, Irene Haas, Marilyn Hafner, and Gerald McDermott.

▶ **WORD FUN** The poet e. e. cummings coined a word that means pretty much the opposite of *vomitrocious, mudluscious.* Neither word is in the dictionary, but nobody needs a dictionary to know what the words mean. On the other hand, when the Time Warp Trio encounter a *vomitorium* in *See You Later, Gladiator,* Jon Scieszka warns that it isn't what you might think it is, and a dictionary will come in handy. Challenge students to invent some words of their own. They can start by following the above patterns: find synonyms for vomit or other negative words and put on the suffix *rocious;* make a list of things they think are wonderful and add the suffix *luscious.* Then they can decide which of their new words sizzle and which don't.

1945 Stephen Roos is born, in New York City. After working ten years for Harper & Row, Stephen quits his job, thinking he'll give himself a year to try writing. About five days before Roos reaches the end of his one-year deadline, Delacorte accepts *My Horrible Secret* for publication. Stephen has written books in several series, including Maple Street Kids and Pet Lovers Club.

EVENT

1884 Beatrix Potter writes in her journal, "Bought a tail-less cockrobin for the exorbitant price of eighteen-pence. Let [it] go in the flower walk, where it hopped into aucuba bush with great satisfaction." Potter's journal is filled with her notes and drawings of the animals in her menagerie.

▶ **WRITING TIP** Invite students to keep journal observations on an animal for one week.

10

Branwell likes his own name because it was his mother's before she got married. She was Linda Branwell, an only child.

E. L. Konigsburg,
Silent to the Bone

BIRTHDAYS

1930 E(laine) L(oeb) Konigsburg is born, in New York City. She signs her books E. L. rather than Elaine because when she began writing she thought it was not important for readers to know whether she was male or female. And one of her favorite writers is E. B. White. But, says, Elaine, if she were starting out today, she would use Elaine.

▶ **WRITING TIP 1** "Finish!" Elaine points out that for writers, as for everybody else, it is much easier to start something than to finish it. One way to help students finish is to give them the ending for which they are to write the beginning and the middle. One source of endings is the *Guinness Book of Records.* Think of the possibilities surrounding the person who grows a fifteen-pound carrot or a thirty-seven-pound radish.

▶ **WRITING TIP 2** Elaine also advises young writers, "Keep a journal."

1934 James Rice is born, in Coleman, Texas. His most popular books are *Cajun Alphabet* and *Cajun Night Before Christmas. Cajun Night Before Christmas* substitutes alligators in the role played by cats and mice in *Night Before Christmas.*

▶ **RESEARCH TIP** Invite students to choose a popular song that is sung in school and then write a parody, substituting words that will reflect their ethnic background or the region of the country in which they live.

1943 Stephen Gammell is born, in Des Moines, Iowa, where he grows up. Even as a young boy Stephen thinks pencils and stacks of paper are better than toys. His work demonstrates a great range of emotion, from the sinister and scary drawings in *Scary*

Stories to Tell in the Dark to the joyous celebration of *Song and Dance Man*, a Caldecott Medal book. Although he has illustrated dozens of books for other authors, Stephen has written just five of his own. He confesses, "I hate writing, and find it terribly difficult. I often come up with ideas, but . . . it is such a chore."

EVENT

1897 The *New York Times* publishes its front-page slogan for the first time, "All the News That's Fit to Print." Years later, the newspaper runs a contest for people to come up with a better slogan, but management decides no entries improve on this one.

▶ **THINK ABOUT IT** Invite students to come up with a class slogan.

FEBRUARY

Nothing is always.

Jane Yolen,
The Girl Who Loved the Wind

BIRTHDAY

1939 Jane Yolen is born, in New York City. Jane sells her first children's book on her twenty-second birthday and then becomes one of the most prolific writers of children's books, writing over two hundred books in a variety of forms, ranging from the Commander Toad science fiction series for young readers to literary fairy tales such as *The Girl Who Cried Flowers and Other Tales* to sensitive free verse to historical novels. Jane says that the great words are *good, evil, courage, honor, truth, hate,* and *love.* Jane does not keep a journal. "Journal writing is writing to be kept hidden. I write to be read openly." Asked to name her favorite authors, Jane says, "Robert Louis Stevenson, Rudyard Kipling, John Donne, James Thurber, Hans Christian Andersen, T. H. White, Oscar Wilde, Louisa May Alcott, Natalie Babbit, Patricia MacLachlan, Patricia McKillip, Diana Wynne Jones." Then she adds, "And many, many others."

▶ **READ MORE 1** In an open letter to her daughter and granddaughters at the beginning of *Not One Damsel in Distress: World Folktales for Strong Girls,* Jane says she wrote this book because growing up, she didn't have it herself. Jane says, "For the longest time I didn't know that girls could be heroes, too. . . . This book is for you because in it are folktales about heroes—regular sword-wielding, spear-throwing, villain-stomping, rescuing-type heroes who also happen to be female."

▶ **READ MORE 2** Bothered that something was "horribly wrong" at the moral center of "Rumplestiltskin," with the only upright character in the tale sacrificed in the end, Jane writes "Granny Rumple," included in the collection *Sister Emily's Lightship.*

FEBRUARY

Read your work aloud!
This is the best advice I
can give you.

Judy Blume

BIRTHDAYS

1809 Abraham Lincoln is born. His favorite foods are steak, apples, and pecan pie. After the Lincolns move into the White House, many people send gifts. Two of the favorite gifts are goats named Nanny and Nanko. The President's sons hitch the goats to carts or kitchen chairs and drive them through the main floor of the White House. One time Tad harnesses Nanko to a chair and drives through the East Room during a White House reception.

▶ **READING TIP** Invite students to choose a favorite animal anecdote from a book and read it aloud to the class.

1938 Judy Blume is born, in Elizabeth, New Jersey. Her favorite books as a child are *Madeline* and the Betsy-Tacy series, by Maud Hart Lovelace. Judy is not alone in her passion for Betsy-Tacy; the series has sold sixty-five million copies. Judy starts her own writing by imitating Dr. Seuss. Judy says *Starring Sally J. Freedman As Herself* is her most autobiographical work. "Sally was the kind of kid I was at ten. My brother was like Douglas, Sally's brother." Judy points out that Fudge is based on her own son Larry.

▶ **READING/WRITING CONNECTION** Judy says even though kids groan when she tells them that rewriting is what she enjoys most, it's true. She also offers this advice: "Read your work aloud! This is the best advice I can give you. When you read aloud you find out how much can be cut, how much is unnecessary. And nothing teaches you as much about writing dialogue as listening to it."

1945 David Small is born, in Detroit, Michigan. Seeing a mural about the auto industry painted by the Mexican artist Diego Rivera convinces David to become an artist: "I suddenly realized the very real power artists have to shape our vision of the world." David struggles through many schools, making mediocre grades, pushed along by teachers who had faith in his artistic talent. He says he found a real home in the art department at Wayne State University. "I felt I had suddenly been washed ashore in a country where people spoke my own language." David illustrates his own hilarious books as well as those of others. His illustrations for Sarah Stewart's *The Gardener* are awarded the Caldecott Honor, and David wins the Medal for *So You Want to Be President.* Sarah is David's wife. They have an Airedale named Simon and a cat named Otis.

1950 Chris Conover is born, in New York City, an only child. Both of her parents are artists, and art is an important part of the household. In college she studies fine art and printmaking but has no formal training in illustration. While watching a W. C. Fields movie, Chris gets the idea for *Six Little Ducks*.

1957 Rick Walton is born, in Utah. He works as a cook in a Mexican restaurant, a secretary, a missionary, a teacher, and a computer software writer. Now he describes himself as the "happy author of more than thirty books for children." These books include picture books, poetry, and a number of joke books coauthored by his wife, Ann: *Dumb Clucks! Jokes About Chickens; Fossil Follies! Jokes About Dinosaurs; Kiss a Frog! Jokes About Fairy Tales, Knights, and Dragons; Something's Fishy! Jokes About Sea Creatures; What a Ham! Jokes About Pigs;* and *What's Your Name Again? More Jokes About Names* are just some of the titles. He lives in Provo, Utah.

▶ **ALL ABOUT NAMES** A few jokes about names from Rick's book can get students thinking about names—and coming up with their own riddles.

Q: Who goes a long way?

A: Miles

Q: Who always has a cold?

A: Isaac

19-- Jacqueline Woodson is born, in Columbus, Ohio. Before she begins to write full time, she is a drama therapist for runaways and homeless children in New York City. She loves writing beginning in fifth grade, but an English teacher in seventh grade has the biggest influence, telling Jacqueline that she writes really well. Jacqueline says, "I wanted to write about communities that were familiar to me and people that were familiar to me. I wanted to write about communities of color. I wanted to write about girls. I wanted to write about friendship and all of these things that I felt like were missing in a lot of the books that I read as a child." Asked who her favorite writers are, Jacqueline names Mildred Taylor, James Baldwin, Toni Morrison, Phyllis Reynolds Naylor, Patricia MacLachlan, and Rosa Guy.

▶ **WRITING TIPS** Jacqueline says even when it's hard, you "really have to write every single day, at least for thirty minutes—just sitting down and writing in your diary or writing a letter to a friend or writing a poem or anything, but just try to practice writing every day."

1987 The United States Postal Service issues a 14-cent stamp honoring Julia Ward Howe.

FEBRUARY

13

Wow, wow, wow. Wow.

Simms Taback,
on being told he has been
awarded the Caldecott Medal

BIRTHDAYS

1881 Eleanor Farjeon is born. Most of her many volumes of poetry are out of print, but individual poems are frequently anthologized. One popular poem begins and ends with these two lines:

Cats sleep
Anywhere

1892 Grant Wood is born, near Anamosa, Iowa. He studies at the Art Institute of Chicago and in Paris. He is director of the WPA art projects in Iowa and teaches at the State University of Iowa. His most famous painting is *American Gothic,* a painting in which stern people in a stylized landscape present a rigid, decorative image of the rural Midwest. Grant says, "All the really good ideas I ever had came to me while milking a cow."

▶ **THINK ABOUT IT** Invite students to finish the sentence, All the really good ideas I ever had come to me while. . . .

1924 Ouida Sebestyen is born, in Vernon, Texas. She uses the West as the setting in most of her novels. She submits her first manuscript to a publisher when she is twenty but doesn't get published for thirty-five years. After that first rejection, Ouida cleans houses and does odd jobs while collecting more rejection notices. After many rejections, *Words by Heart* is accepted for publication in 1979.

1932 Simms Taback is born, in New York City. His *Joseph Had a Little Overcoat* is awarded the Caldecott Medal. He says that when he heard the news, "I had to lay down for about ten minutes, just to sort of . . . wow. All you can say is 'Wow, wow, wow.' You walk around the room for about ten minutes. 'Wow.'"

1945 William Sleator is born, in Havre de Grace, Maryland. He grows up in University City, Missouri. At age six, he types his first story. Titled "The Fat Cat," it reads: "Once there was a fat cat. Boy was she fat. Well, not that fat. But pretty fat." In school, William puts a twist on assignments. When asked to write about a holiday, he writes about "The Haunted Easter Egg." William says that a lot of fun of writing science fiction is learning about such phenomena as behavior modification and black holes. Known for his science fiction, William is also a composer for the ballet and for film.

1947 Janet Taylor Lisle is born, in Englewood, New Jersey. Her books are set in the everyday world but peppered with magic: cats dance, miniature elves hide in the backyard. Janet says, "I believe in the unknown. There is a great deal we don't know about our world, like how big the universe is or what makes our brains work. Perhaps the human brain isn't smart enough or sensitive enough to detect certain secrets. I think of magic as that which is still waiting to be discovered. I put it in my books so that readers (me included) won't forget to keep a sharp eye out."

EVENT

1635 Boston Latin School, the first public school in the United States, is established.

▶ **WRITING TIP** Students may not be able to establish a school, but they can make suggestions of how to change the one they go to. Encourage students to come up with practical plans for reform. They can write letters to the administration and to the board of education with their ideas.

▶ **READ MORE** Invite students to read books about schools. For the younger set, start with *The Librarian from the Black Lagoon*, by Mike Thaler; *Never Spit on Your Shoes*, by Denys Cazet; *The Day the Teacher Went Bananas*, by James Howe; the Miss Nelson series, by Harry Allard and James Marshall; and *Lily's Purple Plastic Purse*, by Kevin Henkes. For middle graders, there's *The Burning Questions of Bingo Brown*, by Betsy Byars; *My Teacher Is an Alien*, by Bruce Coville; *Skinnybones*, by Barbara Park; *There's a Boy in the Girls' Bathroom*, by Louis Sachar; *The Goof Who Invented Homework and Other School Poems*, by Kalli Dakos; and lots more. You could spend a year just on the genre of literature about school. What fun!

FEBRUARY

14

Happy Valentinesaurus Day!

Bernard Most,
Happy Holidaysaurus!

BIRTHDAYS

1952 George Shannon is born, in Caldwell, Kansas. He earns a master's degree in library science and works for five years as a children's librarian before becoming a professional storyteller. His inventive Stories to Solve books are folktales from various cultures with riddles or puzzles for young readers to solve.

1953 Paul Zelinsky is born, in Evanston, Illinois. Paul's mother is a medical illustrator, and he draws a lot as a boy, learning different techniques of printmaking in high school. But Yale is where he learns to take children's books seriously—in a class taught by Maurice Sendak on the history and making of children's books. Paul's Caldecott Honor books include *Hansel and Gretel*, *Rumpelstiltskin*, and *Swamp Angel*; his *Rapunzel* is a Caldecott Medal book. Paul points out that all his work with folktales shows him that there is no such thing as an "original" version; folktales and fairy tales are always changing. Paul remembers William Pene du Bois and Robert Lawson as favorite childhood authors. But he says, "If you dropped me on a desert island with just one book of my choosing, I'd make it a blank book, and hope my pen would never fail me."

▶ **READING TIP** Ask students to decide, if you had only so many books in your classroom (make the number equal to the number of students in your class), what should these books be? Should each student get to choose a special book or would it be better for the class to collaborate on the selections?

▶ **RESEARCH TIP** Paul provides detailed and detailed notes on the creation of *Rapunzel* online: *http://www.penguinputnam.com/Author/AuthorFrame/0,1018,00.html?0000028534_MIS*

EVENT

A.D. 270 It is believed by some that St. Valentine is beheaded on this day. In *Happy Holidaysaurus!* Bernard Most suggests celebrating Happy Valentinesaurus Day!

▶ **WRITING TIP** Students can celebrate this day by creating pop-up Valentine cards. Joan Irvine has written two wonderful book containing easy-to-follow directions for making many varieties of pop-ups: *How to Make Pop-Ups* and *Super Pop-Ups*. Encourage students to make cards for school helpers.

▶ **READ MORE** *Olive You! and Other Valentine Knock-Knock Jokes You'll A-door*, by Katy Hall and Lisa Eisenberg, is a winner. Most of the riddles will travel far beyond Valentine's Day and the lift-the-flap format will inspire young readers to imitation. *Mush! The Complete Book of Valentine Words*, by Lynda Graham-Barber, offers interesting holiday lore.

One time there was a
woman had two
daughters

and they kept a hired
girl. They treated this
girl mean.

Richard Chase,
"Ashpet," in *Grandfather Tales*

BIRTHDAYS

1904 Richard Chase is born, in Huntsville, Alabama. His collections of Southern folktales, *Grandfather Tales* and *The Jack Tales*, are classics. The *Grandfather Tales* contain several Cinderella variants; in one of the *Jack Tales*, Jack is a Cinderella figure.

▶ **READING/WRITING CONNECTION** Invite students to read different versions of the Cinderella tale. Ask them to study the language carefully, looking for words that make a story seem old-fashioned or modern.

▶ **OUT LOUD** Richard Chase points out that he'd rather tell the stories than write them down. Invite students to tell a favorite fairy tale or folktale. How do their versions of the same tale differ from one another?

1928 Norman Bridwell is born, in Kokomo, Indiana. Norman isn't good at sports; his high school shop teacher doesn't want him to handle tools and instead hands him a pad of paper and tells him to draw. Norman's high school art teacher doesn't like his work, but he is determined to make art his life's work. After attending the John Herron Art Institute and Cooper Union Art School, he works as a commercial artist, illustrating filmstrips and designing fabric. Then, in 1962, Norman publishes a small paperback, *Clifford, the Big Red Dog*. It is a huge hit with young readers, and Norman writes sequels.

EVENT

1984 In Chicago, Lincoln Park Zoo officials have to rename Eric the orangutan. After she gives birth, it is clear that Eric should be called Erica.

▶ **READ MORE** Invite students to find and read books about orangutans. Here are a few suggestions: *How to Babysit an Orangutan*, by Tara Darling; *Little Bobo*, by Serena Romanelli; and *Orangutan's Playtime*, by Laura Gates Galvin. If orangutan books are in short supply, branch out to chimpanzees and gorillas. A good place to start is *My Life with Chimpanzees*, by Jane Goodall.

Yellow is the color of
the sun

The feeling of fun. . . .

Mary Le Duc O'Neill,
"What Is Yellow?," *Hailstones
and Halibut Bones*

BIRTHDAYS

1908 Mary Le Duc O'Neill is born, in New York City. Mary says she writes *Hailstone and Halibut Bones* "almost by accident." For years, she has been jotting down feelings and "wisps of ideas" about colors. Then, when she is unable to meet a project deadline, her editor stops by, asking if she has any other work. Mary tells her no but invites her to leaf through items in the desk drawer. The editor sees possibilities for a book in the scraps of paper about color. That book becomes *Hailstone and Halibut Bones*.

▶ **READ MORE** *Color Me a Rhyme*, by Jane Yolen, pays tribute to colors in nature, real and imagined.

1931 Edward Packard is born, in Huntington, New York. He writes books in the Choose Your Own Adventure series.

▶ **READING REFLECTION** Challenge students who love this format to "figure out" how Edward structures these books. Challenge them to create a chart of how an adventure is arranged. Ask students how this is different from the plots of regular books.

1973 Ursula Nordstrom, director of Harper & Row's department of books for boys and girls from 1940 to 1973, writes to a child who has expressed dismay over the death of E. B. White's Charlotte, saying, "When I read the manuscript I felt exactly the way you now feel. I didn't want Charlotte to die, and I too cried over her death." Ursula continues, "What I think you and I both should keep in mind is that Charlotte had a good and worthwhile life. And she was a true friend to Wilbur. . . . This may not be of much comfort to you now, but perhaps as time goes by you will understand why E. B. White had to tell Charlotte's story the way he told it."

FEBRUARY

17

"I don't know what I am at all. If I'm second-grade arithmetic and seventh-grade reading and third-grade spelling, what grade am I?"

The teacher laughed. "You aren't any grade at all, no matter where you are in school. You're just yourself, aren't you?"

Dorothy Canfield Fisher,
Understood Betsy

BIRTHDAYS

1879 Dorothy Canfield Fisher is born, in Lawrence, Kansas. She attends Ohio State University and the Sorbonne, in Paris, and she receives her doctorate in romance languages from Columbia University. *Understood Betsy* is set in Vermont, where Dorothy lives with her husband and children.

▶ **THINK ABOUT IT** Invite students to consider whether grade levels and report grades tell anything important about who they are. Invite students to create alternative report cards. What important things happen at school that don't show up on the report cards?

1928 Robert Newton Peck is born, in Vermont. He is raised there and sets many of his stories there. He often writes about the hard times of the Depression, which he experiences as a boy. Besides being a writer, Robert is a lumberjack, hog butcher, paper mill worker, and advertising executive.

1942 Michael McCurdy is born, in New York City. He attends the School of the Museum of Fine Arts, where David McPhail is his roommate for a year, and gets an MFA from Tufts University. Nearly two hundred books for adults and children feature his drawings and wood engravings.

1948 Susan Beth Pfeffer is born, in New York City. She begins her writing career while a student at New York University, writing *Just Morgan* during her last semester. Her more than sixty books include novels for middle graders and historical fiction. Susan Beth is the author of the Portraits of Little Women series; she also writes young adult novels.

▶ **WRITING TIP** Susan Beth notes that loving to tell stories is her inspiration for writing. Invite students to tell a story: "a food I really hate" or "a food I really love" story. After they've told it, ask them to write it, retaining the spirit of the telling.

1957 Jonathan Allen is born, in Luton, England. His favorite books as a child include *Thomas the Tank Engine, Paddington, William, Narnia,* and *Winnie-the-Pooh.* Jonathan says his career as an illustrator is inspired by cartoons. "I always liked comics, Warner Brothers cartoons, James Thurber's drawings, *Punch* cartoons. . . . I liked people who made me laugh. I was quite good at making people laugh so I suppose that's why I ended up doing funny stuff." Although Jonathan starts out illustrating other people's stories, he is soon writing his own—so he'll have something to illustrate. Cats appearing on Jonathan's Cat of the Week website include Harold, Scrabster, Bad Brenda, Bert, Percival, Elsie, Game Show Gordon, Cuthbert, Monitor Mog, Maxine, Luciano, Kevin, and Duane.

▶ **READING TIP** Encourage students to bring in favorite comics and cartoons to share with one another in a cartoon-reading bonanza.

> I want my books to always be about something that is important to me. . . .
>
> Toni Morrison

BIRTHDAYS

1859 Solomon Rabinowitz is born, in Russia. He takes his pen name, Sholom Aleichem, from the traditional greeting of Jews, meaning "peace unto you." Sholom writes in Yiddish, picturing Jewish life. His *Tevye the Dairyman* is dramatized in the Yiddish Theater in New York and in the Broadway musical *Fiddler on the Roof*. Sholom suffers from triskaidekaphobia, fear of the number 13. His manuscripts never have a page 13. He died on May 13, but his headstone in Mount Carmel Cemetery, Glendale, New York, reads "May 12a, 1916."

1931 Toni Morrison is born, in Lorain, Ohio, the second of four children. Her birth name is Chloe Anthony Wofford. Toni says that no matter what she writes, she "begins in Ohio." That's where her beginnings always are. Toni's novel *Beloved* receives many awards, including the Pulitzer Prize. She receives the Nobel Prize for Literature in 1993. Toni says, "I want my books to always be about something that is important to me, and the subjects that are important in the world are the same ones that have always been important."

▶ **RESEARCH TIP** Encourage students to make a list of five things that are important to them—and then to go find books on at least two of these topics.

1949 Barbara M. Joosse is born, in Grafton, Wisconsin. Barbara says, "I write about heroes. Heroes are people who do something that is beyond comfort. Heroes stretch themselves, solving their own problems with dignity."

▶ **READ MORE** Ask students to consider what books they have read lately that show heroes who match Barbara's definition.

EVENT

1852 Henry David Thoreau notes in his journal, "I have a commonplace-book for facts and another for poetry, but I find it difficult always to preserve the vague distinction which I had in mind, for the most interesting and beautiful facts are so much the more poetry and that is their success. I see that if my facts were sufficiently vital and significant . . . I should need but one book of poetry to contain them all."

▶ **RESEARCH TIP** Challenge students to find poems that contain a lot of facts. Poems about animals and bugs are a good place to begin. Students will need to check the poet's facts by consulting dictionaries and/or reference books. If your library has a copy of Mary Ann Hoberman's out-of-print *A Little Book of Little Beasts*, children can enjoy a master of this form. If your library doesn't have it, try interlibrary loan. This book is worth searching for. When students compare a dictionary definition of a mole with Mary Ann's poem, they become believers in the principle that good poems often contain accurate information.

> . . . things I learn seem to turn on a light in the little room in my mind.
>
> Amy Tan

BIRTHDAYS

1903 Louis Slobodkin is born, in Albany, New York. When he is a junior in high school, Louis persuades his parents to let him quit school. He goes to school every day but refuses to do any work. His parents watch the zeroes pile up and decide to let Louis quit. He gets a job as a bellhop and saves money to study at the Beaux Arts Institute of Design, in New York City. Louis is already an eminent sculptor when he illustrates *The Moffats,* by Eleanor Estes. He illustrates other books for her, including *The Hundred Dresses*. His illustrations for James Thurber's *Many Moons* receive the Caldecott Medal.

1917 Carson McCullers is born, in Columbus, Georgia. Her name at birth is Lula Carson Smith. After high school she enrolls in creative writing courses at Columbia University, and she has a story published in *Story* magazine that same December.

1952 Amy Tan is born, in Oakland, California. Her parents, Chinese immigrants, are determined Amy will be a doctor, but at age thirty-three, she begins her career as a fiction writer. In looking at an essay she writes at age eight, "What the Library Means to Me," Amy reflects that her writing style has not changed much. She still tries to be as direct as possible, writing the way she talks. She likes metaphors. Here is how Amy's essay begins: "My name is Amy Tan, eight years old, a third grader at Matanzas School. It is a brand new school and everything is so nice and pretty. I love school because the many things I learn seem to turn on a light in the little room in my mind."

EVENTS

1857 Henry David Thoreau writes in his journal, "A man cannot be said to succeed in this life who dares not satisfy one friend."

▶ **THINK ABOUT IT** Ask students to make lists of what friends do for one another. This might evolve into the class production of a Friends Are For . . . book.

1944 The concluding episode of the cartoon "Pluto Catches a Nazi Spy," begun on February 2, 1944, is drawn by Floyd Gottfredson.

FEBRUARY

20

I need myself a Toady.

Mary Blount Christian,
The Toady and Mr. Miracle

BIRTHDAY

1933 Mary Blount Christian is born, in Houston, Texas. A prolific author, she writes the Sebastian (Super Sleuth) series, featuring Sebastian, an English sheepdog, and John Jones, the human detective who owns him.

EVENT

1888 Vincent Van Gogh moves to Arles, in southern France, writing to his brother, "I need sunlight and warmth. I want my paints to be bright with sun, sea, and sky."

▶ **READ MORE** *Camille and the Sunflowers,* by Laurence Anholt, is based on an actual encounter of a small boy named Camille and the painter. Anholt includes reproductions of Van Gogh's "Sunflowers" and portraits of Camille and his family.

FEBRUARY

21

All his kin are farmers in the valley, but Shenandoah Noah doesn't like farming.

Jim Aylesworth,
Shenandoah Noah

BIRTHDAYS

1943 Jim Aylesworth is born, in Jacksonville, Florida. Jim is the author of such widely appealing books as *Hanna's Hog, One Crow, Shenandoah Noah,* and *Hush Up!* Among the long-time, award-winning first-grade teacher's favorite books to read to his students are Beatrix Potter's *The Tale of Peter Rabbit* and Dr. Seuss's *The Sneetches.*

1954 Francisco Xavier Alarcón is born, in Wilmington, California. As a child Francisco moves back and forth to Mexico, going to school in both countries. Francisco enjoys the stories of the ancient and mythical world his full-blooded Tarascan Indian grandfather tells him. He is inspired to write poems by the songs his grandmother sings. Francisco's bilingual volume, *Laughing Tomatoes/Jitomates Risueños,* takes its title from a poem in which he terms tomatoes "the happiest of all vegetables" ("los vegetales más felices de todos"). Francisco says tomatoes on the vine are "Christmas trees in spring."

1828 The *Cherokee Phoenix* is published, the first Native American newspaper published in both English and Cherokee. It is published until October 1935.

▶ **READING TIP** Encourage students to explore bilingual books. Challenge them to collaborate on writing their own.

1878 The first telephone book is issued, in Connecticut. Fifty names are listed.

▶ **READING TIP** The telephone book can make for interesting reading. Ask for the donation of old phone books. Then encourage students to browse—and see what they find. You might tell them that many writers use the phone book as their primary source for finding character names. If you want to nudge older students into examining the values of a community, ask them why there are more bars and beauty salons than bookstores in the yellow papers. Ask them to investigate other "values" revealed in the yellow pages.

1944 Anna Mary Robertson Moses, popularly known as Grandma Moses, observes, "I like to finish off a painting and then study it for a week or ten days."

FEBRUARY

22

Nobody shrinks.

Florence Parry Heide,
The Shrinking of Treehorn,
illustrations by Edward Gorey

BIRTHDAYS

1892 Edna St. Vincent Millay is born, in Rockland, Maine. She is the eldest of three daughters. The St. Vincent is in honor of St. Vincent's Hospital, in New York City, where her mother's brother was taken when he was very badly injured. Mrs. Millay is so grateful that she names her first baby for the faraway hospital. When Vincent (for that's what her family calls her) is seven, her father leaves the family. She grows up to become one of the most popular poets of her time and a master of the sonnet form.

▶ **WRITING TIP** By definition, a sonnet contains fourteen lines, typically five-foot iambics rhyming in a set pattern. Invite students to try variations on the sonnet structure. For starters, they can write a one-beat sonnet: fourteen lines of single-syllable words. They can increase complexity by varying the number of beats in a line and the rhyme scheme.

▶ **READ MORE** *Edna St. Vincent Millay,* edited by Frances Schoonmaker and illustrated by Mike Bryce, contains a biography of the poet and a lovely selection of her poems.

1925 Edward Gorey is born, in Chicago. He attends the Art Institute there. He receives a degree in French from Harvard. Edward says he writes his humorous books in the nonsense tradition of Lewis Carroll and Edward Lear. He also illustrates other people's work, including John Ciardi's poetry, Florence Parry Heide's *The Shrinking of Treehorn,* Beatrice Schenk de Regnier's *Red Riding Hood,* and Edith Tarcov's *Rumpelstiltskin.* (Fans of PBS's *Mystery* will recognize Gorey's distinctive style.) Students may enjoy knowing that Edward is the sort of grown-up who doesn't do his homework. He drives his editor, Ursula Nordstrom, nuts by not turning his manuscripts in on time. She writes to him, "I wonder if you will remember me? Perhaps my name is vaguely familiar to you? I am the editor at Harper and Row who wanted you to finish your book, *List,* so that we could publish it. . . . Really, Mr. Gorey, I think it would be easier for you to finish the above-mentioned book than to have to receive mournful phone calls from me. . . . Won't you start the New Year RIGHT and finish your book? . . . I think you go to movies all the time. Please pull yourself together. . . ."

▶ **WRITING TIP** Edward says as years have gone by he's decided not to suffer the trouble of revising. "Now I think first ideas are just as good as endless revisions."

▶ **THINK ABOUT IT** When Edward died, in 2000, he left the majority of his estate to a charitable trust to benefit animals and other creatures. Money goes to needy cats and dogs and to various invertebrates, including insects and bats. One recipient is a bat conservancy in Austin, Texas.

Every morning, when R. R. woke, the first thing he did—before he polished his glasses, before he combed his moustache and his few strands of hair, even before he yawned—was choose a hat.

Laura Geringer,
A Three Hat Day

BIRTHDAYS

1633 Samuel Pepys is born, in London, England. He is known as the writer of the greatest diary in the English language, chronicling the daily life of an observant young man who likes to have a good time. Failing eyesight forces him to stop writing in 1669. Samuel writes the diary in what is known as Shelton shorthand, a sort of code writing introduced in 1626. The diary is donated to Magdalene College, Cambridge, but not "discovered" until 1818. Small sections are published over the years. The complete diary, ten volumes, is not published until 1970.

▶ **READING/WRITING CONNECTION** Invite a few student volunteers to read code books and then teach the class a code. Then students can try writing notes in codes—and breaking them. Students may be interested to know that Beatrix Potter also wrote her journal in code.

1932 C(arole) S(chwerdtfeger) Adler is born, in the Bronx, New York. After eight years as a middle school English teacher, her first novel for middle-grade children, *The Magic of the Glits*, is published and wins the Golden Kite Award and the William Allen White Award. Adler becomes a full-time children's book author and more than forty books follow.

1948 Laura Geringer is born, in New York City. A teacher, a newspaper reporter, a book reviewer, and an editor, she is also the author of a number of books for young readers, including a series of retellings of myths. In her book *Yours 'til the Ice Cracks*, Laura offers a book of sweet and funny valentine sayings, including *Yours 'til the grass grows greener* and *Yours 'til the desert disappears*.

EVENT

1935 *The Band Concert*, the first Mickey Mouse cartoon in color, is released. Famed conductor Arturo Toscanini remembers this as his favorite cartoon.

"Wolf! Wolf!" cried the frightened boy, but no one came.

Jerry Pinkney,
"The Shepherd Boy and the
Wolf," in *Aesop's Fables*

BIRTHDAY

1786 Wilhelm Grimm is born in Germany. In addition to the famous *Fairy Tales*, he and his brother plan and launch a sixteen-volume German dictionary.

EVENT

1998 *Aesop: The Complete Fables* is published in a translation by Robert and Olivia Temple. It causes a sensation, because it is uncensored. It includes a hundred stories not ordinarily found among previous translations of Aesop's sixth-century B.C. tales. Aesop was born a slave about 620 B.C., in Greece, and his clever wisdom has been passed down orally through generations until around two hundred stories were gathered into a collection.

▶ **READ MORE** Jerry Pinkney says in his childhood his parents use the powerful themes from fables to teach him and his siblings about human folly and virtue. When Jerry grows up, he creates a beautiful book, *Aesop's Fables*.

FEBRUARY

25

Columbus set sail
without fear

On the seaworthy Santa
Maria. . . .

Edward Swift Mullins,
The Big Book of Limericks

BIRTHDAYS

1914 Frank Bonham is born, in Los Angeles. Suffering from asthma as a child, he says, influences his writing. It means he can't pursue a career as a reporter; instead he goes to a mountain cabin and writes. He writes books for adults and television scripts for twenty years. Then he starts writing for children. Frank is delighted to discover that all subjects "work" for children. He researches gang activity for a year and a half before writing *Durango Street*.

1919 Jeanne Bendick is born, in New York City. She illustrates many nonfiction books and offers this advice: "I learned, where there are investigations or experiments involved, to do them myself before I try to illustrate them." Jeanne points out that the thickness of a rubber band or the placement of a paper clip "can make the difference between a working model and a disappointment," so the illustrator has a serious responsibility to be absolutely accurate.

1922 Edward Swift Mullins is born, in Sanford, Maine. As a very young boy Edward knows he wants to be an artist. At age nine, he begins attending classes at the New England School of Art, in Boston. He writes and illustrates *Animal Limericks* and *The Big Book of Limericks*. Edward demonstrates that you can write a limerick about anything or anyone. One of his begins like this:

> Columbus set sail without fear
> On the seaworthy Santa Maria. . . .

You really have to adjust your reading of *Maria* to make this one work!

► **READ MORE** Students may be interested to know that Isaac Asimov and John Ciardi, both fond of limericks, collaborated on a collection for adults that is both witty and naughty. More suitable for the classroom are Edward Lear's classics and *Uncle Switch: Loony Limericks*, by X. J. Kennedy, a screwball collection.

► **READING/WRITING CONNECTION** Point out to students that to write a limerick, they need to read a bunch of them—very carefully, figuring out the rhythm and the rhyme scheme. Encourage students to write limericks about something they are studying.

1942 Cynthia Voigt is born, in Boston, the second of four children. Cynthia remembers liking Nancy Drew and the Black Stallion books as a child. She discovers *The Secret Garden* in her grandmother's house, and she cherishes it. Another special book is *The Mouse and His Child*, by Russell Hoban. Although she knows she wants to be a writer, Cynthia works as a secretary and in an advertising agency and then becomes an English teacher. To her surprise, she discovers that this is a job she likes a lot. Teaching inspires Cynthia to write books. "I had to make a reading list for my students, so I went to the library and starting reading the books beginning at A, and ending up at Z!" *Homecoming* is her first book. *Dicey's Song* is awarded the Newbery Medal. Cynthia says Dicey is the child she would like to have been and Gram is the lady she would like to become. Cynthia also observes that Dicey takes the challenge of shepherding everyone down Route 1 from Bridgeport to Crisfield "because she has to. It's a real, recognizable dilemma, not some burst of fantasy. Kids can identify with that and immediately see the implications in their own lives."

► **WRITING TIP** Cynthia agrees with Aristotle that "character is the easiest thing to do and plot is the hardest."

► **READING TIP** "Teachers should read out loud to students so that reading is a treat—it's a present."

EVENT

1998 The Indiana State Legislature passes a resolution designating the period October 7, 1998, to October 7, 1999 "The Year of Riley," commemorating native son James Whitcomb Riley. (See October 7.)

FEBRUARY
26

Dear Diary, You are new and beautiful in your kente cloth cover. Cool, cool!

Sharon Bell Mathis,
*Running Girl: The Diary of
Ebonee Rose*

BIRTHDAY

1937 Sharon Bell Mathis is born, in Atlantic City, New Jersey. She is delighted when her family moves to the Bedford-Stuyvesant section of Brooklyn, New York, and she has her own fire escape. Sharon says she reads Richard Wright's *Black Boy* on that fire escape. And then she immediately reads it six more times that year. Sharon says Wright opens her eyes to other black writers. "I 'borrowed' *The Negro Caravan . . .* from the Brooklyn Public Library for almost two years before I, guiltily, returned it!" Sharon's *The Hundred Penny Box* is a Newbery Honor book.

▶ **READING/WRITING CONNECTION** When Sharon gets stuck on her own writing, reading is the answer. "I get away from my typewriter—for a few days—and read one, two, or three books. Later, perhaps in a week, I am able to create again."

EVENT

1938 Arna Bontemps writes the editor of *The Horn Book,* agreeing to her request to write an article for the journal. "So if you will send the copies you mentioned of back issues, I'll do my best to suggest something suitable."

▶ **READING/WRITING CONNECTION** Arna provides a good role model for young writers when he asks the editor to send him sample issues to study before he attempts to write his own article. He is an established writer and he knows the importance of knowing the reader.

FEBRUARY
27

Why don't you speak for yourself, John?

Henry Wadsworth Longfellow,
"The Courtship of Miles
Standish"

BIRTHDAYS

1807 Henry Wadsworth Longfellow is born, in Portland, Maine. When he's in college Henry writes his father, telling him he wants to be a writer. Called by Walt Whitman "the universal poet of all young people," Henry becomes the first poet in the United States to earn a living from royalties. He is paid $3,000 each for such poems as "The Song of Hiawatha," "The Courtship of Miles Standish," and "Paul Revere's Ride."

1902 John Steinbeck is born, in Salinas, California. His mother, a teacher, fosters John's love of reading. An avid reader, John enrolls in Stanford University, but his attendance is sporadic. He works painting houses, picking fruit, and at a dozen other jobs. Hired as a newspaper reporter, he gets fired for making up details instead of sticking to the facts. In 1937, John follows a group of migrant workers headed west from Oklahoma. This becomes the inspiration for *The Grapes of Wrath.* In a variation on "the dog ate my homework" story, John's setter puppy chews up half of the first draft of *Of Mice and Men,* which John has worked on for two months.

1925 Kenneth Koch is born. He revolutionizes the teaching of poetry by working in New York City classrooms.

▶ **READING/WRITING CONNECTION** In his books *Rose, Where Did You Get That Red?* and *Wishes, Lies, and Dreams: Teaching Children to Write Poetry,* Kenneth observes that children's responses are deepened by reading and writing poetry at the same time. He gives children suggestions for writing poems of their own in some way like the poems they are studying. "We would read the adult poem in class, discuss it, and then they would write. Afterward, they or I would read aloud the poems they had written."

1935 Uri Shulevitz is born, in Warsaw, Poland. At age twenty-four, Uri comes to the United States, studying painting at the Brooklyn Museum Art School. Uri mixes his own oil paints from oil pigments and studies old masters at the Metropolitan Museum of Art. Before he begins illustrating *The Treasure*, Uri experiments with oil, egg tempera, colored inks, and opaque watercolors. Finally he decides on a transparent watercolor technique. Uri says all the experimentation enriches his work: "Nothing was wasted after all." *The Treasure* becomes a Caldecott Honor book.

▶ **READING/WRITING CONNECTION** Uri says that some years ago when nearby areas enjoyed a mild winter, his neighborhood had sixteen snowfalls. "But instead of complaining about the weather, I made a picture book about it, and called it *Snow*." It is another Caldecott Honor title. In *Snow*, Uri writes

> All snowflakes know
> is snow, snow, and snow.

Invite students to use this pattern in their writing: "All _____ know/understand/see/ dream of is _____, _____, and _____." Patterns like this offer students great power as writers, propelling their prose from the mundane to the literary.

Why, sometimes I've believed as many as six impossible things before breakfast.

Lewis Carroll,
Alice's Adventures in Wonderland

BIRTHDAYS

1797 Mary Lyon is born in Buckland, Massachusetts, one of seven children. Her father dies when she is five. When she is seven, Mary does chores to pay for her room and board so she can live near where the school is located. Although she leaves school at thirteen, Mary has more education than most girls of that time. Because of her excellent reputation as a student, Mary is offered a teaching job when she is seventeen. Mary campaigns for higher education for women and in 1837 founds Mount Holyoke Female Seminary, later Mount Holyoke College. At that time, there are 120 colleges for men in the U. S. but none for women. Mary instructs each incoming student to bring with them a Bible, an atlas, a dictionary, and two spoons. The school day lasts 16 hours, starting at 5 A.M.

1829 Sir John Tenniel is born, in England. He is the political cartoonist for *Punch*, a satirical magazine. Today he is known for his illustrations for Lewis Carroll's *Alice's Adventures in Wonderland* and *Through the Looking-Glass and What Alice Found There*. After John produces ninety-two drawings for the books, Lewis likes only one, Humpty Dumpty. Lewis wants John to use real animals as models for the animals in the drawings, but John refuses, insisting that the animals in Alice must come from imagination, not nature. He tells Lewis he no more needs a model for drawing than Lewis needs a multiplication table to do a math problem. Lewis likes the logic of that argument and agrees the drawings can be fanciful.

MARCH

What is the opposite of flying?

For birds it would be just not trying.

Richard Wilbur,
"Opposites"

BIRTHDAYS

1921 Richard Wilbur is born, in New York City. A highly regarded Pulitzer Prize–winning poet, he also writes clever verse for children. While in college, Richard spends the summers riding the rails around the United States in freight cars, visiting forty-six states. He serves in the frontline infantry during World War II and is also the cryptographer for his unit. Richard says that as a boy every year he reread the same three books: Lewis Carroll's two stories about Alice and Mark Twain's *Huckleberry Finn.*

▶ **READING/WRITING CONNECTION** Perhaps it's not surprising that Richard was a cryptographer during the war. As a poet, he helps us see things in words that we haven't noticed before. Ask students, *How are poems like secret codes? How are they different?* Richard's book *The Disappearing Alphabet* shows what happens when letters start disappearing. If there were no *n*s, for example, birds would have *wigs* instead of *wings.* Challenge students to come up with some more *If there were no . . .* observations about letters and words.

1945 Barbara Helen Berger is born, in Lancaster, California, in the Mojave Desert. But she grows up in Seattle, where it rains a lot. Barbara's father combines his professions of physician and artist and becomes a medical illustrator. She remembers microscopes, jars of weird specimens, and a skeleton in his basement workshop. After studying art in college, including a year in Italy, Barbara takes a class taught by Jane Yolen and learns how to write children's books. Barbara says her paintings contain secrets.

▶ **WRITING TIP** Barbara spends a lot of time saying her books out loud. "I'm finding out how the words feel in my mouth. I'm finding out how they sound. I'm finding out if the words like being next to each other or not. I'm finding out how the words want to sing."

EVENTS

1890 Sherlock Holmes makes his American book debut when a U. S. edition of *A Study in Scarlet* is published. Holmes's remark when he meets Dr. Watson, "You've been to Afghanistan, I perceive," introduces readers to the famous Holmes method of deductive thinking. Holmes insists that with this method, he can make far-reaching deductions from the smallest piece of evidence. In another story, Holmes cries, "Data! data! data!"

▶ **READ MORE** Invite volunteers to share with the class information about their favorite mystery series, with special focus on structure. Are there certain elements that always appear in a Nate the Great? In a Sebastian Sleuth? In an Encyclopedia Brown? In a Nancy Drew?

1977 Samantha, Ezra Jack Keats's red Persian cat, is born. American poet T. S. Eliot says that all cats have three names. Mark Twain's mother had twenty cats, and Mark inherits her love for them. Some of his cats' names are Blatherskite, Sour Mash, Stray Kit, Sin, Satan. Mark's daughter Susy says, "The difference between Papa and Mamma is, that Mamma loves morals and Papa loves cats."

▶ **READ MORE** In *I Am the Dog/I Am the Cat*, illustrated by Barry Moser, Donald Hall creates a hilarious and affectionate portrait in contrasts. Michael J. Rosen's

PURR . . . Children's Book Illustrators Brag About Their Cats is also a very good read, giving some insider info about illustrators—and cats.

1982 *Cricket Magazine*, launched in September 1973, publishes its 100th issue. These days, *Cricket* publishes information about contests on its webpage: http://www.cricketmag.com

2000 Douglas Florian's *Mammalabilia* is published. It is filled with Douglas's characteristic visual delight and word play. For instance, he describes a giraffe as "rubbernecker, double-decker, cloud-checker, and star-trekker"; the beaver is a "wood-chopper, tree-dropper, tail-flopper, and stream-stopper."

▶ **WORD FUN** Here is a little quiz about the mule. If the "rule" of the mule is "stay," can students figure out the rhyming words describing its voice, hue, and fuel?

MARCH

2

"Nothing," I said, growing red as a beet,

"But a plain horse and wagon on Mulberry Street."

Dr. Seuss,
And to Think That I Saw It on Mulberry Street

BIRTHDAYS

1904 Theodor Seuss Giesel—Dr. Seuss—is born, in Springfield, Massachusetts. He begins using his mother's birth name Seuss when he becomes editor-in-chief of the college humor magazine at Dartmouth College. His manuscript for *And to Think I Saw It on Mulberry Street* is rejected by twenty-nine publishers. When published, it is an immediate hit. In 1957, Dr. Seuss writes *The Cat in the Hat* to prove that a book written with a limited vocabulary can be fun. Dr. Seuss's books have sold more than one hundred million copies around the world.

▶ **READ MORE** Read Across America Day is a national reading campaign urging children across America to read a book on the evening of Dr. Seuss's birthday. You can start with *Hooray for Diffendoofer Day!* by Seuss with some help from Jack Prelutsky and Lane Smith. ("Our teachers are remarkable/they make up their own rules.")

1931 Tom Wolfe is born, in Richmond Virginia. His book *The Right Stuff,* about the early years of the U. S. space program, contributes a new phrase to the language.

▶ **THINK ABOUT IT** Ask Harry Potter fans what phrase they think he will bring to the language.

1940 Tom Eaton is born, in Wichita, Kansas. Tom says he was always the class artist, from kindergarten all the way through school. He credits his fifth-grade teacher with being his first great editor as well as someone who inspired an interest in storytelling. Because she read aloud each day from books such as the adventures of Richard Halliburton and the fictional tales of Doctor Doolittle, Tom has retained a lifelong affection for these books. The author and illustrator of many books, Tom writes and draws nine pages for *Boys' Life* magazine every month.

EVENTS

1887 Twenty-year-old Anne Sullivan begins to teach six-year-old Helen Keller. Until now, the uncontrollable behavior of this blind and deaf child has baffled everyone. Within a month of this meeting, Anne discovers a frightened and intelligent child eager to communicate, and helps Helen make the connection between objects and words.

▶ **READ MORE** Invite volunteers to find out more about sign language—and to bring that information to the class. *Helen Keller: Rebellious Spirit,* by Laurie Lawlor, is a provocative depiction of a strong-willed girl who grows up to be a woman of strong convictions.

1916 While serving in the military, J. R. R. Tolkien writes his fiancee, "I have done some touches to my nonsense fairy language. . . ."

3

You must have a garden
wherever you are.

Patricia MacLachlan,
Sarah, Plain and Tall

BIRTHDAYS

1919 Ann Bishop is born, in Illinois. She is the originator of theme riddle books, and her titles include *Noah Riddle?*; *The Riddle Ages*; *Annie O'Kay's Riddle Roundup*; *Wild Bill Hiccup's Riddle Book*; *Chicken Riddle*; and *Cleo Catra's Riddle Book*. Ann says she writes riddle books because even poor readers enjoy riddles so much they will read a whole book of them—and discover that sometimes they like to read. For all children, riddles extend language awareness and stimulate creative thinking. Of the riddles she has created, Ann likes this one best:

> What was the name of the cow that jumped over the moon?
> Madame Butterfly.

1933 Leo Dillon is born, in Brooklyn, New York. See March 13 for more information about this talented illustrator.

1938 Patricia MacLachlan is born, in Cheyenne, Wyoming. As a child, Patricia has a very strong fantasy life, inventing many make-believe brothers and sisters. At age nine, she writes in her diary that she has seventeen boyfriends. "That's how I learned to play out themes, to develop characters, to hear other voices," she explains. A former teacher, Patricia is the Newbery Medal–winning author of such books as *Sarah, Plain and Tall*; *Arthur, for the Very First Time*; *The Facts and Fictions of Minna Pratt*; and *Seven Kisses in a Row*.

▶ **WRITING TIP** Patricia reads aloud everything she writes. "I need to have the voices of the characters whisper in my ear." Patricia's stories begin with a character. "This character begins talking to me, and I start putting it down on paper." Patricia advises children who want to be writers to "read a lot and to read lots of different books."

▶ **READING TIP** Encourage children to keep a reading log for two weeks, reading a different type of book every day: one day, biography; one day, natural science; one day, poetry; one day, sports; one day, an almanac; and so on. For each book, they can record something of interest—an amazing fact, a nice turn of phrase, a puzzling word. Encourage students to reflect on these different kinds of reading: for example, do some types of books require slower reading?

1951 Peter Roop is born, in Winchester, Massachusetts. Peter is a teacher and, with his wife Connie, is the author of such easy-read historical novels as *Buttons for General Washington*, *Keep the Lights Burning, Abbie*, and the chapter book *Ahyoka and the Talking Leaves*. He is also the author of riddle books: *Go Hog Wild! Jokes for Down on the Farm* and *Going Buggy! Jokes About Insects*.

▶ **WRITING FUN** Challenge students to write some riddles with *hog wild* as the punch line.

EVENTS

1814 John Keats's first volume, *Poems*, is published, one year after he passes his medical and druggist exams. John had left school at age sixteen to be apprenticed to a surgeon for four years, but soon after he completes the exams, he devotes his life to writing poetry. Probably his most famous lines are the closing of "Ode on a Grecian Urn":

> "Beauty is truth, truth beauty"—that is all
> Ye know on earth, and all ye need to know.

Where does Dogzilla keep her car?

In a barking lot.

1906 Meindert DeJong is born, in Wierum, the Netherlands. He moves to Grand Rapids, Michigan, when he is eight. Meindert works at many jobs, including teaching, masonry, grave digging, and poultry farming. For many years Meindert works in a Grand Rapids church, writing in his spare time. In 1955, Meindert wins the Newbery Medal for *The Wheel on the School*. During the 1950s his books are awarded four Newbery Honor awards.

1940 Suse MacDonald is born, in Evanston, Illinois. After studying art in college, Suse enjoys illustrating textbooks for a living. When her second child starts school, Suse goes back to school too, attending the New England School of Art and Design and the Art Institute of Boston, and her focus shifts to more abstract work. She says a typography course is the catalyst for her first picture book. "My assignment was to turn a letter of the alphabet into a representation of something. I turned an A into an owl. Afterwards I thought, if I can turn an A into an owl, why not turn A into something that begins with A." Suse's *Alphabatics* wins a Caldecott Honor award.

▶ **WRITING FUN** Challenge students to turn the letters in their first name into objects.

1953 Peggy Rathmann is born, in St. Paul, Minnesota. She grows up in the suburbs with two brothers and two sisters. She says she "attended colleges everywhere, changing her major repeatedly." She finally discovers that what she wants to do is draw. One of her nieces writes about her in *The Horn Book* magazine, "I have learned a lot from my Aunt Peggy, but I think the most important thing is that you must do something you really enjoy. It may take you a long time to find it, but only settle for something that is right for you." Peggy is the author and illustrator of the Caldecott Medal book *Officer Buckle and Gloria*.

1957 David A. Carter is born, in Salt Lake City, Utah. David observes that he is born "at the foot of the Wasatch Mountains, home to some of the best powder skiing in the world. I have been an artist and a skier ever since." Attending Utah State University on an art scholarship, David studies illustration and art. While working at Intervisual Communications as a graphic designer and pasteup artist, he learns the fine art of paper engineering and pop-up bookmaking. Since starting his own business in 1987, David has created around forty pop-up books. He enjoys working with young children, showing them how to make their own pop-ups.

▶ **WRITING FUN** Challenge students to create a pop-up card based on an incident from a familiar book. Fairy tales are a good source of inspiration. Making a pop-up of *Little Red Riding Hood*'s wolf's mouth, for example, provides an opportunity to put a message in his mouth. Once students are proficient at card making, they can try the challenge of creating a book. Remind them that planning is important. Excellent resources include *How to Make Pop-Ups*, by Joan Irvine; *The Elements of Pop-Up: A Pop-Up Book for Aspiring Paper Engineers*, by David Carter; and *Pop-O-Mania: How to Create Your Own Pop-Ups*, by Barbara Valenta.

1966 Dav Pilkey is born, in Cleveland, Ohio. He remembers reading *Georgie the Ghost* and *Harold and the Purple Crayon* as a young boy. Dav says his favorite subjects in school are recess and lunch, and he holds his school's all-time record for amount of time spent in the principal's office. Diagnosed as having Attention Deficit Disorder and Severe Activity Syndrome, by the end of first grade Dav is the undisputed king of funny noises and holds the classroom record for the number of crayons he can stick up his nose at one time (a record he still holds to this day). Dav notes, "There was never any room in school for creativity or spontaneity. It seemed like all they were teaching us was conformity and blind obedience." In 1997 Dav wins a Caldecott Honor for *The Paperboy*. His twenty-sixth book, *The Adventures of Captain Underpants*, is a novel based on books he wrote in elementary school while sitting out in the hallway. Dav says he usually ended up in the hallway every day, so he made sure the desk out there was well supplied with paper and markers.

EVENT

1845 Henry David Thoreau's friend Ellery Channing writes, "My dear Thoreau, the handwriting of your letter is so miserable, that I am not sure I have made it out."

MARCH

There was once a baby koala so soft and round that all who saw her loved her. Her name was Koala Lou.

Mem Fox,
Koala Lou

BIRTHDAYS

1853 Howard Pyle is born, in Wilmington, Delaware. He is the oldest of four children. In school he is a daydreamer, drawing and writing on imaginary topics that have nothing to do with the lessons. Howard loves *Grimm's Fairy Tales*, *A Midsummer Night's Dream*, and *The Arabian Nights*. Although an artistic career is frowned on by his Quaker religion, Howard persuades his family to let him try. He finds art school disappointing—the techniques taught are too imitative. "When I left art school I discovered, like many others, that I could not easily train myself to creative work. . . ." Nonetheless, at age twenty-three, Howard leaves work in his father's leather business and goes to New York to pursue a career in art. Probably his most famous illustrations—still in print today—are those he does for *The Merry Adventures of Robin Hood*, which first appear in 1883. Howard's illustrations are popular in Europe. A twenty-nine-year-old painter named Vincent Van Gogh writes his brother, Theo, "Do you know an American magazine called *Harper's Monthly*? There are things in it which strike me dumb with admiration, including sketches of a Quaker town in the olden days by Howard Pyle."

1946 Merrion Frances "Mem" Fox is born, in Melbourne, Australia. When Mem is six months old, her missionary parents move to Rhodesia, now called Zimbabwe. Over five years and through nine rejections, she rewrites her first story twenty-three times. The book stars a mouse, but eventually Mem changes the lead character to a possum, and the published book is the popular *Possum Magic*, the best-selling children's book ever in Australia. Mem says her favorite of her own books is *Koala Lou*, because she is Koala Lou; it is the story of her and her mum, whom Mem refers to as "a female Tarzan." Even though *Koala Lou* contains only 410 words, Mem rewrites it forty-nine times before she gets it just the way she wants it.

EVENT

1847 Sixteen-year-old Emily Dickinson writes a friend about starting a new term at school: "[I] am studying Algebra, Euclid, Ecc[lesiastical] History & reviewing Arithmetic again, to be on the safe side of things next autumn."

MARCH

What artists are featured at the Dogopolis Museum of Art?

Find the answers in *Art Dog,*
by Thacher Hurd

BIRTHDAY

1949 Thacher Hurd is born, in Burlington, Vermont. He grows up in Mill Valley, California. The son of famous children's book writers and illustrators Edith Thacher Hurd and Clement Hurd, Thacher's own books are Reading Rainbow–featured titles. Thacher and his wife, Olivia, run Peaceable Kingdom Press, publisher of cards, posters, and calendars featuring art from well-known children's books. The name comes from the Hurds' farm in Vermont, where they spend summers.

▶ **WORD FUN** Leonardo Dog Vinci is one artist whose work is featured at the Dogopolis Museum. Can students come up with other possibilities? Invite them to study art books for names they can transform.

MARCH

Whose woods these are
I think I know.

Robert Frost,
"Stopping by Woods on a
Snowy Evening"

BIRTHDAY

1949 Jane Dyer is born. She teaches second grade and kindergarten and then leaves teaching to illustrate reading textbooks. Jane advises, "Spend some time each day dreaming." She says her artistic mentors are Jessie Wilcox Smith, Maxfield Parrish, Carl Larsson, and Maud and Miska Petersham. Jane says nearly every character in her illustrations is based on someone she knows, including her dog Woolly.

EVENTS

1834 Henry David Thoreau, a freshman at Harvard, signs a petition protesting Harvard's grading system.

▶ **THINK ABOUT IT** Ask students their opinions of grades. Invite them to create report cards for some favorite literary characters. How would Goldilocks rate? Ramona? Junie B. Jones? the boy in Stone Fox? Maniac Magee? And so on.

1923 One of Robert Frost's best-known poems, "Stopping by Woods on a Snowy Evening," is published in the *New Republic*. It begins "Whose woods these are I think I know."

▶ **OUT LOUD** Read the poem aloud—even if there isn't snow on the ground.

▶ **THINK ABOUT IT** Susan Jeffers illustrates a picture book version of Frost's poem that includes a surprise. Read the book and decide if you agree with Susan's interpretation of the poem. She doesn't alter any words but by putting Santa Claus in the illustration, she certainly changes the meaning. Challenge artists in the class to illustrate a stanza in the poem in a way that changes the meaning.

MARCH

"This is the end of
everything" (he said)
"at least it is the end of
the career of Toad,
which is the same thing;
the popular and
handsome Toad, the
rich and hospitable
Toad, the Toad so free
and careless and
debonair!"

Kenneth Grahame,
The Wind in the Willows

BIRTHDAYS

1859 Kenneth Grahame is born, in Edinburgh, Scotland. Orphaned at the age of five, he lives with his grandmother and later becomes a successful banker. Bedtime stories Kenneth tells his son Alastair about Mole, Rat, and Toad become *The Wind in the Willows*. Alastair is nicknamed Mouse, and when he goes on vacation, the stories continue in letters: "My darling Mouse, Have you heard about the Toad . . . ? He was never taken prisoner by brigands at all. It was all a horrid low trick. . . ." A. A. Milne says, "One does not argue about *The Wind in the Willows*. The young man gives it to the girl with whom he is in love, and if she does not like it, asks her to return his letters. The older man tries it on his nephew, and alters his will accordingly. The book is a test of character."

1914 Ethel Johnston Phelps is born, in Long Island City, New York. She is the author of *Tatterhood and Other Tales*.

▶ **READING/WRITING CONNECTION** Invite students to read three versions of the Cinderella story. For starters, they might try some of these: *Cendrillon: A Caribbean Cinderella* and *Little Gold Star: A Spanish American Cinderella*, both by Robert D. San Souci; *Raisel's Riddle* (celebrating the story of Esther), by Erica Silverman; *Cinderella* (set in the 1920s), illustrated by Roberto Innocenti. They should compare one important scene, such as how the fairy godmother figure renders aid. Then they can try writing a modern update of that scene.

1931 Dorothy Kennedy is born, in Milwaukee, Wisconsin. With her husband, X. J. Kennedy, she authors *Knock at a Star* and *Talking Like the Rain*.

▶ **WRITING TIP** The Kennedys refer to "word music," pointing out that poets pay as much attention to the sound of a word as to its meaning. Invite students to make a list of five or ten words they like the sound of.

1965 Robert Sabuda is born, in Michigan. He says he has known he would be an artist ever since he ate a whole box of crayons. While still a young boy, he makes his mom a pop-up book of *The Wizard of Oz*. Robert says the difference now is he gets paid to make messes. Robert says, "I would love to do *The History of Humankind* as a pop-up with volumes 1 through 150."

▶ **WRITING TIP** See March 4 for resources for making pop-up books.

MARCH

I have an appointment with April.

George Santayana

BIRTHDAY

19-- Joan Lexau is born. In such books as *The Dog Food Caper*, *The Rooftop Mystery*, and *Don't Be My Valentine*, she makes mysteries available to early readers.

EVENTS

1852 Henry David Thoreau notes in his journal: "Cloudy but springlike. When the frost comes out of the ground, there is a corresponding thawing of the man. . . . These March winds, which make the woods roar and fill the world with life and bustle, appear to wake up the trees out of their winter sleep and excite the sap to flow."

1952 Harvard professor George Santayana writes, "I am . . . counting on the Spring weather. . . ." Later in the month, while lecturing to a crowded classroom at Harvard, Santayana spots a forsythia in a patch of snow outside the window. Walking to the classroom door, he says, "I shall not be able to finish that sentence. I just have discovered that I have an appointment with April."

▶ **THINK ABOUT IT** Ask students to picture what an "appointment with April" might look like—in drawings or words.

MARCH

All the animals went back to sleep.

All except the cock and Little Peep.

They stayed awake and argued.

Jack Kent,
Little Peep

BIRTHDAY

1920 Jack Kent is born, in Burlington, Iowa. He is the author-illustrator of *There Is No Such Thing as a Dragon* and *Jim Jimmy James*. He also illustrates a number of easy-read fairy tales and folktales.

EVENT

1774 Thomas Jefferson writes in his account book, "pd. mr Cole's Ned for a gall[o]n of peas 5/." In his gardening journal, he notes, "sowed a bed of Early & a bed of Marrow-fat peas." In a letter to a friend Thomas notes, "No occupation is so delightful to me as the culture of the earth, and no culture comparable to that of the garden."

▶ **READING/WRITING CONNECTION** Probably the most famous ditty about peas is an anonymous folk rhyme:

> I eat my peas with honey,
> I've done it all my life.
> It makes the peas taste funny,
> But it keeps them on my knife.

Eat Your Peas, by Kes Gray, is a funny account of the bribes offered to a kid to get her to eat her peas. Invite students to look for poems about peas—and to write their own. They might start with short rhymes: *Peas/Please* or *Peas/Displease.*

MARCH

It was on a dreary night of November that I beheld the accomplishment of my toils.

Mary Shelley, *Frankenstein*

BIRTHDAYS

1893 Wanda Gag is born, in New Ulm, Minnesota. She is the eldest of seven children. Wanda makes paper dolls and furniture for her siblings, and she writes them stories as well as homemade holiday cards. Wanda's father dies when she is fourteen, and to raise money for the family she draws postcards and place cards to sell in a local drug store. She also sends submissions to *The Junior Journal,* a Sunday supplement to *The Minneapolis Journal.* Wanda receives a scholarship to the Art Students League of New York, but her mother's death leaves her responsible for her siblings. She has to settle for a job painting designs on lampshades. In an autobiographical sketch, Wanda writes that she went to art school, joined the army, lived in Paris for six years, traveled to Africa and Mexico, went to the Orient and India. None of this but the painting of lampshades ever happened. Wanda's book *Millions of Cats* is announced in *Publishers Weekly,* September 8, 1928, as "Stories and pictures of an old man and an old woman who wanted a cat to live with them so they would not be lonely. $1.25." The book receives immediate rave reviews and continues to be popular over the years. Patricia Polacco says the story she enjoys the most as a child is *Millions of Cats.* "I love her illustrations."

1914 Harold Rosenthal is born, in New York City. He writes *Five Hundred Five Football Questions Your Friends Can't Answer.*

▶ **THINK ABOUT IT** Challenge students to come up with five questions their friends can't answer. Then they can combine their questions into a class anthology.

EVENTS

1818 Mary Shelley's *Frankenstein* is published. When Mary is eighteen years old, she and her future husband, the poet Percy Bysshe Shelley, are visiting Lord Byron when Byron challenges them and other guests to write a ghost story. Mary is the only one in this group of writers who finishes a story.

1986 The *San Antonio Express* publishes a column crediting Ignacio Anaya, chef at the old Victory Club, in Piedras Negras, Mexico, as the person who created *nachos* in the 1940s for some Texas women in town for shopping. An editor for the *Oxford English Dictionary* pursues this anecdote and eventually comes up with the recipe—and the story—of nachos. Dictionary editors are very diligent in verifying word origins.

MARCH

Poetry, poetry!

Rearranging right at the heart level,

where standardized tests often don't go.

Naomi Shihab Nye (editor), *Salting the Ocean*

BIRTHDAYS

1936 Virginia Hamilton is born, in Yellow Springs, Ohio, a station on the Underground Railroad. Named for her grandfather's home state, Virginia remembers, "My mother said that her father sat his ten children down every year and said, 'I'm going to tell you how I escaped from slavery, so slavery will never happen to you.'" Virginia's parents are great storytellers, and they pass this heritage and culture and pride in history on to her. Virginia notes that her family "filled the air with stories and gossip and tall tales. And when they couldn't remember the details of the real events, they substituted their own imaginative fictions. Thus they created and recreated who they were and where they had come from and what they hoped to be." Virginia says the Ohio landscape and the Ohio sky feed her "heart and mind and writing."

1952 Naomi Shihab Nye is born, in St. Louis, Missouri. Her name means "shooting star" in Arabic. Her father is Palestinian, and Naomi regrets that she did not learn Arabic as a child. At age six, Naomi writes a poem about visiting Chicago. She is thrilled when her teacher lets her hang it in the hall. At seven, Naomi sends a poem about a cat named Cricket to *Wee Wisdom*, and when it is published, the school principal asks Naomi to read it over the intercom. Naomi has been publishing poems ever since. She says, "I believe poetry is basic to our lives—as in 'getting back to basics.'" Naomi publishes her own poetry, edits anthologies, and has led poetry workshops in most of the fifty states. *Salting the Ocean*, illustrated by Ashley Bryan, is a spectacular anthology of a hundred poems written by students in grades 1–12 with whom Naomi has worked in her travels.

▶ **WRITING TIP** Naomi says poetry is a conversation with yourself as well as a conversation with the world. She advises students to sit down with a piece of paper. "Begin talking and see what speaks back." Naomi adds, "We need to talk to ourselves more, and we also need to *listen* to ourselves more."

▶ **READING/WRITING CONNECTION** "The Traveling Onion" begins, "When I think how far the onion has traveled/just to enter my stew today, I could kneel and praise/all small forgotten miracles." Invite students to find some other "small forgotten miracle" and to take a very close look at it. Then write about it.

▶ **READING TIP** "Reading a poem aloud slows you down, and when you slow down you are likely to read it more than one time. . . . We *need* this slow experience with words, as well as those quick and jazzy ones."

EVENT

1901 Steel magnate Andrew Carnegie gives New York City $5.2 million dollars to build sixty-five branch libraries. Having just sold his Carnegie steel company for $250 million dollars, he has decided to build libraries.

And now, dear friends, relatives, and enemies, the Westing game begins.

Ellen Raskin,
The Westing Game

BIRTHDAYS

1916 Ezra Jack Keats is born, in Brooklyn, New York, the son of Polish immigrants. He is the youngest of three children. When Jack is four or five he covers the kitchen table with drawings. Instead of getting angry, his mother says they are much too nice to wash off; instead, she covers them with a special tablecloth to protect them. When Ezra is told that *The Snowy Day* has won the Caldecott Medal, he asks, "What is the Caldecott?" He soon finds out and is thrilled.

1928 Ellen Raskin is born, in Milwaukee, Wisconsin. When she is twenty-one, she moves to New York City to work as a graphic designer. She illustrates over a thousand book jackets before writing her own first book, *Nothing Ever Happens on My Block*. In her Newbery Medal acceptance speech for *The Westing Game*, Ellen says she writes for readers "curious enough to read slowly, and the slower the better for my books." Ellen worries about authors' personalities becoming more important than their books. "Meeting a writer," she insists, "is not a substitute for reading a book. It is the book that lives, not the author." Asked about her creative method, she says, "I rewrite and rewrite. And rewrite!"

▶ **READING REFLECTION** Ask students to list five books they read slowly and five books they read fast. Invite them to talk about the reasons a book might get on one list or the other.

1933 Diane Dillon is born, in Glendale, California. This Caldecott Medal–winning illustrator collaborates with her husband Leo Dillon to create the illustrations for such books as *Why Mosquitoes Buzz in Peoples' Ears; Ashanti to Zulu: African Traditions; Who's in Rabbit's House; The People Could Fly: American Black Folktales;* and *The Tale of the Mandarin Ducks.* For *Pish, Posh, Said Hieronymus Bosch,* the Dillons' son Lee joins the collaboration, contributing a silver-, bronze-, and brass-sculptured frame for each of the book's illustrations. Diane and Leo have created more than forty books. *The Girl Who Spun Gold,* a West Indian variant on the Rumpelstiltskin tale, is their third collaboration with Virginia Hamilton. In a story with gold as a strong theme, they create a wonderful richness of gold by using special techniques.

1933 Thomas Rockwell is born, in New York City. Thomas remembers reading comic books for free all afternoon on the steps of Howard's General Store, on Route 7, in rural Vermont, where he grows up. After graduating from college and working for a gardening magazine in New York City, he moves to a home beside a dairy farm outside Poughkeepsie, New York, and helps his famous father write his autobiography. He also writes his own book about his father's work: *The Norman Rockwell Album.* Thomas says reading *The Oxford Book of Nursery Rhymes* to his own son Barnaby reminds him how much he likes children's book, and so he writes his own, illustrated by his wife Gail Sudler, *Rackety-Bang and Other Verses.* Thomas says reviews for the book are awful, but this doesn't stop him. He writes *How to Eat Fried Worms,* which not only receives a better reception, it wins ten awards.

1957 Lisa Campbell Ernst is born, in Bartlesville, Oklahoma. She enjoys drawing and making up stories about the animals in her neighborhood. She makes little books out of scrap paper, stapling the pages together. Lisa says that her parents' love of reading aloud planted in her the idea that stories are meant to be shared. After illustrating books for other authors, she illustrates her own book, *Sam Johnson and the Blue Ribbon Quilt,* launching her career as a writer as well as an illustrator.

▶ **READ MORE** In Lisa's *Little Red Riding Hood: A Newfangled Prairie Tale,* the well-known heroine rides a bicycle and has a robust, tractor-riding grandmother who doesn't need saving; *Goldilocks Returns* is an update on another familiar fairy-tale character.

▶ **READING/WRITING CONNECTION** Invite students to describe the day in the life of a fairy-tale character who decides to visit your school.

Wherever they's a fight so hungry people can eat, I'll be there. Wherever they's a cop beatin' up a guy, I'll be there.

John Steinbeck,
The Grapes of Wrath

BIRTHDAYS

1889 Marguerite DeAngeli is born, in Lapeer, Michigan. She trains as a singer in Philadelphia but says she's had an "itch to draw, the longing to put things down in words" as far back as she can remember. Along with raising six children, Marguerite begins illustrating other people's books. In 1935, she writes her own book, *Ted and Nina Go to the Grocery Store.* Marguerite writes numerous books about the foreign born. She writes the Newbery Medal–winning *Door in the Wall,* the story of a crippled boy in thirteenth-century England.

1920 Hank Ketcham is born, in Seattle, Washington. He creates the "Dennis the Menace" comic strip.

EVENTS

1939 John Steinbeck's novel *The Grapes of Wrath* is published. This story of the Joad family, farmers from Oklahoma who leave the Dust Bowl to find a new life in California, is a searing account of poverty and social protest. The Pulitzer Prize–winning novel is made into an acclaimed movie.

2000 At one minute past midnight, the *Oxford English Dictionary* joins the dotcom revolution, launching its online edition, *OED Online*. The day before, in the library of London University, Thomas Murray, the five-year-old great-great-great-grandson of Sir James Murray, the first OED editor, becomes the first person to use *OED Online*.

MARCH

Funny thing was, I used to like Porter Dotson fine when he was just the feller down the street who ran the newspaper. He was funny and friendly. Then he married my mama two years ago, and I stopped liking him.

Ruth White,
Belle Prater's Boy

BIRTHDAYS

1932 Barbara Cohen is born, in Newark, New Jersey. As a child she tells people she wants to be a writer, but after earning her M.A. from Rutgers University, she becomes a high school English teacher, though she does write a weekly newspaper column. Finally, she has ideas for fiction and she leaves teaching to become a full-time writer. She is the author of such books as *The Carp in the Bath Tub*, *Molly's Pilgrim*, and *Thank You, Jackie Robinson*.

1942 Ruth White is born, in Whitewood, Virginia. The daughter of a coal miner who dies when she is six, she feels grateful to a public school system that helps her and her three sisters go on to a better life. Ruth says even before she starts school she knows she will be a writer someday. She thinks she'll write about princesses and faraway places, but after she grows up she finds herself writing about her own Appalachian region. Author of the Newbery Honor book *Belle Prater's Boy*, Ruth is a teacher and a librarian. She says, "I will always work in the public school system and try to give back something of what was given to me."

EVENTS

1926 A. A. Milne signs a contract for *Winnie-the-Pooh*. Later, Milne's son Christopher Robin notes, "If anyone wonders why in the stories so much time seems to be spent in trees or up trees, the answer is that this, in real life, is how it was." Christopher's father writes to friends just after Christopher's seventh birthday, "At the moment he is mad on tree-climbing, which he really does rather well and pluckily, even after doing the last eight feet (downwards) on his head the other day."

▶ **WRITING/READING CONNECTION** Invite students to write five sentences about tree climbing. Then they should find a poem about tree climbing. Does the poem give them any ideas about revising their sentences?

1989 Two books by Jim Arnosky, *I Was Born in a Tree and Raised by Bees* and *Sketches Outdoors in Summer*, receive certificates of commendation as outstanding nature books for children by the John Burroughs Association.

MARCH

Dark ain't so bad if you know what's in it.

Sid Fleischman,
The Whipping Boy

BIRTHDAYS

1920 Sid Fleischman is born, in Brooklyn, New York. He grows up in San Diego, California. At age seventeen, he publishes a book for magicians. After graduating from high school Sid travels around the United States, working as a magician. In addition to the Newbery Medal–winning *The Whipping Boy*, Sid is the author of such popular books as the McBroom series, *By the Great Horn Spoon*, and *The Scarebird*.

▶ **OUT LOUD** Read some of the McBroom books out loud—to reveal the wonders of a master stylist and a very funny writer.

1928 William Mayne is born, in Kingston-upon-Hull, England. Living near a place associated with King Arthur, he brings to his work an interest in Arthurian legends that "have location." He says, "I have always been interested in the naming of places, why they were called this, that, and the other." His book *Earthfasts* features a *bog-*

gart, which is a northern English dialect word for a mischievous poltergeist. J. K. Rowling features boggarts in her Harry Potter stories.

EVENTS

1827 *Freedom's Journal*, the nation's first African-American newspaper, is published, in New York. Editors declare on the front page, "We wish to plead our own cause. Too long have others spoken for us." The paper is published weekly until March 28, 1829. Issues of the paper are available online at <*http://www.shsw.wisc.edu/library/aanp/freedom*>.

1850 Nathaniel Hawthorne's *The Scarlet Letter* is published. Priced at seventy-five cents, it sells six thousand copies in its first printing, making Nathaniel more money than any other book he's written in twenty-two years. But the book also makes him unpopular in his hometown of Salem, Massachusetts.

MARCH

17

Go wind, blow
Push wind, swoosh.

Lilian Moore,
Go Wind

BIRTHDAYS

1909 Lilian Moore is born, in New York City. As a teacher, she discovers she has a talent for helping children learn to read. Then she becomes the first editor at Scholastic's Arrow Book Club. While editing books for children, she begins to write a line of books known as "easy readers." Lilian makes her mark as a poet, helping children find wonder in ordinary things. Among her notable titles are *I Feel the Same Way*, *I'll Meet You at the Cucumbers*, and *Something New Begins*.

1934 Zibby Oneal is born, in Omaha, Nebraska. She is the author of such young adult novels as *The Language of Goldfish* and *A Formal Feeling*. Zibby recalls liking to be by herself—sitting under a tree in her backyard and making up stories while her sister and friends went roller-skating. "I was a solitary child—no doubt about it—but no one ever worried over that. My parents understood that a writer needed solitude." Zibby says the stories she made up were usually set in places like Paris or Bangkok. Noting that her first published book is set in Omaha, Zibby points out that "sooner or later most writers return in some way to what they know best."

1953 Ralph Fletcher is born, in Plymouth, Massachusetts. He is the oldest of nine children. Ralph says when he receives a master's degree in writing at Columbia University he doesn't plan on writing children's books but in working with children, helping them find ideas for their writing, he ends up falling in love with the books himself. Ralph now writes highly regarded and popular poetry and novels for children. In *Flying Solo*, Ralph tells the story of what happens to a class of sixth graders when the substitute teacher never shows up.

▶ **WRITING TIP** Ralph recommends that students keep a writer's notebook with them so they can write at any place and any time. He says, "Write about what amazes/surprises/angers you. Write about what you wonder about. Write about what you notice or what you overhear. Write lists. Draw and doodle." Invite students to make a list: food they like, food they hate, good names for dogs, places they'd like to visit, favorite sports players, things that would improve school, whatever. Encourage them to choose any category they like—and make a list.

EVENT

1957 Parsons School of Design students Leo and Diane Dillon are married. They refer to their work as created by "the artist Leo and Diane Dillon," though Leo admits this collaboration does not come easy: "It was years and years before we could pass a piece of work back and forth between us and not get into a fight." He says Diane has an incredible eye for color. He recalls once when she suggested doing something in pink and orange. "If we do it in pink and orange," I said, "that will be the end! I can't live with someone who'd do anything in pink and orange. We'll have to get a divorce!" He adds, "We did it in pink and orange, of course." In their 1976 Caldecott Medal acceptance speech the Dillons affirm, "We believe that the role of the illustrator is not simply to duplicate the text, but to enlarge on it, to restate the words in our own graphic terms." In 1991, their son Lee collaborates with them for the first time, on *Pish, Posh, Said Hieronymus Bosch*, by Nancy Willard.

MARCH

18

The sun is nervous
As a kite. . . .

John Updike,
"March," *A Child's Calendar*

BIRTHDAYS

1932 John Updike is born, in Shillington, Pennsylvania. He studies at Harvard College and the Ruskin School of Drawing and Fine Art. Famous as a Pulitzer Prize–winning novelist, he has written more than forty books for adults. He also writes occasional verse for children, including *A Child's Calendar*. Each poem celebrates the qualities that make a time of the year unique.

▶ **WRITING TIP** Invite students to choose some aspect of spring and to try writing a metaphor. John Updike says the sun is a nervous kite. What else might it be?

1950 Douglas Florian is born, in New York City. Douglas notes, "I grew up surrounded by art. My father was an artist, and our New York City apartment looked like an art gallery. Landscapes, seascapes, and portraits covered the walls, and the smell of linseed oil filled the air." After college, Douglas publishes hundreds of drawings in the *New York Times*, an experience he finds exciting but too rushed. He decides to look for work that is less hurried, and children reap the benefits in the inventive books he creates. Douglas combines poems with paints to produce a wonderful mix of language play and visual delight. In *Beast Feast*, the verbal antics include the walrus made walrusty by salty sea water and the baby kangaroo "fast asleep/Inside its kangaroom."

▶ **WORD FUN** Challenge students to coin other kangaroo words like *kangaroom*.

EVENTS

1885 Mark Twain notes in a letter that the Concord, Massachusetts, public library has "given us a rattling tiptop puff which will get into every paper in the country. They have expelled Huck from their library as 'trash and suitable only for the slums.' That will sell 25,000 copies for us for sure." *The Adventures of Huckleberry Finn* continues to be one of the most frequently banned books.

▶ **READ MORE** Nat Hentoff's young adult novel *The Day They Came to Arrest the Book* is a fictionalized account of a modern-day challenge to *The Adventures of Huckleberry Finn*. Students can also explore censorship in *Maudie and Me and the Dirty Book*, by Betty Miles. In *Nothing but the Truth: A Documentary Novel*, Avi addresses freedom of speech issues—and the shoddy way the media covers such issues.

1888 In a letter to friend and fellow artist Emile Bernard, Vincent van Gogh describes the countryside of Provence in the south of France: "Water forms patches of a beautiful emerald or a rich blue in the landscape. . . . The sunsets have a pale orange color that makes the fields appear blue. The sun a splendid yellow. And all this though I have not seen the country yet in its usual summer splendor."

▶ **READ MORE** In Neil Waldman's fantasy *The Starry Night*, a young boy shows Vincent van Gogh around his hometown of New York City. In this quite extraordinary volume, familiar Big Apple landmarks are rendered in Van Gogh's style.

1923 A *New York Times* reporter asks George Leigh Mallory, "Why do you want to climb Mount Everest?" Mallory explains his repeated attempts to reach the top: "Because it's there." In 1924, Mallory and his partner disappear on Everest during his third expedition on the unforgiving mountain.

▶ **READ MORE** In his stunning, prize-winning *The Top of the World: Climbing Mount Everest*, Steve Jenkins uses crushed-paper and cut-paper collage to document a climb to the top of Mount Everest, including the equipment used by climbers and how the cold and altitude affect their bodies.

1951 E. B. White writes his editor Ursula Nordstrom, letting her know he has finished a new book, *Charlotte's Web*.

▶ **OUT LOUD** Invite students to choose short passages of *Charlotte's Web* to read aloud.

MARCH

It is said, O King of the Age, that there once lived a poor tailor in a certain city in China. This tailor had a son, called Aladdin.

The Arabian Nights,
translated by Sir Richard
Francis Burton,
retold by Neil Philip

1821 Sir Richard Francis Burton is born, in Torquay, Devonshire, England. Richard grows up in France, England, and Italy, educated by tutors. At Oxford University, he wants to study subjects that interest him—such as Arabic and philosophy—instead of the required curriculum, so he is expelled. This doesn't prevent Richard from learning twenty-five languages, writing forty-three volumes on his extensive travels, and translating thirty volumes, including *The Arabian Nights, or The Thousand and One Nights*, a collection of stories from Persia, Arabia, India, and Egypt.

▶ **OUT LOUD** Read aloud a story from *The Arabian Nights*.

1872 Susy Clemens is born. When she is thirteen, she writes a biography of her famous father, who is best known by his pen name, Mark Twain. Twain treasures her creation. He says of her spelling: "I cannot bring myself to change any line or word. . . . The spelling is frequently desperate but it was Susy's and it shall stand. I love it and cannot profane it. To me it is gold. To correct it would alloy it, not refine it. It would spoil it. It would take from it its freedom and flexibility and make it stiff and formal." Twain adds, "She learned languages easily; she learned history easily; she learned music easily; she learned all things easily, quickly and thoroughly except spelling. She even learned that after a while. But it would have grieved me but little if she had failed in it—for although good spelling was my one accomplishment I was never able to greatly respect it."

▶ **SPELLING TIP** After thirteen-year-old Joanne Lagratta, from Clintonville, Wisconsin, wins the 64th National Spelling Bee by spelling *inappetence* and *antipyretic*, she tells reporters she doesn't study word lists. Joanne says she learns spelling from reading. "I read some books over and over again." Invite students to share their own spelling methods (and miseries).

1939 Lucy Bate is born, in Washington, D. C. In *Little Rabbit's Loose Tooth*, a rabbit makes the most of losing a tooth.

▶ **WRITE MORE** Invite students to share their own stories about when and how they lost their teeth.

▶ **READ MORE** In *Throw Your Tooth on the Roof: Tooth Traditions from Around the World*, Selby B. Beeler provides fascinating lore about what happens to lost teeth in other cultures.

1968 In response to children's letters, Harper & Row editor Ursula Nordstrom prepares a form letter: "Thank you so much for your letter asking us to publish some more books like *Where the Wild Things Are*. We think this is a fine idea and have sent your letter to the author, Mr. Sendak, in the hopes that he will like the idea too."

MARCH

20

A green thing is sprouting

And that's why I'm shouting

Beatrice Schenk de Regniers,
*Happy Birthday, Dear First Day
of Spring!*

BIRTHDAYS

1900 Carl Withers is born, in Sheldon, Maryland. In *A Rocket in My Pocket,* Carl collects over four hundred verses created by children and passed along for generations—jump-rope rhymes, link rhymes, tongue twisters, riddles, and all kinds of verbal nonsense. "I love my wife and I love my baby,/I love my biscuits sopped in gravy" and "A skunk sat on a stump./The stump thunk the skunk stunk;/the skunk thunk the stump stunk" are just two examples.

1926 Mitsumasa Anno is born, in a small mountain village in Japan. Influenced by M. C. Escher, Anno wants *Topsy-Turvies: Pictures to Stretch the Imagination* to challenge readers to see things in new ways. Anno says that a professor of mathematics claims that he found twelve "impossibilities" in the book. But, says Anno, "is anything really impossible in the world of the imagination?" Anno insists that "impossible" is a word used only by grown-ups. "Nothing is impossible to the young, not until we become caught in the problems of living and forget to make-believe."

1937 Lois Lowry is born, in Honolulu, Hawaii. Her father is an Army dentist, and Lois lives all over the world as she is growing up. She remembers when she was eight her mother reading *The Yearling* aloud to her and her sister. It was a book that changed how she felt about books. Among Lois's more than twenty-five books are the Newbery Medal books *The Giver* and *Number the Stars*, as well as *The One Hundredth Thing About Caroline, Us and Uncle Fraud, Taking Care of Terrific,* and the Anastasia series. Lois describes herself as a shy, quiet child, one who goes off by herself and makes up stories. Although this young girl rarely shows her stories to anyone else, they give her great pleasure. When she goes to summer camp, she has a notebook in which she writes "private stuff," the way Anastasia Krupnik does years later.

▶ **READ MORE** Lois's many fans always ask her where she gets her ideas, so after publishing twenty-four books, she tells them by writing *Looking Back: A Book of Memories.*

1954 Louis Sachar is born, in East Meadow, New York. He is the Newbery Medal–winning author of such middle-grade fiction as *Holes, There's a Boy in the Girls' Bathroom, Sixth-Grade Secrets*, and the Wayside School series. Louis writes his first children's story as an assignment in high school. It is about a mean teacher named Mrs. Gorf who turns her students into apples. His teacher suggests he write another story. While attending the University of California, Louis works as a teacher's aide, supervising the playground. Kids call him Louis the yard teacher. He points out that Louis the yard teacher is in *Sideways Stories from Wayside School,* and the kids are in there too. On a book tour Louis meets a guidance counselor in a school he visits in Texas. She later becomes his wife. Fans will remember the important adult in *There's a Boy in the Girls' Bathroom.* Louis' favorite authors are E. L. Doctorow, J. D. Salinger, Kurt Vonnegut, Dostoyevski, Tolstoy, Flannery O'Connor, Kinky Friedman, Rex Stout, E. B. White, William Saroyan, John Steinbeck, and Dr. Seuss. Louis says, "These are mostly adult authors, which is only fitting, since I am mostly an adult."

1997 Jon Agee appears at the thirtieth-anniversary Children's Book Festival, in Hattiesburg, Mississippi. Jon creates his first books when he is four years old, "Book" and "The Little Boy Who Said He Knew Everything." He studies filmmaking and painting at Cooper Union School of Art. In addition to highly acclaimed picture books, Jon has created books of palindromes—phrases that read the same both forward and backward. The titles are themselves palindromes: *Go Hang a Salami! I'm a Lasagna Hog!* and *So Many Dynamos!* He is also the author of a book of anagrams: *Elvis Lives and Other Anagrams.*

▶ **WORD FUN** Challenge students to figure out which is easier to write, a palindrome or an anagram, and why.

MARCH

The *Oxford English Dictionary* remains the world's greatest repository of the English language.

Jonathon Green,
Chasing the Sun: Dictionary Makers and the Dictionaries They Made

BIRTHDAYS

1825 Fitzedward Hall is born, in Troy, New York. Trained as a civil engineer, he leaves college just before his Harvard class graduates—he goes off to find his brother, who has run away to India. In India Fitzedward becomes fascinated with Sanskrit, which he studies and later teaches, first in India and later at King's College, London; he also edits texts on Sanskrit and Hindi grammar. His enormous contributions to the *Oxford English Dictionary* are acknowledged in the preface. To make contributions to the *OED*, readers send in sentences that show word usage. Each quotation must be written on a separate sheet of paper labeled with the word the quotation is exemplifying and must include the date, author, title, and page of the work being cited. Readers are instructed, "Make a quotation for every word that strikes you as rare, obsolete, old-fashioned, new, peculiar, or used in a peculiar way." Readers are also told, "Make as many quotations as you can for ordinary words, especially when they are used significantly, and tend by the context to explain or suggest their own meaning."

▶ **RESEARCH TIP** Invite students to organize a vocabulary notebook employing a version of the *OED* notation system that works for them.

1936 Margaret Mahy is born, in Whakatane, New Zealand. A prolific author, Margaret says she has wanted to write books for as long as she can remember. Margaret's many novels, picture books, and poetry volumes include *The Birthday Burglar and a Very Wicked Headmistress, The Tricksters, The Haunting, The Man Whose Mother Was a Pirate, Nonstop Nonsense*, and *17 Kings and 42 Elephants.* Margaret says her famous *The Boy Who Was Followed Home* draws on her childhood desire to have animals like her. She says the story, like most of her stories, is based on a kernel of truth and then exaggerates that truth. Margaret concedes that it would be easier for the boy to be followed home by guinea pigs, but hippopotamuses are a lot more fun.

▶ **THINK ABOUT IT** Invite students to figure out why hippopotamuses "are a lot more fun." Then they can create more-fun/less-fun animal lists for story possibilities.

1953 David Wisniewski is born, at South Ruislip Air Force Base, Middlesex, England, the son of a U. S. Air Force officer. David remembers enjoying comic books as a boy, followed by Jules Verne, Ray Bradbury, Robert Heinlein, and J. R. R. Tolkien. Ray Bradbury continues to be his all-time favorite author, and his all-time favorite book is *The Martian Chronicles.* After running out of tuition money for college, he attends the Ringling Brothers and Barnum & Bailey Clown College. David illustrates original folktales with wonderfully intricate cut-paper artwork, cutting the paper with an X-acto knife. He uses a thousand blades to create one book. In his Caldecott acceptance speech for *Golem*, David talks about his art: "Though demanding, making words and pictures fit and flow in narrative harmony is enormously satisfying. Few other professions are as metaphysical: the thoughts and images of one mind are transformed into a solid object which, when opened, conveys them to thousands of other minds. What a privilege! What an opportunity! What a responsibility."

▶ **READ MORE** In *The Secret Knowledge of Grown-Ups,* David reveals the real reason grown-ups tell kids to "Eat your vegetables," "Drink plenty of milk," "Comb your hair," "Don't jump on your bed," "Don't bite your fingernails," and so on.

1959 Peter Catalanotto is born, on Long Island. He is the second of five children. When his kindergarten teacher asks him what he wants to be when he grows up, Peter says he's already an artist. Peter's whole family loves to draw, and there is a wall in the basement for the children to draw on. When they run out of wall space, their parents paint the wall white, and the children start drawing all over again. Peter especially likes painting comic book heroes such as Spider-Man.

1964 Lisa Desimini is born, in Brooklyn, New York. One of her early memories as an artist is copying a Tom and Jerry cartoon because she loves the colors, the shapes, and the expressions on their faces. She keeps copying images she likes until finally she begins copying images out of her own imagination. Later she goes to the School of Visual Arts, in New York City. Lisa says her favorite thing to draw is houses.

▶ **WRITING/ART CONNECTION** Ask students to draw a house for homework—it can be theirs or just a house they find interesting. Ask students to write a paragraph about something they hadn't noticed about the house before they started drawing it.

MARCH

22

Moo says, "I've been thinking. What does the farmer have that we don't have?"

"Hands and feet?"

"No," says Moo. "Boots and a hat."

Denys Cazet,
*Minnie and Moo Go
to the Moon*

BIRTHDAYS

1846 Randolph Caldecott is born, in Chester, England. He likes to draw, whittle, and mold things in clay. At age fifteen, he leaves school to work as a clerk in a bank. Six years later he transfers to a bank in Manchester and attends art classes at night at the Manchester School of Art. His sketches appear in various magazines, gradually including American magazines. Then he does illustrations for sixteen children's books that make him famous. Randolph Caldecott is Maurice Sendak's favorite illustrator. In Maurice's words, "He is the king."

▶ **ART TIP** There are a number of books about the work of illustrating books. *What Do Illustrators Do?,* by Eileen Christelow; *Talking with Artists* (three volumes), by Pat Cummings; *A Caldecott Celebration,* by Leonard Marcus; *Wings of an Artist,* by Julie Cummins; and *From Pictures to Words,* by Janet Stevens, are some.

1938 Denys Cazet is born, in Oakland, California, the son of a banker. As his occupation Denys lists work as a gardener, writer, mail carrier, warehouse worker, cable line worker, cook, stock clerk, and process server. He is an elementary teacher and librarian for fifteen years. He remembers large (French) family gatherings that are part Renaissance fair, part circus, with stories being told and retold.

EVENTS

1842 Henry David Thoreau writes in his journal, "Nothing can be more useful to a man than his determination not to be hurried."

▶ **READ MORE** D. B. Johnson's prize-winning *Henry Hikes to Fitchburg* is an amusing and touching illustration of how Henry put the precept of not being hurried into practice.

1961 Short story writer Flannery O'Connor writes a friend, "My nest-watching activities have begun as I have four geese setting."

▶ **READ MORE** Recommended reading about nests ranges from Dav Pilkey's zany *The Silly Gooses* to the sumptuous oversized adult volume *The Nest: An Artist's*

Sketchbook, in which Maryjo Koch provides life-size illustrations of bird nests, eggs, and feathers rendered in actual size, a volume sure to increase reverence for nests.

1980 Katsumi Suzuki wins the longest nonstop jump-rope marathon. Traditionally, jump rope is a street game done to a chant or rhyme:

> I had a little Teddy Bear, his name was Tiny Tim.
> I put him in the bathtub to see if he could swim.
> He drank up all the water, he ate up all the soap,
> He died the next morning with a bubble in his throat.

The rhymes are not always polite. For example:

> I see London, I see France.
> I see somebody's underpants.

▶ **WRITING TIP** Invite students to compile a class collection of jump-rope rhymes.

▶ **READ MORE** *The Jump-Rope Book,* by Elizabeth Loredo, provides directions for various moves as well as rhymes for rollicking jumping. *Anna Banana: 101 Jump-Rope Rhymes,* by Joanna Cole, is fun to read even if you don't want to jump. *Jump-Rope Magic,* by Afi Scruggs, illustrated by David Diaz, shows how an intrepid girl's passion for jump-rope rhymes transforms the neighborhood spoilsport. Quite a hoot from an author with a doctorate in Slavic linguistics.

MARCH

23

I grew to love Ruby and to be awed by her. It was an ugly world outside, but I tried to make our world together as normal as possible. Neither one of us ever missed a day. It was important to keep going.

Barbara Henry, Ruby Bridges's teacher, quoted in *Through My Eyes,* by Ruby Bridges

BIRTHDAYS

1857 Fanny Farmer is born. When a stroke prevents her from going to college, she turns to cooking. Her *Boston Cooking School Cook Book,* first published in 1896 and still in print, is one of the best-known and most popular American cookbooks.

▶ **READING/WRITING CONNECTION** Invite students to bring in a favorite recipe and compile a class collection. They might decide on a theme such as favorite chocolate recipes, favorite desserts, favorite salads, and so on. In *Writers in the Kitchen,* compiled by Tricia Gardella, children's book authors share memories of their favorite recipes. Ashley Bryan confesses, "When it comes to cooking and recipes . . . I'm sunk! I have no mind for cooking and couldn't begin to spell out a recipe for anything beyond . . . and barely . . . a toasted cheese sandwich!" Mark Teague agrees, saying he can make instant oatmeal. Paula Danziger says her favorite recipe is Cheerio necklaces, which in her childhood meant she could "accessorize and munch each day." On the other hand, Crescent Dragonwagon can cook. She gives her recipe for Cuban Black Bean Soup, which she and her husband liked so much they served it at their wedding reception.

1912 Eleanor Cameron is born, in Winnipeg, Manitoba, Canada. After three years in Ohio, where her father tries to farm, the family moves to Berkeley, California. Eleanor says that a sense of place is all-important, and much of her work is informed by Berkeley, San Francisco, Yosemite, the redwoods, the Monterey Peninsula. Like her character Julia Redfern, Eleanor becomes a reference librarian so she can support her writing. Eleanor's son David tells her about a dream he had, and Eleanor writes the Mushroom Planet series.

1857 Thomas Garrett, a Quaker and chief operator of the Underground Railroad's eastern line in the slave state of Delaware, writes to William Still, a free black man of Philadelphia:

> Esteemed Friend, William Still:
>
> I have been very anxious for some time past, to hear what has become of Harriet Tubman. The last I heard of her, she was in the State of New York, on her way to Canada with some friends, last fall. Has thee seen or heard anything of her lately . . . ?

▶ **READ MORE** *"Dear Friend": Thomas Garrett & William Still,* by Judith Bentley, provides an account of two men who formed an alliance as "friends of humanity" to help slaves travel north on the Underground Railroad.

2000 Ruby Bridges's *Through My Eyes* wins the Bank Street College of Education award as the best nonfiction children's book that "advances humanitarian ideals and serves as an inspiration to young readers." Norman Rockwell depicted Ruby's experience integrating a New Orleans elementary school forty years previously on a *Saturday Evening Post* cover. Ruby was six years old on that memorable school day. Rockwell pictures one little girl walking to school, surrounded by four federal marshals.

MARCH

24

When Papa lost a job, a terrible sort of sadness came down over things. In some way that she couldn't explain herself, Franny felt that by staying close, by talking and making herself loudly present, it helped to make something awful seem less awful.

Mary Stolz,
The Noonday Friends

BIRTHDAY

1920 Mary Stolz is born, in Boston. She grows up in New York City. She is the author of such novels as the Barkham Street series, *Emmett's Pig,* and *The Noonday Friends.* Her picture books include *Storm in the Nigh; Zekmet, the Stone Carver;* and *A Wonderful, Terrible Time.* Mary says she loves to read and she loves to write. She says when she is asked what book she'd take to a desert island, she realizes she won't go anyplace where there isn't a public library.

EVENTS

1852 Emily Dickinson writes to her brother about the unusual weather: "You would'nt [sic] think it was spring, Austin, if you were at home this morning, for we had a great snowstorm yesterday, and things are all white, this morning. It sounds funny enough to hear birds singing, and sleighbells, at a time."

1905 At age seventy-seven, Jules Verne, probably the most widely read novelist in the world, dies. Forty years before, Verne made a deal with his publishers to produce two novels a year for the rest of his life. For this he was guaranteed $4,000 annually. When he dies, he is twelve books ahead of his contract.

▶ **WRITING TIP** Invite students to do what Verne did. Fascinated by engines as a boy, as a writer he trains himself to observe carefully how machinery works. Ask students to study a machine and then write about it.

▶ **READ MORE** David Macaulay's *The New Way Things Work* is considered the masterpiece of writing describing the workings of machinery.

1911 The Central Children's Room of the New York Public Library opens.

▶ **READ MORE** *The Inside-Outside Book of Libraries,* by Julie Cummins, illustrated by Roxie Munro, provides an insider's view of U. S. libraries—from the tiny public library on Ocracoke Island, North Carolina, to the library aboard a U. S. Navy aircraft carrier to the Berkeley Public Library tool-lending library.

1962 C. S. Lewis writes to a young fan, "I was at three schools (all boarding schools) of which two were very horrid. I never hated anything so much, not even the front line trenches in World War I. Indeed the story is far too horrid to tell anyone of your age."

MARCH

25

As for Mrs. May, I must have named her that because I knew some English teacher would write and ask me why. I think you folks sometimes strain the soup too thin. . . .

Flannery O'Connor,
letter to a professor of English,
in *The Habit of Being: Letters of Flannery O'Connor,* selected and edited by Sally Fitzgerald

BIRTHDAYS

1867 John Gutzon Borglum in born. He is the sculptor and creator of the Mount Rushmore memorial figures, in South Dakota. Borglum begins work on Mt. Rushmore in the 1920s but doesn't complete it. His son finishes the monument in 1941, the year the elder Borglum dies. Huge heads depicting Presidents Washington, Jefferson, Lincoln, and Theodore Roosevelt are carved into the mountain. George Washington's head is sixty feet from chin to forehead. The heads are carved to the scale of a person 465 feet tall.

▶ **READ MORE** *Rushmore,* by Lynn Curley, is an enticing picture-book account suitable for all ages.

1925 (Mary) Flannery O'Connor is born, in Savannah, Georgia. Flannery says that her life climax occurs when she is six. Pathe News visits her farm and shoots a newsreel of Flannery with a chicken that walks backward. Flannery spends most of her life in Milledgeville, Georgia, where she raises peacocks and writes. In addition to penning celebrated stories, she is known as a consummate letter writer.

EVENTS

1760 Just a few weeks before his seventeenth birthday, the results of his entrance exam are reviewed and Thomas Jefferson is admitted to the College of William and Mary, in Williamsburg, Virginia. More than six feet tall, an unusual height in those days, Tom is known as Tall Tom to his friends.

▶ **READ MORE** Nicknames are a powerful and provocative topic of many books—*Hello, Sweetie Pie,* by Carl Norac, for primary graders; *The Sixth-Grade Nickname Game,* by Gordon Korman; and the interesting-to-all-ages *The Complete Book of Sports Nicknames,* by Louis Phillips and Burnham Holes; *From Abba Dabba to Zorro: The World of Baseball Nicknames,* by Don Zminda; *Nicknames and Sobriquets of U. S. Cities, States, and Countries,* by Joseph Nathan Kane and Gerard L. Alexander; *The Dictionary of Historic Nicknames,* by Carl Sifakis; and *Twentieth-Century American Nicknames,* by Laurence Urdang.

1882 The first public demonstration of pancake making takes place, in New York City.

▶ **READ MORE** Challenge students to find poems and stories about pancake making. There are lots of great titles. For starters, try *Pancakes, Pancakes!,* by Eric Carle; *Mr. Wolf's Pancakes,* by Jan Fearnley; *Curious George Makes Pancakes,* by the H. A. and Margret Reys; *Perfect Pancakes, If You Please,* by William Wise and Richard Egielski; and *The Clever Cowboy,* by Angela McAllister.

▶ **READING/WRITING CONNECTION** In *Acorn Pancakes, Dandelion Salad, and Other Wild Dishes,* Jean Craighead George offers unusual recipes. Invite students to write their own pancake recipes, real or imaginary.

1945 Sylvester, the animated cat fated to futility in his pursuit of Tweetie Bird, makes his first appearance in a television cartoon.

MARCH 26

The ear is the only true writer and the only true reader.

Robert Frost

BIRTHDAYS

1874 Robert Frost is born, in San Francisco. America's most beloved poet recalls, "When I was young I was so interested in baseball that my family was afraid I'd waste my life and be a pitcher. Later, they were afraid I'd waste my life and be a poet. They were right." Frost takes great risks in pursuing his dream of being a poet, but he insists, "The middle of the road is where the white line is—and that's the worst place to drive." When asked to explain a poem he had recited, Robert asked, "What do you want me to do? Say it over again in worser English?"

▶ **WRITING TIP** Robert Frost advises, "Life is tons of discipline. Your first discipline is your vocabulary; then your grammar and your punctuation. Then, in your exuberance and bounding energy you say you're going to add to that. Then you add rhyme and meter. And your delight is in *that* power."

1911 Tennessee Williams is born Thomas Lanier Williams, in Columbus, Mississippi. After graduating from the University of Iowa, he becomes one of America's most famous playwrights.

▶ **ALL ABOUT NAMES** Invite students to consider what state or country they might choose as a nickname.

EVENT

1962 Robert Frost celebrates his eighty-eighth birthday at the White House, where President John Kennedy presents him with a special medal voted by Congress. Robert's first book of poetry in fifteen years, *In the Clearing*, is officially published.

MARCH 27

On an island not too far away and in a time not so long ago lived a secret tribe called the ciguapas. They made their homes under water in cool blue caves hung with seashells and seaweed.

Julia Alvarez,
The Secret Footprints

BIRTHDAYS

1901 Carl Barks is born, in Merrill, Oregon. He grows up on his family's farm, learning to draw by taking a correspondence course. In 1935, Carl sees an ad for cartoonists needed at Walt Disney Studios, in Hollywood. He quits his job, packs his bag, and heads for Hollywood. He works on many cartoons featuring Donald Duck, and when Western Publisher gets the rights in 1942 to publish Walt Disney characters in comic books, Carl starts illustrating Donald Duck. For more than two decades he draws the monthly ten-page Donald Duck segment for *Walt Disney Comics & Stories*. Carl likes to point out that he takes Donald from a noisy, quarrelsome movie brat and turns him into Everyman. He gives Huey, Dewey, and Louie their distinctive personalities, and creates Scrooge McDuck and Ducksburg, the town where Donald and crew live. Some of Donald's other biographical details include the fact that he has a twin sister Della, is primarily raised by Grandma Duck, and later raises his triplet nephews. Donald has a pet St. Bernard named Bolivar and a puppy named Behemoth.

▶ **WORD FUN** Comics have special words that get to the point fast. Invite students to bring in words from comics and comic strips that convey meaning with economy: *Whap! Zam! Pow! Gazooks!*

1922 Dick King-Smith is born, in Bitton, Gloucestershire, England, son of a paper mill director. Dick works as a farmer and a teacher before becoming a writer. Both his careers inform his writing. Teaching tells Dick what kinds of stories children like to read, and farm animals give him something engaging to write about. Dick himself has kept plenty of animals: cows, horses, pigs, goats, hens, ducks, geese, guinea fowl, rabbits, guinea pigs, mice, rats, budgerigars, zebra finches, cats, and dogs. Dick says a typical day for him is to sit down in his very small study in his very old house (dating from 1635) and scribble in longhand. In the afternoon, he types out what he has written in the morning on an old typewriter, using the one-finger method. In the evening Dick reads the day's work to his wife, "seeking her approval."

1950 Julia Alvarez is born, in New York City. She lives in the Dominican Republican until she is ten. When she moves back, the United States seems like an unfriendly place, a place where she will never fit in—until her teacher asks students to write a story about themselves. Julia writes about her cousins, the smell of mangoes, the color of the hummingbirds. She finds herself going more and more to the world of her writing, and finds it's a place she likes to be.

▶ **READ MORE** Julia bases her first children's book, *The Secret Footprints*, on an ancient Taino Indian folktale from the Dominican Republic.

Event

1902 A newspaper writer uses the name Chicago Cubs to fit into the headline of a story about a team that has been called the Chicago White Stockings, the Colts, and the Orphans. This new name sticks, and in 1907 it becomes the official team name.

▶ **READ MORE** *The Complete Book of Sports Nicknames,* by Louis Phillips, will be riveting for sports fans, who can report interesting stories to the rest of the class.

MARCH

I'm in charge of celebrations.

Byrd Baylor

Birthdays

1924 Byrd Baylor is born, in San Antonio, Texas. Now living in Arizona, Byrd says, "I feel at home with the cliffs and mesas and rocks and open skies. I'm comforted by desert storms." Byrd points out the importance of careful observation of horned toads and coyote trails, adding, "I learn what I can, and that is what I write about." In her personal notebook, Byrd includes 108 celebrations, listed by date and time. She has established rules for these celebrations: it must be a celebration of nature, something you plan to remember for the rest of your life, and it must be something so special that you think of it for the rest of the day.

▶ **WRITING TIP** Invite students to keep their own celebration notebooks, finding things to celebrate during one week. Ask them to establish a criterion for declaring a celebration.

1966 Doreen Cronin is born. A New York lawyer who collects antique typewriters, Doreen draws on both her profession and her hobby when she writes *Click, Clack, Moo: Cows That Type*. Some cows find an old typewriter and start sending demands to Farmer Brown. *American Lawyer Media* publishes an article about the book, noting that it is a *New York Times* best-seller. Doreen and her fiancé, also a lawyer, argue over the meaning of the tale. She says, "It's about the power of education and writing." He says, "You're out of your mind. It's a book about unions."

Events

1592 Johann Amos Comenius produces the first picture book for children.

▶ **READ MORE** Make this a day of celebrating beautiful picture books. Each child can share a favorite.

1927 Teachers at P.S. 58, in Manhattan, fine children five cents apiece for grammar errors such as "ain't" and "he don't." There are also fines for talking and chewing gum, but "violated grammar" is the chief source of revenue to the school fund. *Time* magazine reports a defect in the system: "Thrifty pupils come to regard bad grammar as a luxury." An eight-year-old brags about his dime, "Momma gave me two ain'ts for my birthday."

2000 The paperback edition of *Peacebound Trains,* by Haemi Balgassi, is released. When the U. S. government launches its Korean War 50th Anniversary website to commemorate the opening of the Korean War Memorial, in Washington, D.C., an online edition of this book appears on the site.

MARCH 29

Every day we have been ready to start for our depot 11 miles away but outside the door of the tent it remains a scene of whirling drift. We shall stick it out to the end, but we are getting weaker, of course, and the end cannot be far. It seems a pity, but I do not think I can write more.

Robert Falcon Scott, in his diary

EVENTS

1879 In the British magazine *Vanity Fair,* Lewis Carroll introduces a new word game. He calls it doublets. Today we call it word ladders. One starts with a word and, by changing one letter at a time (while keeping the other letters in the same order) changes that word into another word, often the opposite of the original:

head, heal, teal, tell, tall, *tail*
hate, rate, rave, cave, cove, *love*

▶ **WORD FUN** Challenge students to get from *pig* to *sty,* from *four* to *five,* and from *ape* to *man.* Then they can invent their own word-ladder challenges.

1912 British explorer Robert Falcon Scott makes the last entry in his diary during his expedition to the South Pole. Hit by a nine-day-long blizzard, members of the expedition freeze to death in their tent.

1952 E. B. White writes his editor about *Charlotte's Web,* "Whether children will find anything amusing in it, only time will tell." After he reads a scholarly analysis of the book, E. B. White admits, "It is an extraordinary document, any way you look at it, and it makes me realize how lucky I was (when I was writing the book) that I didn't know what in hell was going on." When someone asks him about the difference in writing for children and for adults, he replies, "Anyone who writes down to children is simply wasting his time. You have to write up, not down. Children are demanding. They are the most attentive, curious, eager, observant, sensitive, quick, and generally congenial readers on earth. . . . In *Charlotte's Web,* I gave them a literate spider, and they took that."

MARCH 30

As soon as I was old enough to eat grass, my mother used to go out to work in the daytime and come back in the evening.

Anna Sewell, *Black Beauty*

BIRTHDAYS

1820 Anna Sewell is born, in Britain. Her only book, *Black Beauty,* is published in 1877, a year before her death. Made into a movie several times, once by Thomas Edison, and illustrated by various artists, including Susan Jeffers, the book continues to capture children's interest.

1942 Charles Keller is born, in New York City. He is the author of many popular riddle books, including *Alexander the Grape, Ballpoint Bananas,* and *Remember the A la Mode!* Here's an example of one of his riddles:

How many *i*s do you use to spell Mississippi?
None. I can do it blindfolded.

▶ **READING FUN** Invite students to make reading riddles aloud a part of the day: Every day for the last five or ten minutes, volunteers stand up in front of the class and read or recite a riddle.

▶ **MORE FUN** Start the day with a riddle: write a riddle question on the board before school. All day, students can write possible answers. You will all discover that student answers are often much better than the answer in the book.

1766 Thomas Jefferson notes in his garden journal, "Purple hyacinth begins to bloom." Thomas keeps this garden journal from 1766 to 1824, making careful observations of everything that happens in his garden. We learn for example, that he plants eight varieties of peas; then we learn when the peas are up, when they blossom and pod, and when they are ready for the table.

▶ **READ MORE** Invite students to find and read a book about gardening. Plenty of sumptuous volumes are available—Mary Azarian's *A Gardener's Alphabet;* Chris Van Allsburg's *The Garden of Abdul Gasazi;* forestry graduate Henry Cole's *Jack's Garden;* Douglas Florian's *Vegetable Garden;* and Gail Gibbons's *From Seed to Plant.*

1858 A patent is issued to Hyman Lipman, of Philadelphia, for a pencil with an attached eraser.

▶ **READ MORE** Show students that kids are inventors too! *Brainstorm! The Stories of Twenty American Kid Inventors,* by Tom Tucker, and *The Kid Who Invented the Popsicle and Other Surprising Stories About Inventions,* by Don Wulffson, are good places to start.

1983 The first California condor chick born in captivity is hatched, at the San Diego Zoo. A second one hatches a week later.

▶ **READ MORE** *On the Brink of Extinction: The California Condor,* by Caroline Arnold, and *The Condor's Egg,* by Jonathan London, explain why this is considered an extraordinary event.

1987 One hundred and twenty-four years after his birth, Dutch painter Vincent van Gogh's *Sunflowers* sells at Christie's in London for $39.9 million. The painting is one of six Van Gogh painted on this subject. Sadly, Van Gogh does not have success with his paintings during his lifetime.

▶ **READ MORE** *Camille and the Sunflowers: A Story About Vincent Van Gogh,* by Laurence Anholt, is based on a true incident—and gives a glimpse of the creation of some of the sunflower paintings.

▶ **RESEARCH TIP** Faith Ringgold's joyful painted story quilt "The Sunflower Quilting Bee at Arles" can be seen online: *http://www.artincontext.org/artist/ringgold/D15.htm*

MARCH

There was a miller who left no more estate to the three sons he had than his mill, his donkey, and his cat.

Arthur Lang, "The Master Cat," *The Blue Fairy Book*

BIRTHDAYS

1844 Andrew Lang is born, in Scotland. After extensive anthropological research in folklore, Lang produces *The Blue Fairy Book* in 1889, the first of twelve edited fairy-tale collections with different colors in their titles: blue, red, green, yellow, pink, gray, violet, crimson, brown, orange, olive, lilac. Andrew explains that unlike some adults, he does not believe fairy tales are harmful to children; he believes that children "know very well how much is true and how much is only make-believe."

▶ **OUT LOUD** Read one of the Lang tales aloud. The text of a number of the fairy tales is available online: *http://www.belinus.co.uk/fairytales/FaerypiecesFamous.htm*

1926 Beni Montresor is born, in Bussolengo, Italy. Beni grows up looking not at picture books but at stained-glass windows in churches—visual stories created long ago for people who didn't know how to read. When Beni makes books today he thinks of those windows of his childhood. After studying at the Verona Art School and the Academy of Fine Arts, Beni designs sets and costumes for movies, for the Metropolitan Opera, and for the New York City Ballet. Then he turns to picture books, winning the Caldecott Medal for Beatrice Schenk de Regniers's *May I Bring a Friend?* His illustrations for *Little Red Riding Hood,* with the wolf devouring the little girl, cause great controversy. (Not only does the wolf eat Little Red, we then see her floating inside his belly.) A picture preceding the devouring scene is online: *www.calvin.edu/~hett/Red%20Riding%20Hood/Montresor%20LRRH.html*

EVENTS

1732 The first books are ordered for the Library Company of Philadelphia, the first circulating library in the United States. This lending library is organized by Benjamin Franklin. Fifty people contribute forty shillings each to buy the first books. Then they pay ten shillings a year to belong. A shilling was about fourteen cents. The first free public library is the Juvenile Library of Dublin, New Hampshire, established in 1822.

▶ **READ MORE** Hold a read-a-thon of books featuring libraries and librarians. For starters, *Library Lil*, by Suzanne Williams, illustrated by Steven Kellogg, is about a tall-tale librarian who can balance a set of encyclopedias in the palm of one hand and toss a motorbike over her head like an apple core; *Tomas and the Library Lady*, by Pat Mora, is based on the true story of the man who become chancellor of the University of California at Riverside and the librarian who changed his life. For the mystery crowd, there's everything from *The Deserted Library Mystery*, by Gertrude Chandler Warner (The Boxcar Children No. 21), to *Meg MacKintosh and The Mystery in the Locked Library*, by Lucinda Landon, to *Murder at the Library of Congress*, by Margaret Truman.

1905 Sherlock Holmes is revived. In 1893, weary of six years of writing about his fictional hero, Arthur Conan Doyle had sent Sherlock over the Reichenbach Falls in Switzerland in a fight with the evil Moriarity, apparently the end of a glorious career. For twelve years, Arthur ignores pleas for a sequel. Finally, though, he relents and *The Return of Sherlock Holmes* is published today.

▶ **THINK ABOUT IT** Ask students about book series they can't get enough of.

 **APRIL**

APRIL

 1

April Fool's Day:
"Bumpy dumb
horseplayziness!"

William Cole

BIRTHDAYS

1755 Anthelme Brillat-Savarin is born, in Belley, France. He works for thirty years on the *Handbook of Gastronomy*, also known as *Physiology of Taste*, published in 1825 at his own expense. The book contains observations on the art of cooking and the pleasures of eating, as well as delightful anecdotes about food.

▶ **READING/WRITING CONNECTION** Invite students to read cookbooks and poems about food. Then they can bring in a recipe for a favorite dish and write an anecdote about eating this food. In *Writers in the Kitchen*, by Tricia Gardella, children's book authors share memories of their favorite recipes. The book includes Joseph Bruchac's memory of his grandmother's dandelion greens and Mark Teague's admission that if it weren't for peanut-butter-and-jelly sandwiches, he'd be in trouble. Evidence that poets like to write about food can be found in *Never Take a Pig to Lunch*, selected and illustrated by Nadine Bernard Westcott; *Popcorn* and *Candy Corn* and *Cornflakes* by James Stevenson; and *Yummy! Eating Through a Day*, selected by Lee Bennett Hopkins.

1933 Jan Wahl is born, in Columbus, Ohio. While his parents attend college, he spends a lot of time with both sets of grandparents, making up stories to amuse himself and, later, to amuse his five brothers. A prolific writer, Jan brings his enjoyment of fantasy and whimsy to an account of the true story of sixty-seven-million-year-old Sue, the largest and most complete Tyrannosaurus rex ever found, in *The Field Mouse and the Dinosaur Named Sue*. The real Sue resides in the Field Museum, in Chicago.

▶ **READ MORE** *A Dinosaur Named Sue: The Story of the Colossal Fossil,* by Pat Relf with the Sue Science Team of the Field Museum, follows the work of the experts as they uncover Sue's story.

▶ **READING REFLECTION** Invite students to find a nonfiction book about dinosaurs. Then they can read some dinosaur poems, say, Jack Prelutsky's *Tyrannosaurus Was a Beast* and William Wise's *Dinosaurs Forever*. What facts can they find in these poems? Can they separate the fact from the fantasy?

1947 Francine Prose is born, in Brooklyn, New York, the daughter of two physicians. Known as a writer for adults, Francine's children's book *You Never Know* is based on the ancient legend of the Lamed-vavniks. According to Jewish tradition, there are, at every moment, in every generation, thirty-six righteous individuals living in secret throughout the world. They never make their presence known unless there is some threat to the community, and after the danger is over, they disappear. Francine brings this legend to life with wit and wonder: "A few months after Schmuel left, a new cobbler came to Plotchnik. His name was Yakov, and he was poor, but no one called him Poor Stupid Yakov. Everyone was kind to him. After all, you never know." "You never know" is a great message for children—and for the adults who teach them.

EVENTS

1872 The Chicago Public Library is created. In 1991, it moves from its famous and beautiful old building, decorated with stained glass and mosaics by the artist Louis Comfort Tiffany, to an impressive and very large new building, named for Chicago's first Black mayor, Harold Washington.

▶ **READ MORE** *The Library,* by Sarah Stewart and David Small, is dedicated to and about the real life of a librarian, Elizabeth Brown, a woman whose life centers on reading. When "volumes climbed the parlor walls/And blocked the big front door/She had to face the awful fact/She could not have one more." So she donates her collection to the town, turning her home into a library where, of course, she continues to read.

1964 John Updike is elected to the American Academy of Arts and Letters. At age thirty-two, he is the youngest person ever elected to membership. His *Child's Calendar,* reprinted in 1999 with illustrations by Trina Schart Hyman, is named a Caldecott Honor book. John begins his *April Poem,* "It's spring! Farewell/To chills and colds!"

▶ **WRITING FUN** Invite students to continue an April poem that begins, *It's spring! Hello . . .*

1981 *On Market Street,* by Arnold and Anita Lobel, is published, offering an unforgettable shopping spree from A to Z.

▶ **WRITING FUN** Encourage students to invent their own up-to-date alphabetic shopping spree: what will they acquire from A to Z? To increase divergent thinking, offer the challenge of themed lists, lists for literary characters, and so on.

APRIL

2

"But the Emperor has nothing on at all!" cried a little child.

Hans Christian Andersen,
The Emperor's New Clothes

BIRTHDAYS

1805 Hans Christian Andersen is born, in Odense, an island off the coast of Denmark. He is the only child of a poor shoemaker and a washerwoman. Hans's father loves to tell stories, and he often reads his son stories from *The Arabian Nights* and the fables of LaFontaine, as well as Danish literature.

▶ **READING TIP** Invite students to read Hans Christian Andersen's *The Emperor's News Clothes.* Then invite them to read one of several divergent versions, such as Stephanie Calmenson's *The Principal's New Clothes* and Kathryn Lasky's *The Emperor's Old Clothes. The Emperor's New Clothes: An All-Star Retelling of the Classic Fairy Tale,* published in 1998 by Harcourt Brace for the benefit of the Starbright Foundation, is accompanied by an audio CD and includes contributions by a host of celebrities ranging from Liam Neeson and Harrison Ford to General Norman Schwarzkopf and is illustrated by a host of favorites, including Maurice Sendak, Mark Teague, Graeme Base, and William Joyce. There are lots of terrific surprises.

1954 Amy Schwartz is born, in San Diego, California, the daughter of a newspaper columnist and a professor of chemistry. In elementary school, Amy adapts her favorite picture books into theater productions. Shy in real life, she enjoys hamming it up on stage. But drawing and painting are her real passions. Although she receives acclamations for both her writing and her illustrations, Amy says "I actually think of myself as an illustrator first, I suppose because I do more illustrating than writing."

▶ **WRITING TIP** Amy says it's good to know that writing is something you don't have to do from start to finish all on your own. You can get advice from other people. She notes that in her own writing, she is helped first by teachers and friends and later by her agent and her editor.

▶ **WRITING FUN** In *Bea and Mr. Jones,* Bea, a kindergartner, and her father, a businessman, are both bored—so they change places. Invite students to make a list of ten things that might happen if they were to change places for a day with an adult of their choice. What do they hope the adult would learn from the exchange?

▶ **READ MORE** Mary Rodgers's *Freaky Friday* is the classic change-of-identity story. A thirteen-year-old girl wakes up one morning to find herself in her mother's body.

1969 Harper & Row editor Ursula Nordstrom writes to first-time author John Steptoe, telling him she has signed the print order for *Stevie*. Ursula acknowledges that this is routine part of her job, but "today when I signed yours I had an especial feeling of joy. This is the beginning of a very wonderful career, in painting and in books too."

▶ **READ MORE** John Steptoe's Cinderella tale, *Mufaro's Beautiful Daughters: An African Tale*, is a Caldecott Honor book, as is his *The Story of Jumping Mouse: A Native American Legend*.

APRIL

You should know that for years I had wondered who Miss Alaineus was.

Debra Frasier,
Miss Alaineus: A Vocabulary Disaster

BIRTHDAYS

1783 Washington Irving is born, in New York City. The son of immigrants, he is named for George Washington. While studying law, he writes essays about New York society and the theatre using various pseudonyms: Diedrich Knickerbocker, Geoffrey Crayon, Gent, Jonathan Oldstyle, Friar Antonio Agrapida, and Launcelot Langstaff. *The Legend of Sleepy Hollow* and *Rip Van Winkle* appear as serials, and Washington becomes the best-known figure in American literature, both at home and abroad. Charles Dickens says, "I don't go upstairs to bed two nights out of seven without taking Washington Irving under my arm."

1953 Sandra Boynton is born, in Orange, New Jersey. She creates popular greeting cards as well as such inventive picture books as *A Is for Angry, Chloe and Maude,* and *Hester in the Wild.*

▶ **WORD FUN** *A Is for Angry* is a book of animals and adjectives. Challenge students to come up with their own alphabet of animals paired with adjectives beginning with the same letter. They can also add a verb if they are feeling creative.

1953 Debra Frasier is born, in Vero Beach, Florida. She spends her childhood swimming, walking on the beach, building sand castles, making forts out of driftwood. After earning an art degree from Florida State University, Debra studies textiles at Penland School of Crafts, in North Carolina. She builds wind sculptures for several museums and works as a paper-cutout artist. Debra says she reads all of Vera Williams's books to her daughter. "They're about strong women and love and all the real things that are important for young girls to know." Debra creates the art for *Miss Alaineus: A Vocabulary Disaster* out of objects she finds in her fifth-grade daughter's desk—markers, notebook paper, pencils, glue, and scissors.

▶ **WORD STUDY** In *Miss Alaineus: A Vocabulary Disaster*, the narrator talks about people whose names may or may not be taken literally: For example her teacher is "Mrs. Page, who is not a single side of a printed sheet of paper usually found bound in a book." One of her classmates is Forrest, who "is not a thicket of trees." Challenge students to take a close look at the names of peoples they know—and make a list of those who, like Mrs. Page and Forrest, do not match the definition of their names.

EVENTS

1451 Johannes Gutenberg uses movable type to print a book.

1848 The Massachusetts legislature passes a law enabling Boston to levy a tax for a public library, creating a funding model for public libraries across the country.

▶ **READ MORE** Here's another chance to celebrate books and reading. Ask students to find books featuring the importance of reading. You can start with *The Wednesday Surprise,* by Eve Bunting.

It seems that some years before the Blue Snow (which every old logger remembers because of a heavy fall of bright blue snow which melted to ink, giving folks the idea of writing stories like these, so they tell) Ol' Paul was logging on what was then known as the Whistling River.

Glen Rounds,
Ol' Paul The Mighty Logger

BIRTHDAYS

1906 Glen Rounds is born, near Wall, South Dakota, the son of a rancher. He attends the Kansas City Art Institute, serves in the U. S. Army during World War II, and works as a mule skinner, cowboy, sign painter, railroad section hand, baker, carnival medicine man, and textile designer. Glen's more than fifty books expand upon popular American tall tales or tell original tales of the West. Glen says that in writing and illustrating *Ol' Paul, the Mighty Logger*, instead of researching old Paul Bunyan tales, "I made them up as I went along." Then, since his publisher, Holiday House, is just starting out and doesn't have a sales force, Glen and his bride fix up their station wagon as a combination sleeping quarters and warehouse, load it with copies of *Ol' Paul* and barnstorm the country, working with booksellers and librarians to spread the word about the book.

▶ **READING/WRITING CONNECTION** Invite students to read some tall tales and then to write one of their own, using at least one of the elements they've noticed. Tall tales often tell about the origins of things: logging, dry ice, the Grand Canyon, bookkeeping. Invite students to write a tall tale explaining the origin of something they use or a common geographical feature of their region.

1932 Johanna Reiss is born, in Winterswijk, the Netherlands. As she writes in *The Upstairs Room*, a Newbery Honor book, ten-year-old Johanna and her sixteen-year-old sister are hidden from the Nazis by a Christian couple who risked death with their brave and compassionate actions. For two and a half years, the two girls stay hidden in an upstairs room.

▶ **READ MORE** *Forging Freedom*, by Hudson Talbot, is the compelling true story of Jaap Penraat, who is determined to protect his Jewish friends and neighbors in Amsterdam from Nazi persecution.

1942 Elizabeth Levy is born, in Buffalo, New York. She works as an editor and researcher for ABC, as an editor, and as a public relations writer. Her novel *Lizzie Lies a Lot* draws on Elizabeth's own experience of being caught in a lie by her grandmother. Elizabeth says writing the Something Queer mystery series satisfies her own desire for comfortable adventure: mystery writers, she notes, always know that "in the end everything will be solved."

EVENT

1946 Three girls at the Jackson School, in Chicago, write to Robert McCloskey, asking him why, when he talks about four robbers all through the *Homer Price* chapter titled "The Case of the Sensational Scent," there seems to be an extra robber in the illustration on page twenty-five: "Did you put him there on purpose to see if children are good detectives?" Robert McCloskey writes a funny reply, available at <http://www.hbook.com/exhibit/hunt.html>. Robert admits that he had a lot of counting to do in that book, he was in a hurry, and he "forgot to count for just long enough for that robber to get into bed."

5

Directly opposite him, on the other side of the enclosed space, were two doors, exactly alike and side by side. It was the duty and the privilege of the person on trial to walk directly to these doors and open one of them.

Frank R. Stockton,
"The Lady, or the Tiger?"

BIRTHDAYS

1834 Frank Stockton is born, in Philadelphia, Pennsylvania. He works as a wood-graving illustrator and as an assistant on the popular children's periodical *St. Nicholas Magazine.* The author of imaginative children's tales, Frank's most famous work is "The Lady, or the Tiger?" Frank receives thousands of letters asking him to tell who is behind the door. Even Rudyard Kipling asks, threatening to lure Frank into a jungle. "We'll lay you on your back and have one of our very biggest elephants stand over you and poise his ample forefoot directly over your head. Then I'll say in my most insinuating tones, 'Come now, Stockton, which was it—the lady or the tiger?'"

1934 Richard Peck is born, in Decatur, Illinois. He is a teacher, a professor, and a textbook editor. *A Long Way from Chicago* is a Newbery Honor book and its sequel, *A Year Down Yonder,* wins the Medal.

EVENT

1887 In Tuscumbia, Alabama, teacher Anne Sullivan achieves a major breakthrough with her blind and deaf pupil, Helen Keller, when Helen understands the meaning of the word *water,* which Annie conveys by spelling the word into Helen's hand using the Manual Alphabet and having her touch the water.

▶ **READ MORE** Laurie Lawlor's *Helen Keller: Rebellious Spirit* reaches beyond the icon and shows readers the real life of this extraordinary child.

6

Horrible Hairy Hogs
Hurrying Homeward
on Heavily Harnessed
Horses

Graeme Base,
Animalia

BIRTHDAYS

1926 Gail Kane is born, in Latvia. Born Eli Katz, he emigrates to New York with his family at age three. At age fifteen, he drops out of high school to work at MLJ, the publishers of Archie comics, penciling comic books, which is the first stage in drawing comics. After figures are penciled in, artists go over the lines in ink, someone else adds words, and then someone else adds color. In his long career Gail draws tens of thousands of pages of such superheroes as Atom, Green Lantern, Hulk, Captain Marvel, and Spider-Man. Kane says it took him twenty-five years of daily practice to perfect the artistic principles of perspective and figure drawing.

1938 Joel Rothman is born, in New York City. He is the author of *Secrets with Ciphers and Codes.*

▶ **READ MORE** Invite students to find out how to construct secret codes. They may be interested to know that in the 1790s Thomas Jefferson invented a code machine, a cipher disk with two wheels. Each wheel contains an alphabet and numbers on their edges. Nearly identical cipher devices are still used by the Army and Navy.

1942 Alice Bach is born, in New York City. In her book *The Smartest Bear and His Brother Oliver,* Ronald learns the contents of an encyclopedia to be smarter than his brother.

▶ **RESEARCH TIP** Invite students to choose an alphabet letter out of a hat. Then they should browse in that volume of an encyclopedia and report back to the group five interesting facts they learn in entries starting with their letter.

1958 Graeme Base is born, in Amershame, England. His family moves to Australia when he is eight. He writes his first book, *Book of Monsters,* when he is eight, using colored pencils for the illustrations. His favorite authors are J. R. R. Tolkien, A. A. Milne, and Kenneth Grahame. Graeme works for three years on the alphabetic *Animalia.* One eager reader has found 2,400 alphabetic items. Graeme's own favorite page is the Horrible Hairy Hogs, with the Lazy Lions running a close second. Graeme gets the idea for his very popular *The Eleventh Hour* while reading Agatha Christie novels one summer. He travels extensively collecting ideas, basing *The Entrance Hall* on St. Peter's in Rome, spending a month in the game parks of Kenya and Tanzania, and so on. Graeme's favorite food is stuffed roulade of wildebeest with a light garnish of squid ink.

▶ **WRITING/DRAWING TIP** Graeme says if you hope to write and illustrate books, "Sell the TV."

▶ **DRAWING FUN** Advise students to keep a sketchbook for a week, finding at least five things to draw each day. At the end of the week, ask students to think about whether this assignment has caused them to "see" familiar things in new ways—or if it caused them to take new routes.

APRIL

Little feet of children
blue with cold,

how can they see you
and not cover you. . . .

Gabriela Mistral,
"Little Feet"

BIRTHDAYS

1889 Gabriela Mistral is born, in Vicuna, Chile. The first Latin-American woman to win the Nobel Prize for literature, she takes her name from her two favorite poets, Gabriele D'Annunzio and Frederic Mistral.

▶ **ALL ABOUT NAMES** Invite students to figure out a pen name incorporating the names of two favorite poets.

1929 Donald Carrick is born, in Dearborn, Michigan. While in high school Donald works as an apprentice sign painter, painting billboards on weekends. Later, he collaborates with his wife, Carol, on thirty-seven picture books. She writes, he illustrates. Scientific accuracy is important to both of them. Donald always works from live models, and this sometimes means crayfish living in the turkey roaster and a turtle in the bathtub. A number of their books star their own son Christopher and his dog: *Sleep Out, Lost in the Storm, The Accident, The Foundling.*

1941 Alice Schertle is born, in Los Angeles, the daughter of a real estate investor and a teacher. Alice loves *Mary Poppins, The Wizard of Oz, The Black Stallion,* and *King of the Wind.* Alice writes a lot in elementary school and her stories have one thing in common: they get off to "a roaring good start" but they end somewhere in the middle; she never knows how to end the stories. Alice grows up to write stories with a middle and end as well as a roaring good start. She also writes poetry.

▶ **WRITING TIPS** Alice suggests, "Try writing the last half of a story first, and then go back and write the beginning." Edna Ferber always wrote the last line of her novels first; so did Katherine Anne Porter.

▶ **READING/WRITING CONNECTION** In *How Now, Brown Cow?* Alice observes that "cow" rhymes with "bough" but not with "rough." Invite students to explore what "cow" does and doesn't rhyme with. Then they can do the same thing with cow-related words. Anyone who isn't convinced that English spelling isn't tough should read a (very funny) poem "English Is Tough Stuff," posted at the North Atlantic Treaty Organization headquarters near Paris: see *http://www.milk.com/random-humor/english_poem.html*

The mules strained forward strongly, hoofs stomping, harness jingling. The iron blades of the plow sang joyously as it ripped up the moist, black Kansas earth with a soft crunching sound, turning it over in long, smooth, root-veined rectangles.

Harold Keith,
Rifles for Watie

BIRTHDAYS

1903 Harold Keith is born, in Lambert, Oklahoma. A seventh-grade teacher whose favorite authors are Charles Dickens, O'Henry, and Mark Twain, Harold's hobbies are long-distance running, trout fishing, and singing in a barbershop quartet. Harold gets a list of rebel Civil War veterans still living in Oklahoma and interviews twenty-two of them. Then he works five years on a book that reflects their memories. Harold compares writing this book to long-distance running. "You have to keep going even after you grow dead tired." He says he never gets tired of this book though, and *Rifles for Watie* wins the Newbery Medal.

▶ **WRITING TIP** Interviewing adults can be a powerful aid to student writers. Ask students to interview three adults, asking them about the most difficult spelling word they ever learned, how they learned the nine times tables, or whatever. Provide students with an interview format and conduct practice sessions before sending them out into the field.

▶ **ALL ABOUT NAMES** In *Rifles for Watie,* Jefferson Davis Bussey has trouble when he goes to serve in the Northern army—because of his first and middle names. Invite students to invent other names that might not suit certain life situations.

1938 Ruth Chew is born, in Minneapolis, Minnesota. She is the author/illustrator of *Do-It-Yourself Magic.*

▶ **READ MORE** Invite student volunteers to find books on magic in the library and to learn a trick to perform in front of the class. There's no better way to encourage close reading of a text.

1939 Trina Schart Hyman is born, in Philadelphia. In her acceptance speech for the 1985 Caldecott Medal for *Saint George and the Dragon*, Trina says, "There is an old, unwritten, but very sensible rule in children's book publishing that says you must never let the author and the illustrator meet, at least not until after the book is on its way to the printer. It's a good rule because authors and illustrators almost never agree on how a book should be illustrated and, besides, they usually hate each other on first sight anyway." But Trina wanted to meet Margaret Hodges, the book's author, and in that meeting, she says, "something magical happened to the landscape. I swear that the light changed. The trees became enchanted princesses; the clouds became castles; and the fairies came out of the flowers. It was a case of love at first sight, again. You can see this scene for yourselves on the back of the jacket for *Saint George.*" In the nine months she works on the book, Trina learns about ancient herb-lore, wild flowers, how ancient Celts and Britons lived, pre-Arthurian armor and weapons. "I learned a lot about lizards and dinosaurs and other strange and wonderful reptiles. . . . I learned that Arthur Rackham drew the best dragons in the world."

▶ **READ MORE** An online source gives students a look at Rackham's art as well as some biographical information. Even though there are no dragons, it is very well worth viewing: *http://www.pitt.edu/%7Eenroom/illustrators/rackimg.htm*

1952 Steven Schnur is born. A professor at Sarah Lawrence College and literary editor of *Reform Judaism*, Steven writes novels for middle readers. His two volumes of acrostic poems, *Autumn* and *Spring,* offer ingenious possibilities for children to exercise their own creativity.

▶ **WORD FUN** Invite students to use Schnur's poetry pattern. Choose words associated with spring. Write one of these words vertically, using these letters as the beginnings of poetic lines. For example, here's a start. What could come next?

April showers
Pass, bringing
R
I
L

1794 Thomas Jefferson notes in his Garden Book, "our first dish of Asparagus." The previous October he had noted planting the asparagus and covering it with a thick coat of tobacco suckers and manure.

1871 Robert Louis Stevenson, twenty years old, tells his father that he is giving up his engineering studies to become a writer. The family had expected Robert to carry on the Stevenson family tradition of lighthouse design.

▶ **READ MORE** Invite students to dip into Robert's verse or adventure tales.

APRIL

Please tell Onion John that the whole idea is to build him a regular, respectable house. There can't be any four bathtubs in the living room.

John Krumgold,
Onion John

BIRTHDAY

1908 Joseph Krumgold is born, in Jersey City, New Jersey, the son of a man who runs movie theaters. Joseph moves to Hollywood and writes movie scripts. He adapts one script, about New Mexican sheep farmers, into a children's book. *And Now Miguel* is awarded the Newbery Medal in 1954. Joseph's second book, *Onion John*, is also awarded the Newbery.

▶ **THINK ABOUT IT** When townspeople decide to build Onion John a house, it seems like a good and kind idea. But they insist the house should have only one bathtub. And Onion John wants four—one bathtub to store his beets, another for newspapers, and so on. Ask students to consider: when you do something to help a person, who gets to decide just how things should go?

APIRL

Where do dinosaurs still follow cavemen?

In the dictionary.

David Adler,
The Dinosaur Princess and Other Prehistoric Riddles

BIRTHDAYS

1897 Eric Mowbray Knight is born, in Menston, Yorkshire, England. Although Eric is born into a wealthy family, fortunes change when his father dies, and his mother sends the four young boys to various relatives so she can work as a governess. Eric leaves school at age twelve to become a textile mill laborer. When he is fifteen, after a twelve-year separation, the family is reunited in the United States. Eric's best-known work is the one children's book he writes, *Lassie Come Home*, a story based on his own dog, Toots. The book has been adapted into eight motion pictures and six television series and continues to be reissued in different formats.

1924 Selma Boyd Acuff is born, in Chicago. She writes *Footprints in the Refrigerator* and *I Met a Polar Bear*.

▶ **WRITING FUN** Invite students to write a paragraph titled *Footprints in the _____*.

▶ **READING REFLECTION** Celebrate provocative titles students find in their reading: Ask students to contribute to a Great Titles bulletin board, posting titles they find intriguing.

1947 David Adler is born, in New York City. A former math teacher, David is a prolific author, writing riddle books and the popular Cam Jansen mystery series, among others. David says he makes his main character a girl because he likes to work against stereotypes. David points out that Cam has the characteristics generally attributed to boys: she's curious and she's assertive. When he starts to write his first mystery David remembers a classmate from elementary school who seemed to have a photographic memory and he thought, "Wouldn't such a great memory be helpful in solving mysteries?" David acknowledges that Cam's friend Eric "is based on me. I'm the more timid child being led into the Cam adventures by my more adventurous friend."

▶ **READING FUN** David says his favorite clue is in *Cam Jansen and the Triceratops Pops Mystery*, adding, "I won't tell you the clue; I want you to read the book and try to find it yourself."

EVENT

1941 An editor at Street and Smith publications writes twenty-one-year-old Isaac Asimov, saying "I wish you'd come into the office and talk over 'Nightfall' with me. I am planning to take the story, but there are some parts of it which need changing. The ending is very good, but the beginning is slow." After this first publication, Isaac writes more than three hundred books, which are spread over nine of the ten major categories of the Dewey Decimal System. The only category in which Irving does not have a book is Philosophy/Psychology.

APRIL 11

Fight or die.

Graham Salisbury,
Jungle Dogs

BIRTHDAYS

1908 Leo Rosten is born, in Lodz, Poland. He comes to America as a small boy. His best-known book, *The Joys of Yiddish*, is a comic dictionary of Yiddish words and their many nuances. Susan Ohanian is a research assistant for Leo; she consults with scholars at the Jewish Theological Seminary on word derivations for this dictionary. The dictionary lists twenty-nine meanings for the word *oy*. Leo says "*Oy* is not a word; it is a vocabulary. It is a lament, a protest, a cry of dismay, a reflex of delight."

1944 Graham Salisbury is born, in Philadelphia, Pennsylvania. He grows up in Hawaii. He has been a musician, teacher, graphic artist, and commercial manager. Graham says his love for writing is really his love for reading. Hawaii has changed a lot since Graham was a boy, and he tries to paint word pictures of the Hawaii he remembers. Graham's second novel, *Under the Blood-Red Sun,* wins the Scott O'Dell Award for Historical Fiction.

EVENT

1863 Young newspaper reporter Mark Twain writes to his sister: "Pamela, you wouldn't do for a local reporter because you don't appreciate the interest that attaches to *names.*"

▶ **READ MORE** Invite students to read a page from the phone book, looking for interesting names. Point out that some authors use the phone book as a source of names for their characters.

APRIL 12

Spanish is a matter Of "¡Ay Dios!"

Gary Soto,
Canto Familiar

BIRTHDAYS

1907 Hardie Gramatky is born, in Dallas, Texas. After high school, Hardie works his way through Stanford University and the Chouinard Art School, in Los Angeles, by working in a bank, as a logger, and illustrating a comic strip. After working six years as an animator at Walt Disney Studios, Hardie moves to New York, where his studio overlooks the East River. Watching the tugboats, he gets the idea for his first and most famous book, *Little Toot*.

1910 Paul Showers is born, in Yakima Valley, Washington. Paul writes a series of books offering a simple introduction to such topics as the heart, teeth, eyes, blood, and sleep. His *What Happens to a Hamburger* explains nutrition and the digestive system.

▶ **RESEARCH TIP** Invite students to choose a part of their bodies, then research it and write a short report based on what they find. For a gross, hilarious account of a kid who thinks his body is falling apart, invite students to read *Parts,* by Tedd Arnold.

1916 Beverly Cleary is born, in McMinnville, Oregon. This popular Newbery Medalist keeps a notebook in which she jots down ideas as they occur to her. In her memoirs, Cleary says that her own experience of being put in the low reading group in school has given her special sympathy for children who have difficulties in school.

▶ **READ MORE** Beverly has written a two-volume memoir, *A Girl from Yamhill* and *On My Own Two Feet.*

1952 Gary Soto is born, in Fresno, California. Not having books growing up, Gary regards his own emergence as a poet as "sort of a fluke." After working as a laborer, Gary enters college intending to major in geography. An encounter with Alan Ginsberg and Lawrence Ferlinghetti leads him to poetry. Gary says, "I was lucky to discover at nineteen what I wanted to do." A prize-winning poet, Gary brings much of his Mexican-American heritage to his children's books, carefully setting his stories in specific sections of Fresno, near the color tile plant and the Safeway distribution center where he grew up.

EVENT

1914 George Bernard Shaw's play *Pygmalion* opens in London. Later it becomes the basis for a famous musical, *My Fair Lady,* starring Julie Andrews. Audrey Hepburn plays Eliza in the movie version, although Marnie Nixon sings all but one of her songs.

APRIL

13

The ponies were exhausted and their coats were heavy with water, but they were free, free, free!

Marguerite Henry,
Misty of Chincoteague

BIRTHDAYS

1899 Alfred Butts is born, in Poughkeepsie, New York. An architect without a job during the depression, he invents a board game he eventually calls Scrabble. An executive at Macy's sees the game in 1952 and begins carrying it in the store. For years, Butts receives three cents on every set sold. The set contains one each of the letters Q, J, K, and X. It contains twelve Es. According to the *Guinness Book of Records,* the highest score ever recorded is 1,049. The highest single-move score is Dr. Saladin Karl Khoshnaw's 392 for the word CAZIQUES, in a competition in Manchester, England.

▶ **WORD FUN** Give students an opportunity to examine letter frequency. Ask them what letter they think is used more often in the books they read. Which appears most in their own writing? Which appears least often? Challenge them to design a method for figuring out the answers.

1902 Marguerite Henry is born, in Milwaukee, Wisconsin. She sells her first story when she is eight years old. This Newbery winner, who grows up in a home with no pets, writes more than fifty books, including *Misty of Chincoteague.* Marguerite writes about dogs, foxes, and other animals, but she is the poet laureate of horses. Marguerite does a lot of research for her stories. *Misty of Chincoteague,* for example, depicts the history surrounding a herd of wild ponies living on an island. The story weaves facts with legend and has lots of heart. Misty actually lives with the Henrys for several years. The popularity of this Newbery Honor book is proven in its reissue in 2000, fifty-three years after its first appearance, in a deluxe edition that includes photographs of Marguerite and Misty. One of the photos shows Misty celebrating her first birthday with neighborhood children—she's eating an oatcake.

EVENT

2000 Judith Caseley's *Praying to A. L.* is released. Judith says, "When I was a little girl, I fell in love with Abraham Lincoln. I was drawn to the kindness and melancholy I saw in his face. My sister Jean and I prayed to a framed portrait of him that hung on our bedroom wall. . . . It was a private act of communion, and we called him A. L."

APRIL **14**

I guess you've heard how amazing rich our farm is. Anything will grow in it—quick. Seeds burst in the ground, and crops shoot right up before your eyes. Why, just yesterday our oldest boy dropped a five-cent piece, and before he could find it, that nickel had grown to a quarter.

Sid Fleischman,
McBroom's Wonderful One-Acre Farm

BIRTHDAY

1945 Susan Saunders is born, in San Antonio, Texas. She is the author of picture books and several series, including *Fifth Grade S.T.A.R.S., Sleepover Friends, Treasured Horses Collection,* and *Black Cat Club.*

EVENTS

1822 Sir Walter Scott entertains George IV when the king visits Edinburgh. The king gives Sir Walter a glass goblet. Sir Walter puts it in his coat and later in the day, when he sits down, he crushes the precious souvenir of their meeting.

▶ **THINK ABOUT IT** Invite students to consider a "most embarrassing moment" and then write about it.

1828 Twenty-two years in the making, Noah Webster's *American Dictionary of the English Language* is published. It is the first dictionary of American English, containing 12,000 "Americanisms" that have never appeared in any dictionary. Many dictionaries now contain *Webster* in the title, but that doesn't mean they have anything to do with the original dictionary writer. Book titles cannot be copyrighted, and anyone who wants to use Webster's name can do so.

▶ **WORD FUN** Ask student teams of three or four to start work on a dictionary. For starters, they should decide on the ten most important words for their dictionary. What ten words can they not get through the day without?

1992 Sid Fleischman's *Jim Ugly* is published. Jim Ugly is "a big sandy mongrel, part elkhound, part something else, and a large helping of short-eared timber wolf."

1999 Karen Romano Young's first novel, *The Beetle and Me,* is published. In high school, Karen writes a picture book called *The Blue Volkswagen.* Years later, she wonders where that old Beetle might be. Karen published her first writing in fourth grade, a poem titled "My Secret Place." It appears in the local newspaper. Karen notes that she has kept a diary since she was nine.

APRIL **15**

He made over a hundred photographs during the two-day storm. He called the storm a gift from King Winter.

Jacqueline Briggs Martin,
Snowflake Bentley

BIRTHDAY

1945 Jacqueline Briggs Martin is born, in Lewiston, Maine. Jackie says she has always loved the sounds of words. "One of my earliest memories is of my mother waking me up in the morning with an explanation of the 'runcible spoon' in Edward Lear's *The Owl and the Pussycat,* which we had read the night before." Jackie says there weren't many books in her house but she remembers a Paul Bunyan tall tale, *Snow White and Rose Red,* the Uncle Wiggily books, and a collection of Hans Christian Andersen tales. She likes the names of the Holstein cows on the family farm: Riceland Marathon Indigo, Riverflat Blanche Wisconsin, Kearsage Helen Dauntless. She also likes the names of the Maine rivers Nezinscot, Androscoggin, Damariscotta, and Kennebec. Jackie says that to write about Wilson Bentley's life in *Snowflake Bentley* she needed to "hear his voice." She read his own writing and read magazine interviews.

▶ **RESEARCH TIP** Invite students to choose a category of names in your region to examine: towns, rivers, plant life, or something else provocative.

EVENTS

1755 Samuel Johnson's *Dictionary* is published. An advertisement in newspapers states that word meanings are shown "by examples from the best writers."

1981 Robert Quackenbush's *Detective Mole and the Halloween Mystery* is published. It wins the 1982 Edgar Allen Poe Special Award.

2000 The University of California, Berkeley, celebrates its library's nine millionth acquisition. For this acquisition the library selection committee wants a volume that makes a statement that books in a traditional format are "very important, are sought after, and offer an experience, both tactile and intellectual, that a computer screen does not." The selection committee chooses *Aboriginal Portfolio*, by James O. Lewis, this country's first attempt at a true-to-life depiction of the American Indian. The book includes seventy-two hand-colored lithographs that portray Indian chiefs, mostly in their ceremonial garb. When the book, published in 1836, arrives, conservators in the library's preservation laboratory repair tears using cooked Japanese wheat paste and Japanese handmade paper.

APRIL

16

[I] knew that I'd probably have to stay after school for the next zillion years picking off every dang piece of gum I'd stuck all over the place. From where I was on the floor I saw lots of wads poking out from under cafeteria tables and seats. I wasn't sure, but it looked like one of them moved.

Eleanora E. Tate,
Don't Split the Pole

BIRTHDAYS

1890 Gertrude Chandler Warner is born, in Putnam, Connecticut. At age five, Gertrude decides she wants to become an author. Each Christmas, she writes a story as a present for her grandfather. Poor health forces Gertrude to leave high school in her sophomore year and she studies with a tutor. While sick at home, she thinks up the story of *The Boxcar Children*, but the first adventure isn't published until 1942. Some adults protest that the children are having too good a time without any parental control, but children love the books, so Gertrude writes eighteen of them. After her death, children keep asking for more, so other writers continue the Boxcar adventures.

1912 Garth Williams is born, in New York City. His illustrations for the Little House books, *Stuart Little*, and *Charlotte's Web* are some of the most famous images in children's literature. To gain the necessary background for illustrating the Little House books, Garth visits Mr. and Mrs. Wilder and then follows the route the Ingalls family took in their covered wagon. In Garth's words, "Illustrating books is not just making pictures of the people and articles mentioned by the author; the artist has to see with the same eyes. For example, an architect would have described the sod house on the bank of Plum Creek as extremely primitive, unhealthy, and undesirable—nothing to seal the walls from dampness, no ventilation, no light. But to Laura's fresh, young eyes, it was a pleasant home, surrounded by flowers and with the music of a running stream and rustling leaves. She understood the meaning of hardship and struggle, of joy and work, of shyness and bravery. She was never overcome by drabness or squalor. She never glamorized anything; yet she saw the loveliness in everything. This was the way the illustrator had to follow—no glamorizing for him either; no giving everyone a permanent wave."

1948 Eleanora Tate is born, in Canton, Missouri. She is raised by her grandmother. Her favorite childhood books are the Oz books and the Little House books, books she continues to reread. In her teens Eleanora discovers James Baldwin, Langston Hughes, Gwendolyn Brooks, and Lorraine Hansberry. "I was especially in awe of Ms. Brooks and Ms. Hansberry because they were women, and they looked like me!" Eleanora says the old schoolbooks of her childhood that placed African Americans in a negative light convinced her that she'd grow up and write books with positive African-American characters. Eleanora writes everywhere—on the porch, in bed, at the beach, in the car, at restaurants. She starts out with a number-two pencil or flair-tip pen and a wide-lined notebook. After her first draft she goes to the keyboard. Eleanora notes that she collects nicknames. "Every time I go to a school, I tell students I want to hear their nicknames. So I get nicknames: Skeeter, Lizard, Gummy Bears, Mickey Mouse, Pepper. . . . They send me these lists. I save them, and when I'm working on another manuscript, I look at those lists and pull some of those names."

▶ **WRITING TIP** Eleanora advises young writers: "Write and rewrite, and write and rewrite, and rewrite, and rewrite, and rewrite. . . ."

▶ **WRITING FUN** In *Don't Split the Pole: Tales of Down-Home Folk Wisdom,* Eleanora bases folksy tales on proverbs such as "slow and steady wins the race" and "big things come in small packages." Encourage students to pair up and write dialogue between two animals that emerges from (or results in) a proverb.

▶ **ALL ABOUT NAMES** Gordon Korman also asks students for nicknames. *The 6th Grade Nickname Game* is dedicated "To the schools I've visited; thanks for the nicknames."

1984 Amelia Atwater-Rhodes is born, in Silver Spring, Maryland. Always writing stories, when Amelia is in third grade she reads Christopher Pike's *The Last Vampire* and she's hooked. Amelia says she likes vampires because "you can do whatever you want with them." On her fourteenth birthday her first novel, *In the Forest of the Night,* is accepted by the Delacorte Press. Amelia says she has at least twenty more stories in her computer that aren't finished yet. Her English teacher is her agent. Amelia's mother, a high school principal, says she has "had a fantastic imagination all her life."

EVENT

1960 Noted short-story writer Flannery O'Connor writes, "My mind is so free and unburdened that I am fixing to clean up my desk."

▶ **WRITING TIP** Invite students to clean their desks, taking notes on the contents. Then they can write a reflection on what they find.

APRIL

17

The Scroobious Pip went out one day

When the grass was green and the sky was gray.

Edward Lear, "The Scroobious Pip"

BIRTHDAYS

1952 Daniel Hayes is born, in Troy, New York, the son of a dairy farmer. He remembers rereading *Huckleberry Finn* and *Great Expectations* in college and being amazed by how "how clever, how intelligent, and how funny writers like Mark Twain and Charles Dickens really were." Daniel begins studying his favorite writers' styles so he can sound like a writer. Then, when he does sound a bit like his favorite writers, he works at developing his own voice. "After I finished my first book, *The Trouble with Lemons,* a story told by thirteen-year-old Tyler McAllister, friends would read it and say things like, 'That's really amazing! It sounds just like you.'" Daniel notes that it has taken him a long time—and a lot of work—to learn to sound like himself.

1952 Jane Kurtz is born, in Portland, Oregon. When she is two years old her parents move to Maji, a small town in the southwest corner of Ethiopia. She remembers it as a beautiful country with a fascinating history and a tradition of hospitality and pride. Growing up, Jane's favorite books are *Charlotte's Web, Winnie-the-Pooh, Black Beauty,* and *Caddie Woodlawn.* Jane comes back to the United States to go to college, but it takes her twenty years to tell her Ethiopia stories. Her children's book *Fire on* the Mountain, illustrated by E. B. Lewis, is a retelling of an Ethiopian folktale she heard as a child. She sends photographs to Lewis, and he photographs Ethiopian families in Philadelphia where he lives to help him create the illustrations in the book.

EVENTS

1868 Edward Lear begins writing "The Scroobious Pip," scribbling it on the back side of notes he's written on his two-month Corsica tour. He also makes over three hundred drawings on this tour. Nancy Ekholm Burkert, who later illustrates a wondrous version of this poem, examines Edward's manuscript at Harvard University's Houghton Library, in Cambridge, Massachusetts. She notes, "No subtlety of leaf, light, rock, or human existence escaped his perceptive brush and pen." She also notes that in the hundred years between Lear's writing the verse and her illustrating it, at least a hundred species of animals have become extinct.

1873 Mark Twain writes, "The moment the spring birds begin to sing . . . I get the fidgets. . . ."

▶ **WRITING TIP** Invite students to write their own *The moment the spring . . .* sentences. They might want to conduct interviews, asking adults what "first sign of spring" they look for. A provocative way to sow seeds for thinking is to invite students to order flower seeds for a particular writer's garden. This exercise has possibilities from primary grades through high school. A high schooler in Virginia's McCormick's class, for example, ordered seeds for Alice Walker: baby's breath for her only daughter, bachelor(ette) buttons to represent the single life, and lots of purple flowers for her most popular work. Another student planned an astronomer's garden: moonflower, comet, star grass, cosmos, and so on.

APRIL

18

Listen, my children, and you shall hear

Of the midnight ride of Paul Revere.

'Twas the eighteenth of April in '75 . . .

Henry Wadsworth Longfellow

BIRTHDAYS

1934 Ida Luttrell is born, in Laredo, Texas. She is author of *Mattie and the Chicken Thief* and the Tillie and Mert series about a skunk and a mouse who are best friends.

1951 Chris Demarest is born, in Hartford, Connecticut. He earns a degree in painting from the University of Massachusetts. Chris finds success as a freelance illustrator for newspapers and magazines and then draws the art for the *Reader's Digest* column "Laughter, the Best Medicine." Chris illustrates books for other writers as well as his own books. Chris is well suited to create a book called *Firefighters A to Z*, because he is a member of a volunteer fire department. Using an alphabetical format for offering information, the text begins, "A is for Alarm that rings loud and clear, B is for Boots stowed in our bunker gear." Chris says his motive as a writer is entertainment. "Whether it is with a single cartoon or an entire book, I try to leave my readers with a warm smile and the feeling they've been included in the joke."

▶ **RESEARCH TIP** The alphabet format provides a useful organizing device for information on just about any topic. Invite student teams to research a topic and then organize their information in an ABC format. Such an exercise helps students develop their "find the main idea" skills.

1775 Paul Revere and Will Dawes start their famous "midnight ride" around 10 P.M., warning American patriots between Boston and Concord, Massachusetts, that "the British are coming."

▶ **READ MORE** In addition to Longfellow's famous poem, written in 1861 and interpreted for children by illustrators ranging from Nancy Winslow Parker to Ted Rand, there are numerous juvenile biographies of Paul Revere. Not to be missed are *America's Paul Revere,* by Esther Forbes; *And Then What Happened, Paul Revere?,* by Jean Fritz; and *Paul Revere,* by George Sullivan.

1842 Emily Dickinson thanks a friend for writing, referring to the letter as "one precious little 'forget-me-not' to bloom along the way."

▶ **READ MORE** There are a number of children's editions of Emily's poems, including *I'm Nobody! Who Are You,* illustrated by Rex Schneider, and *A Brighter Garden,* illustrated by Tasha Tudor. *Emily,* by Michael Bedard, illustrated by Barbara Cooney, offers a view of Emily's childhood. *The Mouse of Amherst,* by Elizabeth Spires, herself a noted poet, offers a poetic conversation between Emily and a talented mouse living in the wainscoting of her bedroom.

1961 E. B. White explains in a letter that "questing is more important than finding, and a journey is more important than the mere arrival at a destination." White explains that the importance of searching "the perfect and unattainable" is why he has never answered the question of whether Stuart Little ever gets back home.

APRIL

19

What do you call a mummy that sleeps all day?

Lazybones!

Katy Hall and Lisa Eisenberg,
Mummy Riddles

BIRTHDAYS

1902 Jean Lee Latham is born, in Buckhannon, West Virginia. She becomes fascinated by facts about Nathaniel Bowditch, who had to leave school when he was ten. At age twelve he was apprenticed to a ship chandler and could not leave the premises, day or night, without permission. Despite the hardship of his early beginnings, Nathaniel Bowditch wrote a book on nautical calculation that's still the sailor's Bible and received a master's degree from Harvard. When Jean hears that her book about this remarkable man, *Carry On, Mr. Bowditch,* has won the Newbery award, she confesses she has to look up *Newbery* in the encyclopedia. Then she calls her sister to borrow some winter clothes for a trip to New York.

1949 Lisa Eisenberg is born, in Flushing, New York. With Katy Hall, she is the author of many popular riddle books.

▶ **READING FUN** Invite students to choose a riddle, practice it, and recite it to the class.

19-- Sharon Dennis Wyeth is born, in Washington, D.C. Sharon has been a family counselor, an actress, and a writer for the children's television show *Reading Rainbow.* Her picture book *Something Beautiful* is based on a memory of when she is eight and asks her mother for "something beautiful." She still has her mother's gift, a small white china pitcher with a golden handle and a golden rose embossed on it. She also treasures her mother's reminder that "I already had something even more beautiful—the something beautiful I had inside." On the Loose Leaf Book Company website (<http://www.looseleafbookcompany.com/archives/2050/journal.html>), Sharon keeps an audio journal (with transcript) of her process of writing a book. The journal begins as Sharon starts major revisions on her first draft, which has been accepted for publication.

20

We love you,
Diffendoofer School . . .

You are so
diffendooferous . . .

Dr. Seuss (with some help from
Jack Prelutsky and Lane Smith),
Hooray for Diffendoofer Day!

BIRTHDAY

1945 Mary Hoffman is born, in Eastleigh, Hampshire, England. As a little girl she wants to be a garage mechanic, but she changes her mind and studies English literature at Cambridge University and linguistics at the University of London. The author of more than seventy books for children, her best-known titles are *Amazing Grace* and *Boundless Grace*, both of which are turned into musical plays and performed in Minneapolis, Minnesota. Mary says, "Grace is really me—a little girl who loves stories." And this is how the Grace's story starts: "Grace was a girl who loved stories."

▶ **READING REFLECTION** Invite students to list the stories they love. What are the top-ten class favorites? Invite students to think about what qualities a story has to make it "tops" for them.

EVENT

1998 *Hooray for Diffendoofer Day!*, by Dr. Seuss (with some help from Jack Prelutsky and Lane Smith), is published. The incomplete manuscript about an unusual school is tacked on Dr. Seuss's bulletin board when he dies. Janet Schulman, Dr. Seuss's longtime editor, says, "Jack and Lane are very similar in some ways. They're Ted-like kids who never grew up. They have a childlike way of looking at things." At Diffendoofer School, kids learn things not taught at other schools: listening, smelling, laughing, tying knots, how to put a saddle on a lizard, how to teach a frog to dance, and so on.

▶ **THINK ABOUT IT** Invite students to create a curriculum that they'd like to learn, a curriculum they don't think is taught at any other school.

▶ **WRITE ABOUT IT** Invite students to write a letter to the principal and/or the board of education recommending one change in the current curriculum.

21

What's another name
for Chinese
brontosaurus stew?

One-ton soup.

Joanne Bernstein and
Paul Cohen,
*Why Didn't the Dinosaur Cross
the Road?*

BIRTHDAYS

1900 Walter Blair is born, in Spokane, Washington. Walter teaches English at the University of Chicago for more than thirty-five years. He is one of the first American scholars to take humor seriously. His enthusiasm for oral stories leads to *Tall Tale America: A Legendary History of Our Humorous Heroes*, a book read by children as well as adults.

▶ **READING/WRITING CONNECTION** Invite students to browse in the "tall tale" section of the library. Tall tales are a rich source of metaphor and simile. After students read about someone being "scareder than a raccoon looking down a rifle barrel," a girl who "lit the sky with lightning from her eye," and Paul Bunyan's chewing popcorn sounding "like a couple hundred coffee grinders all going at once," they'll get the idea and clamor to write metaphoric whoppers of their own. To get them started, ask for similes: as cold as, as hot as, as ugly as, as noisy as, as strong as, as big as, as brave as.

1943 Joanne Bernstein is born, in New York City. A kindergarten teacher and professor of education, Joanne is the author, with Paul Cohen, of popular riddle books as well as *Fiddle with a Riddle: How to Write Riddles*.

1946 Kathleen Karr is born, in Allentown, Pennsylvania. She grows up on a chicken farm in New Jersey. A teacher, she responds to her students' request to write a book for them and discovers she loves writing children's fiction. Kathleen particularly enjoys historical settings—likes the challenge of re-creating a time and place, which includes being aware of specific language patterns as well as all the other elements that make one time period different from another. She likes to dig around in old letters and build a life from the bits and pieces she finds there.

EVENT

1888 Vincent van Gogh writes to his friend Emile Bernard, also an artist, "I am working on nine orchards: one white; one pink, almost red; one white-blue; one grayish pink; one green and pink. . . ."

▶ **WRITE ABOUT IT** Invite students to write a passage about colors in a particular place.

Maurice's room measured six long steps in one direction and five in the other.

Paula Fox,
Maurice's Room

BIRTHDAYS

1923 Paula Fox is born, in New York City. Calling herself "a traveling child," Paula attends nine schools before she is twelve, seldom seeing either of her parents. For two years Paula goes to a one-room school in Cuba. Paula says her nomadic childhood leads her to rediscover the "freedom, solace, and truth" of public libraries. Paula holds a number of jobs, including a lathe operator at a Bethlehem Steel plant and a reporter. She becomes a fifth-grade teacher and a prize-winning author. In the opening words of her Newbery Medal acceptance speech for *The Slave Dancer*, Paula notes, "Nearly all the work of writing is silent. A writer does it alone." Paula points out that for a writer, being preoccupied with how she feels and why she feels it "is an effort carried out against formidable enemies: habit; inertia; the fear of change and what it will entail; the wish to preserve our idiot corners of safety, of being 'right'; and self-righteousness—the most dangerous of all. . . ." She continues: "Once we accept the responsibility of our connection with others, we must accept that we are like them even in our differences."

▶ **WRITE ABOUT IT** Challenge students to try Paula Fox's opening to *Maurice's Room* for a piece of writing of their own. Tell them to measure their rooms, their desks, or anything else—and to use these dimensions as the first line in a little piece.

1943 Eileen Christelow is born, in Washington, D.C. In *What Do Authors Do?* Eileen takes readers through the nitty-gritty of producing a book, from the author's idea to an author signing at a bookstore. Eileen shows that even when authors are writing about their own pets, a lot of writing involves sitting and thinking, searching out more information, asking people questions. She shows that writers write a lot, and they throw away a lot. She shows that writers get rejected. *What Do Illustrators Do?* takes a similar approach to answering that question.

EVENT

1868 Charles Dickens leaves the United States after a five-month reading tour. While Dickens was on the tour, twelve-year-old Kate Douglas Wiggins sat beside him on the train from Portland, Maine, to Boston. She told him she admired his novels but skipped "some of the very dull parts." Kate grows up to become the author of the popular *Rebecca of Sunnybrook Farm*.

▶ **READING REFLECTION** Invite student pairs to role-play sitting next to a famous author on a plane, train, or bus. What would they say? What would the author say?

23

Shall I compare thee to a summer's day?

Thou art more lovely and more temperate . . .

William Shakespeare

BIRTHDAY

c. 1564 William Shakespeare is born, in Stratford-on-Avon, England, the third of eight children. He is acclaimed as the greatest playwright who has ever lived. Little is known about Will's boyhood. At age eighteen, he marries Anne Hathaway, and they have three children. In 1594, Will becomes an actor and playwright in London. He is the author of at least 36 plays and 154 sonnets.

▶ **READ MORE** Diane Stanley's *Bard of Avon: The Story of William Shakespeare* is a good place to start in an exploration of the Bard.

▶ **WRITING CONNECTION** Challenge students to compare themselves to a month or season of the year. Point out that it can be a negative or positive comparison.

EVENTS

1902 The sun sinks on Robert Falcon Scott's first Antarctic expedition, not to reappear until August 22. A member of the crew, Ernest Shackleton, produces the "South Polar Times" to entertain the crew, bringing out five issues during the Antarctic winter. Ernest sets up an editor's office on board the ship *Discover*. The paper includes riddles, a sports page, and articles containing scientific information.

▶ **THINK ABOUT IT** Ask students to consider what they would put in a classroom newspaper. Will the proposed contents change depending on whether the newspaper is for parents or for students?

1908 Poet Carl Sandburg writes to Lillian Steichen: "Ten thousand lovebirds, sweet-throated and red-plumed, were in the garden of my under-life. There on ten thousand branches they slept as in night-time. You came and they awoke . . ." Carl and Lillian marry on June 15, 1908.

1942 President Franklin Delano Roosevelt tells the American people, "We all know that books cannot be killed by fire. People die, but books never die. . . . In this war, we know books are weapons."

▶ **READING REFLECTION** Ask students to interpret this statement. Ask students which books today might be weapons.

24

"And now," cried Max, "let the wild rumpus start!"

Maurice Sendak,
Where the Wild Things Are

BIRTHDAYS

1776 Robert Bailey Thomas is born. He founds *The Farmer's Almanac* in 1792 and publishes it every year for fifty-four years. Almanacs containing astronomical and navigational data as well as holidays and proverbs date to ancient times, probably the first publications in most societies. Egyptians called almanacs carved on wooden sticks or stone slabs "fingers of the sun." Thomas's almanac is the first American almanac to contain agricultural information and long-range forecasts interspersed with humorous anecdotes and homespun verse. It is the longest continuously published journal in the United States. *The Information Please Almanac* starts in 1947, stating as its purpose to answer "virtually all the questions the general reader might ask it."

▶ **READ MORE** Invite students to browse in almanacs—and report two interesting facts to the class.

1788 Ammi Phillips is born, in Colebrook, Connecticut (now Interlaken, Massachusetts). He is a prolific and successful portrait painter, probably self-taught. While working on an exhibition of American folk art at the Metropolitan Museum of Art, where Ammi's painting *Portrait of a Little Girl in a Red Dress with Cat and Dog* is displayed, Nicholas B. A. Nicholson, an expert on Russian art, gets the idea for a picture book. The result is *Little Girl in a Red Dress with Cat and Dog*, illustrated by Cynthia von Buhler, about a little girl who tells what happens when she poses for a portrait done by Mr. Ammi Phillips.

1911 Evaline Ness is born, in Union City, Ohio. She grows up in Pontiac, Michigan. She works in fashion design before launching a career illustrating children's books. Evaline writes and illustrates the Caldecott Medal book *Sam, Bangs & Moonshine*. She says of this book, "I decided Sam would be a liar, the same kind *I* was when *I* was a child, except that I made up new lies for her to tell."

1937 Evelyn Wolfson is born, in New York City. She is the author of *From Abenaki to Zuni: Growing Up Indian*.

▶ **WORD FUN** Challenge students to make an alphabetic list of items in the classroom in a way that will reflect what it's like to be a student in this room.

EVENTS

1800 President John Adams approves $5,000 for the purchase of "such books as may be necessary for the use of Congress," thus giving Congress a library and the institution we now call the Library of Congress. This first collection arrives from London in 1801, 740 books and 3 maps. In 1802, President Thomas Jefferson, who has his own impressive personal library, makes plans to expand the Library of Congress. Today, the Library has holdings numbering nearly 119 million items, including music, video, and digital materials as well as books. Students can visit the Library of Congress on line at *http://www.americaslibrary.gov*

1963 Maurice Sendak completes a draft of *Where the Wild Things Are*, one of the most popular and influential books of our time.

▶ **READING REFLECTION** Ask students what lesson they think kids learn from this book. Does it say anything about their own lives?

1997 The work of Remy Charlip is celebrated at the annual spring program of the Library of Congress Children's Literature Center. Remy's popular books include *Fortunately; Mother, Mother, I Feel Sick, Send for the Doctor Quick, Quick, Quick;* and *Arm in Arm*. Remy's longtime friend, Vera B. Williams, introduces Remy, saying, "Remy has influenced me and my work since I've known him."

APRIL

25

Only the busy beetle

Tap-tapping in the
wall. . . .

Walter De La Mare,
"Some One"

BIRTHDAYS

1873 Walter De La Mare is born, in Charlton, Kent, England. In 1908, Walter receives a royal grant, allowing him to devote himself entirely to writing. He is considered the most distinguished lyric poet writing for children in the first half of the twentieth century. Joan Aiken remembers her mother reading *Peacock Pie* aloud. "I still know many of those poems by heart," she recalls. Walter receives the Carnegie Medal and, in a rare tribute, the entire June 1957 of *The Horn Book Magazine* is devoted to an appreciation of his work.

▶ **THINK ABOUT IT** Ask students their opinions of government funding for poets and musicians, so they can spend their time writing poetry and creating music—instead of trying to earn a living.

1927 Alvin Schwartz is born, in Brooklyn, New York. Alvin says he's known all his life that he wants to write. After studying journalism in college, Alvin works as a reporter and a writer for an opinion research organization before becoming a freelance writer. A collector of folklore, ghost stories, superstitions, jokes, riddles, and tongue twisters, Alvin has published more than fifty books to fascinate children and their teachers, including *Cross Your Fingers, Spit in Your Hat; The Cat's Elbow; All of Our Noses Are Here and Other Noodle Tales; Busy Buzzing Bumble Bees and Other Tongue Twisters; Fat Man in a Fur Coat; I Saw You in the Bathtub and Other Folk Rhymes;* and *Chin Music and Witcracks.* Writing in the *New York Times,* William Cole observes that *Tomfoolery: Trickery and Foolery with Words* "elevates foolishness to a form of art."

▶ **WRITING FUN** "Don't be mean, jellybean" is one type of rhyming folk wisdom Alvin collects. Challenge students to invent ten short, pithy, rhyming "Rules for Living," a fun and folksy version of *Poor Richard's* advice.

▶ **OUT LOUD** Invite students to pair up and read folk rhymes collected by Alvin Schwartz to each other. They can then share good stories or rhymes with the class.

1949 George Ella Lyon is born, in Harlan, Kentucky, a small coal town in the mountains of Eastern Kentucky. She starts writing poetry in second grade, getting her love of poems from hearing her mother reading them aloud. "My mother often played with words, delighting in their possibilities as she talked, and she also played imagination games with me." George Ella points out that publication does not come easy. She starts sending out manuscripts in 1972; *Mountain,* her first book, is published in 1983.

▶ **WRITER'S TIP 1** Read all you can.

▶ **WRITER'S TIP 2** Keep a writer's notebook where you practice paying attention. Keep it as a scrapbook and you can paste in things to help you remember.

EVENT

1901 New York becomes the first state to require license plates for cars. Each plate carries the initials of the car's owner and costs $1. Today people pay extra money to get these "vanity plates" with special letters or numbers that relate to a car's owner. More than 7,000 car owners entered *Parade* magazine's vanity plates contest. Here are some of the puzzles: IRIGHTI; RUD14ME?; XQQSME; H20UUP2?

Right Between the Eyes; Are You the One for Me?; Excuse Me; What Are You Up To?

▶ **WRITING FUN** Invite students to create their own vanity plate. They can research license plates and see how many letter and number combinations the typical plate has. They might research the economical use of letters to convey meaning by reading *CDB,* by William Steig.

"**I want readers to know that love and friendship make a difference.**"

Patricia Reilly Giff,
Lily's Crossing

BIRTHDAYS

1935 Patricia Reilly Giff is born, in Brooklyn, New York. Patricia's favorite books as a child include *Little Women, The Secret Garden,* the Black Stallion books, and the Nancy Drew series. Patricia brings her experiences as a longtime teacher to books such as her Polk Street School series. Giff confides that her husband, Jim, a detective with the New York City police, is Detective Garcia in *Have You Seen Hyacinth Macaw?* Her children and her cats often appear in her books. Patricia's favorite foods are baked potatoes and chocolate candy.

▶ **WRITER'S TIP** Write! Write every day!

▶ **THINK ABOUT IT** Invite students to "notice" for a week a difference a friend has made, then share this with the class.

1938 Lee Bennett Hopkins is born, in Scranton, Pennsylvania. He remembers, "I hated school and everything associated with it, including books and reading." Fortunately, a teacher introduces Lee to the magic of books and the theater, changing his life. Lee compiles poetry anthologies that make short poems accessible to beginning readers. His two novels, *Mama* and *Mama and Her Boys,* are semiautobiographical.

▶ **READING REFLECTION** Invite students to compile a class anthology of favorite poems. They should talk over some of the responsibilities of compiling such a work. Point out that Lee's anthologies, including *School Supplies* and *Yummy! Eating Through a Day,* are organized around themes.

APRIL

27

To the tiger in the zoo

Madeline just said, "Pooh-pooh."

Ludwig Bemelmans,
Madeline

BIRTHDAYS

1898 Ludwig Bemelmans is born, in the Austrian Tyrol. When he comes to America at age sixteen, he gets a job as a waiter at the Hotel Astor, but he doesn't last long. "I broke too many dishes." In his Caldecott acceptance speech for *Madeline's Rescue,* Ludwig explains how he was looking for a different audience than that afforded him as a gallery artist. "I wanted to paint purely that which gave me pleasure . . . and one day I found that the audience for that kind of painting was a vast reservoir of impressionists who did very good work themselves, who were very clear-eyed and capable of enthusiasm. I addressed myself to children." Judy Blume remembers *Madeline* as her favorite book: "I loved that book! I loved it so much I hid it in my kitchen toy drawer so my mother wouldn't be able to return it to the library. Even after the overdue notices came I didn't tell my mother where the book was. . . . I thought the copy I had hidden was the only copy in the whole world. I knew it was wrong to hide the book but there was no way I was going to part with *Madeline.*"

1947 Barbara Park is born, in Mount Holly, New Jersey. Barbara says, "From first grade on, whenever a funny thought hit me, I would happily blurt it out for the whole class to hear. Unfortunately, not many of my teachers appreciated my sense of humor as much as I did." Barbara admits that in elementary school she finds writing assignments "about as enjoyable as a hearty helping of Brussels sprouts." Barbara says as an adult she finds writing books for kids the perfect way she can pretend to be a grown-up and "still blurt out funny stuff for the whole class to hear." Barbara says she enjoys writing about "uncool" kids, kids never quite in control. She wants her readers to see that "the moments of laughter and joy in life more than make up for the sadness." Barbara adds, "If my books hold any message for the young reader, I hope it is simply that when they see the name Barbara Park, they associate it with fun."

▶ **WORD FUN** Invite students to follow Barbara's example, coming up with images to show their attitudes about school subjects: *Writing assignments are about as enjoyable as* _____; *Math homework is about as enjoyable as* _____; and so on.

EVENTS

1983 Zoologist Dr. Bob Mason first sees 18,000 garter snakes emerge from their underground dens in Manitoba, Canada.

▶ **READ MORE** *The Snake Scientist,* by Sy Montgomery, provides fascinating information about Dr. Mason's snake studies.

▶ **RESEARCH TIP** Invite students to research a snake of their choice—and to share their findings.

1990 *Beneath a Blue Umbrella,* by Jack Prelutsky, is published. The illustrations, by Garth Williams, make it one of the top-ten illustrated books on the *New York Times* annual list. From "Ida Rose dressed in polka-dot clothes" to "Anna Banana who walks on her hands from Montana to Maine," there are lots of clever rhymes and hijinks.

Up a tree. This phrase comes from raccoon hunting. Dogs would chase a raccoon and force it up a tree. Then it was helpless.

Marvin Terban,
*In a Pickle and Other
Funny Idioms*

BIRTHDAYS

1925 Barbara Juster Esbensen is born, in Wisconsin. She says she has considered herself a writer since the age of ten. Then, when she is fourteen, she writes an anti-war poem, and her English teacher, herself a published poet, tells her, "You are a writer." Barbara says those words change her life. She knows her total love of words must mean something.

▶ **READ MORE** Invite students to read *Words with Wrinkled Knees*, a volume of poems showing how animal names point to their characteristics.

▶ **WRITING TIP** Barbara's *Celebration of Bees: Helping Children to Write Poetry* is a book for teachers, containing wonderful advice. Here's one tip. "Explore different beginning words for poems." Barbara points out that although *the* is a useful and necessary word, "it gives the effect, sometimes, of a heavy, dull, clumpiness that can slow down an otherwise lively poem."

1926 Nelle Harper Lee is born, in Monroeville, Alabama, the youngest of four children. She studies law at the University of Alabama and works as a reservation clerk with Eastern Air Lines. She gives up her job to write full time, submitting a manuscript in 1957. An editor urges her to rewrite it, and, with the help of the editor, she works another two and a half years on it. In 1961, *To Kill a Mockingbird* is published. It is Harper Lee's only published book.

1934 Lois Duncan is born, in Sarasota, Florida. At age ten, she begins submitting stories to magazines, selling her first story at age thirteen. Throughout high school she writes for *Seventeen Magazine*. Lois says that her favorite writer growing up is Rudyard Kipling. "The rhythm of his writing affected me as if it were music. When I turned ten, all I wanted for my birthday was a volume of his poetry, which I received and cherish to this day. The magic of his *Just So* stories enchanted me, and I was mesmerized by *The Jungle Book*."

1940 Marvin Terban is born, in Chelsea, Massachusetts. He writes a series of word-play books that also inform children about language, including *Eight Ate* and *In a Pickle*. *Too Hot to Hoot* is a collection of palindrome riddles.

▶ **WORD FUN** Challenge students to invent a palindrome. Here's one of Marvin Terban's: NO LEMON. NO MELON.

▶ **WRITING TIP** In *Funny You Should Ask: How to Make Up Jokes and Riddles and Word Play*, Marvin suggests listing homonyms side by side and then using these sound-alike words to make up jokes and riddles like this headline: CHICKENS ARRESTED FOR FOWL PLAY!

1950 Amy Hest is born, in New York City. She grows up in the suburbs. Amy works as a librarian before she begins her book-writing career. A number of Amy's books focus on a child's relationship with a grandparent or other relative. Amy says, "All writers, I suspect, are excellent spies. At least they ought to be." In two of her books, Amy lets the reader become a spy of sorts by presenting the story mostly in the form of a notebook filled with letters, drawings, and private thoughts of the main character.

▶ **WRITING TIP** Invite students to keep a "spy notebook" for a week or two. They should write down what they see and hear in places like the cafeteria, the trip to school, and so on. Remind students that this is not meant to invade anyone's privacy but meant to be a fun record of daily activities that take on new significances when one writes them down.

▶ **READING/WRITING CONNECTION** Louise Fitzhugh's *Harriet the Spy* features a girl whose journal is made public without her knowledge.

1983 Barbara Cooney accepts the National Book Award for *Miss Rumphius*. She acknowledges that Miss Rumphius is her alter ego. When Rosemary Wells tells her daughter that she is appearing at the 1989 *Horn Book* ceremonies with Barbara, her daughter shouts, "Barbara Cooney! *The* Barbara Cooney? The *Miss Rumphius* Barbara Cooney? . . . Tell her I love her, Mom. Tell her she's written my all-time favorite book."

APRIL

When I was in the sixth grade, I kissed a girl for the first time. She was gigantic. I remember kind of holding her by the elbows and standing on my tiptoes so I could peck her on the cheek. I didn't know what else to do because none of the love stories I'd read covered the topic of romance between a shrimp and a giant. Years later, I decided to remedy the situation. Somehow the shrimp Sammy Carducci took over the story.

Ronald Kidd,
*Sammy Carducci's Guide
to Women*

BIRTHDAYS

1937 Jill Paton Walsh is born, in London, England. She is the eldest of four children. Her given name is Gillian. Jill says Hitler made her a writer, because when she was sitting in air-raid shelters in England "there was nothing to do but read." Jill's favorite memory is the lighthouse in St. Ives Bay seen from her bedroom window in her grandmother's house. She studies at Oxford in "the twin looming presences of C. S. Lewis and Tolkien," and so has a liking for "dragons, magic, and strong story lines." Later, when she needs intellectual stimulation while taking care of a howling baby who doesn't talk yet, Jill starts writing a book. She says until that moment she hadn't known she is a writer. The book isn't good, but she is convinced to keep trying. Jill is the author of such books as *Fireweed, Gaffer Samson's Luck*, and *The Green Book*—books, Jill says, that are "fully adult while being fully accessible to children."

▶ **WRITING TIP 1** Read a lot.

▶ **WRITING TIP 2** Keep a notebook. Write in it every day something you have seen or heard.

▶ **WRITING TIP 3** Keep reading a lot.

1948 Ronald Kidd is born, in St. Louis, Missouri. Among his titles for middle graders are *The Glitch*, a computer fantasy, and *Second Fiddle*, a Sizzle and Splat Mystery. Ronald, the author of *Sammy Carducci's Guide to Women*, says that the shrimp Sammy Carducci has the same problems he had as a sixth grader. "He made me laugh. I hope he does the same for you. Just don't take his advice."

1953 Nicole Rubel is born, in Miami, Florida. Nicole says her favorite book when she is small is *Macaroon,* by Julia Cunningham, illustrated by Evaline Ness. "There is a wonderful scene in the story where Macaroon lies in the bathtub with a plate of cookies. It's the scene I always refer to when I think of bliss." Among Nicole's most popular illustrations are the Rotten Ralph series, written by Jack Gantos. Nicole notes that her illustrations are influenced by Matisse. She also illustrates the Katy Hall/Lisa Eisenberg Riddles series and many others. She writes and illustrates the Sam and Violet books about twin kittens, inspired, she says, by her relationship with her own twin sister.

▶ **READING/WRITING CONNECTION** Invite students to share their own picture of bliss they have encountered in books—either in words or pictures.

EVENT

1962 President John F. Kennedy greets Nobel Prize winners at a White House dinner in their honor, commenting, "I think this is the most extraordinary collection of talent, of human knowledge, that has ever been gathered at the White House—with the possible exception of when Thomas Jefferson dined here alone."

▶ **READ MORE** Leonard Everett Fisher's *Monticello* gives a good picture of Jefferson and his accomplishments. When Jefferson is distraught over the way the Continental Congress is editing and rewriting his draft of the Declaration of

Independence, Benjamin Franklin says, "This puts me in mind of a story." That story, told in *The Hatmaker's Sign: A Story by Benjamin Franklin*, by Candace Fleming and Robert Andrew Parker, is a wonderful parable about writing and editing.

APRIL

30

Fire came to Earth long before living things, so it's no surprise that both plants and animals have ways of dealing with this powerful natural force.

Dorothy Hinshaw Patent,
Fire: Friend or Foe

BIRTHDAYS

1904 Hubert Davis is born, in Richland, Virginia. The title of one of his books offers challenge for a word game: *A January Fog Will Freeze a Hog.*

▶ **WORD FUN** Invite students to use Hubert's idea and create funny rhymes for the other eleven months.

1940 Dorothy Hinshaw Patent is born, in Rochester, Minnesota. Dorothy gets started writing books because she wants to use her Ph.D. in zoology but she also wants to stay home with her children. Since her first book is published in 1973, Dorothy has written about 130 highly respected books on meticulously researched topics, including *All About Whales, Appaloosa Horses, Arabian Horses, Dolphins and Porpoises, The Lives of Spiders,* and *Mosquitoes.*

▶ **READING/WRITING CONNECTION** Invite students to choose a book by Dorothy. Before they read it, ask them to write three questions they hope she answers. Then they can see if she does it!

M A Y

MAY

Words are used to think with, to write with, to dream with, to hope and pray with. And that is why I love the dictionary. It endures. It works. And, as you now know, it also changes and grows.

Andrew Clements,
Frindle

BIRTHDAYS

1923 Joseph Heller is born, in Brooklyn, New York. His novel *Catch-22* brings a new term into the language. A catch-22 is the predicament that occurs when the only solution to a problem is prevented by a circumstance inherent in the problem. An example: you can't get a job without experience, but the only way to get experience is to get a job. In Heller's novel, military life is filled with catch-22s. An educational catch-22 is that children's reading skill is improved and enhanced by their hearing stories read aloud, but increasingly read-aloud time is abandoned so there will be more time to teach reading skills.

▶ **WORD FUN** In Andrew Clements's *Frindle*, fifth grader Nicholas Allen invents a new word for "pen." Ask students to invent a new term for a common classroom item—and see if they can get their classmates to use it.

▶ **READ MORE** *2107 Curious Word Origins, Sayings and Expressions from White Elephants to Song Dance* by Charles Earle Funk makes for good read-aloud material on entomology.

1950 Marisabina Russo is born, in Queens, New York. She remembers, "In sixth grade I read *The Diary of Anne Frank* and decided to keep a journal. I keep one to this day."

EVENTS

1881 An article in the *Gazette des Beaux Arts* on this date discusses a "special painter" of exceptional talent whose eye captures on canvas the "seductive extravagances" of the world of ballet. "Monsieur Degas treats the subject as a master, and knows precisely how a ribbon is tied on a dancer's skirt, the way the tights wrinkle over the instep and the tension given to the silk attached to the ankle."

▶ **READ MORE** *Degas and the Little Dancer: A Story About Edgar Degas,* by Laurence Anholt, gives young readers an appreciation of the man and his art. Pamela Duncan Edwards says if she hadn't been "dismissed" from ballet class when she was five—because of flat feet—she would be a prima ballerina. In *Honk! The Story of a Prima Swanerina*, Pamela relives her dreams through Mimi Swan. Henry Cole's illustrations are wonderful.

1930 On the occasion of Mother Jones's one hundredth birthday, congratulations for the activist pour in from all over the world. Even her detractors acknowledge she lives by her motto: "Pray for the dead, and fight like hell for the living."

1931 The Empire State Building is dedicated, in New York City. At 1,250 feet, it is today no longer the tallest building in the world, but it still captures people's imagination.

▶ **READ MORE** David Macaulay's *Unbuilding* provides a fictional look at what would be involved in dismantling this icon. *The Empire State Building*, by Craig A. Doherty and others, describes, in detail, what was involved in building it.

1950 Poet Gwendolyn Brooks becomes the first African American to win the Pulitzer Prize, for *Annie Allen*.

▶ **OUT LOUD** Read aloud a poem by Gwendolyn Brooks. Here's one:

I am Kojo. I am A Black.
And I Capitalize my name.

— "I Am A Black," from *Children Coming Home*

1957 Michael Bond writes a friend, "I have just completed the rough draft of a book-length children's story. It is about the adventures of a bear called Paddington and I think it has possibilities."

MAY

a million daffodils
trembling in the
sunshine

Bobbi Katz,
"Spring Is"

BIRTHDAY

1933 Bobbi Katz is born, in Newburgh, New York. A social worker and freelance writer and editor, Bobbi is also known as the author of poetry collections for children. Bobbi says, "I write for children because I hope to join those writers and artists who delight, sensitize, and give hope to children."

▶ **WRITING TIP** Use Bobbi Katz's poetic image as a springboard: invite students to interview people, asking them to complete the phrase *Spring is . . .* Make a butcher paper–covered wall of *Spring is* images.

EVENT

1611 The King James Bible is published. King James I had appointed a group of scholars to produce a new version of the Bible. It becomes the authorized version for the Church of England.

MAY

"You sure are brave,"
said Alex. "I like wolf
spiders, but I wouldn't
have let that one into
my coat. That's the
biggest, hairiest wolf
spider I've ever seen."

Mavis Jukes,
Like Jake and Me

BIRTHDAY

1947 Mavis Jukes is born, in Nyack, New York. This popular author of picture books and middle-grade titles starts her career as a teacher. After five years, she decides she wants to change the world, and she goes to law school. But in the end, she decides not to practice law, that the way to change the world is to become a writer.

▶ **READING REFLECTION** Invite students to think of a book that has changed their opinion about something.

▶ **WRITING TIP** Mavis Jukes notes that details are important for writers. She advises young writers to notice some details in their everyday life.

▶ **WRITING CHALLENGE** Invite students to describe in writing what's inside their desks, their refrigerators, a drawer at home, or some other storage space in a way that reveals something about their personalities.

EVENT

1863 Poet Walt Whitman makes one of his many visits to help sick and wounded Civil War soldiers in hospitals around Washington, D.C. Walt fills forty little notebooks with what he calls "impromptu jottings in pencil." His entry on this day: "Sunday Evening, Armory Sq. Hosp. Ward D. to 5 wounded or sick with fever &c. distributed a small pot of nice apple jelly—fed 1 who were very weak with a spoon."

4

A is the Art that was
stolen at night. . .

Z is asleep . . . and a job
that's well done.

Doug Cushman,
The ABC Mystery

BIRTHDAY

1953 Doug Cushman is born, in Springfield, Ohio. Doug says that like many book author/illustrators he grows up "looking at comic strips and comic books." In high school Doug entertains his classmates by making them comic books that transform teachers into zany superheroes. He sells these books for five cents apiece. Doug cautions that people shouldn't think that just because a book is easy to read that it's also easy to write. *The Mystery of King Karfu* took him three years to write. Doug's fans won't be surprised to learn that he loved mysteries as a child and he still loves them. Sometimes the solution to the mystery he writes surprises even Doug. He explains, "In *The Mystery of the Monkey's Maze* I thought I knew who the thief was . . . until I finished the book dummy. I suddenly realized that someone else was the real culprit. I was just as surprised as the reader."

▶ **READ MORE** Invite students to bring in a book that surprised them.

EVENTS

1774 Thomas Jefferson, who keeps a gardening journal in which he records the planting and growth of produce, notes that he is eating the first dish of peas from the early planting. By July 13 he will note the "last dish of peas." Over the years Jefferson grows 15 varieties of peas and, in all, 450 varieties of vegetables, fruits, nuts, and herbs in this garden.

▶ **READING/WRITING CONNECTION** In Kes Gray's *Eat Your Peas*, Mom tries to bribe Daisy with ice cream, a new bike, and a baby elephant—and more—if she will just eat her peas. Invite students to write Mom a letter advising her how to handle the situation.

1967 Maurice Sendak falls seriously ill in England. Friends send him lots of books—including all of Laura Ingalls Wilder's Little House books. Maurice is enthusiastic, noting, "Calmly and clearly she illustrates the courage necessary to live an ordinary life. She is not concerned with fantasy heroics but with falling down and getting up, being ill and slowly recovering. What is important, she says, is to continue. In persevering, you will discover triumphs." On June 28, 1983, Maurice accepts the Laura Ingalls Wilder book award from the American Library Association.

1989 Illustrator Marylin Hafner begins her first collaboration with her brother Edward, on *Sports Riddles*.

▶ **WRITING CHALLENGE** Invite students to take a sports phrase—such as *a long fly ball* or *next at bat*—and turn it into the punch line of a riddle they write. Here's an example:

> What is an infielder's favorite insect?
> *A pop fly.*

5

Oh, Caterpillar, where
will you hide

After tonight sets today
aside?

J. Patrick Lewis,
"May"

BIRTHDAYS

1910 Leo Lionni is born, in Amsterdam, Holland, an only child. He comes to the United States in 1939 and has a long, successful career in graphic design. While riding on a commuter train, Leo tears scraps of paper from a magazine, then gives them identities to amuse his grandchildren. This is the start of a career that produces more than thirty books, including four Caldecott Honor books: *Frederick, Swimmy, Alexander and the Wind-up Mouse,* and *Inch by Inch.* Leo says, "Painting is really very mysterious." When asked what artists he admires, he says, 'I think it's impossible today not to have Picasso as a hero, a role model." The writing of a book takes longer than the drawing, says Leo, because "the possibilities are so infinite always.

You find yourself in this big word-ocean, whereas with pictures you find yourself in a small lake."

▶ **READING TIP** Vivian Gussin Paley's *The Girl with the Brown Crayon* is must reading for teachers. She provides a riveting/inspiring account of what happens when kindergartners undertake a yearlong study of Leo Lionni's work.

▶ **READING REFLECTION** Leo is glad he is an only child. Limerick writer Edward Lear (see May 12) is one of twenty-one children. Invite students to consider these topics:

Find a fairy tale, folktale, or myth about an only child. How does this character's being an only child shape the story?

Now find a fairy tale, folktale, or myth about a family with three or more children. How does the size of the family shape the tale?

1942 J. Patrick Lewis is born, in Gary, Indiana. His twin brother is twenty minutes older. A professor of economics, he writes his first children's book after seeing a white rainbow in Cumberland Falls, Kentucky. His first book of poems, *A Hippopotamusn't*, is published in 1990. Patrick names Edward Lear, Lewis Carroll, A. A. Milne, and Walter de la Mare as his great influences.

▶ **WRITING TIP** Patrick says, "Good writing means choosing strong verbs. I'll spend hours, sometimes days searching for just the right verb, and when it comes, it's very nearly heaven."

▶ **WORD FUN** Invite students to make a list of animal names. Then they should try to change these names by adding on to the end. For example, what have you got when you've got an elephantenna? Or a kangaroof?

▶ **ALL ABOUT NAMES** Patrick offers a lot of fun with names: *Ridicholas Nicholas* gets a book title all to himself. And then there's "Donna Iguana" and "Paula Koala." Invite students to look for rhymes or coined words to go with their names.

1950 Todd Strasser is born, in New York City. His best subjects in school are math and science. He is a horrible speller and says "Thank God for computer programs that check spelling." He is sent to reading tutors because he reads "below grade level." He notes, "My reading comprehension was, and probably still is, terrible, and I was never able to memorize a speech from Shakespeare." Todd is the author of such young adult novels as *Angel Dust Blues, Friends Till the End*, and *The Accident*. Todd says, "Sometimes I think I write young adult books because I'm still trying to resolve the conflicts of my own youth."

▶ **WRITING TIP** Todd points out that "writing is mostly rewriting," adding that rewriting means comparing his own writing with some standard he holds in his head. How do we create such a standard? By reading.

MAY

6

What do you call a
he-man tortilla chip?

A macho nacho.

Giulio Maestro,
*Macho Nacho and Other
Rhyming Riddles*

BIRTHDAYS

1914 Randall Jarrell is born, in Nashville, Tennessee. He is a novelist, critic, and poet before he translates a Grimm fairy tale. Then he writes several children's books. Maurice Sendak loves Randall's *The Bat-Poet*, calling it "one of the great fables about the life of the artist."

1929 Dave Anderson is born, in Troy, New York. His titles *The Story of Basketball* and *The Story of Football* include a history of the respective sports as well as an analysis of strategies.

▶ **READ MORE** Invite sports buffs to find three interesting historical facts about a sport they love.

1935 Ted Lewin is born, in Buffalo, New York. When he is eleven, he paints an oil portrait of President Truman and sends it to him. He reads all of Edgar Rice Burroughs's Tarzan books. He earns money to attend Pratt Institute by wrestling and continues to wrestle part-time for ten years after college. In *Touch and Go*, Ted tells stories gleaned from his travels to Australia, India, Nepal, Botswana, Namibia, Kenya, Uganda . . . and lots more places. Among the photographs is one of Ted with a boa constrictor wrapped around his neck.

1942 Giulio Maestro is born, in Greenwich Village, New York City. In addition to coauthoring books with Betty Maestro, he illustrates a series of amusing and informative books about words by Marvin Terban and a series of his own riddle books, including *Macho Nacho and Other Rhyming Riddles*.

▶ **WORD FUN** Rhyming riddles, also known as *hink pinks* and *hinkety pinketies*, teach children a lot about language. Challenge students to write the riddles for these answers: *peas, please,* and *cow chow.* Next they can invent their own questions and answers.

1955 Barbara McClintock is born, in Flemington, New Jersey. Barbara says she drew so much as a child that by second grade she had a callous on the index finger of her drawing hand—from holding pencils and crayons. As a young adult Barbara isn't sure how to make art her career, so she calls Maurice Sendak and asks him. Maurice tells her how to put together a dummy book and advises her to move to New York. Barbara notes that her finely detailed pen-and-ink and watercolor artwork is strongly influenced by such nineteenth-century artists as Grandville, Delacroix, Dore, Leech, and Caldecott. Barbara says she loved *The Little Princess* as a young girl and as an adult welcomed the chance to create a picture-book adaptation. "The story is rich in visual imagery, is very dramatic, and is set in a time period that I especially enjoy." To acquire necessary information, Barbara and her twelve-year-old son go to London to photograph and sketch houses, trees, rooms, and streets that she will use in her illustrations. They spend an afternoon in Charles Dickens's house and visit museums to look at such things as costumes and eating utensils. Barbara says her son notices details she's missed.

Events

1877 Crazy Horse, the Sioux Indian chief who helped defeat General Armstrong Custer at the Battle of Little Big Horn, surrenders to government forces. He says, "We preferred our own way of living. . . . All we wanted was peace and to be left alone."

▶ **READ MORE** In *The Life and Death of Crazy Horse*, Russell Freedman brings his usual thoroughness to the story.

1995 On her birthday Kristine O'Connell George receives a letter accepting for publication her first poetry collection, *The Great Frog Race and Other Poems*. Kristine's website (<www.kristinegeorge.com>) is filled with a rich collection of ideas for aspiring young poets. Kristine includes ideas for balloons poems, billboard poetry, cookie poems, gift-wrap poems, basket-of-poems, fabulous first lines, flashlight poetry, and lots lots more. Among her many insights, Kristine explains that the original definition of an anthology is "a gathering of flowers."

▶ **WRITING TIP** Kristine advises young writers to keep a notebook close—even on vacation. "Keep writing—every day! But, don't go back and read your work for one week. Or, a month. Sometimes an idea you thought wasn't very good when you first wrote it down turns out to be a VERY GOOD idea!" Kristine points out that writers often put their work away for a while. "Then, when they go back and read what they have written they get NEW ideas! MORE ideas! BETTER ideas!"

MAY

7

> "Hoorah! Safe at last!"
> Let no man boast
> himself that he has got
> through the perils of
> winter till at least the
> seventh of May."
>
> Anthony Trollope,
> in his journal

BIRTHDAY

1932 Nonny Hogrogrian is born, in the Bronx, New York. She is awarded the Caldecott Medal for *Always Room for One More* and *One Fine Day*. *The Contest* is a Caldecott Honor book. Nonny says, "Children's books should be as beautiful as they possibly can be. Kids grow up on picture books, and they should see beauty in them."

▶ **READ MORE** Invite students to find a beautiful book in the library to share with the group.

EVENT

1961 Faber and Faber publishes Ted Hughes' first children's book *Meet My Folks,* full of rhyming poems about imaginary relatives.

MAY

8

> Douglass reached out to
> embrace almost every
> issue that concerned
> Americans troubled by
> injustice, inequality,
> and racism. He was, of
> course, a major figure
> among the abolitionists.
> But he also took part in
> many other reform
> movements—for
> women's rights, for
> labor, for temperance,
> against war and capital
> punishment. . . .
>
> Milton Meltzer (editor),
> *Frederick Douglass: In His
> Own Words*

BIRTHDAYS

1938 Milton Meltzer is born, in Worcester, Massachusetts. The first reading he remembers enjoying is the comic strip "Gasoline Alley." Milton recalls that his parents had neither the time nor the money for books; they read only the newspaper. He loves Saturdays at the public library. He "holes up in the bedroom and read myself into a daze." Milton remembers, "What I liked most were adventure stories that took me out of my skin. And biographies. I was always trying on a new hero for size—explorer, reporter, detective." Milton writes about many influential Americans—from Thomas Jefferson to Mary McLeod Bethune, from Mark Twain to Langston Hughes.

▶ **READ MORE** Milton tells his own story in the memoir *Starting from Home: A Writer's Beginnings*. It is an engrossing tale of the child of immigrant parents growing up in New York City.

1924 Tana Hoban is born, in Philadelphia, Pennsylvania. Photographer and author, she concentrates on showing objects from everyday life. Tana says, "The way I have learned to focus on ordinary objects is the connection between children, my work, and me. Every concept I want to share with children is obvious in everyday life: shape, size, color, relationship, comparison and—emotion."

EVENT

1862 At Henry David Thoreau's funeral, his friend Ralph Waldo Emerson quotes from Thoreau's unpublished writings, "Nothing is so much to be feared as fear." In 1933, President Franklin D. Roosevelt echoes this sentiment in his first inaugural address, saying, "The only thing we have to fear is fear itself."

▶ **READING/WRITING CONNECTION** In *Higher on the Door*, James Stevenson recalls his own boyhood fears and manages a humorous take on children's very real fears. It is an excellent model for children to use to write about their own fears. Another way to approach fear is to ask the class to make a list of common fears. Then students can select one and write a letter of advice to someone who suffers that fear.

9

A hundred dresses! Obviously the only dress Wanda had was the blue one she wore every day. So what did she say she had a hundred for?

Eleanor Estes,
The Hundred Dresses

BIRTHDAYS

1860 J(ames) M(atthew) Barrie is born, in Kirriemuir, Scotland. He works as a journalist before moving to London in 1885. After his first book is published, Barrie carries it around in his pocket, taking it out often to make sure the ink hasn't faded. The author of *Peter Pan*, the story of a boy who doesn't want to grow up, Barrie says of himself, "I am not young enough to know everything." In later life, when struck by writer's cramp, Barrie, being ambidextrous, switches hands. He says that what he writes with his left hand has an eerier quality than what he writes with his more rational right hand.

▶ **LOOKING AT ART** The Cooper Edens compilation of *Peter Pan* invites young readers to examine the images of F. D. Bedford as well as those of other early twentieth-century artists who have illustrated the book. Invite students to look at the differing ways illustrators picture the same story. Ask them to talk about the differing effects of, say, the wolves of Edward Gorey, Paul Caldone, and James Marshall's renditions of *Little Red Riding Hood*.

1906 Eleanor Estes is born, in West Haven, Connecticut. She works as a librarian until her first book, *The Moffats*, is published. She says her own childhood in a rural town in Connecticut is very similar to that of the children she writes about in the Moffat books; the Newbery Medal–winning *Ginger Pye* is about Eleanor's own dog. Eleanor remembers climbing trees, fishing, exploring small rivers in rowboats. She says, "I like drawing and painting and also I like to sit and look at the ocean and the sky and do nothing."

▶ **THINK ABOUT IT** Invite students to think about their favorite "do nothing" thing.

1914 Keith Robertson is born, in Dows, Iowa. Although he enjoys algebra, geometry, trigonometry, and calculus in school and works as a refrigeration engineer, Keith knows early on that he wants to write. Keith gets a job selling children's books to bookstores. While traveling, he begins to write books, quitting his job after he sells his first manuscript. A prolific writer, Keith's most famous books are the Henry Reed series. Keith explains that his books have no great message, no sermon to preach; their purpose is to entertain readers. "If a book of mine can make just one young person discover that reading can be a pleasure, then I feel it has been a success."

EVENTS

1880 In Hartford, Connecticut, where he lives, Mark Twain buys a copy of *Sir Gibbie*, written by his British friend George MacDonald. Some months later, Mark sends a copy of his own *Life on the Mississippi* to George, asking if George will send him in return *Back of the North Wind*. Mark explains that his children "have read and read their own copy so many times that it looks as if it had been through the wars."

▶ **READING REFLECTION** Ask students to name books they read more than once. Do these books have anything in common?

1944 Thirteen-year-old Aranka Siegel and her Hungarian family arrive at Auschwitz. Aranka and her older sister are separated from their parents and five brothers and sisters and never see them again. Later they emigrate to the United States. In *Upon the Head of the Goat*, Aranka depicts the emotions of a young Jewish girl caught up in the events that destroy the world she knows. In *Grace in the Wilderness*, she describes how she and her sister learn to live again.

2000 Scholastic announces that Dav Pilkey's Captain Underpants series has sold 6.3 million copies. The title of the "Fourth Epic Novel" in this series is *Captain Underpants and the Perilous Plot of Professor Poopypants*. All the epics are narrated by rambunctious fourth graders George and Harold. The humor underlying the use of the word *epic* deserves some discussion.

MAY

10

I loved when Dad talked to me like I was grown-up. I didn't really understand half the junk he was saying, but it sure did feel good to be talked to like that!

Christopher Paul Curtis,
The Watsons Go to Birmingham—1963

BIRTHDAYS

1947 Caroline Cooney is born. Caroline begins writing as a young housewife sitting home with two babies. "I had to find a way to entertain myself." Now, much of Caroline's inspiration comes from her extensive volunteer work with teenagers at school and church. Caroline finds that kids want stories with happy endings. "They want hope, want things to work out, want reassurance that even were they to do something rotten, they and the people around them would still be all right."

1949 Robert Blake is born, in Paterson, New Jersey. His *101 Elephant Jokes* is a classic of the genre.

▶ **READING/WRITING/LISTENING FUN** Challenge students to post all the elephant jokes they can find. Remind them that older people are a good resource. Challenge students to convert other animal riddles into elephant riddles.

1953 Christopher Paul Curtis is born, in Flint, Michigan. For thirteen years after high school, he works on the assembly line hanging eighty-pound car doors on automobiles. He says, "I can't tell you how much I hated it." In his spare time Christopher begins work on *The Watsons Go to Birmingham—1963*. He says writing during breaks takes him away from being in the factory. "I didn't like being there so I would sit down and write. It was much like reading, it would take me away from where I was." After *The Watsons* is published, Christopher works in a warehouse. But he notes that inside he knows he's a writer. "Whatever else I've done, I'm Christopher Curtis/Writer." *Bud, Not Buddy*, set in the segregated, Depression-era Midwest, is awarded the Newbery Medal.

EVENTS

1815 Thomas Jefferson notes in his diary, "$187 spent on books." Two months later, he spends another $550.

1963 Maurice Sendak decides to try a new title for the book he started working on in 1955, changing *Where the Wild Horses Are* to *Where the Wild Things Are*. Over time, "Wild Horses" has become "Wild Animals," "Wild Beasts," and finally "Wild Things." This transition seems to break with the received wisdom about good writing. Maurice's title has moved from most specific to most general.

1869 At Promontory Point, Utah, the governor of California drives the last spike, a gold one, to complete tracks for the first transcontinental railroad, linking the Mississippi River to the Pacific Coast.

▶ **READ MORE** *Ten Mile Day and the Building of the Transcontinental Railroad*, by Mary Ann Fraser, provides a full portrait of the day the train crew laid more than ten miles of track, emphasizing the multicultural backgrounds of the workers involved. In 1879 Robert Louis Stevenson makes a dramatic trip across the United States on the transcontinental railroad to meet the woman he loves, who is gravely ill. Jim Murphy's *Across America on an Emigrant Train*, an NCTE Orbis Pictus winner, intertwines the story of Stevenson's trip with a history of the transcontinental railroad.

1883 Sitting Bull, Indian chief and Sioux leader in the Battle of the Little Bighorn, is released from prison.

▶ **READ MORE** Both *A Boy Called Slow: The True Story of Sitting Bull,* by Joseph Bruchac, and *To See with the Heart: The Life of Sitting Bull,* by Judith St. George, provide stirring portraits of a boy who goes from a child called "slow" to a young warrior whose courage in defeating the Crow earns him his father's vision name Tatan'ka Iyota'ke—Sitting Bull.

1970 Referring to the fact that a Caldecott winner is expected to make acceptance speeches, William Steig writes Paul Heins, "I would almost rather die than have to formally address a group of people larger than two in number. I've successfully avoided doing so for 50 years; I've been depressed ever since January & will not realize happiness again until after June 30th when my trial is over. . . ."

1999 Shel Silverstein dies. Take a moment to remember and pay tribute to a beloved poet prankster whose verse takes children seriously. He gave us much.

2000 Robert Pinsky ends his third term as U. S. poet laureate with a reading from his work. Robert's Favorite Poem Project has heightened awareness of the Library of Congress's role as the home of America's poetry archives. The *News Hour,* on PBS, includes Favorite Poem Project video segments on Monday evenings.

▶ **OUT LOUD** Begin and/or end every day with a favorite poem. Invite students to read aloud their favorites; invite people who work in the school or visit the school to drop by and read their favorites. Solicit people from the community to drop by with an offering.

MAY

Her name was April Hall, but she often called herself April Dawn.

Zilpha Keatley Snyder,
The Egypt Game

BIRTHDAYS

1927 Zilpha Keatley Snyder is born, in Lemoore, Pennsylvania. She is raised in California. Her favorite books as a child include *Smoky the Cow Horse, Doctor Dolittle, Peter Pan,* and *The Secret Garden.* At age eight, Zilpha decides to become a writer herself. She says that for her, writing stories always begins as a "form of self-entertainment." Zilpha says getting ideas is a habit. "It is the habit of taking bits and pieces of reality and building on them for your own entertainment."

▶ **WRITING TIP** Zilpha says she has a "map complex." After she has collected some scattered notes about a new character, she draws town plots, "clarifying for myself the location of the protagonist's home in relation to other pertinent sites—such as the location of his or her school, best friend's home, sites of important happenings, etc." Zilpha also draws floor plans of a house if the house is important in the story.

▶ **DRAWING/WRITING CONNECTION** Invite students to draw a floor plan of the classroom or a room in their homes. Then they can write a paragraph about the room. Invite them to talk about how drawing first affects the writing.

1949 Peter Sis is born, in Brno, Czechoslovakia (now the Czech Republic), the son of an artist and a filmmaker. He grows up in Prague. In 1982, Peter is allowed to travel to Los Angeles to work on a film project about the Summer Olympic Games. He refuses to return to Czechoslovakia. Someone shows Peter's work to Maurice Sendak, who introduces him to the art director of Greenwillow books, and Peter's career as a children's book illustrator begins. Peter says that an important concept in his work is that children should have choices. Water is his favorite thing to draw.

▶ **ART CHALLENGE** Invite students to draw their favorite thing.

1981 The original production of *Cats* opens, at the New London Theatre, in the West End of London, England. *Cats,* with music by Andrew Lloyd Webber, is based on fourteen poems in T. S. Eliot's *Old Possum's Book of Practical Cats.* It becomes the longest running musical in the history of the British theater and also the longest running show on Broadway.

MAY

The reason Dad said: "Oh NO! Not owls too" was because I already had some pets.

Farley Mowat,
Owls in the Family

BIRTHDAYS

1812 Edward Lear is born, in London, one of twenty-one children. His childhood is not a happy one. He is sickly, suffering frequent asthma and epilepsy attacks at a time when there is no effective treatment. When Edward is thirteen, his father is sent to debtor's prison and Edward has to go to work. At age nineteen he works as a draftsman for the London Zoological Society, and his paintings of birds are among the first color plates of animals ever published in Great Britain. For many years, Edward earns his living drawing and painting animals, and for a time teaches drawing to Queen Victoria. But his dream of becoming a renowned landscape painter never comes true; instead he becomes known throughout the world as Mr. Nonsense. Lear calls himself Derry Down Derry "who loved to see little folks merry." And make children merry he does. As he writes to a friend, "If a man aint able to do any great service to his fellow critters, it is better (than nothing) to make half a million children laugh." Limerick Day is named in honor of the birth of this great writer of limericks.

▶ **WRITING FUN** Sooner or later nearly everybody tries writing a limerick. If children read a few, they will see that many limericks have similar beginnings:

There was once a boy of Quebec . . .
There was a young lady from Gloucester . . .
There was an old man from Calcutta . . .

Challenge students to write a limerick incorporating a geographical place.

1921 Farley Mowat is born, in Belleville, Ontario, Canada, an only child. Farley's parents are supportive of his love of wildlife. He keeps a pet rattlesnake in a drawer and also has Jitters the squirrel, Wol the owl, a Florida alligator, several cats, and hundreds of insects. At the age of thirteen, Farley writes a weekly nature column for the Saskatoon *Star-Phoenix*. Farley's dog Mutt becomes the hero of *The Dog Who Wouldn't Be*. His autobiographical *Never Wolf Cry* and *Owls in the Family* are great books to read aloud, popular with adults and children alike.

1937 Betsy Lewin is born, in Pennsylvania. The things she likes to draw best as a child are horses, elephants, fish, pirates, and people peeking out from behind trees. As an adult Betsy most likes drawing animals. She continues to love Ernest Shepherd's illustrations for *Winnie-the-Pooh*. Betsy illustrates books for many authors, including those of her husband, Ted Lewin.

1949 Janice Lee Smith is born, in Fowler, Kansas. Among her chapter books are those featuring Adam Joshua and the school troubles he faces.

▶ **READING REFLECTION** Ask students to make a list of the books about school experiences that most "tell it like it is." Challenge them to come up with a good plot idea to send their favorite authors.

1961 Jennifer Mary Armstrong is born, in Waltham, Massachusetts, the daughter of a physicist and a master gardener. She has always known she would be an author. Jennifer tells people that Neil Armstrong is her father because "I was born making up lies and honed my fibbing skills all through school and college. . . . Now I make a living at it; it's called writing fiction. It's my calling! That's the truth." After college,

Jennifer edits juvenile books and also writes for the Sweet Valley High series. Discovering she has a knack for writing, Jennifer decides to work on her own projects: series books, picture books, historical fiction, and nonfiction. For both fiction and nonfiction, library research is essential to Jennifer. "For *Mary Mehan Awake*, I had to research nineteenth-century photography, Abe Lincoln's funeral, train lines at the end of the Civil War, Niagara Falls, the rivers of Manitoba and Ontario, and a boxful of other things." Jennifer's *Shipwreck at the Bottom of the World* wins the NCTE Orbis Pictus award for nonfiction and is a Boston Globe-Horn Book Honor book.

▶ **WRITING TIP** Jennifer advises, "Learn to enjoy the revision process. It's an important part of being a writer."

EVENT

1986 Pat Hutchins's *The Doorbell Rang* is published. Pat says she has known from an early age that she wants to be an artist. She is encouraged by an older couple who give her a chocolate bar for each picture she draws.

MAY

Local townspeople gave each of the recruits four dollars and a New Testament as they marched off to war amid the cheers of their neighbors.

Clinton Cox,
Undying Glory

BIRTHDAY

1938 Francine Pascal is born, in New York City. Francine says that from her early childhood she confides in a diary (which she still keeps), not in people. A prolific author, her most famous books are those in the Sweet Valley High series, which have sold more than sixty-five million copies. Francine describes them as "a soap opera in book form." *Perfect Summer* becomes the first young adult novel to make the *New York Times* bestseller list. Spin-off series include Sweet Valley Kids, Sweet Valley High thrillers, and Sweet Valley Twins. Francine even writes *The Wakefields of Sweet Valley*, a novel covering five generations of the family over one hundred years. A stable of writers now produce the various series, but Francine does the plot outlines and keeps track of the characterizations.

EVENTS

1863 The 54th Regiment of Massachusetts, the "Glory regiment," swears in its 1,000th African-American recruit. These recruits come from 22 states; the oldest is 47, nine are 16 years old. The regiment's 29 officers are all white. Abraham Lincoln observes, "Without the military aid of black freed men the war against the South could not have been won."

▶ **READ MORE** *Undying Glory*, by Clinton Cox, vividly chronicles the struggles of this regiment.

1933 Outside the University of Berlin, in the presence of 40,000 cheering people, 25,000 books are burned on the grounds that they are contrary to the goals of Hitler's National Socialism. As Ray Bradbury points out in *Fahrenheit 451*, "Remember, the firemen are rarely necessary. The public itself stopped reading of its own accord." There are a number of Internet sites providing information about censorship:

> http://www.humanities—interactive.org
> http://www.ala.org
> http://www.cs.cmu.edu/people/spok/most-banned.html

Astoundingly, the list of most-challenged books in public schools and libraries in the 1990s includes many of the most highly regarded children's books.

1916 Sholom Aleichem dies, but the date on his tombstone in Mount Carmel Cemetery, Glendale, New York, reads "May 12a." The Russian-born Yiddish author suffered from triskaidekaphobia, fear of the number 13. His manuscripts never had a page 13.

MAY 14

> "How did you get to New York?" asked Tucker Mouse.
>
> "It's a long story," sighed the cricket.
>
> "Tell me," said Tucker, settling back on his haunches. He loved to hear stories. It was almost as much fun as eavesdropping.
>
> George Selden,
> *The Cricket in Times Square*

BIRTHDAYS

1927 Robert Andrew Parker is born, in Norfolk, Virginia. An accomplished jazz performer on clarinet, saxophone, and drums, he studies art at the Chicago Art Institute and Atelier 17, in New York. Robert has painted everything from fruit plantations in Central America for *Fortune* magazine to the art for a movie about Vincent Van Gogh to more than forty children's books.

1929 George Selden Thompson is born, in Hartford, Connecticut. He uses his first two names because when he is starting out there is already a writer named George Thompson. George knows from an early age that he wants to be a writer. He writes more than fifteen books, but *The Cricket in Times Square* is the one people remember. One night in the Times Square subway station, George hears a cricket's chirp, and he gets the idea of a lost cricket who is homesick. George's own favorite among his titles is *Tucker's Countryside*. Harry and Tucker travel to Chester's home in a Connecticut meadow to save it from a building project. Asked what work he finds most inspirational, George replies, "So far as inspiration goes—present, past, and future—I have only one: *The Lord of the Rings* and *The Hobbit*." In his words, "No one else will ever again go that high, that far!"

▶ **OUT LOUD** Read a chapter from a George Selden book aloud.

EVENT

1817 Eighteen-year-old Mary Wollstonecraft Shelley completes *Frankenstein*. Written as a challenge from friends and published a year later, this story of a man whose hunger to create life drives him to build a monster has inspired many film versions. The film following most closely to Mary's story, made in 1995, stars Robert DeNiro and Kenneth Branagh.

MAY 15

> Dorothy lived in the midst of the great Kansas prairies, with Uncle Henry, who was a farmer, and Aunt Em, who was the farmer's wife.
>
> L. Frank Baum,
> *The Wonderful Wizard of Oz*

BIRTHDAYS

1856 L(yman) Frank Baum is born, in Chittenango, New York. He doesn't like his first name, preferring to be known as Frank. Mostly educated at home, he also attends the Syracuse Classical School. A dreamer more than a businessman, Frank manages a chain of theaters, works as an actor, and opens a variety store. He feels sorry for people who can't pay their bills, and with 161 nonpaying customers, his store goes bankrupt. Frank has trouble finding a publisher for *The Wonderful Wizard of Oz*, because it is judged "too radical" a change from traditional children's books. Finally, a small publisher agrees to bring out the book—if Frank and the illustrator pay all the expenses. The book is immediately a success and letters from enthusiastic children convince Baum to write thirteen more Oz books.

1931 Norma Fox Mazer is born, in New York City. She describes herself as a "middle sister in a three-sister sandwich." Before age thirteen, she wants to be a nurse. After thirteen, she chooses writing for a career. She says that she puts herself "somewhere" in all of her many books. Norma points out that with her first book, published in 1973, she writes two hundred pages of notes before she gets a page she can use in the book. Now, decades later, she is more experienced about what a book needs and doesn't need to take a lot of notes before she begins writing.

1936 Paul Zindel is born, in Staten Island, New York. He moves with his single working mother fifteen times after his father deserts the family. Paul says he is born as a writer when his first story, "A Geometric Nightmare," is published in the school newspaper. Paul's writing about the way teenagers think is informed by his work as a chemistry teacher. In 1965, Paul's play *The Effect of Gamma Rays on Man-in-the-Moon Marigolds* wins the Pulitzer Prize. Charlotte Zolotow, an editor who sees the play, urges him to try a young adult novel. *The Pigman* becomes an instant classic. More than twenty years later, Paul titles his autobiography *The Pigman and Me,* noting, "Eight hundred and fifty-three horrifying things had happened to me by the time I was a teenager."

▶ **WRITING TIP** Paul advises writers to start with a bang. Sometimes he asks kids to nibble on imaginary chocolate-covered ants: "Now think of all the adjectives that you're feeling when you're nibbling on those ants."

1938 Nancy Garden is born, in Boston. She is an only child. The most memorable books of her childhood are Rudyard Kipling's *Jungle Book,* Anna Sewell's *Black Beauty,* and A. A. Milne's Pooh books. A teacher and editor, Nancy has also worked in theater. Nancy says, "I write for young people because I like them, and because I think they are important."

1951 David Almond is born, in Newcastle-upon-Tyne, England. David knows from age seven that he wants to be a writer, and once he starts going to the library he wants to see his books on the shelves. After publishing a number of books for adults, David's debut in children's literature, *Skellig,* wins Great Britain's Whitbread Prize. David says the first sentence of the story, "I found him in the garage on a Sunday afternoon," intrigues him. David isn't sure what the boy has found, but he knows he has the start of the children's book he's been wanting to write. David likes writing for children because "children are capable of accepting all sorts of possibilities as long as the parameters of reality are in place." David says in children's books, "light has to triumph over darkness, life has to triumph over death. I write in the expectation that things will turn out all right."

▶ **THINK ABOUT IT** Challenge students to think about what age audience they would like to write a book for—and why.

EVENTS

1855 Walt Whitman registers *Leaves of Grass* with the United States District Court. Then he brings the copyright notice to the Brooklyn printing office of James and Thomas Rome, where he is working on the first, privately printed edition. Later, Walt's brother George comments, "I saw the book, but I didn't read it at all—didn't think it worth reading. Mother thought as I did."

1900 On L. Frank Baum's forty-fourth birthday, *The Wonderful Wizard of Oz* is printed, and the world of Dorothy and the Yellow Brick Road, magic slippers, and Toto comes into being. As Martin Gardner observes in the preface to *The Annotated Wizard of Oz: Centennial Edition,* by Michael Patrick Hearn, "You might suppose that Judy Garland made the novel famous, but it was the other way around. It was Baum's imagination that made Judy famous." The list of writers expressing affection for *Oz* is long and impressive. It includes Ray Bradbury, Angela Carter, Arthur C. Clarke, F. Scott Fitzgerald, Shirley Jackson, Salman Rushdie, James Thurber, William Styron, John Updike, Gore Vidal, and Eudora Welty.

1949 Anna Mary Robertson Moses, popularly known as Grandma Moses, is invited to tea at the White House with President and Mrs. Truman. Grandma Moses later recalls the visit: "After the tea we had a terrific thunderstorm, so we sat down on a couch to wait till the shower was over. President Truman sat beside me and said, 'Don't be afraid, as this is a large building and has many lightning rods on it.'"

▶ **READ MORE** *The Year with Grandma Moses,* by W. Nikola-Lisa, and *Grandma Moses: Painter of Rural America,* by Zibby Oneal, expand young readers' appreciation of the famous painter. Children who focus on the thunderstorm part of the anecdote will enjoy Patricia Polacco's *Thunder Cake,* in which Babushka helps a young girl overcome her fear of thunderstorms.

MAY

Whiteblack the penguin was worried. He was the Chief Storyteller on Station W-O-N-S. Spelled backwards it read S-N-O-W.

Margret and H. A. Rey,
Whiteblack the Penguin Sees the World

BIRTHDAYS

1906 Margret Elizabeth Rey is born, in Hamburg, Germany. On a June day in 1940, with her husband Hans Augusto, Margret leaves Paris on bicycle, trying to get out of the city before the Nazis arrive. They carry nothing but warm coats and their book manuscripts—including *Curious George.* (In those days, George was called Fifi.) Margret says, "We believe we know what children like. We know what we liked as children, and we don't do any book that we *wouldn't* have liked."

▶ **WORD FUN** In *Whiteblack,* the Reys create a place name by spelling a common word backward, a devise also used by Samuel Butler in the adult book *Erewhon.* Challenge students to find some words that make different words when spelled backward.

1928 Betty Miles is born, in Chicago. She spends her early years in Baghdad, Iraq, where her parents are missionaries. Betty says her early literary influences are Lewis Carroll, Edward Lear, James Thurber, and P. G. Wodehouse. In college, Betty is editor of the school paper. The author of such middle-grade books as *Maudie and Me and the Dirty Book* and *The Trouble with Thirteen,* Betty tries to show that young people of courage can make a difference in dealing with such difficult problems as friendship, racial discrimination, and censorship.

1944 Caroline Arnold is born, in Minneapolis, Minnesota, the daughter of social workers. Trained as an artist, her plan is to write books that she illustrates herself, but her highly respected books on natural science topics lend themselves to color photographs. In 1997, Caroline celebrates the creation of her hundredth book.

▶ **READING/WRITING CONNECTION** Ask students to examine half a dozen Arnold titles. Then challenge them to write an editorial memo of elements needed to write a nonfiction book about animals.

1950 Bruce Coville is born, in Syracuse, New York. Bruce says the best thing his father ever did for him was read *Tom Swift in the City of Gold* aloud. "It is the only book I can ever remember him reading to me, but it changed my life. I was hooked on books." Bruce says that after reading *Winnie-the-Pooh,* "I suddenly knew that what I really wanted to write was children's books." While trying to get published, Bruce works as a toy maker, camp counselor, grave digger, and magazine editor. He also teaches second and fourth grades. Looking at some of Bruce's book titles may indicate why Halloween is his favorite holiday: *The Ghost in the Third Row, My Teacher Is an Alien, My Teacher Fried My Brains.* Bruce refers to himself as "an absolute bookaholic." His cats' names are Spike, Thunder, and Ozma. His dog is Booger.

1763 James Boswell and Samuel Johnson meet in London, England, beginning the most famous biographer-subject relationship in history.

▶ **READING TIP** Invite students to celebrate Biography Day by choosing a biography to read.

1848 Emily Dickinson writes to a friend, "The older I grow, the more do I love spring and spring flowers." A reclusive poet, she lived all her life in Amherst, Massachusetts. In her lifetime, she published just seven poems. After her death, nearly two thousand more poems are found. On the radio show *Prairie Home Companion*, Garrison Keillor claimed any Emily Dickinson poem can be sung to the tune of "The Yellow Rose of Texas"—and then he demonstrated by singing "Because I Could Not Stop for Death."

1866 The first nickel is issued by the U. S. Mint. It is 75 percent copper and 25 percent nickel.

▶ **READ MORE** *Bunny Money*, by Rosemary Wells, is a funny story about what happens when money runs through bunny siblings' fingers. *Money, Money, Money*, by Nancy Winslow Parker, explains the meaning of the art and symbols on U. S. paper currency. *The Denver Mint* (in the SRA Math CrossSections series), by Susan Ohanian, contains lots of information about coins.

1893 H. L. Wagner patents a new improved typewriter. The sentence "The quick brown fox jumps over the lazy dog" is often used to test typewriters—because it contains every letter in the alphabet.

▶ **WRITING FUN** Challenge students to invent a sentence that contains every letter in the alphabet.

MAY

He was sitting in a bushplane roaring seven thousand feet above the northern wilderness with a pilot who had suffered a massive heart attack and who was either dead or in something close to a coma. He was alone. In a roaring plane with no pilot he was alone.

Gary Paulsen,
Hatchet

BIRTHDAYS

1929 Eloise Greenfield is born, in Parmele, North Carolina. She grows up in Washington, D.C., the second oldest of five children. Eloise has always loved to read, but she doesn't consider writing until she is in her thirties. She notices the shortage of books about African-American life, knowing this shortage is a tragedy. With the goal of giving "children words to love, to grow on," she writes easy-to-read biographies of such famous African Americans as Rosa Parks, Paul Robeson, and Mary McLeod Bethune. As Eloise tells *Horn Book*, "It is necessary for Black children to have a true knowledge of their past and present, in order that they may develop an informed sense of direction for their future."

1939 Gary Paulsen is born, in Minneapolis, Minnesota. Because his father is a military man, Gary never spends more than five months in any one school. He remembers school as "a nightmare." Gary's parents drink a lot and he finds a refuge in books, snuggling by the furnace in the basement with a quart of milk, peanut-butter sandwiches, and books. At fourteen, Gary runs away from home and travels with a carnival. When asked where his stories of Eskimos, plane crashes, survival, dogsled races, and hunting expeditions come from, Gary answers, "I've lived them all," adding that he doesn't know how to make things up, that he writes about things he has done. On his way to becoming a popular writer, Gary works as a truck driver, dynamite handler, carpenter, teacher, folksinger, migrant worker, and electronics field engineer. He is proud of completing the Iditarod twice with his dogsled team. Gary receives two hundred letters a day from fans telling him they want more of Brian Robeson's story. Readers want to know what would have happened if Brian hadn't been rescued in *Hatchet*, so Gary writes *Brian's Winter*.

> ▶ **READING TIP** Ask Paulsen fans to write down the first sentence of five of his books. Do they see a pattern? Or is each beginning different?

EVENTS

2000 Sue, the largest and most complete Tyrannosaurus rex ever discovered, goes on exhibition at the Field Museum, in Chicago. Sue's skeleton, sixty-five million years old, was discovered in South Dakota in 1990. Forty-two feet in length, Sue is estimated to have weighed seven tons when she lived. Her skull weighs one ton; some of her teeth are as long as bananas. The Field Museum buys Sue for 6.8 million dollars. Jan Wahl gives a whimsical account of the factual story in *The Field Mouse and the Dinosaur Named Sue*. Working with the Sue Science Team of the Field Museum, Pat Relf skips the whimsy but provides a fascinating insider's look at Sue's excavation and restoration in *A Dinosaur Named Sue: The Story of the Colossal Fossil*.

> ▶ **WORD FUN** Invite students to write a rhyme titled "Colossal Fossil." Or invent a riddle using this hinkity-pinky as a punch line.

MAY

18

I, Harry, am an orphan.

Barbara Ann Porte,
Harry's Mom

BIRTHDAYS

1925 Lillian Aberman is born, in Philadelphia, Pennsylvania. Lillian knows as a child that she wants to illustrate books, and she wins a scholarship to art school. But after Lillian marries Russell Hoban and moves to New York, she studies dance with Martha Graham and teaches modern dance. Lillian and Russell collaborate on their first book, *Herman the Loser*, in 1961. Of the fifty books Russell writes for children, Lillian illustrates half. She also illustrates her own books, as well as those of other authors. She creates such characters as Frances the badger and Arthur the chimpanzee.

1943 Barbara Ann Porte is born, in New York City. Growing up, she helps out in her father's pharmacy around the corner from where they live. Her father tells her and her sister, "Read something every day and write something every day, no matter what else you do with your lives." Barbara Ann says, "We did, and we do." Barbara studies agriculture in college, but after her children are born she becomes a librarian. Best known for her Harry books, Barbara has also written numerous books for middle graders and for young adults.

> ▶ **READ MORE** When Barbara Ann learns that illustrator Greg Henry grew up on a chicken farm in Guyana, she is ecstatic, pointing out that she majored in agriculture in college and received a foundation grant based on her own love of chickens. The result is *Chickens! Chickens!*, a buoyant book about following your dreams.

> ▶ **OUT LOUD** Read this passage aloud, asking students to savor the sound and rhythm of the language:

> He drew big chickens and little chickens, fat chickens and thin chickens, red chickens and blue chickens. Sometimes he drew chickens that stood on one leg. He drew chickens in the sunshine and chickens in the rain, chickens on rooftops and chickens pecking grain. That man drew chickens!

1948 Ron Hirschi is born, in Bremerton, Washington. Growing up, Ron spends all his free time "in the woods, at the beach, or out on the water in boats my father made for me." A biologist, Ron has a graduate degree in wildlife ecology. Ron's picture books featuring animal characters in realistic settings promote an appreciation for wildlife. In *Seya's Song*, Ron uses words of Washington's native S'Kallam Indian speakers to describe the life cycle of the salmon. His books such as *City Geese* invite young readers to take a close look at the natural world.

1958 In an interview in the *New York Post*, Robert Frost observes, "Poets are like baseball pitchers. Both have their moments. The intervals are the tough things."

MAY

19

I am for truth, no matter who tells it. I'm for justice, no matter who it is for or against.

Malcolm X

BIRTHDAYS

1925 Malcolm Little is born, in Omaha, Nebraska. When Malcolm is six, the family's house, in Lansing, Michigan, is burned down, and his father, a Baptist preacher, is murdered; Malcolm's mother suffers a mental breakdown, and the eight children are sent to foster care. While serving a prison sentence in his early twenties, Malcolm converts to Islam and changes his name to Malcolm X, the X representing the unknown African tribe of his ancestors who were renamed after they were sold into slavery. Malcolm becomes the activist spiritual leader of a temple in Harlem. He collaborates with Alex Haley on *The Autobiography of Malcolm X*.

▶ **READ MORE** Walter Dean Myers and Arnold Adoff have written highly regarded biographies of Malcolm X.

1930 Lorraine Hansberry is born, in Chicago, the daughter of parents prominent in civil rights issues who challenge Chicago's segregation laws by moving to an all-white neighborhood. When Lorraine's play *Raisin in the Sun* opens in 1959, she becomes the first black woman to have a play produced on Broadway. The play, which depicts the comic and serious aspects of African-American family life, takes its title from a Langston Hughes poem about what happens when dreams get delayed. Lorraine says, "The thing that makes you exceptional, if you are at all, is inevitably that which must also make you lonely."

▶ **THINK ABOUT IT** A dried-up raisin is a powerful metaphor for deferred dreams. Ask students if they can come up with another metaphor for disappointment—or joy.

1933 Tom Feelings is born, in Brooklyn, New York, the son of a taxi driver. Tom has always loved to draw, at first copying characters from comic books and newspaper comic strips. His mother folds sheets of blank paper in half and stitches them at the fold on her sewing machine, telling Tom to draw her a book. After attending the School of Visual Arts, Tom draws a comic strip and then works in Ghana, West Africa, for a number of years. Tom says two things in Ghana that influence his art are the "basically happy, stable, and secure children" and "the colors." In *jambo Means Hello: Swahihli Alphabet Book*, by Muriel Feelings, Tom's illustrations, prepared in black ink, white tempera, and linseed oil, reinforce a lyrical text about the language of forty-five million people in eastern Africa.

▶ **ART TIP** Tom Feelings advises, "Carry a sketchbook wherever you go because it's a record of what you're seeing and feeling."

1954 Elise Primavera is born, in Long Branch, New Jersey. Elise is a huge fan of Christmas and when she can't find "the right" holiday book for a very young friend, she writes *Auntie Claus*, a book that provides a behind-the-scenes look at Santa's operations. Elise says, "I played with words that rhymed, beginning with A: Aunta Claus, Santy Clause, Auntie Claus. And as soon as I said it, the whole character came to mind: an eccentric woman who keeps her Christmas lights on all year long." Saks Fifth Avenue creates dioramas from the book for their holiday store windows, and Rosie O'Donnell stars in the movie.

EVENTS

1785 Twenty-seven-year-old Noah Webster goes to General Washington's home in Mt. Vernon to tell him about the new schoolbook he has written, the *Speller*. He also visits eighty-year-old Benjamin Franklin in Philadelphia. Franklin is very interested in "Americanized" spellings—that is, spelling words the way they are pronounced and simplifying certain British spellings.

▶ **WORD FUN** Invite student teams to come up with a list of ten words whose spelling should be "regularized." You might share with them A. A. Milne's observation from *The House at Pooh Corner*, "You can't help respecting anybody who can spell TUESDAY, even if he doesn't spell it right; but spelling isn't everything. There are days when spelling Tuesday simple doesn't count."

1844 Ralph Waldo Emerson sends some pencils made by Henry David Thoreau and his father, who make pencils for a living, to a friend with this note:

> Dear Caroline,
>
> [I] only write now to send you four pencils with different marks which I am very desirous that you should try as drawing pencils & find to be good. Henry Thoreau has made, as he thinks, great improvements in the manufacture, and believes he makes as good a pencil as the good English drawing pencil. You must tell me whether they be or not. They are for sale at Miss Peabody's, as I believe, for 75 cents the dozen. . . .
>
> Farewell,
> Waldo

1849 "The better part of one's life consists of . . . friendships," writes Abraham Lincoln to his friend Joe Gillespie.

MAY

20

"I'm not a shy little colt," she said. "And I'm not a singing nightingale, neither. I can tote a steamboat on my back, outscream a panther, and jump over my shadow. . . and I like to wear a hornets' nest for my Sunday bonnet."

Mary Pope Osborne,
American Tall Tales

BIRTHDAYS

1935 Carol Carrick is born, in Edgartown, Long Island, New York. Growing up, she is fascinated by the tadpoles and turtles in the pond near her home and by finding out the names of wildflowers she sees in the fields nearby. In college, Carol studies art, but in 1965 she offers to write the text for a book her husband, Donald, is illustrating, beginning a long collaboration. Donald draws beautiful barns in Vermont; Carol researches animals that live in barns. Over the next two decades they create more than thirty-five books together, including many books about the nature they both love. Carol also branches out, writing books for older readers as well as picture books.

1949 Mary Pope Osborne and her twin brother are born, in Fort Sill, Oklahoma. Her father is in the military, and she grows up with two siblings in addition to her twin. Mary goes to college to study drama and then discovers even greater adventure in the study of mythology and comparative religion. A prolific author, she is the author of the Magic Tree House series, among others. *American Tall Tales*, illustrated by Michael McCurdy, is filled with wildly exaggerated and funny stories, including one about Sally Ann Thunder Ann Whirlwind, who can "outgrin, outsnort, outrun, outlift, outsneeze, outsleep, outlie any varmint." Mary explains the inspiration for *Spider Kane and the Mystery Under the May-Apple* and its sequel, *Mystery at Jumbo Nightcrawler's:* Always afraid of spiders in general and big spiders in particular, she discovers a huge spider on the sofa in a cabin she and her husband have bought. "We have to leave now and never come back," Mary insists. Her husband disagrees, and so she decides to overcome her fear. She sets out to gather all the scientific information she can. "But in the process a number of bug names jumped off the page at me—leafwing butterflies, emperor moths, deathwatch beetles. I started making a list of all the names I liked, and a world of mystery and fantasy opened up. At the center was a remarkable detective named Spider Kane, who, in my mind is that same scary creature I saw sitting on my sofa. . . ."

▶ **ALL ABOUT NAMES** Invite students to research a creature that scares them.

1963 Caralyn Buehner is born, in St. George, Utah, the daughter of a judge. She grows up in Salt Lake City, the youngest of five siblings. Caralyn remembers her mother reading *Onion John* and *The Boxcar Children* aloud. When her sisters read the P. G. Wodehouse series, Caralyn knows she is missing quite a bit of the humor, but she enjoys it anyway. Caralyn creates picture books with her husband, artist Mark Buehner. Their *Fanny's Dream* is a wonderful contribution to the Cinderella canon.

EVENT

1916 The first Norman Rockwell cover appears on the *Saturday Evening Post*, "Boy with Baby Carriage." When Norman and his brother are growing up, they sit at the dining room table while their father reads Dickens aloud. Norman draws the characters his father reads about: David Copperfield, Oliver Twist, Uriah Heep.

▶ **DRAWING TIP** A nice exercise for students is to draw a character while the teacher reads aloud. Then they can see whether the characters they "see" are similar or different.

MAY

There are only two types of mammals that lay eggs and this is one of them. Like the duck, it has a bill and webbed feet. . . . Who is it?

Gail Radley,
The Who Is It Book of Mammals

BIRTHDAYS

1951 Gail Radley is born, in Boston, Massachusetts. Her novels for middle graders about family changes include *The Night Stella Hid the Stars* and *Nothing Stays the Same Forever*. Gail says she likes writing for preteens because "they are trying to make sense of the world, to understand it, often while wading through some tough problems." Gail says that books can help these preteens see that they are not alone and that there are answers.

1966 Mark Crilley is born, in Hartford City, Indiana. He is raised in Detroit. Growing up, Mark likes *Mad* magazine and M. C. Escher art. After graduating from college with a major in art, Mark teaches English in Morioka, Japan. One day he takes "The Beast That Ate Morioka," a monster-movie parody he has created, into class. The students enjoy it, so Mark keeps drawing. Using *Alice's Adventures in Wonderland*, *The Wizard of Oz*, and *Charlie and the Chocolate Factory* as inspiration, he comes up with "Akiko on the Planet Smoo," the story of a fourth-grade girl who has extraterrestrial adventures. In 1996, "Akiko" becomes a monthly black-and-white comic book in an "all ages" category: no graphic violence, no objectionable language, but content that is intended to interest adults as well as children—in the manner of "Calvin & Hobbes." In 2000, he publishes two novels in a four-novel series: *Akiko on the Planet Smoo* and *Akiko in the Sprubly Islands*.

EVENTS

1881 Clara Barton founds the American Red Cross.

1927 Charles Lindbergh lands in Paris, France, after making the first solo air crossing of the Atlantic.

▶ **RESEARCH TIP** The quantity of material written at all levels on both Clara Barton and Charles Lindbergh provides excellent research possibilities. Ask students to devise a plan for finding out more information about Clara Barton and/or Charles Lindbergh. Emphasize the research process by posting their ideas of possible sources: biographies, encyclopedias, Internet. Then, as students bring in information, they can post it in appropriate category. Tell students many biographers insist on verifying a fact in at least three different sources before using it.

1986 In an interview in the *New York Times* about becoming a writer, Theodor Geisel—Dr. Seuss—observes, "You can get help from teachers, but you are going to have to learn a lot by yourself, sitting alone in a room."

MAY 22

One morning Toad sat in bed. "I have many things to do," he said. "I will write them all down on a list so that I can remember them."

Arnold Lobel,
Frog and Toad Together

BIRTHDAYS

1859 Sir Arthur Conan Doyle is born, in Edinburgh, Scotland. His father hopes to bring him up as a keen businessman and mathematician, but at an early age Arthur lets everybody knows that he loves Sir Walter Scott and loathes arithmetic. The boy grows up to be a man of adventure and achievement, best known as the creator of Sherlock Holmes and Doctor Watson. Arthur receives a medical degree in 1881, and writes the first Sherlock Holmes story in 1887. He abandons medicine in 1990 and devotes himself to writing more Sherlock Holmes stories.

1933 Arnold Lobel is born, in Los Angeles. He grows up in Schenectady, New York. He studies art at the Pratt Institute, in Brooklyn. Arnold writes *Fables* while laid up with a broken ankle. A few years earlier his editor had suggested that he might be interested in illustrating Aesop, but Arnold declined, saying Aesop is essentially for adults. But the fable idea lingers. Arnold says, "The creation of most picture books for children is not dramatic. It is a matter of daily, patient, single-minded effort. It is a matter of writing some words on a page in a silent room. It is the soft sound of a pencil or a pen sweeping across a bit of drawing paper." As soon as he begins *Fables,* says Arnold, it takes on a life of its own. He makes a list of animals he's always loved: the ostrich, the hippo, the crocodile, and the kangaroo. "Day by day, to my great surprise," says Arnold, "They told me their stories, and I wrote them. . . ." Although he loves to draw, Arnold is jittery about the *Fables* drawings, and he sneaks into the editorial office when he knows the editor won't be there, leaves the drawings on her desk, and sneaks away. *Fables* is awarded the Caldecott Medal.

▶ **WRITING TIP** Lists can be a powerful tool for inspiring writing. Invite students to make a list of animals they like—or animals they dislike. Then invite students to let one or two of those animals tell their story in a fable format.

▶ **READING REFLECTION** Ask students to read a story from *Frog and Toad*. What special quality of friendship do they think Frog offers Toad? And what special quality does Toad offer Frog? What would happen if Encyclopedia Brown, say, or Junie B. Jones or Pinkerton or Bunnicula or Steig's brave Irene or Ogden Nash's Isabel or Rotten Ralph (or anybody else) ended up in the same story? Invite students to role-play a scene.

EVENT

1848 In a letter, Henry David Thoreau observes, "Nothing makes the earth seem so spacious as to have friends at a distance; they make the latitudes and longitudes."

MAY 23

Freedom, New Hampshire, may be a small town, but it sure can produce a big egg.

Oliver Butterworth,
The Enormous Egg

BIRTHDAYS

1898 Scott O'Dell is born, in Los Angeles. Perhaps Scott inherits his storytelling talents from his famous ancestor Sir Walter Scott. Scott says it takes him several months to do the research for each of his books. Then it takes him six months to write a book. His books include the Newbery Medal title *Island of the Blue Dolphins* and three Newbery Honor books. Scott says he likes writing for children because children "have the ability to be someone else, to live through the stories and lives of other people." Scott creates the Scott O'Dell Award for Historical Fiction to encourage other writers of this genre.

▶ **READING TIP** Ask student to create an Honor Roll of Historical Fiction, listing their favorite books.

1910 Margaret Wise Brown is born, in Brooklyn, New York. When Margaret is four her family moves to Long Island Sound where she grows up playing on beaches and in the woods. The middle of three children, the other two are seen as achievers, Margaret as the daydreamer. Her pets include thirty-six rabbits, two squirrels, a collie dog, two Peruvian guinea pigs, a Belgian hare, and seven fish. She also considers a wild robin that returns every spring a pet. Margaret says as a child the stories of *Black Beauty*, *Peter Rabbit*, and *Snow White* all seem so real to her that she doesn't think about the fact that somebody wrote them. Margaret enrolls in the Bank Street teacher education program and is encouraged by Lucy Sprague Mitchell, who believes young children need a special kind of story written just for them. Margaret says her goal is to write a story as true to a child as *Hansel and Gretel* and *Br'er Rabbit*.

1915 Oliver Butterworth is born, in Hartford, Connecticut. He grows up in a rural area. He teaches elementary school for a few years and then, for the rest of his life, teaches college. At the age of forty, Oliver draws on his classroom experiences to write *The Enormous Egg*, a humorous tale of a twelve-year-old who tends a huge egg—out of which a triceratops is hatched. And that's only the beginning of the tale.

▶ **WORD FUN** *Eggs* offer fun word possibilities for creating riddles. Invite students to list all the words they can think of (and find) that begin with *ex*. Then they can change the *ex* to *eggs* to get *eggsplain*, *eggscited*, *eggstraordinary*, and so on. Once they have the word list, writing the riddles is easy.

1936 Peter Parnall is born, in the Big Bend area in Texas. He is well known as the illustrator of many of Byrd Baylor's books and also illustrates his own books, which often reflect time spent on a farm on the Maine coast.

▶ **READ MORE** In *Feet*, Peter invites readers to take a close look at the feet of different creatures. Invite students to consider other "close-ups" they might research.

1941 Brenda Seabrooke is born, in Florida. One of her books has the arresting title *The Vampire in My Bathtub*.

▶ **READING/WRITING CONNECTION** Invite students to write the opening paragraph for a book titled *The _____ in My Bathtub*.

MAY

You wouldn't think we'd have to leave Chicago to see a dead body.

Richard Peck,
A Long Way from Chicago

BIRTHDAY

1912 Alfred Andriola is born, in New York City. He is the creator of the "Terry and the Pirates" and "Charlie Chan" comic strips.

EVENTS

1863 "On 24 May 1863, which was a Sunday, my uncle, Professor Lidenbrock, came rushing towards his house, No 19 Kongstrasse, one of the oldest streets in the old quarter of Hamburg." So opens Jules Verne's *Journey to the Center of the Earth*, one of the most popular of science fiction tales.

1971 Richard Peck quits his job as a junior high English teacher, deciding if he's going to be a writer, he'd better do it. Richard says that "writing isn't self-expression. It's communication." He adds that "professional writing is the craft of communicating with strangers."

▶ **WRITING TIP 1** Richard Peck says that writers don't write from experience but from observation. Invite students to pick a spot in the school and write what they see in ten minutes of observation.

MAY

25

"It's too weird," Arthur said. "My teacher in my house, walking on my carpet, eating from my spoons, and touching my stuff!"

Marc Brown,
Arthur's Teacher Moves In

BIRTHDAYS

1908 Theodore Roethke is born, in Saginaw, Michigan. Much of his adult poetry reveals an acid wit; his verse for children is exuberant and playful, such as the last two lines of "The Bat": "For something is amiss or out of place/When mice with wings can wear a human face."

1940 Ann McGovern is born, in New York City. Ann becomes a celebrated writer of nonfiction. As a result of her interest in scuba diving, she has written many books about creatures that live in the ocean, particularly sharks. She has made numerous sea dives with the subject of *Shark Lady: True Adventures of Eugenie Clark.*

▶ WRITING TIP Ann advises young writers to read a lot, to keep a journal, and to rewrite. Ann says she rewrites her stories at least twenty-five times.

EVENTS

1856 Mark Twain writes a letter in which he complains about being pestered by a chorus of "forty-seven thousand mosquitoes and twenty-three thousand horse flies."

▶ READING/WRITING CONNECTION Sid Flesichman's McBroom tales contain similar specificity about the number of mosquitoes and their size. Invite students to consider how this exaggerated specificity has a humorous effect.

1976 *Arthur's Birthday,* by Marc Brown, is published. Arthur is the only anteater known to be the hero of a popular series of books. Twenty-four years later, in *Arthur's Teacher Moves In*, which Marc dedicates to his own third-grade teacher, Arthur doesn't seem to have aged much. How do students feel about this? Do they want their favorite characters to stay the same—or to grow up?

MAY

26

Mythology teaches you what's behind literature and the arts, it teaches you about your own life.

Joseph Campbell,
with Bill Moyers,
The Power of Myth

BIRTHDAYS

1906 Joseph Campbell is born, in New York City. As a young boy he becomes interested in the stories of the American Indians as a result of watching Buffalo Bill's Wild West Show at Madison Square Garden every year. In his famous work *The Hero with a Thousand Faces*, Campbell develops the theory that myths reveal what people of all cultures have in common.

▶ READ MORE *Wings,* by Christopher Myers, and *Icarus Swinebucke,* by Michael Garland, two books based on the myth of Icarus, provide very different stories, each with arresting art and a message about daring.

1934 Sheila Greenwald is born, in New York City. Sheila says she's been drawing so long that she can't remember *not* drawing. After college, she works for fourteen years illustrating magazine articles and other people's books. Then she becomes a prolific author, illustrating her own books. Sheila's middle-grade novels include *Alvin Webster's Surefire Plan for Success (and How It Failed)* and the Rosy Cole series. Sheila also writes young adult fiction.

EVENTS

1909 Frederick Barrett sets a world marathon record time of 2:42:31.

1925 Ty Cobb is the first baseball player to collect 1,000 extra-base hits.

▶ **RESEARCH TIP** Challenge students to find a reference book (or Internet site) giving information about the current marathon record holder and/or baseball extra-base-hit record holder.

MAY

When a writer chooses a name for characters, she has to believe they couldn't be called anything else. Frankenstein could never be called Andersen.

M. E. Kerr,
Blood on the Forehead: What I Know About Writing

BIRTHDAYS

1927 Mary Jane Meaker is born, in Auburn, New York. All her life Mary Jane has wanted to be a writer. She uses a number of pseudonyms: Vin Packer, Laura Winston, Mamie Stone, M. J. Meaker, Eric Rantham McKay, and M. E. Kerr. Kerr is the author of such middle-grade novels as *Dinky Hocker Shoots Smack; If I Love You, Am I Trapped Forever?; Is That You, Miss Blue; The Son of Someone Famous;* and *Fell.* Why all the noms de plume? Meaker says, "I just like to name myself." She says women walk around with their father's name and their husband's name. She likes to create her own. She adds, "Even Proctor and Gamble doesn't call all its soap Tide."

▶ **ALL ABOUT NAMES** Invite students to create noms de plume.

EVENT

1945 President Harry Truman writes to his mother: "My daughter and her two pals . . . are sleeping in Lincoln's bed tonight! If I were not afraid it would scare them too badly I would have Lincoln appear. The maids and butlers swear he has appeared on several occasions. It is said that even Mrs. Coolidge saw him."

▶ **READ MORE** *The White House* (in the SRA Math CrossSections series, by Susan Ohanian) contains lots of lore about White House residents.

MAY

My name is Emmaline. Before I met Emily, the great poet of Amherst, I was nothing more than a crumb gatherer, a cheese nibbler, a mouse-of-little-purpose.

Elizabeth Spires,
The Mouse of Amherst

BIRTHDAYS

1908 Ian Fleming is born. When Ian is eight, his father is killed in World War I. His first James Bond novel, *Casino Royale,* is written, says Ian, to combat the shock of getting married at age forty-three. Ian borrows the name for his famous hero from James Bond, a Philadelphia ornithologist and author of *Birds of the West Indies.* While writing his book about a British secret agent who has the code name 007, Ian sees the bird book and thinks the author's name is "brief, unromantic, and yet very masculine, just what I needed."

▶ **ALL ABOUT READING** Ask students to take a careful look at the names of three literary characters, offering opinions about each name's suitability.

1952 Elizabeth Spires is born, in Lancaster, Ohio. At age twelve she reads a short story by Flannery O'Conner and decides she will be a writer. An acclaimed poet for adults, Elizabeth writes *The Mouse of Amherst,* a story narrated by Emmaline, a mouse who lives behind the wall in Emily Dickinson's room. Emmaline appreciates Emily's poems—and writes some of her own. Companion volumes *With One White Wing* and *Riddle Road,* both offering puzzles in poems and pictures, invite young readers to use clues in the imagery to guess the riddle.

1895 Beatrix Potter writes in her journal: "The garden is very large, two-thirds surrounded by a red-brick wall with many apricots, and an inner circle of old gray apple trees on wooden espaliers. It is very productive but not tidy, the prettiest kind of garden, where bright old-fashioned flowers grow amongst the currant bushes." In 1909, this garden becomes the setting for *The Tale of the Flopsy Bunnies.*

MAY

29

Seconds before the windshield shattered into a crazed, opaque spiderweb pattern, Nick saw the terrified face that would remain forever imprinted on his mind: eyes wide and unseeing, mouth stretched in a grimace of horror.

Willo Davis Roberts,
Nightmare

BIRTHDAYS

1906 T(erence) H(anbury) White is born, in Bombay, India. An authority on medieval life and legend, his four novels about King Arthur and Merlin are collected in the book *The Once and Future King.* The Broadway musical *Camelot* is based on this book. The first story in the tetralogy is adapted by Disney for the movie *The Sword and the Stone.*

▶ **OUT LOUD** White is wonderful to read aloud.

1922 Eleanor Coerr is born, in Kamsack, Saskatchewan, Canada. She grows up in Saskatoon. She recalls, "When I was very young, drawing was my passion, and I sketched every day after school." But any ideas of becoming a serious artist are snuffed out in high school when an aptitude test shows Eleanor is "best suited for a scientific career." In college she struggles with biology and chemistry. "The only pleasure then was making drawings of the insides of frogs or cross-sections of worms." Realizing she does not want to become a physician, Eleanor becomes first a reporter and later a children's librarian and the author of such popular children's book as *Sadako and the Paper Crane* and the *Josefina Story Quilt.*

1928 Willo Davis Roberts is born, in Michigan. Her family moves a lot. She remembers attending six schools in fourth grade. Willo's favorite books include *Black Beauty, Heidi,* fairy tales, and mysteries. Willo writes thirty-five mystery/suspense books for adults, and then, since *The View from the Cherry Tree* is about an eleven-year-old boy who sees a murder committed, the publishers decide it must be a children's book. She's been writing children's books ever since. Willo says she writes for children the same way as she writes for adults—by getting the suspense as close to the first paragraph as she can.

▶ **WRITING TIP** Willo says, "Never end a chapter in a place where it's easy to stop reading—end on a note where the reader is going to be compelled to turn the page and go into the next chapter to see what happens next."

▶ **READING TIP** Willo says, "Reading mysteries should be fun." Invite students to make a list of fun-to-read titles.

1938 Brock Cole is born, in Charlotte, Michigan. A college instructor of philosophy, Brock is the author-illustrator of picture books, of middle-grade novels, and young adult novels. As a self-taught artist, Brock is especially fond of pencil. He says publishers don't like pencil art because it is difficult to reproduce, but he likes the great subtlety that an artist can achieve with pencil. Brock's favorite illustrators are Edward Ardizzone and E. H. Shepard.

MAY

30

Yet do I marvel at this curious thing

to make a poet black and bid him sing!

Countee Cullen

BIRTHDAYS

1903 Countee Cullen is born Countee LeRoy Porter, in Louisville, Kentucky. When his grandmother and guardian dies, fifteen-year-old Countee is taken into the home of Reverend Frederick Cullen, pastor of Harlem's largest congregation. Countee earns academic honors, including poetry prizes, at New York University and Harvard. Some of Countee's most celebrated poems can be found in *I, Too, Sing America,* edited by Catherine Clinton.

1912 Millicent Selsam is born, in Brooklyn, New York. Her nonfiction books in the A First Look at . . . series, which provide a close look at nature for young readers, include books about birds' nests, caterpillars, dogs, fish, sharks, and mushrooms.

▶ **RESEARCH TIP** Invite students to choose a topic such as birds' nests, caterpillars, or sharks. They should list all the facts they know about this subject. Then they should find a book on the topic and see how much more information they can add to their list.

MAY

31

I like to hear a thunder storm,

A plunder storm,

A wonder storm. . . .

Elizabeth Coatsworth, "Rhyme"

BIRTHDAYS

1819 Walt Whitman is born, in West Hill, New York. He is the second of nine children. During his childhood, Walt's family moves many times as his father looks for work. At age eleven, Walt's formal schooling ends, and he begins work as an office boy for lawyers. When they give him a subscription to a lending library, Walt's real education begins. He reads nonstop and visits museums. When he is twelve, Walt becomes an apprentice on a Long Island newspaper and learns the printing trade. He gets his first article published when he is fifteen. At age seventeen, Walt begins his teaching career in one-room schools on Long Island, becoming a journalist five years later. He publishes *Leaves of Grass* himself, sending a copy to Ralph Waldo Emerson. For the rest of his career, Walt keeps revising this volume, publishing several more editions.

1893 Elizabeth Coatsworth is born, in Buffalo, New York. The author of more than ninety books of poetry and prose, some of her writing draws on her wide travels as a young child. Her Newbery Medal book, *The Cat Who Went to Heaven,* is based on a legend featuring a Japanese artist, his cat, and a Buddhist miracle.

▶ **WORD FUN** Invite students to try out Elizabeth's technique of describing something in the natural world with three rhyming adjectives.

1914 Jay Williams is born, in Buffalo, New York. Jay's storytelling career begins at age twelve when he wins a prize for "the best original ghost story told round the campfire in boy's camp." Best known as the coauthor of the Danny Dunn series, Jay publishes nearly one hundred books. Although the Danny Dunn books are science fiction, the authors are careful to get their science right. His other books include *Everybody Knows What a Dragon Looks Like* and *The Practical Princess.*

J UNE

JUNE

I must go down to the sea again,

To the lonely sea and the sky . . .

John Masefield,
Salt-Water Ballads

BIRTHDAYS

1878 John Masefield is born, in Ledbury, Herefordshire, England. He runs away to sea at thirteen, and draws on this experience in his first volume of poems, *Salt-Water Ballads*. Named Poet Laureate in 1930, John holds the position until 1967.

1889 James Daugherty is born, in Asheville, North Carolina. James studies art in Washington, D.C., Philadelphia, and London. During World War I, he works in New England shipyards camouflaging ships for the U. S. Navy. While his father reads aloud from Shakespeare, Poe, and Dickens, James draws illustrations to go with the stories. James remembers his grandfather telling stories about Daniel Boone. Later his own book about Daniel Boone wins the Newbery Medal.

▶ **READING/DRAWING CONNECTION** Try this illustrate-while-I-read-aloud technique, also used by the Norman Rockwell family, with your students.

1934 Doris Buchanan Smith is born, in Washington, D.C. From the age of eleven, Doris knows she wants to be a writer. Doris's large family includes more than twenty foster children. When they and her five birth children are in school, she gets serious about a career. Doris reminds would-be writers that writing requires discipline, noting that "accepting the fact that the Muse works only in proportion to my endeavors was the hardest thing I've ever done in my life and also the best."

1947 Joyce Rockwood is born, in Ames, Iowa. Joyce says, "I consider myself an anthropologist as well as a novelist. . . . I write primarily about the American Indians, setting my stories in the cultures of the past, relying heavily on anthropological and historical research in order to re-create the reality that has since been shattered by the European invasion." As serious as that sounds, Joyce says she wants above everything for her books to entertain the reader. "My purpose is not to teach, but to offer a powerful human experience."

EVENTS

1843 At age forty-six, a woman given the slave name Isabelle leaves her job as a domestic servant to begin a career teaching against slavery and "doing God's work." To begin her new life, she gives herself a new name: Sojourner, because "I was to travel up and down the land," and Truth, because "I was to declare the Truth unto the people."

▶ **READ MORE** There are a number of books about this woman who is born a slave, is only nine when she is sold for the first time, and becomes a leader and inspiration to all. Patricia McKissack, Anne Rockwell, and David Adler have all written about this remarkable woman.

1938 Superman, the world's first superhero, appears in the first issue of *Action Comics*.

1965 Lloyd Alexander writes the editor of *The Horn Book*, "Well, needless to say I'm delighted you liked *The Black Cauldron*. Seriously delighted, for I value your opinion and it does indeed make me feel encouraged about the project—a rare and wonderful sensation!"

▶ **READING/WRITING CONNECTION** Reminding students that everyone likes to be appreciated, invite them to write a fan letter to a favorite author. Make this an invitation, *not* an assignment. Also point out that it is nice to encourage less well-known authors.

2

"I didn't know I was going to have to eat my words," objected Milo. "Of course, of course, everyone here does," the king grunted. "You should have made a tastier speech."

Norton Juster,
The Phantom Tollbooth

BIRTHDAYS

1929 Norton Juster is born, in Brooklyn, New York. An architect and professor of design, Norton is known to children as the author of the pun-filled *The Phantom Tollbooth*, where Milo, a boy with a lazy mind, enters a world ruled by words and numbers, Dictionopolis and Digitopolis. Another Norton book, *As Silly as Knees, as Busy as Bees*, most definitely delivers on its subtitle, *An Astounding Assortment of Similes*. In 2000, an eighth grader at the North Chatham School creates a Norton Juster website: *http://www9.chatham.k12.nc.us/NCS/Authors/Norton%20Juster/nortonjuster.html*

▶ **READ MORE** For a factual discussion of "eating" words, see Charlotte Foltz Jones' *Eat Your Words*, a fascinating look at word derivations. The reader learns that Caesar salad has nothing to do with the Roman emperor but was originally called aviator salad, how Mary Queen of Scots' poor appetite resulted in marmalade, and lots more.

1938 Helen Oxenbury is born, in England. This winner of the Kate Greenaway Award says she listens almost nonstop to cassettes or the radio while she paints, dramatic readings being her favorite. She says Dickens and Hardy are "perfect to work by." Helen works in a tiny room at the top of a tall house; her husband, John Burningham, works in a room at the bottom of the house. In Helen's words, "We meet in the kitchen for lunch and a grumble." Helen says that since their children, who are art students, like to "borrow" materials, she locks the door to her workroom and hides the key.

EVENT

1854 Anthony Burns, a fugitive slave, is sent back South from Boston. Thousands of protesters appear on the streets. Later, Burns is sold to the people of Boston, who collect money to set him free.

▶ **READ MORE** *Anthony Burns: The Defeat and Triumph of a Fugitive Slave* by Virginia Hamilton gives a powerful account of Anthony's struggles.

3

Zena zeroed in on a Zinnia for Alison.

Anita Lobel,
Alison's Zinnia

BIRTHDAYS

1934 Anita Lobel is born, in Cracow, Poland. Anita and her brother are saved during the persecution of Jews by a Catholic servant who pretends they are her children. Nazis finally discover the children and take them to a concentration camp. The children are reunited with their parents after the war and come to the United States. Lobel, a Caldecott Honor recipient, brings her talents as a textile designer and stained-glass artist to her exuberant paintings. Anita says her own love of drawing and painting flowers and a visit to Vero Beach, Florida, where streets are named Azalea, Bougainvillea, Camellia, etc., inspires *Alison's Zinnia*.

▶ **WRITING FUN** Challenge students to use Anita's pattern in *Alison's Zinnia* for their own work. For another sort of challenge, they can try her geographical pattern in *Away from Home*, which begins, "Adam arrived in Amsterdam." Nicholas Heller employs the same pattern in *Ogres! Ogres! Ogres!* (The book is also notable for Jos. A. Smith's signature bizarre artwork.) Here are a couple of Heller's creations: "Fergusen flips frog's legs on the griddle" and "Gabby gobbles gobs of hummus."

EVENTS

1895 William Morris's Kelmscott Press publishes an edition of Chaucer. Many consider this Kelmscott Chaucer one of the most beautiful books ever published.

▶ **LOOKING AT BOOKS** Invite students to share a book they consider beautiful.

1916 "It must have been a little after three o'clock in the afternoon that it happened—the afternoon of June 3rd, 1916. It seems incredible that all that I have passed through—all those weird and terrifying experiences—should have been encompassed within so short a span as three brief months." Thus opens Edgar Rice Burroughs's *The Land That Time Forgot*.

▶ **WRITING FUN** Invite students to write a paragraph that begins by naming a specific date and time.

JUNE

When you go out into the world, watch out for traffic, hold hands, and stick together.

Robert Fulghum,
All I Really Need to Know I
Learned in Kindergarten

BIRTHDAY

1937 Robert Fulghum is born. He is best known for the best-seller *All I Really Need to Know I Learned in Kindergarten*.

▶ **THINK ABOUT IT** Ask students to list all the important things they learned in kindergarten. Or share "What I learned today."

EVENT

1940 Carson McCullers's *The Heart Is a Lonely Hunter* is published. Carson is twenty-three. She says, "I have more to say than Hemingway and God knows, I say it better than Faulkner."

▶ **THINK ABOUT IT** Students won't appreciate this reference, but writing "in the manner of" a noted writer gives them a similar feeling of pride in their work.

JUNE

Dear Mr and Mrs Bear and Baby Bear,

I am very sory indeed that I cam into your house and ate Baby Bears porij. Mummy says I am a bad girl. . . .

Jane and Allan Ahlberg,
The Jolly Postman or Other
People's Letters

BIRTHDAYS

1919 Richard Scarry is born, in Boston. During his childhood he spends Saturday mornings studying art at the Boston School of the Museum of Fine Arts. During World War II he draws maps for the army. Richard admires the work of Beatrix Potter. He likes Mark Twain's *Huckleberry Finn* so much that he calls his own son Huck after the main character. Richard is the author-illustrator of more than three hundred books, including *The Best Word Book Ever,* designed for children who like lots of detail and lots of busy activity in their books. Richard says his books should be fun for the author and for the child and for the parent, teacher, or babysitter who reads these books aloud again and again. "I try to put as much fun and action as possible into each book so that the reader may find something new each time it is read."

1938 Allan Ahlberg is born, in England. He is the joint author-illustrator, with his wife Janet, of such favorites as *Jeremiah in the Dark Woods, Funnybones,* and *The Jolly Postman*.

▶ **WRITING FUN** Invite students to follow Allan's example and write a letter exchange between two literary characters.

EVENT

1998 Diane Wolkstein officially opens the Central Park story season at the statue of Hans Christian Andersen. An annual tradition, storytelling by Wolkstein and others continues until September 25.

▶ **READ MORE** In *The Emperor's New Clothes: An All-Star Retelling of the Classic Fairy Tale*, film and TV stars from Madonna to Robin Williams each retell one part of the story. Likewise, a large cast of famous illustrators each portray a scene, so that each double-page spread is by a different duo.

▶ **OUT LOUD** Invite student teams to use this same technique to tell a Hans Christian Andersen tale to the class.

JUNE

Poppleton liked nothing better than soaking in a hot tub. When he was tired, he would say, "I need a soak." When he was worried, he would say, "I need a soak." Even when he felt happy, a soak made him happier.

Cynthia Rylant,
Poppleton Has Fun

BIRTHDAYS

1911 Verna Norbert Aardema is born, in New Era, Michigan. She is the third of nine children. Verna says her mother desperately needed help to run the household, "but first she had to get me away from my book." Verna goes into the swamp in back of the house to create stories—and to get out of doing the dishes. She begins writing down those stories. After college, Verna teaches and writes for *The Muskegon Chronicle* for more than twenty years before she becomes the writer and storyteller she'd hoped to become when she was eleven. In 1882, James Earl Jones reads *Bringing the Rain to Kapiti Plain* to inaugurate the PBS weekly program *Reading Rainbow*.

1927 Peter Spier is born, in Amsterdam, Holland. He grows up in Broek-in-Waterland, the setting for *Hans Brinker, or the Silver Skates,* by Mary Mapes Dodge. Peter's father is a journalist and illustrator, and Peter says he can't remember a time when he hasn't been drawing or watching someone draw. When Peter draws a book, he visits the locale where the book takes place. So to create *London Bridge Is Falling Down,* Peter goes to England; for *The Erie Canal,* he drives the length of the canal twice, stopping often to draw. Peter explains, "I can't make things come alive from photographs." A book takes him at least four months to create even though he works sixteen hours a day.

▶ **WRITING/DRAWING CONNECTION** Invite students to write about and/or draw a familiar place near your school. Then they should go look at the place, take notes, and revise their piece.

1954 Cynthia Rylant is born, in Hopewell, Virginia. When she is four, Cynthia's parents send her to live with her grandparents, in Cod Ridge, West Virginia. Cynthia's family doesn't have money for books, and there is no library anywhere near. Reading a Langston Hughes story in college causes Cynthia to change her major from nursing to English. She tries writing what she calls some "stupid little fantasy stories," but then reading Donald Hall's *Ox-Cart Man* changes her whole approach to writing. "I started writing from my heart." Cynthia's son Nat and his large dog are an inspiration for her popular Henry and Mudge series. After Cynthia wins the Newbery Medal for *Missing May,* she buys herself a 1912 Steinway baby grand piano. "I wanted to do something really symbolic," she says. Cynthia's name is a pseudonym and her neighbors don't even know what she does for a living. She doesn't own a computer but writes on yellow legal pads.

I share the desire to plant a masthead for doves . . . to spin a soft Black song . . . to waltz with the children . . . to the mountains of our dreams.

Nikki Giovanni,
Spin a Soft Black Song

BIRTHDAYS

1917 Gwendolyn Brooks is born, in Topeka, Kansas. She grows up on the south side of Chicago. This Pulitzer Prize–winning poet begins writing poems at age seven, and when she is thirteen, her poem "Eventide" is published in *American Childhood* magazine. After graduating from junior college during the Depression, the only work Gwendolyn can find is as a domestic worker and a secretary. But she never stops writing, and in the 1940s her poetry begins appearing in *Harper's, Poetry,* and *The Yale Review.* Gwendolyn says of her first volume of poetry, *A Street in Bronzeville,* "I wrote about what I saw and heard on the street."

▶ **WRITING TIP** Gwendolyn Brooks advises, "Collect words. Read your dictionary every day. Circle exciting words. The more words you know, the better you will be able to express yourself, your thoughts." Invite students to collect exciting words for two weeks. Encourage them to document their collection: when they write a word in their journal, they should note where they find it.

1943 Born Cornelia Giovanni, Jr., in Knoxville, Tennessee, on this date, Nikki Giovanni is raised in Cincinnati, though she spends her summers with her grandparents in Knoxville and attends high school there. Nikki's poems for children explore the many facets of the African-American experience and express her ongoing commitment to social justice.

▶ **READ MORE** In the introduction to *A Dime a Dozen,* Nikki says lots of children ask her, "Where do writers come from?" Nikki says her mother thought it was a horrible idea for her to think of becoming a writer, and her neighbors said, "Writers don't come from 'round here!" Nikki adds, "Looks like they were wrong, doesn't it? That just goes to show, it pays to listen to your own heart."

EVENTS

1769 Daniel Boone and his five companions set up camp on a fork of the Kentucky River. Daniel is captured by Indians but manages to escape.

▶ **READ MORE** *Bewildered for Three Days,* by Andrew Glass, tells a tall tale about Daniel's boyhood. Author's notes at the end give an account of Daniel's actual life. The title draws on the adult Daniel's answer when he's asked whether he's ever been lost. Daniel replies, "No, I was never lost, but I was bewildered for three days."

1955 In a letter to the poet W. H. Auden, Hobbit-creator J. R. R. Tolkien recalls, "I first tried to write a story when I was about seven. It was about a dragon. I remember nothing about it except a philological fact. My mother said nothing about the dragon, but pointed out that one could not say 'a green great dragon,' but had to say 'a great green dragon.' I wondered why and still do. The fact that I remember this is possibly significant, as I do not think I ever tried to write a story again for many years. . . ."

1977 On this day Bruce McMillan finds his remarkable riderless runaway tricycle at the Kennebunkport dump. It later inspires his book *The Remarkable Riderless Runaway Tricycle.*

JUNE

8

"You be careful, Wiley," said Wiley's mama. "The Hairy Man got your daddy, and he'll get you, too, if you don't watch out."

Wiley and the Hairy Man,
as retold by Judy Sierra

BIRTHDAY

1945 Judy Strup is born, in Washington, D.C. In 1985, she changes her last name to Sierra. By age two, she is reciting poems by Robert Louis Stevenson. She remembers "The Walrus and the Carpenter," by Lewis Carroll, and "The Rum Tum Tugger," by T. S. Eliot, as early childhood favorites. By the time she is in second grade, Judy is writing school reports in rhyme.

▶ **READ MORE** Read Molly Bang's retelling of the southern tale *Wiley and the Hairy Man.* Then compare her version and Judy Sierra's.

EVENT

1867 Mark Twain sets off on the journey through Europe to the Holy Land that he later writes about in *The Innocents Abroad.*

▶ **READ MORE** Encourage students to find books in which people write about their travels. Vera Williams's classic *Stringbean's Trip to the Shining Sea* is a good place to start.

JUNE

9

Who? Me? Oh, no, I've got a bellyache.

Donald Duck,
in *The Wise Hen*

EVENTS

1790 *The Philadelphia Spelling Book* is the first book entered for U. S. copyright.

▶ **WRITING TIP** Invite students to write a paragraph about one word they are proud they can spell—and how they learned it.

1934 The cartoon character Donald Duck makes his first film appearance in an animated film titled *The Wise Hen.* Every time the hen asks for help planting and harvesting her cornfield, Donald says, "Who? Me? Oh, no, I've got a bellyache."

▶ **READ MORE** Invite students to read classic versions of *The Little Red Hen* by Paul Galdone, Byron Barton, Margot Zemach, and others. This tale holds great possibilities for story theatre and dramatization. Once they know the classic tale, students will enjoy such variants as Philemon Sturges's *The Little Red Hen Makes a Pizza* and Alvin Granowsty's *The Little Red Hen, Help Yourself, Little Red Hen! (Another Point of View).* Another hen definitely worth noting is *Henny-Penny*, retold and illustrated by Jane Wattenberg. Henny-Penny and her feathered friends search for the king to tell him the sky is falling, but we're not sure whether it's King Kong, King Tut, or Elvis. The illustrations, which feature photos of Jane's own hens, run amok with visual puns.

JUNE

10

How much does it cost to get to where the wild things are? If it is not expensive my sister and I want to spend the summer there. Please answer soon.

From a letter sent by a seven-year-old fan of *Where the Wild Things Are*

BIRTHDAYS

1928 Maurice Sendak is born, in Brooklyn, New York. *Where the Wild Things Are* is the Caldecott Medal winner in 1963. Some adults worry that the monsters in this book are too disobedient and untidy, too scary. Maurice replies that children send him "their own drawings of Wild Things: monstrous, hair-raising visions . . . [that] make my Wild Things look like cuddly fuzzballs." One reviewer suggests, "Boys and girls may have to shield their parents from this book. Parents are very easily scared." Maurice confesses, "I was a very difficult child. I hated school. Even when I was encouraged to do what they thought I wanted to do—write and paint pictures—I had no pleasure, because I was doing it in a schoolroom. . . . My poor parents had to make countless trips to the school principal's office. . . ." Maurice's aim is to live until he is seventeen so he can get out of school. Maurice calls drawing his "salvation."

▶ **DRAWING TIP** Maurice advocates studying other artists, borrowing from them. "What I take, I transform, but basically, borrowing is how you learn . . . what you do is fall in love with other artists, past and present." Invite students to choose an artist to imitate. For two weeks they should draw like this artist. Then ask students to comment on what they learned from this imitation.

19— Clinton Cox is born, in Sumter, South Carolina. He becomes interested in history during the summers he spends with his grandparents, in Oberlin, Ohio. He hears older people talking about the black men from Oberlin who had gone with John Brown on his raid on Harpers Ferry. Clinton also hears his father and other black veterans talking about their experiences in World War II. Growing up, Clinton is bothered that he doesn't find mention of black soldiers in the Civil War in the history books. So he writes *Undying Glory*: *The Story of the Massachusetts 54th Regiment*, finding all kinds of information in primary sources from the National Archives.

EVENT

1928 *Dialogues,* by Alfred North Whitehead, is published. He writes, "Art is the imposing of a pattern on experience, and our aesthetic enjoyment is recognition of the pattern."

▶ **READING FUN** Invite students to bring a literary pattern to share with the class. A pattern can be anything from an alphabet book to Jack Prelutsky rhymes to a cumulative tale (such as *The House That Jack Built*) to the structure of an Amelia Bedelia, Nate the Great, Encyclopedia Brown book. And lots more besides.

▶ **WRITING TIP** Invite students to use one of these literary patterns in their own writing.

One day, while Aaron was combing his hair, he got so mad that he yelled, "HAIR! I HATE YOU!" That hurt hair's feelings. It jumped off Aaron's head and ran out of the bathroom.

Robert Munsch,
Aaron's Hair

BIRTHDAY

1945 Robert Norman Peter Maria Munsch is born, in Pittsburgh, Pennsylvania. He is the fourth of nine children. He says the middle is a bad position, as he gets attacked by both his younger and older siblings. About his name Robert says, "I know it is a weird name but IT IS MY NAME AND I LIKE IT." Robert's favorite cartoon character is Bugs Bunny. Robert daydreams a lot in elementary school, never learning to spell or do math. But he does write poetry. After earning a master's degree in anthropology, Robert starts telling stories to kids when he works in a day-care center, developing a pattern of telling stories aloud many times before finally writing them down.

▶ **READING/WRITING CONNECTION** In Robert Munsch's *Andrew's Loose Tooth*, Andrew has a loose tooth that the dentist, the Tooth Fairy, and a sledgehammer cannot dislodge. Invite students to tell the class about their own loose-tooth experiences. After they've told their stories, they should write them down.

EVENTS

1848 George Eliot writes to a friend who has recommended she read Charlotte Bronte's *Jane Eyre*, "I shall be glad to know what you admire in it . . . the book is interesting—only I wish the characters would talk a little less like the heroes and heroines of police reports."

▶ **WRITING TIP** The idea of looking at characters through the lens of a police report can be fun for young readers. Invite students to choose a fairy-tale character and write a police a report about that character.

1985 Theodor Geisel (Dr. Seuss) receives a doctor of fine arts degree from Princeton University. When he steps up to accept his degree, the graduating class begins to recite from *Green Eggs and Ham*: "I do not like them in a house./I do not like them with a mouse. . . ." Seuss says his books always start as doodles. "I may doodle a couple of animals; if they bite each other, it's going to be a good book. If you doodle enough, the characters begin to take over themselves—after a year and a half or so."

▶ **READ MORE** Hold a Dr. Seuss Day, with everybody sharing a favorite with three friends.

JUNE

12

When I write, I can shake off all my cares.

Anne Frank,
in her diary

BIRTHDAYS

1929 Anne Frank is born, in Frankfurt am Main, Germany. Anne's diary, written when she is thirteen years old, is one of the most famous diaries ever written. Over one million children under the age of sixteen died in the Holocaust. Anne Frank was one of them. Here are two websites for more information: *http://www.annefrank.com* and *http://www.annefrank.nl*

1936 Helen Lester is born, in Evanston, Illinois. After college, she becomes an elementary teacher. Helen is the author of many picture books that explore themes that are important to primary graders. Her book *Author: A True Story* is based on what she tells young audiences on school visits.

EVENT

1970 William Steig writes to Paul Heins, editor of *The Horn Book,* "I hope you'll understand if I tell you that I tend to be a bit 'uptight,' even neurotic perhaps, about being edited. It's not vanity—I don't think I'm a great writer, or even a good one (in fact, I'm not a writer)—but I like to sound like myself when I talk or write. . . . I see the logic of your suggested changes, but don't hate me if I say I like it better my way. Perhaps I've been spoiled by the *New Yorker* where, in forty years, neither my drawings nor their captions have been edited."

▶ **WRITING TIP** Ask students to find a picture to which they can add a caption that sounds just like them, their voice.

JUNE

13

My little horse must think it queer,

To stop without a farmhouse near. . . .

Robert Frost,
"Stopping by Woods on a Snowy Evening"

BIRTHDAY

1820 John Bartlett is born, in Plymouth, Massachusetts. Although he has little formal education, in 1855 John publishes *Familiar Quotations: Being an Attempt to Trace to Their Sources Passages and Phrases in Common.* This quotation source book, grouped by topics, is one of the most-used reference works in the English language. Today's revised edition contains 22,000 entries.

▶ **READ MORE** Invite students to browse quotations at *http://www.biblio mania.com/reference/bartlett*

EVENTS

1789 Mrs. Alexander Hamilton serves ice cream for dessert to George Washington. George likes it so much that in the summer of 1790 he runs up an ice cream bill of about $200, roughly the equivalent of about $6,000 in today's money.

▶ **READ MORE** According to Charlotte Foltz Jones's *Eat Your Words,* it's illegal to carry an ice cream cone in your pocket in Lexington, Kentucky.

1922 After his family goes to bed, Robert Frost stays up all night writing. He has been thinking about a poem that he comes to call "New Hampshire," and during this night he writes the whole thing. The next morning he writes another poem, one about a sad Christmas seventeen years earlier when he was returning home penniless. This poem, written in June about December memories, is probably his most famous. Robert later recalls that even as he wrote "Stopping by Woods on a Snowy Evening," he knew it would be his "best bid for remembrance."

▶ **READ MORE** Natalie Bober's *A Restless Spirit: The Story of Robert Frost* is a biography for children. Ed Young has illustrated "Birches."

JUNE

Your first home will always be the one that you remember best. I have been away from it for over twenty years; and yet I still go back in my dreams.

Laurence Yep,
The Lost Garden: A Memoir

BIRTHDAYS

1945 Bruce Degen is born, in Brooklyn, New York. Bruce says that in *Jamberry*, a book he writes and illustrates, he is the bear as well as the little boy. And berries are his favorite food. Bruce points out that even though his painting style is not strictly realistic, "the shapes that I put into my drawings come from looking at real things." The finished paintings in the Commander Toad books result from "pages and pages of research sketches on toads and frogs." Bruce also illustrates The Magic School Bus series.

▶ **RESEARCH/DRAWING CONNECTION** Invite students to draw a picture of an animal that interests them. Then, after researching that animal they can draw another picture.

1948 Laurence Yep is born, in San Francisco. Laurence says that growing up in a black ghetto in San Francisco while commuting to a school in Chinatown makes him an outsider. Science fiction and fantasy seem "truer" to him as a boy than books about Anglo kids growing up in rural communities. He remembers Andre Norton's *Star Born* as one of his favorite books at age eleven. A bit later he discovers Ray Bradbury's *Martian Chronicles*. When he is eighteen, Laurence sells his first story to a science fiction magazine. Laurence believes all writers are outsiders in some way. Otherwise, why would they write?

▶ **WRITING TIP** Laurence says, "Read a lot. Read to find out what past writers have done. Then write about what you know. Write about your school, your class, about your teachers, your family."

EVENT

1942 Walt Disney's animated film *Bambi* is released.

▶ **READ MORE** The original story *Bambi: A Life in the Woods*, by Felix Salten, was published in 1926. There have been many reissues, including one illustrated by Barbara Cooney.

JUNE

What is green and sour and weighs over five tons?

Picklesaurus

Louis Phillips,
Wackysaurus Dinosaur Jokes

BIRTHDAYS

1927 Betty Ren Wright is born, in Wakefield, Michigan, the daughter of teachers. Her books include *The Dollhouse Murders, Getting Rid of Marjorie, A Ghost in the Window,* and *The Ghost of Room 11*.

▶ **THINK ABOUT IT** Based on these titles, what kind of books do students think Betty writes? Challenge students to compile two lists: books whose titles reveal what they will be about, and books whose titles reveal nothing until after you've read the book.

1939 Brian Jacques is born, in Liverpool, England. His interest in adventure stories begins at an early age as a result of reading Daniel Defoe, Arthur Conan Doyle, Robert Louis Stevenson, Edgar Rice Burroughs, Kenneth Grahame, and Sir Henry

Rider Haggard. When Brian is fourteen his teacher introduces the class to poetry and Brian is inspired to save enough money to buy *The Iliad* and *The Odyssey* in a used-book shop. Brian leaves school at fifteen and sets out to find adventure as a merchant seaman. He writes *Redwall* for the children at the Royal Wavertree School for the Blind in Liverpool, where he delivers milk. Brian says his very descriptive style of writing comes from painting pictures with words so the blind students can see them in their imagination.

EVENT

1784 When James Boswell asks Samuel Johnson if one should finish every book one begins, Samuel answers no: "You may as well resolute that whatever men you happen to get acquainted with, you are to keep them for life."

JUNE 16

It was the summer I was fourteen that I came to know The Man Without a Face. Everybody called him that for the obvious reason.

Isabelle Holland,
The Man Without a Face

BIRTHDAY

1920 Isabelle Holland is born, in Basel, Switzerland, daughter of a U. S. Foreign Service officer. Isabelle says, "I think of myself as a storyteller, and for this I am indebted to my mother." In creating her own stories, Isabelle follows her mother's lead, creating stories that are exciting and entertaining and that also provide insight about real-life problems. Isabelle's novel *The Man Without a Face* is made into a movie starring Mel Gibson.

EVENT

1716 The first volume of Alexander Pope's translation of *The Iliad* is published. A critic complains, "It is a pretty poem, Mr. Pope, but you must not call it Homer."

▶ **READ MORE** Padraic Colum's *Children's Homer* remains the classic retelling for children. Books of Wonder has reissued it as *The Trojan War and the Adventures of Odysseus*, illustrated by Barry Moser. Rosemary Sutcliff's *Black Ships Before Troy: The Story of the Iliad* is also highly regarded.

JUNE 17

Lift ev'ry voice and sing,

Till earth and heaven ring,

Ring with the harmonies of Liberty. . . .

James Weldon Johnson,
"Lift Ev'ry Voice and Sing"

BIRTHDAYS

1871 James Weldon Johnson is born, in Jacksonville, Florida, the son of a head-waiter and a teacher. Since there are no high schools for African Americans in Jacksonville, James and his brother go to Atlanta for high school and college. In 1900, to celebrate Abraham Lincoln's birthday, James writes "Lift Ev'ry Voice and Sing," which his brother sets to music. In 1920, the NAACP adopts the song as the "Negro national hymn." Appointed U. S. consul to Venezuela in 1906, James writes *Autobiography of an Ex-Colored Man*.

1946 Liza Ketchum is born, in Albany, New York, the daughter of a writer-historian and a sheep farmer–conservationist. She starts writing in second grade, writing under the covers with a flashlight when her parents think she is asleep. They are stories about a girl who escapes her troubles by riding off on the back of a white stallion.

EVENTS

1919 *Barney Google*, created by Billy DeBeck, makes its debut in a King Features comic strip. In the strip, Barney is given a horse named Spark Plug, who becomes such a popular part of the strip that many children get nicknamed Sparky. One of these children is Charles "Sparky" Schulz, who grows up to create *Peanuts.* In 1995 *Barney Google* is honored by a U. S. Postal Service commemorative stamp.

1925 The first National Spelling Bee is held.

▶ **READING/WRITING CONNECTION** Invite students to interview adults they know about spelling triumphs and disasters.

1984 According to *McBroom's Almanac,* by Sid Fleischman, "By actual count, 4,678,092,546,190,359,121 fireflies appeared on June 17. Folks needed sunglasses to step outside at night."

▶ **WRITING TIP** Invite students to write two sentences using exaggeration to say something about the weather or other natural phenomena.

2000 J. K. Rowling, author of the phenomenally popular Harry Potter books, receives the Order of the British Empire from Queen Elizabeth.

JUNE

18

Monsieur Bibot, the dentist, was a very fussy man.

Chris Van Allsburg,
The Sweet Fig

BIRTHDAYS

1947 Pam Conrad is born, in New York City. A prolific author, Pam writes both young adult novels and picture books. Pam says that although her books are not autobiographical, "they are each about my life in one disguise or another." Drawing on events in her children's lives, Pam writes picture books as gifts to them. Pam lists her hobbies as needlework, quilting, crocheting, knitting, pug dogs, country music, Ray Charles, jogging, reading, the seashore, the plains.

▶ **READ MORE** In *Animal Lingo,* Pam offers a sampling of what animals "say" in other countries—from the *Jui Jui* of pigs in Venezuela to the *holderolderol* of turkeys in Israel. In *Who Says a Dog Goes Bow-wow?* Hank De Zutter takes the same idea, offering animal sounds in many languages. *Cock-A-Doodle-Doo!,* by Marc Robinson and Steve Jenkins, includes everyday sounds such as passing trains and crowing roosters in twelve different languages. A number of Internet sites explore this topic. Here's one from the linguistics department at Georgetown University: *http://www.georgetown.edu/cball/animals/animals.html*

1949 Chris Van Allsburg is born, in Grand Rapids, Michigan. Two books that mean the most to him as a child are *Harold and the Purple Crayon,* by Crockett Johnson, and *Bartholomew and the Oobleck,* by Dr. Seuss. Chris loves Harold's emphasis on the power of being able to create things with your imagination; he also loves the mystery of the book. He loves the surrealism of *Bartholomew,* the green goopy stuff dropping out of the sky. Chris also remembers the Alice books, both for their story and for Sir John Tenniel's illustrations. The first book Chris checks out of the library on his own is *The Biography of Babe Ruth.* Chris also decides to read the family encyclopedia all the way through, from A to Z; he makes it through D. In addition to creating provocative books, Chris designs a stamp for the U. S. Postal Service.

▶ **WRITING TIP** When asked where he gets his ideas, Chris says, "The fact is, I don't know where my ideas come from. Each story I've written starts out as a vague idea that seems to be going nowhere, then suddenly materializes as a completed concept. It almost seems like a discovery, as if the story was always there. The few elements I start out with are actually clues. If I figure out what they mean, I can discover the story that's waiting."

1951 Connie Roop is born, in Elkhorn, Wisconsin. A longtime science teacher, Connie is the coauthor with Peter Roop of easy-read historical titles featuring real young heroes and heroines. They also write riddle books. Here's a riddle from *Going Buggy! Jokes About Insects:*

What did the mother grasshopper say to her children?
"Hop to it!"

► **WORD FUN** Challenge students to come up with a list of insects. Then they can see that these names elicit many riddle possibilities. What kind of bugs did the knights fight? (*Dragonflies.*) Which bug is related to you? (*An ant.*) Honeybees, ticks, hornets, carpenter ants, for starters, should elicit this type of joke making.

1954 Frane Lessac is born, in Jersey City, New Jersey, daughter of a philosopher and a travel agent. Frane says as a child her lines are never straight and her paintings don't have dimensions, so her art teachers consider her "unteachable." She climbs through the classroom window after school to change her grade in the book. Frane moves to the Caribbean island of Montserrat, which offers the beautiful images that inspire *My Little Island*.

1961 Angela Johnson is born, in Tuskegee, Alabama. She grows up there and in Ohio. She says listening to her teacher read aloud after lunch is magic she doesn't think will ever be repeated. "I asked for a diary that year and have not stopped writing."

JUNE

Bartholdi had decided to make his immense statue out of copper. Copper is lighter and cheaper than bronze, it is very malleable, and it can be beautifully worked in thin sheets.

Lynn Curlee,
Liberty

BIRTHDAYS

1880 W. A. Dwiggins is born, in Martinsville, Ohio. He designs a number of type-faces, including Electra.

► **READ MORE** Encourage students to examine the differing typefaces in books. Often the copyright page includes a note about typeface. It is valuable for children to know that such things don't just happen; they are created. Invite students to consider the effect of the changing typeface in *Squids Will Be Squids,* by Jon Scieszka and Lane Smith. Can they find other books where the typeface is part of the plot?

1921 Patricia Wrightson is born, in Lismore, New South Wales, Australia. She lives on a farm with her parents and older sister. Every night Patricia's father reads Dickens to the family. Patricia enrolls in a correspondence high school for children who live in isolated areas. Patricia fantasizes about legendary creatures in aboriginal mythology.

EVENTS

1885 Packed into 214 crates, the Statue of Liberty arrives in New York, a gift from France.

► **READ MORE** *Liberty,* by Lynn Curlee, is an inspiring account of Lady Liberty's history, from her design to the feat of her construction. Endnotes provide specifications and a timeline. *The Statue of Liberty,* by Leonard Everett Fisher, is another noteworthy resource.

1940 *Brenda Starr,* the first cartoon strip by a woman to achieve syndication, appears in Chicago. Trying to break into the male-dominated cartoon field, Dalia Messick changes her name to Dale. In those days, editors wouldn't even look at work they knew is drawn by a woman. The popular strip becomes the basis for a movie starring Brooke Shields and in 1995 is featured on a postage stamp.

1967 Impressed by the portfolio he has brought to the office, Harper & Row editor Ursula Nordstrom writes to sixteen-year-old John Steptoe, a student at New York's High School of Art and Design, giving him directions on how to prepare a rough dummy. She advises him, "Even if the first dummy you make doesn't seem to have a great big 'plot'—don't worry. It is the emotion which is important." John's teacher had urged him to show his work to publishers. John is eighteen when *Stevie* is published, in 1969.

1978 Jim Davis's lasagna-loving Garfield first appears in his own comic strip.

JUNE

E Pluribus Unum

Latin words on the Great Seal of
the United States
(translation: Out of Many
[States], One [Nation])

BIRTHDAYS

1938 Lynette Vuong is born, in Owosso, Michigan, the daughter of a draftsman and a practical nurse. When Lynette is five years old, her father sets her up with a "castle" of her own, a drafting table in the one-windowed walk-in closet adjoining her bedroom. She creates fanciful stories of children in faraway places At age ten, she writes a fifty-page historical novel titled "The Russian Twins." After marrying a Vietnamese student, Lynette moves to Saigon for thirteen years, learning the language and culture. They leave with their children right before the Communist takeover. Her *The Brocaded Slipper and Other Vietnamese Tales* contains five fairy tales, some of which exemplify themes similar to those in Western fairy tales.

19-- Elaine Stewart is born, in Philadelphia, Pennsylvania. She moves to Dallas, Texas, at age eleven. Elaine's mother reads the poems of Robert Louis Stevenson aloud. When Elaine can read on her own, she loves biographies, Nancy Drew mysteries, Mark Twain, and the Bible. When Elaine and her brother can't agree on a name for a stray dog the family adopts, her mother says they should write poems about dogs—and whoever writes the best poem gets to name the dog. Elaine's brother wins, but around the same time, Elaine's sixth-grade teacher enters one of her poems in a contest, it wins the contest, and she sees her words in print. Today, Elaine describes her career by saying, "I write nonfiction books for curious kids," adding that she is curious about the way things work and knows kids are too.

EVENT

1782 The Great Seal of the United States is adopted. On one side, the seal depicts an eagle clutching an olive branch in one talon and thirteen arrows in the other. In its beak is a ribbon bearing the legend *E Pluribus Unum*. Benjamin Franklin, John Adams, and Thomas Jefferson proposed this motto.

▶ **THINK ABOUT IT** Encourage students to explore mottos (Do they know their state motto?) and to come up with one for the class.

JUNE

The ants worked hard
all summer storing food
for the winter,

while the grasshopper
played his fiddle and
sang,

"Hip, hop, I just can't
stop

I'm a cool grasshopper
and I like to bop!"

Robert Kraus,
Fables Aesop Never Wrote

BIRTHDAYS

1925 Robert Kraus is born, in Milwaukee, Wisconsin. Robert sells his first cartoon at age ten—to the *Milwaukee Journal*. By the age of sixteen he is selling cartoons to *The Saturday Evening Post* and *Esquire*. After producing more than five hundred cartoons and twenty-two covers for *The New Yorker*, Robert starts a company specializing in children's picture books. Robert sometimes writes under the pseudonyms E. S. Silly and I. M. Tubby.

▶ **READ MORE** After students read traditional Aesop fables they will enjoy Robert's contemporary spoof and Jon Scieszka's offbeat *Squids Will Be Squids*. Also try Arnold Lobel's prize-winning *Fables*. Robert's fable titles include: "Sour Crepes," "The City Mouse and the Country Moose," and "The Wolf Who Cried Boy," which shows why readers need to be familiar with traditional fables to get the humor. In the *Ant and the Grasshopper*, Amy Lowry brings a different perspective to a traditional retelling of this fable: she sets the fable in the Imperial Chinese Emperor's Summer Palace, drawing on the four years she lived and worked near the Summer Palace in Beijing, China. In *Ackamarackus*, Julius Lester offers his own sumptuously silly Fantastically Funny Fables.

1957 Berkeley Breathed is born, in Encino, California, the son of an oil equipment executive. A Pulitzer Prize–winning cartoonist (for the "Bloom County" comic strip), his work reaches about forty million readers. In *Edwurd Fudwupper Fibbed Big*, Berkeley presents a cautionary tale about a talented liar—told by his sister.

▶ **READ MORE** There are many noteworthy liars in children's literature, from Evaline Ness's *Sam, Bangs & Moonshine* to Miriam Cohen's *Liar, Liar, Pants on Fire!* to stories featuring Charlotte Cheetham, Skinnybones, Bradley Chalkers, and Gilly Hopkins.

EVENT

1999 Nicole Rubel gives a talk at the Salem Public Library, showing children slides of her studio and telling how she creates the Rotten Ralph illustrations. Nicole is inspired by the paintings of Henri Matisse and by the art deco architecture of her hometown of Miami. Nicole says she finds inspiration for comic storylines from growing up with an identical twin sister.

JUNE

By making your own pop-ups, you will be carrying on a very long tradition. In the 1700s, "novelty books" with flaps, peepholes, and cut-outs were produced to amuse children.

Joan Irvine,
How to Make Pop-Ups

BIRTHDAY

1951 Joan Irvine is born, in Wiarton, Ontario, Canada. She lives in an old church near Wiarton with her family, and she teaches elementary school half-time. After writing nature books and drawing cartoons for a local newspaper, Joan is intrigued by *Robot*, a pop-up book by Jan Pienkowski. She researches pop-up cards and books and begins doing pop-up workshops at schools. Her *How to Make Pop-Ups* is a very complete, easy-to-follow guide for producing stupendous pop-ups.

EVENTS

1890 French painter Claude Monet writes to a friend, "I have again taken up something impossible—water with grass rippling at the bottom. It's fine to look at, but it's madness to want to paint it. Oh well, I'm always getting into such things."

▶ **READ MORE** *Linnea in Monet's Garden*, by Christine Bjork, is a winsome favorite. Other books featuring Monet's artwork are *Once upon a Lily Pad: Froggy Love in Monet's Garden*, by Joan Sweeney, and *A Blue Butterfly: A Story About Claude Monet*, by Bijou Le Tord.

1908 Frederic Remington, a painter noted for his depiction of western landscapes, notes in his diary, "I have now discovered for the first time how to do the *silver sheen* on moonlight." Remington also notes, "I have always wanted to be able to paint running horses so you would feel the details and not see them."

JUNE

Like silent, hungry sharks that swim in the darkness of the sea, the German Submarines arrived in the middle of the night.

Theodore Taylor,
The Cay

BIRTHDAY

1921 Theodore Taylor is born, in Statesville, North Carolina. Theodore's favorite stories are those in a book of Bible stories for children. He likes the fact that adventurous things happen in these stories. When Theodore is thirteen his family moves to Virginia and he gets a job writing about high school sports for the local newspaper.

EVENT

1846 Antoine Joseph Sax patents the instrument he has created, the saxophone.

▶ **ALL ABOUT NAMES** Invite students to invent musical instruments from their names. They should draw a picture of the instrument.

▶ **READ MORE** In *A Chartreuse Leotard in a Magenta Limousine*, Lynda Graham-Barber provides a humorous explanation of over 150 things named after people and places—from Afghan house to zeppelin. Magenta, for example, is a bright purplish-red dye developed in a town near Milan, Italy, named Magenta, and the town is named for a Roman general who stationed his troops there fifteen centuries before the dye is developed.

JUNE

24

So you're ten! Why that's two numbers old!

(As I hope you know without being told.)

John Ciardi, "For Someone on His Tenth Birthday," *The Monster Den*

BIRTHDAYS

1916 John Ciardi is born, in Boston, Massachusetts, the only son of Italian immigrant parents. John says he writes poems for his sister's children and his own—and then for himself. He says the children grew up, but he didn't. In his words, "I wrote for my own childhood." John writes *I Met a Man* for his daughter Myra using a first-grade vocabulary. "I wanted it to be the first book she read through, and she learned to read from it." John believes that poetry and learning both should be fun. John, also a noted poet for adults, says the difference is, "children's poems are *eternal*; adult poems are *mortal*."

▶ **WRITING TIP** John says the rate at which a writer recognizes his own faults is the rate at which he grows as a writer. He also advises that for a writer, "the waste-basket is a prime resource."

1924 Leonard Everett Fisher is born, in New York City. The author-illustrator of such books as *The Alamo, Ellis Island, Monticello, Number Art, The Statue of Liberty*, and *Symbol Art*, Leonard remembers, "I had a studio when I was two years old; it was a closet. We lived in a small apartment. . . . Near the front door was a walk-in closet in which my parents put a Lilliputian table and chair, crayons and pencils. Nothing liquid. I sat in there over the next three or four years under a naked light bulb drawing pictures. My mother could see me from the kitchen and would read to me from *A Child's Garden of Verses* or Mother Goose. She would expect that what I was drawing was in some way related to what she was reading. But there was no connection whatever. By the time I was four or five years old, I was drawing deep sea divers, soldiers, and bloody scenes of World War I."

1930 Charlotte Pomerantz is born, in Brooklyn, New York. Charlotte says if anyone asks her what one book she'd take to a desert island, her answer is "a big unabridged English dictionary." She adds, "This assumes, of course, that the desert island has electricity and running water. Otherwise, I'd exchange the dictionary for a 'how-to' book."

▶ **READING REFLECTION** The famous question "What book would you take to a desert island?" can engage children. What book would they take?

1942 Jean Marzollo is born, in Manchester, Connecticut, the daughter of a town manager and a teacher. Growing up, Jean never thinks about becoming a writer. She is too busy riding her bike or making doll clothes with her friends. Jean becomes a teacher and then editor of *Let's Find Out*, a magazine for kindergartners. She has written more than sixty books for children of all ages, including the popular I Spy series and the 39 Kids on the Block series.

1944 Kathryn Lasky is born, in Indianapolis, Indiana. Her father's family had come to the United States to escape Tsarist Russia, and *Night Journey* reflects this experience. Kathryn was labeled a "reluctant reader" in school. She says she just didn't like the kind of books provided in school, the "See Dick, See Jane" books. What she loved was what her mother was reading at home, *Peter Pan* and *The Wonderful Wizard of Oz*. Kathryn says, "Hands down, my favorite book as a child was *The Secret Garden*." Reflecting on her nonfiction writing, Kathryn quotes Samuel Eliot Morrison's statement that history is one-tenth fact and nine-tenths imagination. She admits, "I have a fascination with the inexact and the unexplainable. I try to do as little explaining as possible, but I try to present my subject in some way so it will not lose what I have found to be or suspect to be its sacred dimension. . . . Facts are quite cheap, but real stories are rare and expensive." Kathryn says the point of being an artist is to be able to get up every morning and "reinvent the world."

EVENT

1896 Harvard University awards John Muir an honorary degree, a tribute to his talents as a naturalist and also to his determination to educate himself. John's father believes the Bible is the only book worth reading, but when John is forced to leave school at age eleven, he persuades his father to buy him a math book and teaches himself algebra, geometry, and trigonometry. When John desperately wants to stay up at night and read, his father insists he must go to bed with the rest of the family— but agrees John can get up whenever he wants. So John starts rising at 1 A.M.—to read.

JUNE

When I was twelve or thirteen years old we had a canary, a cheerful and lively yellow bird whose songs I loved. If he wasn't singing I'd go up to his cage and whistle. The canary would listen carefully and then respond with more of his songs.

Eric Carle,
Flora and Tiger: 19 Very Short Stories from My Life

BIRTHDAYS

1929 Eric Carle is born, in Syracuse, New York. His immigrant family soon moves back to Germany. The question children most often ask this popular picture-book creator is, "Where do you get your ideas?" Eric feels an honest answer to this question is complex. Ideas don't come from just one place but are related to the person's background and education—all his experiences.

1937 Jane Sarnoff is born, in Brooklyn, New York. Her book *Words* gives word origins arranged by subjects such as sports and names. Jane also writes riddle books.

▶ **READ MORE** Stories of word origins are popular with students—and instructive too. In *Why You Say It*, Webb Garrison offers the stories behind over six hundred everyday words and phrases and how their meanings have changed. *2107 Curious Word Origins, Sayings and Expressions from White Elephants to Song Dance*, by Charles Earle Funk, includes four previously published works: *A Hog on Ice, Thereby Hangs a Tale, Heavens to Betsy!,* and *Horsefeathers and Other Curious Words.*

EVENTS

1798 Peter Mark Roget earns his M.D. degree from the University of Edinburgh. Peter's fascination with classifying ideas leads to the work we now know as *Roget's Thesaurus.*

1852 Henry David Thoreau notes in his journal, "There is a flower for every mood of the mind."

▶ **READING/WRITING CONNECTION** Invite students to match flower names with mind moods. They can browse gardening books for provocative names (such delights as blazing star, bleeding heart, candytuft, cowslip, dogtooth violet, lion's-ear, rattlesnake master, for starters). Then ask students to think of what flowers would be particularly appropriate for what authors and illustrators. For example, would they send Indian paintbrush to Paul Goble? The pocketbook plant to Kevin Henkes? The possibilities are limitless. For starters, Anita Lobel's *Alison's Zinnia* has lots of flower names.

1995 In accepting the Caldecott Medal, David Diaz mentions teachers and artists who have influenced his work. One of them is William Steig. "I was immediately drawn in by the depth of characterization he conveys in so few lines."

26

Let the pample moose
grab my galoshes and
the butterflies button
my hair.

Nancy Willard,
*The Moon & Riddles Diner and
the Sunnyside Café*

BIRTHDAYS

1902 Walter Farley is born, in Syracuse, New York. Some of his friends in Queens have horses and Walt loves to ride. Thus, the Black Stallion books are set along the Long Island Expressway. Walt writes *The Black Stallion* while he is in high school, and it is published while he is attending Columbia University. Walt recognizes how much kids love horses, saying, "Many kids would rather ride on the back of a horse than pilot a spaceship to the moon." After writing twenty books in the Black Stallion series, Walter collaborates with his son Steven on *The Young Black Stallion*, and now Steven carries on his father's tradition.

1905 Lynd Ward is born in Chicago, Illinois, the son of a Methodist minister. Lynd begins drawing when he discovers that *ward* is *draw* spelled backward. While studying at Teachers College, Columbia University, he becomes interested in children's books. He says, "I do not consider myself a writer but rather an artist whose stories sometimes need some words." Ward creates his *The Biggest Bear* entirely as a sequence of pictures. Then he adds "a minimum of words . . . to hold it together." Based on summers at Lonely Lake in the backwoods of Canada, this book is awarded the Caldecott Medal.

1925 Barbara Jenner is born, in Brooklyn, New York. Her informational titles include *A Snake-Lover's Diary*, which gives instructions on how to care for snakes.

▶ **THINK ABOUT IT** Ask students to consider why it's interesting to read about how to care for snakes—even if you never plan on owning one. What other things do they enjoy reading about—even though they don't want to do it?

1925 Robert Burch is born, in Inman, Georgia, the son of a bookkeeper. Growing up on a Georgia farm during the Depression gives Robert the setting and circumstances of many of his stories. In *Queenie Peavy*, for example, he shows how a motherless child of a small-town ne'er-do-well covers up deep hurt with outrageous behavior. The heroine of *King Kong and Other Poets* is another misfit with talent.

▶ **READ MORE** Invite students to share with the class books about literary misfits they have enjoyed.

1936 Nancy Willard is born, in Ann Arbor, Michigan. Nancy muses, "When a friend asked me recently who my ancestors were, I told her they were farmers, clockmakers, aristocrats, and scoundrels. I did not tell the truth. My ancestors were squirrels. How else could the members of my family have acquired such a passion for hiding things? Once my mother forgot where she'd hidden the family silver, as squirrels forget where they have buried their acorns. The loss of a dozen place settings was cause for inconvenience but not for alarm. 'They're not lost,' she said. 'They're in the house.'" Nancy adds that the place settings came to light when the piano tuner was called to find out why the piano rasped like a snare drum.

1940 Wallace Tripp is born, in Boston. He grows up in rural New Hampshire and New York. Wallace says most kids draw a lot when they are young, but they don't stick with it. "An illustrator is just a kid who hung on to his pencils." Wallace says he uses 4B to 2H pencils plus "forests of Berol Electronic 350 Scorer pencils." He also uses about six thousand research books when illustrating books. Wallace says lions are his favorite animals, and he wishes they made "more reliable pets."

EVENTS

1284 More than 130 children follow the Pied Piper of Hamlin, never to return home.

▶ **READ MORE** Robert Browning wrote a poem about the incident, and the story has been retold in a number of handsome picture books.

1994 In her Newbery Medal acceptance speech for *The Giver*, delivered at the annual meeting of the American Library Association, in Miami Florida, Lois Lowry says, "But each time a child opens a book, he pushes open the gate that separates him from Elsewhere. It gives him choices. It gives him freedom."

▶ **READNG REFLECTION** Invite students to give examples of choices books offer.

JUNE

27

. . . and no matter what happens when people die,

love doesn't stop and neither will I.

Lucille Clifton,
Everett Anderson's Goodbye

BIRTHDAYS

1872 Paul Laurence Dunbar is born, in Dayton, Ohio, the son of former slaves. In high school, Paul is the only black student in his class. In his senior year he is elected president of the school literary society, serves as editor of the school paper, and writes the lyrics for the class song. Paul wants to go to college, but he needs to earn money to help his mother. While running an elevator, Paul keeps a notebook, jotting down ideas for poems. Among the first to publish poems written in black dialect, Paul's verse evokes lively conversational rhythms.

▶ **READ MORE** *Jump Back, Honey* is a collection of the poems of Paul Laurence Dunbar, lovingly illustrated by Ashley Bryan, Carol Byard, Jan Spivey Gilchrist, Brian Pinkney, Jerry Pinkney, and Faith Ringgold. Each artist provides an anecdote about Paul's poems. An introduction by Ashley Bryan and Andrea Pinkney encapsulates Paul's life and discusses the "problem" of writing in dialect.

1936 Lucille Clifton is born, in Depew, New York. Lucille remembers her father telling stories about her great-great-great grandmother, born of Dahomey people but forced into slavery. Her mother writes poetry and reads it aloud. At age sixteen, Lucille is awarded a scholarship to Howard University. Lucille's first book for children, *Some of the Days of Everett Anderson*, tells the story of six-year-old boy who has a poem for each day of the week and two for Friday. There are several sequels.

▶ **WORD FUN** Start the day with a short poem written on the board. Ask students to copy this poem into a poetry notebook—so that they will own these good words. Once this habit is firmly established, invite student volunteers to choose the poem to post. If this poetry tradition is maintained over months, the benefits will be enormous.

EVENTS

1978 The erasable ballpoint pen is patented.

▶ **WRITNG FUN** Invite students to write a *pour quoi* story about the invention of this pen. Read one of Kipling's *Just So* stories to give them an idea of the genre.

1999 In accepting the Newbery Medal for *Holes*, Louis Sachar says, "I never talk about a book while I'm writing it." In the year and a half he's working on *Holes*, his wife and daughter don't know anything about it, except occasionally he announces he's finished the first draft or the second draft or third or fourth or fifth draft. Louis tells them, "Thank you for leaving me alone when I needed to be left alone." Louis also mentions that he gave the main character the name Stanley Yelnats because he was so caught up in creating the story, he didn't want to stop and think of the main character's last name. So he just wrote the first name backwards, figuring he'd change it. Later, he decides to leave it as is.

▶ **WRITING TIP** "During the first draft, I may only write forty-five minutes a day. Then I have to let it sit twenty-four hours, like a lab experiment, and see what grows from it."

▶ **READING TIP** Louis says, "The book was written for the sake of the book, and nothing beyond that. If there's any lesson at all, it is that reading is fun." This brings to mind what Mark Twain says in the frontispiece of *The Adventures of Huckleberry Finn*: "NOTICE: Persons attempting to find a motive in this narrative will be prosecuted; persons attempting to find a moral in it will be banished; persons attempting to find a plot in it will be shot."

JUNE

Daddy came in,

he sat across from Ma and blew his nose.

Mud streamed out.

He coughed and spit out mud.

If he had cried,

His tears would have been mud too,

But he didn't cry.

And neither did Ma.

Karen Hesse,
Out of the Dust

BIRTHDAY

1934 Bette Greene is born, in Parkin, Arkansas. Because of trouble with spelling and punctuation, Betty gets only average grades, but this doesn't squash her conviction that she's a great writer. Betty says that writers have to believe in themselves. She offers proof of this by pointing out that her favorite of her own books, *Summer of My German Soldier*, was turned down by seventeen publishers before it was published. Betty writes with a fountain pen—with ink from an inkbottle—on legal pads, because she likes the "drama" of the pen. She rewrites on computer.

▶ **WRITING TIP** Betty uses a technique of method acting, drawing on personal experiences to bring out the emotions of the characters portrayed. So, she says, if you're writing about someone who is hungry, then skip a meal or two, taking notes about what it feels like to be hungry.

EVENTS

1987 In accepting the Newbery Medal for *The Whipping Boy*, Sid Fleischman says, "The problem for the writer is not in finding ideas. They are as common as weeds. What to do with the idea that touches you and excites the imagination—that's the writer's problem."

1998 In accepting the Newbery Medal for *Out of the Dust*, Karen Hesse says occasionally adult readers grimace at the events documented in *Out of the Dust*. "They ask, how can this book be for young readers? I ask, how can it not? The children I have met during my travels around the country have astounded me with their perception, their intelligence, their capacity to take in information and apply it to a greater picture, or take in the greater picture and distill it down to what they need from it."

JUNE

And now here is my secret, a very simple secret: It is only with the heart that one can see rightly; what is essential is invisible to the eye.

Antoine de Saint-Exupery,
The Little Prince

BIRTHDAY

1900 Antoine de Saint-Exupery is born, in Lyon, France. Educated at the University of Fribourg, he joins the French air force. He becomes a commercial pilot in 1926. The author of several books for adults, he is best known for *The Little Prince*, popular with both children and adults. This illustrated fable, featuring a boy traveler from asteroid B-612, has sold fifty million copies in 120 languages.

EVENT

1986 In her Newbery Medal acceptance speech for *Sarah, Plain and Tall*, Patricia MacLachlan tells the audience, "My brother William is a fisherman, and he tells me that when he is in the middle of a fogbound sea the water is a color for which there is no name." Patricia adds, "'The water is a color for which there is no name' is my favorite sentence in *Sarah, Plain and Tall*."

▶ **WORD FUN** The Crayola 64-pack contains thirteen varieties of blue: blue, cerulean, sky blue, aquamarine, cornflower, teal, blue green, midnight blue, turquoise, blue violet, navy, cadet, and periwinkle. Invite students to consider the qualities of blue and then to write a description of a blue thing.

JUNE

30

Ever since I read *Charlotte's Web,* by E. B. White, I've wanted to own a pig—a live pig. . . . Maybe I've drawn pigs as a way of making up for not having one.

David McPhail,
*In Flight with David McPhail:
A Creative Autobiography*

BIRTHDAYS

1922 Maureen Mollie Hunter McVeigh is born, in Longniddry, Scotland, daughter of a motor mechanic and a confectioner. Mollie's father dies when she is nine years old. Mollie starts carrying a notebook with her, to write down her thoughts. She draws on these childhood experiences for her novels *A Sound of Chariots* and *Hold on to Love.* Because of family poverty, Mollie has to leave school at fourteen, getting a job in a flower shop. But she goes to night school four nights a week. She says all of her books are about individuals choosing sides in order to take a stand.

1940 David McPhail is born, in Newburyport, Massachusetts. He is one of four children in a family without much money, but his mother tells her children they can do anything they aspire to do. His grandmother cuts out pieces of brown paper bags for David to draw on. After high school David works in a factory and plays in a rock-and-roll band. After art school he illustrates textbooks, waiting for the opportunity to create his own book. Pig Pig is one of his most popular characters. As an artist, David finds it easier to portray character development in animals than people.

▶ **WRITING TIP** David says, "I'm convinced that stories find me, not the other way around—and if I'm not prepared, they move on, perhaps never to return. That's why I try to be ready. I always have pen and paper nearby." Encourage students to carry small notebooks and to take notes of what they see and hear.

EVENTS

1859 French tightrope walker Charles Blondin crosses Niagrara Falls on a 1,100-foot-long cable 160 feet above the water. Twenty-five thousand spectators are watching. Five days later, he crosses again—blindfolded and pushing a wheelbarrow.

▶ **READ MORE** In *Mirette and Bellini Cross Niagara Falls,* Emily Arnold McCully continues the adventures of Mirette and Bellini, which began in her Caldecott Medal book *Mirette on the High Wire,* where Emily depicts the high wire act of Mirette and the "Great Bellini" above the rooftops of Paris—and makes some nice points about conquering one's fears.

1964 In his Caldecott Medal acceptance speech for *Where the Wild Things Are,* Maurice Sendak points out that fantasy gives children the "best means they have for taming Wild Things." Maurice says, "Max is my bravest and therefore my dearest creation. Like all children, he believes in a flexible world of fantasy and reality, a world where a child can skip from one to the other and back again in the sure belief that both really exist." Maurice says in his other picture books Max appears as Kenny, Martin, and Rosie. "They all have the same need to master the uncontrollable and frightening aspects of their lives, and they all turn to fantasy to accomplish this."

1991 In his Newbery Medal acceptance speech for *Maniac Magee,* Jerry Spinelli says that he was asleep at 12:30 A.M., half an hour after midnight, when the phone rang and he was told he had won the Newbery. He and his wife Eileen, also a writer, talked until 4 A.M. about the news. At 7 A.M. they went out for breakfast, where he celebrated with French toast and bacon. He says, "I never get bacon."

JULY

Most of my life I've subscribed to a rule that can be found in the Chinese book of wisdom *I Ching*: perseverance furthers.

Emily Arnold McCully,
Caldecott Medal acceptance
speech

BIRTHDAY

1939 Emily Arnold McCully is born, in Galesburg, Illinois. She is, in her words, a "daredevil child." When Emily wins the Caldecott Medal for *Mirette on the High Wire*, a librarian who remembers being at camp with her when she was nine years old writes, "Those counselors had heart failure when you used to hang from the rafters in the old barn." Emily says her mother, who was a teacher, stood over her when she drew, encouraging her to be accurate. She recalls, "There never was a period of stick figures and happy suns for me, but instead the discipline of daily practice, the elusive goal, the pain of failure. This wasn't a grim ordeal; I did it because I was fascinated and fulfilled." When she is young, Emily draws "two-minute" portraits for twenty-five cents each at Memorial Day town picnics.

EVENT

1975 In his Caldecott Medal acceptance speech for *Arrow to the Sun*, a Pueblo Indian tale, Gerald McDermott worries that children's visual perceptions, "instead of being cultivated, are eradicated." Gerald says it is too easy to blame advertising and television, but that we need to look to the visual experience of the picture book, to distinguish good art from bad art. "A picture book of artistic integrity will often be the only place where a child can expand his imagination and direct his gaze toward beauty."

JULY

Bad things started not long after school had ended and Mom was leaving me home alone all day because she had to work.

Jack Gantos,
Joey Pigza Loses Control

BIRTHDAYS

1919 Jean Craighead George is born, in Washington, D.C. In her Newbery Medal acceptance speech for *Julie of the Wolves*, Jean describes her research on wolves and concludes, "If there is an animal who might raise a human child, it is the puppy-loving, communicative wolf, who is sophisticated enough to share. To me, the ancient statue of Romulus and Remus is a symbol of the continuity between the lower forms of life and civilized man." Jean remembers that her favorite books as a child were *Heidi* and *Bambi*, "The books, not the Disney movie versions." She also remembers *The Adventures of Tom Sawyer* as a favorite. "The wonder of his language spurred my brothers and me on to our own adventures."

1951 Jack Gantos is born, in Mount Pleasant, Pennsylvania. In first grade, he is in the Bluebird reading group, which he later finds out is for slow readers. When Jack is in second grade, his fifth-grade sister gets a diary, and he insists on having one too. When she writes, he writes. He doesn't know what to write, so writes "the date, the weather, and what I ate for breakfast, lunch, and dinner." The family moves to Barbados and Jack begins to write about where he catches bugs, about stamps he collects, about the photographs he's collected. Jack keeps journals all through junior high and high school. Later, when an editor tells Jack to "write about what you know," he looks down at the floor under his desk and sees his "lousy, grumpy, hissing creep of a cat" and thus is born the Rotten Ralph series. Jack also writes books for middle graders and young adults. *Joey Pigza Loses Control* is about a seriously hyperactive boy and how he deals with his family and his school.

1962 Christopher Lynch is born, in Boston, Massachusetts. Chris says his writing in graduate school was going nowhere, and then he was lucky enough to get into Jack Gantos's children's writing class. Chris says he starts with character before story, so "I can walk around with them in my head before it is time to sit down and build a world around them. And when you do that, your characters develop their sound, their personalities, their sense of humor or sadness or outrage well before you actually ask them to 'do' anything." When characters are formed, says Chris, then "the process becomes a great game of 'What if.'"

EVENT

1911 Seventeen canvases for N. C. Wyeth's elaborate edition of Robert Louis Stevenson's *Treasure Island* are due at his publisher's. In choosing what parts of the story to illustrate, Wyeth looks for incidents in which he can develop emotions that the author only hints at. Painting nine hours a day, Wyeth loves the work and is excited about the results.

JULY

3

When I wrote the following pages, or rather the bulk of them, I lived alone, in the woods, a mile from any neighbor, in a house which I had built myself, on the shore of Walden Pond, in Concord, Massachusetts, and earned my living by the labor of my hands only.

Henry David Thoreau,
Walden

BIRTHDAYS

1908 M(ary) F(rances) K(ennedy) Fisher is born, in Albion, Michigan. She is raised in Whittier, California. Growing up, she enjoys cooking meals for her family. She also likes to write so she combines her favorite pastimes and writes about food. She writes about meals she has cooked and meals she has eaten.

▶ **WRITING TIP** Following M. F. K. Fisher's belief that life's small moments are important, invite students to write about a food memory. Perhaps it will be the first time they tasted a strange new food or the pleasure of a birthday cake.

▶ **READ MORE** Invite students to choose a poem about food to read to the class.

1949 Christine McDonnell is born, in Southampton, New York. A longtime librarian, Christine says many of Ivy's adventures in *Don't Be Mad, Ivy* are based on her own childhood. Christine says that using the technique of making the minor character in one book the star of the next one means that she knows the characters well, and "it's nice not to have to say goodbye to them at the end of a book."

EVENT

1845 Henry David Thoreau begins his twenty-six-month stay at Walden Pond, where he has built himself a simple cabin. He keeps journals of this attempt to live a life free of "things." Henry grows vegetables and does odd jobs in a nearby village to support himself, but he spends most of the time looking closely at nature, reading, and writing in his journal.

JULY

There's a fish in the backyard! Hobie! Come see!

Jamie Gilson,
Hobie Hanson, Greatest Hero of the Mall

1804 Nathaniel Hathorne is born, in Salem, Massachusetts, the son of a sailor. Nathaniel's father dies when Nathaniel is four. Instead of going to sea as is the family tradition, Nathaniel enrolls at Bowdoin College, determined to be a writer. He adds a *w* to his name: Ha*w*thorne. His famous works include *Twice Told Tales, House of Seven Gables*, and *The Scarlet Letter*.

1826 Stephen Foster is born, in Lawrenceville, Pennsylvania. He is the ninth of ten children. Stephen hates school but loves reading. Without musical training, Stephen writes his first song at age thirteen. After "Oh! Susanna" becomes a big hit in 1948, Stephen makes a full-time career of writing songs. Geographically speaking, the first line of Stephen's "The Old Folks at Home" should be "Way down upon the Suwanee River"; there is no "Swanee River." But Stephen needs a two-syllable name, so he changes Suwanee to Swanee. People say if he'd ever seen the river, he might not have immortalized it. It runs through swamps in Georgia and Florida and the water is as black as coffee.

1933 Jamie Gilson is born, in Beardstown, Illinois, the daughter of a teacher. Jamie writes her humorous books for middle graders in the first person, from the point of view of children. To keep the voice real in her work, Jamie spends a lot of time in schools, sitting in classes, going on an overnight nature study trip with a fifth-grade class, teaching writing to sixth graders. Jamie says this kind of research is a joy.

▶ **WRITE ABOUT IT** Invite student researchers to spend time in kindergarten or first-grade classes, looking for a "voice" with which to tell what school is like for a child in one of those classes.

1941 Stephen Mooser is born, in Fresno, California, the son of a librarian. When Tricia Gardella is compiling *Writers in the Kitchen* and asks Stephen for a recipe, he contributes Eyeball Soup, which is easy. Heat one can of tomato soup and then plop in ten grapes. "Serve with a diabolical chuckle." Stephen provides a second recipe: Vampire Brain Delight, which starts with spaghetti and spaghetti sauce. When he isn't writing books or heating tomato soup, Stephen likes to go treasure hunting on land and sea expeditions.

▶ **WRITING FUN** Invite students to create a funny recipe.

JULY

When you go owling

you don't need words

or warm

or anything but hope.

Jane Yolen,
Owl Moon

BIRTHDAY

1935 John Schoenherr is born, in New York City. In his acceptance speech for the Caldecott Medal, which he wins for illustrating *Owl Moon*, he observes that Jane Yolen's text expresses his own thrill of sharing special experiences in the woods with his children. "I know the feeling of meeting a wild animal on its own ground. I've been face to face with field mice and Kodiak bears, bull moose and wild geese, wild boar and mountain goats, and of course, owls." John adds his wife has been his best friend, putting up with windstorms, snowstorms, caves, deserts, swamps, mountains, and outdoor plumbing. She has stood fast when threatened by moose, bison, wild boar, and bugs. After all that, he says, "We are still best friends."

EVENT

1955 Marcia Brown receives her second Caldecott Medal, this one for *Cinderella*.

▶ **READING TIP** Invite students to find three different versions of Cinderella and to comment on how the different illustrations give the story a different "feel." Then they can examine the texts and see if they are different or similar. For starters, John Steptoe's *Mufaro's Beautiful Daughters: An African Tale* is very different in content and style from Marcia's book. John's book is a Caldecott Honor book, so students can see that winning similar honors doesn't mean that books have similar artistic visions.

JULY

I always wanted to be somebody. If I made it, it's half because I was game enough to take a lot of punishment along the way and half because there were a lot of people who cared enough to help me.

Althea Gibson,
I Always Wanted to Be Somebody

BIRTHDAY

1946 James Browning Wyeth is born, the grandson of N. C. and the son of Andrew. He is known as Jamie. He leaves school after sixth grade and commits himself to a life of painting.

EVENT

1957 Althea Gibson wins the Wimbledon women's singles tennis title. She is the first black tennis star to win the prestigious event.

1971 Louis "Satchmo" Armstrong dies. His nickname, Satchmo, is a shortened version of "satchel-mouth" and refers to his large lips and huge, puffed-out cheeks when he plays his trumpet. E. B. White so admires Armstrong's musical ability that when he writes a book about a trumpeter swan, he names it Louis.

▶ **ALL ABOUT NAMES** Invite students to tell (and write) how they got their own nicknames.

JULY

"Yahoo!" Freddie Fox shot over the crest of the hill, his skis kicking up a spray of snow behind him.

Wendy Watson,
Tales for a Winter's Eve

BIRTHDAY

1942 Wendy Watson is born, in Paterson, New Jersey. She grows up in rural Vermont, surroundings reflected in her illustrations. Wendy collaborates on many of her books with her sister Clyde Watson.

▶ **READING FUN** Wendy's rhymes are short, fun, and easy to memorize. Encourage students to learn a rhyme today.

EVENTS

1757 Benjamin Franklin publishes *Poor Richard Improved, Being an Almanac &c. for the Year of Our Lord, 1758*. Some of Poor Richard's advice that is still repeated today includes "The early bird gets the worm" and "Early to bed, early to rise, makes a man healthy, wealthy, and wise."

▶ **READING/WRITING CONNECTION** Invite students to collect adages and then choose one to use as the moral for an original fable they write.

▶ **READ MORE** Jim Anton's *Wise Wacky Proverbs: The Truth Behind Everyday Sayings* examines what proverbs really mean—and whether it's fact or nonsense.

1882 *The Adventures of Pinocchio*, by Carlo Collodi, is first published. Among others, Maurice Sendak and William Steig pay great tribute to this book, saying it was a favorite and influential book of their childhood.

1996 In her Caldecott Medal acceptance speech for *Officer Buckle and Gloria*, Peggy Rathmann notes that she wrote and illustrated the story as an assignment for a writing class. The assignment was to write and illustrate a story that could not be understood by reading the text alone. Peggy says that Officer Buckle is the words; Gloria is the pictures. Turning this class assignment into a published book takes Peggy four years. While collecting the 101 safety tips for the endpapers and the bulletin boards, Peggy offers her nieces, nephew, and young friends twenty-five dollars for any safety tip that her editor accepts. Peggy is pleased that elementary school children contribute to an award-winning book.

► **READING FUN** Invite students to read the safety tips in the book and see whether they can think of any more.

1996 In her Newbery Medal acceptance speech for *The Midwife's Apprentice*, Karen Cushman says, "As children are what they eat and hear and experience, so too they are what they read. This is why I write what I do, about strong young women who in one way or another take responsibility for their own lives; about tolerance, thoughtfulness, and caring; about choosing what is life-affirming and generous; about the ways that people are the same and the ways they are different and how rich that makes us all."

JULY

The scene: The Egyptian Sculpture Gallery of the British Museum in London. The time: Now.

James Cross Giblin,
The Riddle of the Rosetta Stone: Key to Ancient Egypt

BIRTHDAYS

1621 Jean de la Fontaine is born, in Chateau-Thierry, France. His more than 240 fables are well known to French schoolchildren.

► **READING/WRITING CONNECTION** Show students that there is a close relationship between fables and proverbs. For example, "Slow and steady wins the race" comes from the fable "The Tortoise and the Hare." Invite student pairs to choose a proverb for which they can create a fable. They can act it out before they write it down. Here are a few possibilities: *people in glass houses shouldn't throw stones; look before you leap; too many cooks spoil the broth; don't count your chickens before they hatch.*

1933 James Cross Giblin is born, in Columbus, Ohio, an only child. A noted editor, he is also a noted nonfiction author.

► **WRITING TIP** James says the trick in writing is to "recognize a good idea when it comes along." Once on a plane he sat next to a chimney sweep. That work sounded fascinating and when he got off the plane James researched chimney sweeps and wrote a book on the topic. Invite students to look for interesting topics for two days, compiling a list of possibilities. Then they can choose one to research.

EVENT

2000 *Harry Potter and the Goblet of Fire* goes on sale at 12:01 A.M., with an initial printing of 3.8 million copies. It becomes the fastest-selling book in publishing history. Bookstores host pajama parties and other extravaganzas for eager customers who have been in line for hours. Thirty-five million copies of the first three Harry books are already in print, in thirty-five languages. Stephen King writes in the *New York Times* that he has waited for this installment "with almost as much interest as any Potter-besotted kid." And he isn't disappointed. When asked how many words are in the first Harry Potter book, J. K. Rowling replies, "Eighty-six thousand, nine hundred and something." She also reveals that Harry "will come of age at seventeen in the final book."

JULY

Before this year I used to sit on the stoop, and my mother used to comb my hair into corn rows almost every day.

June Jordan,
Kimako's Story

BIRTHDAYS

1936 June Jordan is born in New York City. She is a poet and the author of *His Own Where* and *Kimako's Story*.

1941 Nancy Farmer is born, in Phoenix, Arizona. She says growing up in and working at the desk of a hotel on the Arizona/Mexico border was wonderful preparation for writing. She listens to the stories of the guests, who include retired railroad men, rodeo riders, and circus employees. After college, Nancy works in the Peace Corps in India and as a lab technician in Africa.

1842 When writer Nathaniel Hawthorne and his bride Sophia Peabody move into their home in Concord, Massachusetts, they find that their friend Henry David Thoreau has already plowed a garden for them.

1974 Margot Zemach receives the Caldecott Medal for *Duffy and the Devil.* In her acceptance speech she admits, "I would much rather be sitting down behind you than standing here before you, since the way I express myself is by drawing pictures." Zemach mentions that she was very good at roller-skating as a child, noting that it is a good sport for loners.

JULY

10

Mommy says her nose is running.

Fred Gwynne,
The Sixteen Hand Horse

BIRTHDAYS

1875 Mary McLeod Bethune is born, the child of former slaves. She is the fifteenth of seventeen children. With $1.50, Mary founds the Daytona Normal and Industrial Institute for Negro Girls, which becomes Bethune-Cookman College. In 1935, she founds the National Council of Negro Women. A social activist and impassioned speaker and advisor to President Franklin Roosevelt, Mary observes, "I have unselfishly given my best, and I thank God I have lived long enough to see the fruits of it."

▶ **READ MORE** There are a number of good biographies about Mary, including those by Eloise Greenfield, Patricia McKissack, and Milton Meltzer.

1916 Martin Provensen is born, in Chicago. He wins a scholarship to the Art Institute of Chicago, transferring later to the University of California in Berkeley. Martin creates storyboards for Walt Disney for such films as *Fantasia* and *Dumbo.* He meets his wife and collaborator, Alice, when they work in the same animation studio. They create beautiful picture books together for more than forty years, winning the Caldecott Medal for *The Glorious Flight.*

1926 Fred Gwynne is born, in New York City. He is the author of *The King Who Rained, The Sixteen Hand Horse, Chocolate Moose for Dinner,* and *Pondlarker.*

▶ **WORD FUN** Invite students to illustrate familiar phrases that can have more than one meaning. They can imitate Fred Gwynne and show the double meaning through their illustrations for the phrases.

EVENT

1841 Henry David Thoreau writes in his journal, "A slight sound at evening lifts me up by the ears, and makes life seem inexpressibly sere and grand." More than a hundred years later, in July 1954, E. B. White writes a tribute to Thoreau's *Walden,* saying it is his favorite book, one he takes with him everywhere. "I keep it about me in much the same way one carries a handkerchief—for relief in moments of deflux-ion or despair." White gives copies of the book to his wife, to their grandchildren, to friends. He says all graduating college students should be given a copy to help them appreciate the simplicity of Thoreau's life and words.

▶ **READ MORE** Inspired by a passage from *Walden,* D. B. Johnson's *Henry Hikes to Fitchburg* depicts a charming incident in the lives of two friends who have very different approaches to life.

11

I assure you that you can pick up more information when you are listening than when you are talking.

E. B. White,
Trumpet of the Swan

BIRTHDAYS

1899 E(lwyn) B(rooks) White is born, in Mount Vernon, New York. He is the youngest of six children. He never likes his name, saying, "My mother just hung it on me because she'd run out of names. I was her sixth child." From college on, to his relief, he is called Andy. The first president of Cornell was Andrew D. White, and the nickname is bestowed on all students there named White. After graduating from Cornell, Andy writes for the *New Yorker* for the rest of his life. Of *Stuart Little*, White says Stuart's journey is the journey everybody takes "in search of what is perfect and unattainable." Of *Charlotte's Web*, he says, "Before attempting the book, I studied spiders and boned up on them."

▶ **READING/WRITING CONNECTION** In an interview with Lee Bennett Hopkins, Andy says, "In *real* life, a family doesn't have a child who looks like a mouse; in *real* life, a spider doesn't spin words in her web. In *real* life, a swan doesn't blow a trumpet. But real life is only one kind of life—there is also the life of the imagination."

1929 James Stevenson is born, in New York City. He is the author-illustrator of many books, including *July, Emma, If I Owned a Candy Factory, That Dreadful Day, When I Was Nine, The Worst Person in the World,* and *Yuck!* In his autobiographical *Higher on the Door,* James recalls that even though his brother calls him a scaredy-cat and afraid of everything, that isn't true. "The only things I was afraid of were: bees, hospitals, bats, snakes, the dentist, tough kids, iodine on cuts, ticks on Jocko, lightning, the bull that lived in the meadow down the road, and the dark."

▶ **WRITING TIP** Inviting students to list their fears can be a powerful impetus to storytelling. Invite students to list things they are afraid of and things that don't scare them.

1944 Patricia Polacco is born in Lansing, Michigan. She spends the school months in Oakland, California, and her summers in Michigan, near her Babushka's farm. Patricia says her favorite book as a child is *Millions of Cats,* by Wanda Gag. "I loved her illustrations." Because of dyslexia and dysnumeria, schoolwork is difficult for Patricia. Rocking rhythmically in a rocking chair helps her then and continues to help her as an accomplished storyteller and artist. She has twelve rocking chairs in her house, and she keeps writing pads and pens next to them—for when she gets a good idea. Patricia has a Ph.D. in art history, specializing in Russian and Greek painting and iconographic history.

EVENT

1982 Chris Van Allsburg receives the Caldecott Medal for *Jumanji.* In his acceptance speech, Chris thanks a lot of people—including seventeenth-century Dutch painter Jan Vermeer and nineteenth-century French painter Edgar Degas—and children who let him know how much they like his books. Chris says, "Children can possess a book in a way they can never possess a video game, a TV show, or a Darth Vader doll. A book comes alive when they read it. They give it life themselves by understanding it."

JULY

12

"Where shall I sleep, Grandfather?" she asked.

"Where you like," he replied.

Johanna Spryi,
Heidi

BIRTHDAYS

1817 Henry David Thoreau is born, in Concord, Massachusetts. The author of *Walden* and *Civil Disobedience*, Henry David is considered one of the most influential figures in American thought. He speaks out for individual conscience—and spends a night in jail as an act of civil disobedience—and against conformity and the piling up of possessions.

1827 Johanna Spyri is born, in Hirzel, Switzerland. Johanna writes *Heidi* to amuse her young son, drawing on her own childhood for characters and settings. She publishes more than forty additional titles, but this is the one readers remember.

1947 Gayle Pearson is born, in Chicago, Illinois. Gayle enjoys doing research for historical fiction, digging up little-known facts and weaving them into a story. She likes to think about what's different then and now—and why. Gayle believes historical fiction can be one more way to learn.

EVENT

1983 Marcia Brown receives her third Caldecott Medal, this one for *Shadow*. In her acceptance speech Marcia recalls her 1975 trip to East Africa, where she experiences "a land of dazzling light that carved bold shapes relentlessly against mysterious shadow, colorful rocks still displaying the scars of the geological upheavals that had formed them, savannahs of golden grasses, and brilliant sunsets before the sudden fall of night. Proud peoples seemed caught between past and present. Magnificent animals were both hunters and prey. The shadow of scavengers hung greedy over the burning land." Marcia confides, "I trusted children to understand many more emotional levels of shadow than the obvious."

JULY

13

Sing to the sun
It will listen

Ashley Bryan, "Song,"
Sing to the Sun

BIRTHDAYS

1918 Marcia Brown is born, in Rochester, New York, the daughter of a minister. Marcia says as a child she reads and draws constantly. Every Christmas she and her sisters receive paints and crayons and large pads of drawing paper. Marcia remembers the library being an important part of her childhood. When the family moves to a new city, she gets a library card before the family has even unpacked. It seems fitting, then, that Marcia's first four books are created while she is working in the New York Public Library. While working on *Cinderella,* Marcia spends months sketching clothing and furniture in museums and libraries.

1923 Ashley Bryan is born, in New York City. He writes his first alphabet book when he is in kindergarten. "As we learned each letter of the alphabet, we drew a picture for it. The teacher gave us construction paper for the cover and taught us to sew those pages together. That ABC was my first book. I was author, illustrator, editor, publisher, and binder, and I also got rave reviews for this limited edition, one of a kind!" Ashley emphasizes, "As a black American, I have African roots. Retelling and illustrating African tales has kept me close to African sources."

▶ **READ MORE** As an adult, Ashley creates a unique alphabet book: *Ashley Bryan's ABC of African American Poetry*, containing an A-to-Z look at twenty-five poems and one African American spiritual. The selections are short: encourage students to memorize selections of their choice for a choral presentation.

1958 Michael Dooling is born, in Marlton, New Jersey. Growing up, Michael plays baseball, builds tree houses, and has a paper route. Encouraged by his mother, Michael also loves to read and draw. Michael loves adventure stories, mysteries, and especially "period" stories with characters in costumes, such as Sherlock Holmes and Blackbeard. Today, Michael still likes characters in costumes. In fact, he poses in costume as a model for some characters he draws for his books. "Every day at my house is Halloween," Michael says. His family and friends also pose in costume for figures in his books. Michael also travels to historic sites in preparation for illustrating such books as *The Amazing Life of Benjamin Franklin.* He takes his costumes on school visits, giving children a behind-the-scenes look at how he creates a book.

JULY

One bright sunny morning in the shadow of the steeple

By the Relief Office I saw my people;

As they stood hungry, I stood there wondering,

Is this land made for you and me?

Woodie Guthrie,
"This Land Is Your Land"

BIRTHDAYS

1912 Woodrow Guthrie is born, in Okemah, Oklahoma. Everyone calls him Woody. The composer of more than a thousand songs, his most famous one is "This Land Is Your Land." Woody says, "Stick up for what you know is right. This land was made for you and me."

▶ **READ MORE** The spectacular *This Land Is Your Land,* illustrated by Kathy Jakobsen, puts the song that has been called the real U. S. anthem in context, providing the complete lyrics as well as a biographical scrapbook and tribute by folksinger Pete Seeger.

1921 Leon Garfield is born, in Brighton, England. He becomes a biochemist but then leaves this career in 1966 to write full time. Leon says he has a large family, and pieces of all of them have appeared in his books, but not one of them has noticed. Leon says what he loves most of all is a good story.

1927 Peggy Parish is born, in South Carolina. Her fans won't be surprised to learn that she becomes a third-grade teacher (she knows third graders' sense of humor so well). The author of the popular Amelia Bedelia series says, "I don't try to teach anything in my stories—I write just for fun."

▶ **WORD PLAY** Encourage students to take some of the word difficulties Amelia encounters and turn them into riddles.

1953 Laura Joffe Numeroff is born, in Brooklyn, New York, the daughter of an artist and a teacher. Growing up, Laura reads at least six books a week. She has worked as a merry-go-round operator and as a private investigator. Her most popular books are the If You Give a Mouse . . . series.

JULY

If you really want to hear about it, the first thing you'll probably want to know is where I was born, and what my lousy childhood was like, and how my parents were occupied and all before they had me, and all that David Copperfield kind of crap, but I don't feel like going into it, if you want to know the truth.

J. D. Salinger,
The Catcher in the Rye

BIRTHDAYS

1779 Clement Moore is born, in New York City. Professor of Oriental and Greek literature at the Episcopal General Theological Seminary, Moore is best known for the poem that begins "'Twas the night before Christmas," which it is said he wrote for his daughter who was ill. Over the years, many parodies have been written. In *Author Unknown: On the Trail of Anonymous,* Vassar professor of literature Don Foster uses textual analysis to prove that Clement Moore did not write the verse.

1796 Thomas Bulfinch is born, in Newton, Massachusetts. Thomas works as a clerk in the Merchants' Bank of Boston, a job he holds his whole life. He likes the job because it leaves him time for his real love—history and literature. Thomas is best known as the author of *Mythology* and *The Age of Fable.*

▶ **READ MORE** Invite students to read a myth—and to share the story with the class.

EVENTS

1868 Louisa May Alcott finishes *Little Women.*

1951 Little Brown publishes J. D. Salinger's *The Catcher in the Rye.* The novel, a Book-of-the-Month Club selection, creates a sensation and it maintains its popularity over the decades.

JULY

16

I Raise My Voice Most
High, This Night,

in praise of Milk Duds:
most improbably

named candy in its
yellow box. . . .

Arnold Adoff,
Chocolate Dreams

BIRTHDAYS

1935 Arnold Adoff is born, in the South Bronx, New York City. As a child, Arnold remembers reading *Little Women*, Sholem Aleichem, *The Five Little Peppers*, and *The Story of the Chanukah*. His favorite poets are Dylan Thomas, e. e. cummings, Rilke, Marianne Moore, Gwendolyn Brooks, and Robert Hayden. Arnold says, "I want my anthologies of Black American writing to make Black kids strong in their knowledge of themselves and their great literary heritage—give them facts and people and power. I also want these Black books of mine to give knowledge to White kids around the country, so that mutual respect and understanding will come from mutual learning."

▶ **WRITING TIP** Arnold says writing is a small part of what he does. Rewriting is the thing. "I can do as many as seventy-five drafts of a single poem."

▶ **READING TIP** Arnold says because poems say and sing at the same time the reader should read each poem at least three time, the first time for meaning, the second for how it sings, the third for structure.

1952 Richard Egielski is born, in Queens, New York, the son of a police lieutenant. Richard remembers being frustrated as a boy by the fact that if he pressed too hard with his No. 2 pencil on lined, loose-leaf paper, he would make holes in the paper. Plus the lines got in the way. Then, for Christmas, Richard is thrilled to get black charcoal pencils, thick drawing paper, and a gummy, kneaded eraser. He likes drawing pictures based on movies: King Kong, Frankenstein, dinosaurs, medieval knights, Roman soldiers, ships, planes, and flying saucers. He also draws cartoon characters he sees on television and copies cartoon characters from comics in the newspaper. Going on a school trip to an art museum makes Richard imagine himself as an artist. Maurice Sendak, Richard's teacher at the Parsons School of Design, introduces him to writer Arthur Yorinks. Their collaboration, *Hey, Al*, wins Richard the Caldecott Medal. Richard says, "An important teacher is one who exposes you to something new and points out a direction you otherwise might have missed."

▶ **READING/WRITING CONNECTION** Richard's version of *The Gingerbread Boy* gives the tale a big-city twist, with the Gingerbread Boy being chased through New York City by rats, construction workers, and a mounted policeman. Invite students to choose another fairy tale to retell in a city setting.

JULY

17

Do not ask a snake's
advice

Do not bathe in
chocolate pudding

Karla Kuskin,
"Rules"

BIRTHDAYS

1889 Erle Stanley Gardner, the mystery writer best known for his Perry Mason series, is born. After giving up a lucrative law practice to write mysteries full time, Erle writes eighty-two Mason novels and, under the name A. A. Fair, writes twenty-nine novels about the private eye Bertha Cool. Keeping to a strict schedule, Erle writes four thousand words a day, producing a new novel every six weeks. Erle keeps to this schedule well into his eighties.

1932 Karla Kuskin is born, in New York City. When Karla is a young child, she makes up rhymes and her mother writes them down and reads them to her. Karla says having teachers who read poetry aloud at school greatly influences her decision to write poetry herself. Karla writes and illustrates her first book, *Roar and More*, as a part of her thesis at Yale. Karla says, "Writing prose makes me listen for stories. But if I am writing poetry I concentrate more on the rhythms and sounds of words, and on details." Karla notes that "Write About a Radish" begins "as advice to myself on a day when I was determined to write a poem about something nobody else had ever written a poem about."

▶ **READING/WRITING TIP** Ask students to create a class list of topics-you-might-not-think-anybody-would-write-a-poem-about. Once they have a list, encourage students to scour poetry anthologies for poems on these topics.

▶ **WRITING TIP** Although Karla uses rhyme, she advises children against it, because rhyme is such a hurdle. "It freezes all the originality they have, and they use someone else's rhymes. . . . And yet their images are so original." Karla encourages children to get a visual image of the object they are writing about, urging them to write descriptions in short, easy lines.

1946 Chris Crutcher is born, in Dayton Ohio, the son of an Air Force pilot. He grows up in Cascade, Idaho. Although his parents love reading, Chris confesses that he is not well read. "I haven't read the classics in any but comic book form, and I do a horrible job of keeping up with new writers." Chris says in high school he reads only one book. He makes up titles when he writes book reports, choosing authors' names out of the telephone book. But Chris feels that the one book he read, *To Kill a Mockingbird*, influenced his career as a storyteller. "Stories like Harper Lee's were the only kind I had any desire to tell: stories about real life as I see it, about my sense of justice and injustice." Chris has worked as a teacher, school director, therapist, concrete-bridge-beam builder, and gas station attendant. He bases his work on real life as he sees it from his own experience and from working with inner-city kids.

JULY

18

As was the custom in those days, Chief Wu had taken two wives. Each wife in her turn had presented Wu with a baby daughter.

Yeh-Shen,
as retold by Ai-Ling Louie

BIRTHDAYS

1941 Jerry Stanley is born, in Highland Park, Michigan, the son of a saxophonist. Jerry confesses that when he was young the last thing he thought he'd grow up to be is a writer. He hated the lifeless books he encountered in school. In high school, when he passes only woodshop and gym, he is expelled. Later, he attends community college and goes on to earn his Ph.D. in history. Drawn to stories of people who overcome adversity against great odds, Jerry researches the Weedpatch School, opened during the Depression for the children of migrant workers in California, and writes *Children of the Dust Bowl*.

▶ **WRITING TIP** Jerry says, "Good writing requires good thinking and good thinking requires good reading, reading, reading."

1949 Ai-Ling Louie is born, in New York City. The daughter of a teacher, Ai-Ling also becomes a teacher. Ai-Ling first hears "Yeh-Shen," a Cinderella story dating from ninth century B.C. China, from her mother, who had learned it from her mother, who had learned it from her mother. Ai-Ling first writes the tale for her students. Ed Young's illustrations for the published version include a copy of an ancient Chinese text.

▶ **READ MORE** Invite students to read Cinderella tales from other cultures. They can try *Sootface: An Ojibwa Cinderella Story; Cendrillon; Little Gold Star,* by Robert D. San Souci, and *Raisel's Riddle,* by Erica Silverman. Challenge students to then research the culture and look for evidence of some unique cultural details revealed in the tale. For example, if the authors didn't tell them that Sootface is Ojibwa; Raisel, Jewish; and Yeh-Shen, Chinese, how might details in the story reveal this to them?

▶ **THINK ABOUT IT** In her notes to "Cinder Elephant," in *A Wolf at the Door and Other Retold Fairy Tales*, edited by Ellen Datlow and Terri Windling, Jane Yolen confesses that her dislike of the Disney *Cinderella* inspires and informs this tale.

EVENT

1991 At the end of a typical July week, Marty Doyle has done what he has done for the past seven years—given away four thousand books at the Traveler Restaurant off Interstate 84 at the Connecticut-Massachusetts border. The Traveler, which he owns, is billed as the world's only literary roadside restaurant. Marty, a seventh-grade dropout, loves to read. When his wife urges him to get rid of the piles of old books lying around the house, he starts offering them to customers at the restaurant. The idea catches on, and people begin asking for books. Marty starts going to auctions and estate sales, buying ten thousand books at a time. He buys fifty tons of books a year—to give away. Every customer gets a free book, and while waiting for food they can browse in the basement, where Marty has opened a used bookstore.

▶ **THINK ABOUT IT** Invite students to consider where they might give away books. For starters, they might consider homeless shelters, homes for the elderly, hospitals, a school without a library. Then they can conduct a book drive and do it!

JULY

He's a lionhearted man,

he's a road hog in his

car. . . .

Eve Merriam, "Mr. Zoo,"
Chortles

BIRTHDAYS

1713 John Newbery is born. A London bookseller, he is the first English publisher of books for children. The American Library Association names the famed Newbery Medal, given annually for the most distinguished contribution to American literature for children, in his honor.

1916 Eve Merriam is born, in Germantown, Pennsylvania, a suburb of Philadelphia. Eve recalls that as a young child growing up in Philadelphia she is enthralled by the sounds of words, by their musicality, and by the fact that if you say something alliterative like "Peter, Peter, Pumpkin Eater," it can be very funny. Of if you recite something like "The Highwayman came riding, riding up to the old inn door," it is exciting because you can hear a whole orchestra with your voice. Eve thinks taking tap dancing lessons when she is young convinces her to get movement into her poetry. "What can a poem do?" asks Eve. "Just about everything." Often lyrical, often rollicking, always provocative, no one has more fun with words than Eve Merriam and her readers.

▶ **READING TIP 1** Eve says, "Read it aloud! Read it aloud! Read it aloud!"

▶ **READING TIP 2** Eve says, "Read a serious poem. Read a light poem. Keep sharing different types of poems until there is something for all kids to like."

▶ **RECITING OUT LOUD** Invite students to choose an Eve Merriam poem to learn to recite by heart. Then hold an Eve Merriam celebration. Small groups may choose to team up and do a choral rendering of a poem. If the classroom can go online, invite students to submit reviews of their favorite Eve Merriam book at *Amazon.com.*

EVENT

1943 The opening episode in the cartoon series "Mickey Mouse on a Secret Mission" is released. The series continues through October 20, 1943.

20

Once upon a time in a wild Wyoming town there lived a sturdy girl named Fanny Agnes. She worked from sunup to sundown on her daddy's farm, but she had her dreams.

Caralyn Buehner,
Fanny's Dream

BIRTHDAYS

1959 Mark Buehner is born, in Salt Lake City, Utah. He is the youngest of seven children. He remembers his father drawing pictures to entertain him while they sit in church. Mark says he practically lives in a sandbox until he is twelve, turning it into army trenches, forts, and a pizza hut. In school, Mark can't read as well as other children, but he loves to draw. He particularly remembers *Pierre*, a small book by Maurice Sendak. He doesn't just read it; he memorizes it. Mark takes his first oil painting class when he is sixteen and loves it. Mark still prefers to work in oils. He has collaborated on a number of books with his wife, Caralyn.

▶ **READ MORE** The homespun *Fanny's Dream* is a whimsical, wonderful Cinderella variant, with farmer Heber Jensen appearing when Fanny is expecting—or at least hoping for—a fairy godmother. The robust pictures perfectly mirror the text.

EVENT

2000 *Who's in the Hall?*, by Betsy Hearne, is published. Hey! What's up with Willy-Nilly, Wag and Wave, Dizzy-Lizzy, Lowdown-Rowan, Ratty-Ryan, Nelly-Belly, and Wicked-Nick? By the time you get to the end you'll be able to answer this question—and you'll also know who's in the hall.

21

A man can be destroyed but not defeated.

Ernest Hemingway,
The Old Man and the Sea

BIRTHDAYS

1899 Ernest Hemingway is born, in Oak Park, Illinois. A reporter for the *Kansas City Star*, he becomes an ambulance driver for the Red Cross in World War I. In 1953, *The Old Man and the Sea* wins the Pulitzer Prize. In 1954, Ernest is awarded the Nobel Prize for the body of his work. Ernest tells a reporter that he wrote the ending of *A Farewell to Arms* thirty-nine times before he got it right. Toward the end of his career, a back injury forces him to write standing up. Other writers who prefer to be on their feet when writing include Thomas Jefferson, Lewis Carroll, William Saroyan, and Thomas Wolfe. Wolfe is so tall that he puts his yellow pad on top of the refrigerator and writes.

1923 William Wise is born, in New York City. William is a prolific author, mostly of nonfiction titles, including *In the Time of the Dinosaurs* and *Detective Pinkerton and Mr. Lincoln*.

▶ **READ MORE** In *Dinosaurs Forever*, William Wise combines his love of words, science, and dinosaurs in a collection of dinosaur poems. It is instructive for students to find out whether such lines as "It's said the ghost of Stegosaurus/Met a scholar once,/Who sneered, "Your brain was very small!/I'm sure you were a dunce!" are pure fancy for the sake of rhyme or if they embed any factual information. And did the Stegosaurus roam the Earth for fifty million years? Or is Wise making that up? Invite students to become dinosaur sleuths—and learn something about poetry at the same time.

1953 Rika Lesser is born, in Brooklyn, New York, the daughter of a teacher. An eminent translator of German and Swedish poetry as well as the author of her own poems, Rika is fascinated by things that seem more readily expressed in one language than another. Because she likes to learn languages, she's now working on Finnish. Rika's retelling of *Hansel and Gretel* is illustrated by Paul Zelinsky.

EVENTS

1855 Ralph Waldo Emerson writes to Walt Whitman, "I greet you at the beginning of a great career. . . ."

▶ **READING/WRITING CONNECTION** Show students a selection of "first books" by new authors/illustrators. Invite them to choose a favorite and write that author, sending greetings and good wishes at the beginning of a great career.

1976 Leo and Diane Dillon receive the Caldecott Medal for *Why Mosquitoes Buzz in People's Ears.* Peter Parnall's *Hawk, I'm Your Brother* is named a Caldecott Honor book.

JULY

There was once a velveteen rabbit, and in the beginning he was really splendid. He was fat and bunchy, as a rabbit should be; his coat was spotted brown and white, he had real thread whiskers, and his ears were lined with pink sateen.

Margery Williams,
The Velveteen Rabbit

BIRTHDAYS

1844 William Archibald Spooner is born, in London, England. From his name is derived the term *spoonerism,* meaning an accidental transposition of the (usually) initial sounds of two or more words. During World War I, he tells his students, "When our boys come home from France, we will have the hags flung out." He called British farmers "noble tons of soil."

▶ **WORD FUN** Challenge students to invent some spoonerisms.

1849 Emma Lazarus is born, in New York City. The daughter of a wealthy businessman, Emma is touched by the plight of Russian immigrants who have fled to America to escape terrible persecution. Emma's concern for the immigrants inspires a sonnet, "The New Colossus." She compares the ancient Colossus of Rhodes with the Statue of Liberty, which she calls "Mother of Exiles." In 1903, the words of Emma's "The New Colossus" are engraved on a plaque on Liberty's pedestal.

1881 Margery Williams Bianco is born, in London, England, the daughter of a barrister and classical scholar. Her father believes children should be taught to read early and then have no regular teaching until they are ten. Margery loves three volumes of natural history and says, "I knew every reptile, bird, and beast in those volumes long before I knew my multiplication table." After her father's death when she is seven, Margery's family moves to the United States. Writing as Margery Williams, she is the author of the beloved *The Velveteen Rabbit.*

1948 S(usan) E(loise) Hinton is born, in Oklahoma. She writes the phenomenally popular *The Outsiders* when she is sixteen years old, a junior in high school. The publisher decides to use Susan's initials rather than her name—to disguise the fact that this book filled with male characters and violence is written by a young woman. When movies are made of her books, Susan makes cameo appearances.

EVENT

1893 Katherine Lee Bates scribbles the lines of "America the Beautiful" in a notebook while on a trip to Colorado. Katherine, a young professor at Wellesley College, in Massachusetts, has kept a diary since she was nine years old. She continues this habit while riding the train from Boston to Colorado Springs. For example, after seeing Pike's Peak, she writes in her diary, "Most glorious scenery I ever beheld." She also writes a few lines of poetry:

> O beautiful for halcyon skies
> For amber waves of grain
> For purple mountain majesties
> Above the enameled plain!
> America! America! God shed his grace on thee. . . .

▶ **WORD STUDY** Invite students to find out which words Katherine changed in the final version—and think about why she might have made these changes.

▶ **READ MORE** *Purple Mountain Majesties: The Story of Katharine Lee Bates and "America the Beautiful,"* by Barbara Younger, is a moving and provocative human account of the creative process behind a national icon.

JULY

23

Dear Henry,

Please come to my party next Sunday. . . . Don't be late.

Love,
Clara

> Robert Quackenbush,
> *Henry's Important Date*

BIRTHDAY

1929 Robert Quackenbush is born, in Hollywood, California. The two stories that make the greatest impression on him are Hans Christian Andersen's *The Steadfast Tin Soldier* and Oscar Wilde's *The Selfish Giant*. Years later, his first book commissions are to illustrate these very two stories. Robert feels his own "never give up" attitude comes from *The Steadfast Tin Soldier,* his willingness to be compassionate and flexible from *The Selfish Giant*. Robert notes, "Humor became a key to survival in my family when I was growing up during the Depression and World War II. Thus, humor became the keynote of all the books I wrote. . . . I want young readers to know that as long as we keep our sense of humor, our spirits cannot be crushed." Once his son is born, in 1974, Robert dedicates every one of his books to Piet, who is named for the Dutch painter Piet Mondrian and for Pieter Quackenbosch, the family ancestor who came to America from Holland in 1660.

EVENT

1846 In protest over slavery and the United States' involvement in the Mexican War, Henry David Thoreau refuses to pay his $1 poll tax and spends the night in jail. According to legend, Ralph Waldo Emerson visits his friend in jail and asks, "Henry, why are you here?" Henry replies, "Waldo, why are you not here?" In any case, Henry is freed the next day when some unidentified person pays his tax. Henry protests and the constable threatens to use force to get him out of the jail. So, "as mad as the devil," Henry leaves the jail, has a shoe mended in town, attends a huckleberry party, and returns to Walden Pond. Henry's written account of the incident persuades Leo Tolstoi and the young Mahatma Gandhi to advocate civil disobedience.

JULY

24

Joe could not remember a time when he hadn't known Maggie.

> Amy Ehrlich,
> *Maggie and Silky and Joe*

BIRTHDAYS

1942 Amy Ehrlich is born, in New York City. She is the author of *Leo*, the Zack and Emmie books, the Bunnies books, and several young adult novels.

1959 Miriam Nerlove is born, in Minneapolis, Minnesota. She is the author-illustrator of *I Made a Mistake*, verse based on an old jump-rope rhyme, and *I Meant to Clean My Room Today*, excuses presented in verse.

▶ **WRITING TIP** Students enjoy coming up with their own excuses—and then comparing them with the author's.

All of a sudden we find ourselves standing in the shadow of a giant tuna fish sandwich being delicately airlifted by a helicopter. In the distance another helicopter races off with a jumbo pickle in tow.

Judi Barrett,
Pickles to Pittsburgh,
illustrations by Ron Barrett

1911 Ruth Krauss is born, in Baltimore, Maryland. She writes and reads "all the time" as a child. When she is fifteen, she writes in a book in a secret language her parents can't decipher. After graduating from Parson's School of Fine and Applied Arts, Ruth marries author-artist Crockett Johnson, who illustrates her book *The Carrot Seed.* This book begins as a ten-thousand-word story, which Ruth simplifies to ninety-two words. Her other books include *A Hole Is to Dig* and *A Very Special House.*

1937 Ron Barrett is born. He is the coauthor, with Judi Barrett, of *Cloudy with a Chance of Meatballs,* where, in the land of Chewandswallow, fantastic food falls from the skies.

▶ **WORD FUN** The Barretts' *Pickles to Pittsburgh* offers opportunity for alliterative geography. Invite students to create alphabetic lists that contain foods and places: Artichokes to Albany, Broccoli to Birmingham, etc.

1945 Paul Janeczko is born, in Passaic, New Jersey. An English teacher and poet, Paul is the premier anthologist of poetry for young adults. He begins collecting poetry because he isn't satisfied with the anthologies available for students. "Poetry was going through a period of change and I wanted the kids to experience some of that new poetry."

▶ **READING TIP** Paul says, "I've always felt that any kid will read if you give him or her the right stuff, and that applies to poetry as well."

▶ **READING/WRITING CONNECTION** The criterion for Paul's second collection, *Postcard Poems,* is that the poems must be short enough to fit on a postcard to send to a friend. Challenge students to find short poems they like. Ask them to copy the poem on a postcard and send it to someone.

▶ **WRITING TIP** In *How to Write Poetry,* Paul offers lots of advice. He suggests that students try metaphors in their poetry journals for these things: a swiftly flowing river; a calm, blue lake; a snake coiled on a rock; a long, dark hallway; a partially torn basketball net.

1945 Clyde Watson is born, in New York City, the daughter of an art editor who is also an illustrator and a writer. Best known for her work with her sister, illustrator Wendy Watson, Clyde frequently uses details from her childhood in rural Vermont in her writing. One of her best-known works is *Father Fox's Pennyrhymes,* nursery rhymes with a distinctly American flavor. Homespun love, more precious than gold and as common as rain, is at the center of the pennyrhymes in *Love's a Sweet.* Clyde is also a professional violinist.

1966 Rachel Vail is born, in New York City. She is raised in New Rochelle, New York, the oldest of two children. Rachel says one of her talents growing up is eavesdropping. "I wanted to be a spy." After graduating from college, Rachel writes for *Sesame Street.* She tells her friends that if she ever writes a book for kids she will "tell the truth: junior high is not great." She decides to quit her job, move back with her parents, and write a book. In addition to works for younger readers, Rachel is the author of the Friendship Ring series.

▶ **WRITING TIP** Rachel says that being a writer means you write on days when it's hard as well as days when it's fun.

JULY

26

In the days when monsters and giants and fairy folk lived in England, a noble knight was riding across a plain.

Saint George and the Dragon,
as retold by Margaret Hodges

BIRTHDAYS

1796 George Catlin is born, in Wilkes Barre, Pennsylvania. He is the fifth of fourteen children. Going along with his father's wishes, George studies law and begins practicing with his brother. He later recalls, "During the next three years another and stronger passion was getting the advantage of me—that for painting, to which all my love of the law soon gave away. After having covered nearly every inch of the lawyer's table with penknife, pen and ink, and pencil sketches of judges, juries, culprits and spectators, I very deliberately resolved to convert my law library into paint-pots and brushes, and to pursue painting as my future, and certainly more agreeable profession." Between 1831 and 1836, George travels west and paints portraits, visiting the Cheyenne, Sioux, Blackfoot, Crow, Mandan—forty-eight plains tribes in all—learning their language and customs and painting portraits of tribal leaders.

1911 Margaret Hodges is born, in Indianapolis, Indiana. A children's librarian, Margaret says her stories fall into three categories. She writes real-life stories based on the adventures and misadventures of her three sons, picture book retellings of folktales and myths, and biographies written to bring to life little-known characters who have made important contributions. One of her noted books is *Saint George and the Dragon*, for which Trina Schart Hyman's illustrations win the Caldecott Medal.

1950 Dorothy Kingel is born, in Schenectady, New York. She is the author of *Rat Race and Other Rodent Jokes*.

▶ **WORD FUN** Challenge students to invent a riddle for which the term *rat race* is the punch line.

EVENT

1911 N. C. Wyeth writes in a letter, "*Treasure Island* completed!" He has been working for sixteen weeks on the illustrations, producing one large picture a week. He is convinced it is his best work.

JULY

27

Matilda told such dreadful lies

it made one gasp and stretch one's eyes. . . .

Hilaire Belloc,
The Bad Child's Book of Beasts and Cautionary Tales

BIRTHDAYS

1870 Hilaire Belloc is born, in La Celle-Saint-Cloud, France, to a French lawyer father and an English mother. Hilaire becomes a British citizen in 1902. A noted essayist, he is known today for his nonsense verse for children, *The Bad Child's Book of Beasts and Cautionary Tales*.

1912 Scott Corbett is born, in Kansas City, Missouri. Scott says his parents ruined his chances of ever being a great novelist by giving him a very happy childhood. In junior college, Scott reads joke books, studying the technique of joke writing. He is very pleased to earn two dollars per published joke. A prolific writer, Scott writes nonfiction, mystery, and adventure tales. Scott admits that the first pages in *The Lemonade Trick,* from his Trick series, are autobiographical. The book has sold a million copies.

▶ **WRITING TIP** Scott says *What if?* is what makes a story. Start with an everyday situation, and then think of an unusual *What if?* instead of the expected next event.

JULY

28

Once upon a time there were four little Rabbits, and their names were— Flopsy, Mopsy, Cotton- tail, and Peter.

Beatrix Potter,
The Tale of Peter Rabbit

BIRTHDAYS

1866 Helen Beatrix Potter is born, in England. Her notebooks show that as an eight-year-old Beatrix is already keeping careful drawings and notes on her pets. Later, she uses this habit of careful observation to write *The Tale of Peter Rabbit*, who is still the most famous rabbit in the world. His tale is translated into sixteen languages. Among other Potter creations are Squirrel Nutkin, Mr. Tod, Mrs. Tiggy-Winkle, Jemima Puddle-Duck, two bad mice, and Peter's brainier, bolder cousin, Benjamin Bunny, all of whom appear in books bearing their names.

▶ **WRITING/DRAWING TIP** Invite students to practice Beatrix's careful observation technique on a pet of their own—or on a neighbor's pet. They should create careful drawings, with accompanying notes about the animal's behavior.

▶ **WRITING FUN** Beatrix wrote a wonderful, hard-to-find volume, *Yours Affectionately, Peter Rabbit*, in which her characters in various books exchange amusing letters. Children enjoy taking this idea and writing the same sorts of letters.

1932 Natalie Babbitt is born, in Dayton, Ohio. She is the younger of two children and a distant relation of Zane Grey. As a child she reads mostly fairy tales and Greek myths. Her mother reads aloud every night, selecting books from a list of children's classics. Natalie says, "*Alice's Adventures in Wonderland* was read to me when I was nine; it has been my favorite book ever since." The gifted author-illustrator of such Newbery Honor books as *Kneeknock Rise*, *Tuck Everlasting*, *The Devil's Storybook*, and *Goody Hall*, Natalie credits her editor for encouraging her to write. She had thought of herself only as an illustrator. Natalie objects to "fifth graders being lumped together into some great unformed ball of clay called *the child*." Natalie points out that "there are a lot of special things about fifth grade." For one, she says, it is "the last best year of childhood."

▶ **WRITING TIP** Natalie says the creation of each of her stories begins with a word or phrase that strikes a chord with her and from this initial word characters evolve. Invite students to collect words that make them stop and think. At the end of each day, invite students to discard all their words but a couple. Then they can begin the next morning by seeing whether that word takes them anywhere.

EVENT

2000 The first retrospective exhibition of the art of Allen Say opens at the Japanese American National Museum, in Los Angeles, featuring fifty-five original watercolor paintings and pen-and-ink drawings.

▶ **READ MORE** Invite students to bring in books by Allen. The art is wonderful and so are the stories, touching universal emotions as they do.

JULY

29

Gramps says that I'm a country girl at heart and that is true.

Sharon Creech,
Walk Two Moons

BIRTHDAYS

1891 Esther Shepherd is born, in Minneapolis, Minnesota. Her *Paul Bunyan* retells classic legends about the gigantic lumberman.

▶ **READING/WRITING CONNECTION** Invite students to read some Paul Bunyan tales and then try creating their own. What might happen if Paul drove the school bus? Or taught the class? Sally Ann Thunder Ann Whirlwind Crockett uses a bowie knife as a toothpick. Suggest to students that they open their tale with a similar strong image.

1937 Betsy Smith is born, in Omaha, Nebraska. Two of her titles are *A Day in the Life of a Firefighter* and *A Day in the Life of an Actress*.

▶ **WRITE MORE** Invite students to interview someone who has an interesting job, then write a piece using the day-in-the-life-of structure.

1945 Sharon Creech is born, in Cleveland, Ohio, to a large family. She grows up in the suburbs "with hordes of relatives telling stories around the kitchen table." She says she learns to "exaggerate and embellish" because if you didn't, your story was drowned out by a more exciting one. As a child she loves reading American Indian myths, Greek myths, and the King Arthur legends. With her two children, Sharon moves to England to teach and gets the idea for *Walk Two Moons,* a Newbery Medal book, from a fortune cookie: "Don't judge a man until you've walked two moons in his moccasins."

▶ **WRITING TIP** Sharon says kids shouldn't think they have to know the whole story when they start. "Start with a person and a place and start thinking, 'Who do they know?' or 'What would happen to them?' 'What are they like?' If you start describing all that, the story will come."

1952 Kathleen Krull is born, in Fort Leonard Wood, Missouri. When she is fifteen she is fired from her part-time job at the library. She's reading too much when she should be working. The day after she graduates from college she begins a career as a children's book editor. While holding down the editorial job, she writes the Trixie Belden series. Kathleen says she loves writing the Lives of . . . series because it allows her to "snoop behind the closed doors of my favorite groups of really strange people."

▶ **READ MORE** The subtitle tells a lot about Kathleen's approach in *Lives of Extraordinary Women: Rulers, Rebels (and What the Neighbors Thought).* Children who read this book will be able to answer these questions: Which Egyptian queen bathed in donkey's milk? Which world leader did other people's laundry, by hand? Which military heroine was sued for rejecting a marriage proposal?

▶ **READING/WRITING CONNECTION** Invite students to prepare a book report that reveals three provocative questions the book answers.

EVENT

1924 A letter Beatrix Potter writes to a friend reveals that there is a real Jemima Puddle-Duck as well as a fictional one: "I am very fond of my garden. It is a regular old-fashioned farm garden, with a box hedge round the flower bed, and moss roses and pansies and blackcurrents and strawberries and peas, and big sage bushes for Jemima."

JULY

30

What a gem in a bird's egg. . . .

Henry David Thoreau

BIRTHDAY

1818 Emily Bronte is born, in Thornton, Yorkshire, England, the daughter of a rector. When Emily is six her mother dies and she and Charlotte, two years older, are sent to join their older sisters Maria and Elizabeth at the Clergy Daughters' School, in Cowan Bridge. The school is the model for the infamous Lowood School in Charlotte's novel *Jane Eyre.* When the older sisters become ill, all the children are sent home. The children write tiny volumes about Angria, a mythical kingdom they have created. In 1946, the sisters' verses are published, at their own expense, as *Poems by Currer, Ellis, and Acton Bell.* Emily's novel *Wuthering Heights* is published in 1847.

EVENTS

1852 Henry David Thoreau writes in his journal, "What a gem in a bird's egg, especially a blue or a green one, when you see one broken or whole in the woods! I noticed a small blue egg this afternoon washed up by Flint's Pond and half buried by white sand, and as it lay there, alternately wet and dry, no color could be fairer, no gem could have a more advantageous or favorable setting."

▶ **WRITING TIP** Invite students to observe the world closely on their way to school tomorrow and then to write a paragraph about something that has a special color.

1991 First Lady Barbara Bush presents a gift to the children of Russia—a bronze statue of eight ducklings, a copy of Nancy Schön's sculpture *Make Way for Ducklings,* which stands in the Boston Public Garden as a tribute to Robert McCloskey's long-popular children's book of the same name. "There's something magical about the thought of American children loving and playing with the ducks in Boston while children in Moscow are doing the same," says Mrs. Bush.

JULY

This is the true and real story of what happened when Grandpa came to live with us and took my room and how I went to war with him and him with me and what happened after that.

Robert Kimmel Smith,
The War with Grandpa

BIRTHDAYS

1921 Lynne Reid Banks is born, in London, an only child. She is evacuated to Canada during World War II. Lynn admits that she is a "reluctant reader" as a child but loves the stories her mother tells her or reads to her. Lynn says her own three sons, now adults, are "personated" in the Indian in the Cupboard series.

1930 Robert Kimmel Smith is born, in Brooklyn, New York. Robert is eight years old when he reads his first book. It convinces him he loves reading and that he wants to become a writer. When he is ten, he sends a joke to a magazine and is thrilled when they pay him thirty-five dollars. But he credits his daughter with getting him started. He starts telling her a bedtime story about a boy who can eat as much chocolate as he wants. Each night he adds to the story. After two weeks, his daughter urges him to write it down. Robert's first book, *Chocolate Fever,* is the result. This title sells nearly two million copies. *Jelly Belly* comes from Robert's own experience of being the fattest kid in fifth grade. When a group of fifth graders ask Robert to write about an average kid who doesn't like school, *Mostly Michael* is the result. When he isn't writing, Robert loves to cook and is a fanatical baseball fan.

▶ **WRITING TIP** Robert starts with a hero and an opening situation. He discovers the story along with his characters.

EVENT

1703 Daniel Defoe is locked in a pillory frame before London's Temple Bar because authorities are furious about a satire he wrote. He is held in Newgate Prison and displayed in the pillory, head and hands locked in place. This is sixteen years before he writes his masterpiece *Robinson Crusoe.*

AUGUST

The ripened corn is now ready to eat. It is picked by everyone, including mothers who work in the fields while their babies, bound on cradleboards, are hung on nearby tree branches.

Michael McCurdy,
An Algonquian Year: The Year According to the Full Moon

AUGUST 1

Call me Ishmael.

Herman Melville,
Moby-Dick

BIRTHDAYS

1819 Herman Melville is born, in New York City. When Herman is seven, his father writes a relative, "He is very backward in speech and somewhat slow in comprehension, but you will find him . . . of a docile & amiable disposition." Herman's father believes he needn't push Herman too hard because his son can go into commerce and won't need "much book knowledge." Twelve when his father dies, Herman leaves school at fifteen to earn money for his impoverished family. At age twenty, he signs on as a cabin boy on a ship headed for England. Working on a whaler is so difficult that he and another sailor jump ship at the Marquesas Islands. Melville writes popular books about his experiences.

1944 Gail Gibbons is born, in Oak Park, Illinois. Gail, her husband, and his children build a home on three hundred acres in Vermont. Her experiences with such things as driving trucks, operating a dairy, and harvesting maple syrup have given her the factual background for her informative and popular books.

▶ **READING TIP** Make a list of the titles of available books by Gail. Ask students to select a title and then write three questions they think the book might answer. Then they should read the book and find out if they are right.

EVENT

1900 A clerk at the Library of Congress's copyright office opens a letter that reads, "Enclosed please find check for $2.20 for which please enter for copyright and send certificates of same the two following books." The first is *The Navy Alphabet*; the second is *The Wonderful Wizard of Oz*, both by L. Frank Baum. In 2000, Henry Holt publishes the one-hundredth anniversary edition, illustrated by Michael Hague, who says that as a child there were three places he wanted to visit: England in the days of King Arthur, the Wild West of Hopalong Cassidy, and the wonderful land of Oz.

▶ **READ MORE** *The Annotated Wizard of Oz* reproduces the original 1900 edition in its exact form, with an introduction and extensive notes by Michael Patrick Hearn, who says this is the "quintessential American fairy tale."

AUGUST 2

"Maybe [Howie] will write books one day just as I have," Harold says. "Anything is possible."

James Howe,
Bunnicula Strikes Again

BIRTHDAYS

1936 Judy Morris is born, in Orange, New Jersey. The title of her novel for middle graders gives students something to think about: *The Kid Who Ran for Principal*.

▶ **WRITE ABOUT IT** Invite students to come up with plans for changing the school if they are named principal next week. Once they come up with their plans, they can write campaign speeches.

1946 James Howe is born, in Oneida, New York. James and his wife, Deborah, collaborate on *Bunnicula*. They sit around the kitchen table, one talking while the other writes frantically. James says, "As we inspired each other's thinking, the ideas overlapped, until there were sentences, phrases, even, that were truly the creation of two people." The titles of some of the sequels hint at the word play involved, revealing to young readers that puns are often based on sound as well as sense: *The Celery Stalks at Midnight, Howliday Inn, Rabbit-Cadabra!, Harold and Chester in the Fright Before Christmas*.

▶ **WORD FUN** *Bunnicula* is a name derived from combining *bunny* and *Dracula*. Invite students to create other horrific combinations. Include some discussion about word roots, prefixes, and suffixes.

EVENTS

1776 The Declaration of Independence, submitted to the Continental Congress on June 28 and accepted on July 4, is formally signed. Today, each page is protected in a bulletproof glass and bronze case filled with inert helium to displace damaging oxygen.

▶ **READ MORE** Jean Fritz's *Will You Sign Here, John Hancock?* gives insider information and Russell Freedman's *Give Me Liberty! The Story of the Declaration of Independence* explains that a document we take for granted was a dangerous political statement involving profound personal risks to its signers and supporters. The Declaration of Independence may be viewed on the National Archives website: *http://www.nara.gov/exhall/charters/declaration/decmain.html*

1858 The first letter boxes for mail collection are installed in Boston and New York City.

▶ **CELEBRATE** Celebrate this event by taking a class walk to a mailbox and dropping in a class letter to someone.

AUGUST

I watch how other things travel

to get an idea how I might move.

Naomi Shihab Nye, "Observer, "
Come with Me:
Poems for a Journey

BIRTHDAY

1926 Mary Calhoun is born Mary Huiskamp, in Keokuk, Iowa. Mary enjoys listening to her mother tell stories and decides at age seven that she will be an author. The big brick house near the Mississippi River where she grows up, which was built by her great-grandfather, is very like the house in which her Katie John books are set. Mary also writes a series featuring Henry, a resourceful Siamese cat.

▶ **WRITING TIP** Invite students to write a paragraph about the building in which they live.

EVENTS

1989 On the eighth day of his Antarctic expedition Will Steger's journal entry takes note of the greatest danger, the deep crevasses that "line the perimeters of Antarctica like protective moats."

▶ **READ MORE** Will collaborates with Jon Bowermaster to write *Over the Top of the World,* a picture book about another dramatic trek, this time to the Artic.

2000 *Come with Me,* by Naomi Shihab Nye, is published. The book contains sixteen poems about journeys, internal and external. The poems are illustrated by Dan Yaccarino's mixed-media collages.

▶ **WRITING TIP** Invite students to follow Naomi Shihab Nye's travel directions, choosing an animal from which they would like to get "directions" for moving. (They might also choose a vehicle.) They should write some images they associate with this animal. What verbs seem to fit?

AUGUST

4

What is done cannot be undone, but one can prevent it happening again.

*Anne Frank,
diary entry*

BIRTHDAY

1946 Joyce McDonald is born, in San Francisco, the daughter of a police lieutenant. Joyce says she grows up in a house with book-filled shelves in almost every room. When she is six Joyce writes her own book—six pages with crayon illustrations held together by a safety pin. When Joyce is seven, she is thrilled when her mother pecks out one of Joyce's stories on a typewriter even though she doesn't know how to type. "It may well have been one of the most important things she ever did for me, because her message was loud and clear. She liked what I had written."

1948 Nancy White Carlstrom is born. Among her many books are the Jessie Bear series, illustrated by Bruce Degen.

▶ **WORD FUN** A Jessie Bear book about color has this rhyme: "Hoorah for me/ Hoorah for you/Hoorah for blue." Challenge students to come up with short rhymes about other colors. Ask them whether some colors are easier to rhyme than others— and why.

EVENT

1944 Anne Frank is arrested by Nazis in Amsterdam.

▶ **READ MORE** In addition to Anne's diary, *Anne Frank: The Diary of a Young Girl,* there are several biographies, including *Anne Frank: Life in Hiding,* by Johanna Hurwitz, with illustrations by Vera Rosenberry, and *Anne Frank: Beyond the Diary: A Photographic Remembrance,* by Ruud van der Rol and Rian Verhoeven.

AUGUST

5

What's that—?
A bat!

*Conrad Aiken,
"The Bat"*

BIRTHDAY

1889 Conrad Aiken is born, in Savannah, Georgia. Known as an author for adults and the father of the popular children's author Joan Aiken, he is also the author of a volume of poetry for children, *Cats and Bats and Things with Wings.*

▶ **READ MORE** Some people like bats; other people fear them. Edward Gorey liked them so much that in his will he left a lot of money to a bat sanctuary. Invite students to list why they do or do not like bats—and then do some research to prove or disprove these feelings.

EVENT

1979 A letter from a fourteen-year-old girl is printed in the Dear Abby newspaper column. Her list of don'ts for parents includes "Don't ever search your kid's room" and "Don't choose their friends for them."

▶ **WRITING TIP** Invite students to compile a list of don'ts for their teacher.

AUGUST

6

You must do something to make the world more beautiful.

*Barbara Cooney,
Miss Rumphius*

BIRTHDAY

1917 Barbara Cooney and her twin brother are born, in Room 1127 of a large hotel in Brooklyn Heights, New York, a hotel built by their grandfather. They live on Long Island during the school year and in Maine during the summer. In her 1980 Caldecott Medal acceptance speech for *Ox-Cart Man,* Barbara notes that "most children have the souls of artists. Some of these children stubbornly keep on being children even when they have grown up. Some of these stubborn children get to be artists." Barbara hates TV. When she sees her family watching it, she pulls the plug out and cuts off the cord. Of her more than one hundred books, Barbara says, "*Miss*

Rumphius, Island Boy, and *Hattie and the Wild Waves* are the closest to my heart. These three are as near as I ever will come to an autobiography."

▶ **DRAWING TIP** Barbara says, "I draw only the things I know about. I draw from life whenever possible, and do not invent facts."

EVENT

1762 "Sandwich Day" is often celebrated on the birthday of John Montagu, the fourth Earl of Sandwich, but this is the day he actually makes the sandwich. In the middle of one of his famous around-the-clock gambling sessions, the earl doesn't want to leave his cards for a meal and so he orders a servant to bring him some cold meat between two slices of bread. And thus the sandwich is born.

▶ **ALL ABOUT NAMES** Kids can read more fascinating stories about names in *The Name's Familiar: Mr. Leotard, Barbie, and Chef Boyardee,* by Laura Lee. Students can find out for whom the guppy, the Honda motorcycle, and the thesaurus are named. And lots more!

AUGUST

I think how you look is the most important thing in the world. If you look cute, you are cute; if you look smart, you are smart, and if you don't look like anything, then you aren't anything.

Betsy Byars,
The Summer of the Swans

BIRTHDAYS

1927 Maia Wojciechowska is born, in Warsaw, Poland. She leaves her homeland during World War II. After time in France and England, her family settles in Los Angeles. Then Maia moves to New York City to become a writer. When her manuscript of short stories is rejected, she tosses all her money—one dime—off the Brooklyn Bridge. She works as a tennis coach, a private detective, and a beautician. Years after giving up on becoming a writer, she turns an early short story about bullfighting into the prize-winning *Shadow of a Bull.* Maia's *Alice* is an update of Lewis Carroll's *Through the Looking Glass and What Alice Found There;* it stars a chess-playing African-American girl.

1928 Betsy Byars is born, in Charlotte, North Carolina, the younger of two sisters. She shares her birthday with Thomas J., the abandoned child in *The Pinballs.* Betsy describes herself as a happy, busy child. She says that her first-grade teacher Miss Harriet's reading of *The Adventures of Mabel* is better than anybody had ever read a book before or since. Betsy plans on working in a zoo when she grows up. She wants to grow up so she can have as many pets as she wants. She makes lists of all the pets she will have.

▶ **WRITING TIP 1** Betsy says characters' names are crucial. "The names have to be right or the characters won't come to life." And, says Betsy, the characters are the most important element in the story.

▶ **WRITING TIP 2** Betsy says it takes about two years to write a book—one year to write it and a second year to polish it.

▶ **READ MORE** Once students read the opening to Betsy's *Me Tarzan,* your classroom may never be the same again (of course they need to read it out loud):

Dorothy threw open the kitchen door.
AHHHHHH-AHH-AHH-AHHHH
AHH-AHH-AHH-AHHHHHHHHHHHH!

1942 Gary Edward Keillor is born, in Anoka, Minnesota, the son of a railway mail clerk and a carpenter. Professionally known as Garrison, he becomes the host and writer of the radio program *A Prairie Home Companion.* He also writes two picture books featuring his trademark zany rhymes: *Cat, You Better Come Home* and *The Old Man Who Loved Cheese.* The worse the cheese smells, the better Wallace P. Flynn loves it, "So his daughter moved to Oklahoma/To escape the aroma."

▶ **WORD FUN** Garrison employs other fun geographical rhymes: *Arkansas/Halitosis Law; Louise/Hebrides.* Challenge students to come up with their own geographical rhyming couplets.

1948 Marty Appel is born, in Brooklyn, New York. His *The First Book of Baseball* offers the basic rules of play and tips on playing.

▶ **WRITING TIP** Challenge students to write the directions for playing a game. Then invite them to read one another's directions and comment on them.

The baby bird had to go home, but first it had to learn to fly.

Jan Pienkowski,
Bel and Bub and the Baby Bird

BIRTHDAYS

1896 Marjorie Kinnan Rawlings is born, in Washington, D.C. Marjorie goes to school in Wisconsin, is a journalist in Louisville and Rochester, and in 1928, settles in Cross Creek, Florida. "The people so charmed me I determined to write about them, and if I failed, not to write anymore." When she makes her first sale, in 1931, earning $750, Marjorie uses the money to install indoor plumbing, the first in Cross Creek. In *The Yearling* Jody Baxter comes of age in the big scrub country that is now the Ocala National Forest. It receives the Pulitzer Prize in 1938.

1936 Jan Pienkowski is born, in Warsaw, Poland, into a family of architects and artists. At age eight he makes his first book—as a present for his father. Featuring a horse and cart, the story is about road rage. When Jan is ten, he moves with his parents to England and goes to school for the first time. He is very impressed by the comics, and later he is one of the first to use the strip cartoon in children's books. Jan studies the classics and English literature at Cambridge. A two-time winner of the Kate Greenaway medal for illustration, Jan illustrates the popular *Meg and Mog* series and pioneers the modern pop-up book, creating eighteen titles.

EVENT

1872 Thirteen-year-old Theodore Roosevelt writes in the natural history notebook he keeps, "A nest of the gray squirrel was situated in a chestnut tree. . . . The nest contained three young, whose eyes were not yet open. . . ." Before he goes off to Harvard, Theodore preserves hundreds of birds. He gives more than two hundred of his specimens to the Smithsonian Institution. A snowy owl, a spurwinged lapwing, a crocodile bird, and a white-tailed lapwing, mounted when he is thirteen, are on display at the American Museum of Natural History in New York City. When Theodore goes off to college, he takes a large (live) turtle with him. He also takes a few snakes.

▶ **WRITE ABOUT IT** Invite students to keep a natural history notebook for two weeks, making observations about wildlife they observe. At the end of this period they can reflect on whether or not keeping such a notebook has changed the way they look at the world.

▶ **WRITING TIP** Ask students to choose one item from their notebook—something they can observe again. This time they should find out as much as possible and write about it.

9

Mary Poppins sighed with pleasure, however, when she saw three of herself, each wearing a blue coat with silver buttons, and a blue hat to match. She thought it was such a lovely sight that she wished there had been a dozen of her or even thirty. The more Mary Poppins the better.

P. L. Travers,
Mary Poppins

BIRTHDAYS

1593 Izaak Walton is born, in Staffordshire, England. At age sixty, he writes *The Compleat Angler,* one of the most famous books in English letters. Izaak discusses every aspect of fishing and a contemplative life.

▶ **READING/WRITING CONNECTION** Invite students to find poems and stories about fishing that will inform their own remembrances on the topic. DK Publishing offers an enticing photo-filled volume, *Young Fishing Enthusiast,* by John Bailey. It has lots of practical information—choosing the right rod and tackle, how to prepare bait, and so on. *Kids' Incredible Fishing Stories,* by Shaun Morey, reads like fiction but the author insists it's nonfiction. Donald Graves, author of a dozen books on writing for teachers and parents, offers a fishing memory for young readers in "The Night Before Fishing Season Opens" in *Baseball, Snakes, and Summer Squash;* the dustjacket has a picture of young Don with his catch. Don's simple, understated language of anticipation offers students a model for crafting their own remembrances.

1898 P(amela) L. Travers is born, in Maryborough, Queensland, Australia. At age eighteen, Pamela travels to Britain to discover her roots and never leaves. Her Mary Poppins series is translated into more than twenty-five languages, sells in the millions, and is made into a movie in 1964.

1909 Norma Farber is born, in Boston. Norma's early writing is for adults. She begins writing for children in the 1960s, writing most of these books in rhyme. The enchanting *As I Was Crossing Boston Common,* for which Norma receives the National Book Award, is one of the first alphabet books to extend the range of an appropriate audience. Narrated by a turtle who relates his experiences as he encounters an alphabetic line of beasts, fish, and fowl, the creatures—from the angwantibo to the zibet—are far from ordinary.

1931 Seymour Simon is born, in New York City. Many of Seymour's ideas for his more than one hundred books grow out of his twenty-three years of teaching science to middle graders. "Interesting questions come up in class discussions." Seymour credits his years with students with helping him develop his direct, conversational writing style. In addition to nonfiction books on science, Seymour writes the Einstein Anderson series, in which the main character is a science whiz kid who solves local mysteries.

▶ **WRITING TIP** Seymour Simon says, "I try to write the way I talk. I think about what effect my sentences will have if they are read aloud." Invite student teams to read original pieces to each other and then write a paragraph of how hearing their words did (or did not) inspire some changes.

1944 Patricia McKissack is born, in Smyrna, Tennessee. Patricia grows up listening to her mother reading poetry and her grandparents telling stories. Her grandfather uses Patricia's and her brother's and sister's names in the stories. Since all the characters are smart, brave, daring, and clever, Patricia grows up believing that she, too, is smart, brave, daring, and clever. Patricia remembers her pride when her third-grade teacher puts a poem she has written up on the bulletin board. Patricia's own favorite poem is Paul Laurence Dunbar's "Little Brown Baby," and the first book she writes is a biography of Paul Laurence Dunbar. In the 1980s Patricia leaves teaching to write full time, and her husband Fredrick joins her. Fred does the research, Pat the writing. Together, they have written more than fifty books.

▶ **RESEARCH TIP** Invite students to form writer-researcher teams. Each should research and write up two topics, switching roles on the second topic. (For starters, "animals" is a recommended topic.) Then they should write a paragraph or two about what they learned about the different roles. What tips can they take from this experience to help other researchers/writers? They can write these tips in the form of a memo.

1952 Hazel Hutchins is born, in Calgary, Alberta, Canada. Hazel says, "I like words—how they sound and feel. I love the way ideas in fiction open so many doors in my mind."

▶ **WRITING TIP** Hazel advises, "Always write about things you're intrigued by, not just about things you know."

EVENTS

1930 Betty Boop debuts, in the animated cartoon *Dizzy Dishes*.

1973 Steven Kellogg completes the illustrations for *The Island of the Skog*, "after," he notes, "nine years of rewriting."

AUGUST

I both wished and feared to see Mr. Rochester on the day which followed this sleepless night: I wanted to hear his voice again, yet feared to meet his eye.

Charlotte Bronte,
Jane Eyre

BIRTHDAY

1931 Thomas J. Dygard is born, in Little Rock, Arkansas. He writes well-regarded sports books such as *The Rebounder, Second Stringer,* and *Infield Hit*. The books include the excitement of play-by-play description but also grapple with important social and personal concerns.

▶ **READING/WRITING CONNECTION** Invite baseball fans to try writing about a recent game. They will soon discover the importance of compression and the need for variety in describing events. Students can compare their account with newspaper accounts, trying to figure out which are more important—nouns or adjectives.

EVENTS

1664 Noted diarist Samuel Pepys visits Edward Cocker, a master calligrapher and writing teacher. In later eras authors don't care about their penmanship. The story goes that noted newspaperman Horace Greeley had such bad handwriting that an employee he fired used the dismissal letter as a letter of recommendation for his next job. While he was in college, Nathaniel Hawthorne wrote a letter home, asking his family, "What do you think of my becoming an author . . . ? Indeed, I think the illegibility of my handwriting is very author-like." In contrast, Edgar Allan Poe was thought to have the most elegant penmanship of any noted writer.

1824 When she is eight years old, Charlotte Bronte's widowed father sends her and her younger sister Emily off to Cowan Bridge School. This dreadful school becomes the model for the infamous Lowood School in Charlotte's *Jane Eyre*.

▶ **READ MORE** Encourage students to compile a list of books about awful teachers and awful schools—from *Miss Nelson* on. Bruce Coville's *My Teacher Is an Alien* is so popular it inspires an entire line: *My Teacher Glowed in the Dark, My Teacher Fried My Brains*, and so on.

Before we knew what was happening, we were wooshed out of the tank and into a pipe that carries water to our city.

Joanna Cole,
The Magic School Bus at the Waterworks

BIRTHDAYS

1908 Don Freeman is born, in San Diego. He moves to New York to work as a professional musician. Don has always drawn everything he sees, and one night he is sketching fellow passengers on the train and forgets his trumpet on the train. He studies at the Art Students League, and his sketches of Broadway events appear in the *New York Times* and other newspapers. A librarian friend sees a book he has drawn for his son and convinces him to send it to a publisher. For every book, when the deadline for finishing the manuscript approaches, Don checks into a hotel so he won't be distracted.

▶ **READING/WRITING CONNECTION** Most students won't have the luxury of checking into a hotel to avoid distraction, but it is a topic worth thinking about. Invite students to write each other memos with Tips for Avoiding Distraction as the subject line.

1933 Terry Berger is born, in New York City. Terry's books include *Black Fairy Tales*, a collection of tales from Africa, and *Ben's ABC Day*.

▶ **WRITING TIP** Invite students to try Terry's idea: describe their day using an ABC format. They may want to tie their ABC schedule to the clock.

1944 Joanna Cole is born, in Newark, New Jersey. As a child, Joanne loves watching insects, and her favorite subject in elementary school is science. She says Ms. Frizzle in the Magic Schoolbus series is like her favorite teacher Miss Blair but also like Joanna herself. "Ms. Frizzle likes to learn about science and she likes to explain it to children, just as I like to explain it in my books." Joanne says the character in the books she feels closest to is Arnold. Like Arnold, Joanne spends most of her time reading and writing.

▶ **WRITING TIP** Ask students to take a look at the word *wooshed* in the quote that begins this day. Then as them to consider other ways water can move—and what words describe this.

EVENT

1885 A headline runs in the *The World*: "ONE HUNDRED THOUSAND DOLLARS: TRIUMPHANT COMPLETION OF THE WORLD'S FUND FOR THE LIBERTY PEDESTAL." In five months, 121,000 people have contributed $102,000 for the pedestal for the Statue of Liberty. As he promised, Joseph Pulitzer, owner of *The World*, publishes the name of every contributor in the paper.

▶ **READ MORE** In *Liberty*, Lynn Curlee gives a detailed account of Lady Liberty's history.

You ain't got nothing to back you up 'cept what you got in your heart.

Walter Dean Myers,
Scorpions

BIRTHDAYS

1859 Katherine Lee Bates is born, in Falmouth, Massachusetts. Katherine loves stories and rhymes from a very early age. Her mother gives her a red leather diary when she is nine, and Katherine loves writing in it. Diary keeping is a habit she maintains, and jotting down impressions of the scenery when she travels west on the train helps her create the lyrics for "America the Beautiful."

▶ **READ MORE** *Purple Mountain Majesties: The Story of Katherine Lee Bates and "America the Beautiful"* is an informative account of Katherine's life and her creative process in penning the lyrics.

1867 Edith Hamilton is born, in Dresden, Germany. She is educated at Miss Porter's Finishing School for Young Ladies, in Farmington, Connecticut. Edith earns B.A. and M.A. degrees in Latin and Greek at Bryn Mawr College. After retiring from teaching, she writes the highly regarded *The Greek Way* and *The Roman Way* and is made an honorary citizen of Athens, Greece.

▶ **READ MORE** Invite students to read Greek and Roman myths. Good places to start are *D'Aulaires' Book of Greek Myths; The Gods and Goddesses of Olympus,* by Aliki; and *Greek Gods and Goddesses,* by Geraldine McCaughrean and Emma Chichester Clark.

1923 Ruth Stiles Gannett is born, in New York City. She receives a degree in chemistry from Vassar College. Between jobs as a medical technician, a waitress, and a ski lodge worker, Ruth writes the whimsical *My Father's Dragon,* which is named a Newbery Honor book. Ruth writes two sequels. All three books are illustrated by Ruth's stepmother, Ruth Chrisman Gannett. Ruth Stiles says her books come out of a happy childhood, adding, "I do not write for children so much as for my own pleasure."

1930 Mary Ann Hoberman is born, in Stamford, Connecticut. Mary Ann remembers singing songs she's made up as she swings in her backyard. Mary Ann says the book that first pointed her in her life's direction is *Modern American Poetry,* edited by Louis Untermeyer. She "borrows" it from her uncle's bookshelf—and sixty years later, she still has it. The book is still a touchstone for her. She says this 900-page book, including 145 poets, each one represented by two to thirty poems, shows her that poetry comes in all forms and cadences and subject matter and points of view. A poet for adults as well as children, Mary Ann also works as a newspaper reporter and editor.

▶ **READING TIP** As a child, Mary Ann memorizes hundreds of the poems in the Untermeyer volume. She points out that "a poem committed to memory in childhood is a lifetime treasure."

▶ **OUT LOUD** Invite students to memorize special poems, and schedule their presentations as a regular part of the school day.

1937 Walter Dean Myers is born, in Martinsburg, West Virginia. After his mother dies when he is three, Walter moves to Harlem, where he is raised by foster parents. One day his teacher finds Walter reading a comic book and tears it up. But she replaces it with a pile of books from her own library. Walter remembers this as "the best thing that ever happened to me." Knowing his family can't afford to send him to college, Walter drops out of high school and joins the army. When he gets out of the army, he loads trucks and works at the post office. And he writes at night. Now, he gets up between 4:30 and 5:00 A.M. and walks about five miles. Then he starts writing. "I try to get ten pages done. Once I do my ten pages, that's it." Author of popular fiction, Walter Dean is also the author of the nonfiction *Now Is Your Time!,* a book about the African-American struggle for freedom. As he says, "I claim the darkest moments of my people and celebrate their perseverance." For fun, Walter plays the flute and does crossword puzzles.

▶ **WRITING TIP** Walter outlines the story first. Then he cuts out pictures of all the characters, which his wife puts into a collage to go on the wall above the computer. Then, every time Walter walks into the room, he sees the characters.

1955 Ann M. Martin is born, in Princeton, New Jersey, the daughter of an artist and cartoonist for *The New Yorker* and a preschool teacher. She remembers her childhood being filled with books. Some of her favorites include *A Cricket in Times Square,* the Mary Poppins books, the Mrs. Piggle-Wiggle books, the Dr. Dolittle books, and Marguerite Henry's horse books. Ann writes with a fountain pen on lined paper. She writes outlines for each book—an overall framework outline and a chapter-by-chapter outline. "An outline is like a road map. I always know where I am going." Her editors help her think up plots for the more than two hundred books in the Babysitters' Club series, but Ann does about seventy-five percent of the writing. Ann says she is most like Mary Anne, the shy, quiet one.

▶ **WRITING TIP** Ann says she never listens to music while she's writing. "I need absolute silence in order to write."

1993 Sara Holbrook's dog Mike is born. Mike's picture is on the cover of Sara's poetry volume *The Dog Ate My Homework*. Read the title poem and you will learn that the dog not only ate the homework but also "garbaged down everything/left in his path."

AUGUST

My name is the symbol of my identity and must not be lost.

Lucy Stone

BIRTHDAYS

1422 William Caxton is born, in Kent, England. On November 18, 1477, he publishes the first book to be printed in England.

▶ **CELEBRATE** Ask children for ideas on how to celebrate book publishing.

1818 Lucy Stone is born, in West Brookfield, Massachusetts. A determined abolitionist and women's suffrage pioneer, Lucy shocks people by keeping her name when she marries. She founds the *Woman's Journal*, the chief publication of the women's movement, a journal she edits for more than twenty years. In 1858, in Orange, New Jersey, Lucy refuses to pay taxes because women are not allowed to vote.

▶ **RESEARCH TIP** Jean Fritz has profiled Lizzie Stanton; Susan B. Anthony is featured in a number of biographies. Where's Lucy's book? Students may want to right a wrong. A first step will be digging up information.

AUGUST

The outlook wasn't bright for the Mudville nine that day. . . .

E. L. Thayer,
"Casey at the Bat"

BIRTHDAYS

1863 E(rnest) L(awrence) Thayer is born, in Lawrence, Massachusetts. When, one hundred years later, on October 6, 1963, the New York Yankees suffer one of the most humiliating defeats in their history, losing the World Series in four games straight to the former Brooklyn Dodgers, the newspaper headline reads "The Mighty Yankees Have Struck Out." Another headline on the same page, reporting good news from the New York Stock Exchange reads "But There's Still Joy in Mudville." Both headlines come from Ernest's popular poem "Casey at the Bat." Before writing the poem, Ernest makes a brilliant record as a philosophy major at Harvard. After college, he writes humor columns for the *San Francisco Examiner*, where "Casey" appears on June 3, 1888.

▶ **READ MORE** The poem is an old chestnut, but it's fun, and notable illustrators offer their distinct versions: Christopher Bing, Gerald Fitzgerald, Patricia Polacco, Barry Moser, Wallace Trip.

▶ **OUT LOUD** Challenge sports buffs to tell what happens to the Mudville Nine in the manner of a modern-day sportscaster.

1918 Alice Provensen is born, in Chicago. In 1991, her *Punch in New York* is named one of the year's best illustrated books by the *New York Times*, marking the eighth time this Caldecott Medal illustrator has won this honor.

▶ **RESEARCH TIP** Alice's *The Buck Stops Here: The Presidents of the United States* depicts each president surrounded by symbols, headlines, and episodes from his administration. It is a marvel of selecting and arranging information—and of information compression. Students might take a look at two other easy-read volumes on the presidents—*Mr. President: A Book of U.S. Presidents,* by George Sullivan, and *Ask*

Me Anything About the Presidents, by Louis Phillips—and compare the ways writers select, arrange, and write about information.

1950 Gary Larson is born, in Tacoma, Washington. Growing up, Gary is an avid fan of comic books as a child and *Mad* magazine as an adolescent. His pets include snakes, frogs, and tarantulas. As a child Gary likes to draw animals. After college he plays jazz guitar and banjo and works at a music store. Realizing he hates his job, Gary tries drawing cartoons, and he gets a syndication contract for a regular cartoon feature called *The Far Side.* His cartoons run in more than 1,900 newspapers worldwide in more than seventeen languages.

▶ **READ MORE** People often ask Gary where he gets his ideas. In *The PreHistory of the Far Side* Gary talks about lots of his cartoons and where ideas do and don't work. For example, "I won't go into the bizarre details, but I once had a close call involving a rather large Burmese python that I had raised from a baby (the snake)." In this book, Gary does what few artists do: he talks about mistakes as well as his successes.

AUGUST

15

At first when I saw
horses fly

I thought it SUPER
DOOPER.

But SPLAT!!

Richard Michelson,
*A Book of Flies Real or
Otherwise,* drawings by
Leonard Baskin

BIRTHDAYS

1771 Sir Walter Scott is born, in Edinburgh, Scotland. He is credited with inventing the historical novel. "I care not who knows it—I write for the general amusement."

1858 Edith Nesbit is born, in Britain. She is playwright Noel Coward's favorite writer, and he always carries several of her books with him. Edith's work has a wonderful blend of realism and magic. Among her best-known works are *The Railway Children.*

1922 Leonard Baskin is born, in New Brunswick, New Jersey. Widely known as a printmaker, draftsman, and book designer, Leonard is most highly acclaimed for his sculpture. A Caldecott Honor artist for *Hosie's Alphabet,* Leonard collaborates with Richard Michelson for *A Book of Flies Real or Otherwise.* Leonard's illustrations are as witty as Richard's poems.

▶ **WORD FUN** Invite students to come up with literal interpretations of fruit flies, horse flies, fire flies, and as many other "unusual" flies as they can locate. Then they can illustrate and write pseudo-dictionary descriptions of these flies.

1948 Theresa Nelson is born, in Beaumont, Texas. She remembers walking with her five brothers and five sisters to school and passing the biggest, richest house in Beaumont, Texas. "We were almost kin to the widow lady who lived there—her son had married Aunt Pat, our daddy's sister. Which made us close enough to brag, but not close enough to ever actually be invited inside." Theresa visits the library often. Jo March in *Little Women* is her favorite heroine. Theresa becomes an actress, traveling a lot with her actor husband. She thinks all this travel is what makes "place" so important in her writing.

▶ **WRITING TIP** When a headline, "The Empress of Elsewhere," in an upside-down newspaper catches Theresa's eye, she picks up the newspaper to read the story. Then she sees that she has misread the headline. But she likes her version better, so she writes it in her notebook—even though she has no idea what it might mean. A year later, she thinks of that title—and of the old iron gate in front of the richest house in Beaumont, Texas.

▶ **WRITING TIP** Invite students to scan newspaper headlines—and write down three that offer intriguing possibilities for stories. They don't have to write the stories, just recognize "possibilities."

1950 Lucinda Landon is born, in Galesburg, Illinois. Lucinda says, "Writing the Meg Mackintosh series gives me the opportunity to combine a love of drawing with my love of mysteries. It's fun to design books with the clues hidden in both the text and the black and white illustrations."

AUGUST 16

Somebody loves you.

Eileen Spinelli,
*Somebody Loves You,
Mr. Hatch*

BIRTHDAYS

1909 Marchette Chute is born, in Hazelwood, Minnesota. She is the middle daughter of three. Marchette is raised on 450 acres on Lake Minnetonka, twelve miles from Minneapolis, and is homeschooled until she is eleven. After she moves to New York City and starts work on a biography of Geoffrey Chaucer, Marchette develops her research method. She arrives at the New York Public Library every morning at nine, where she finds the information and the resources she needs. Then she walks home and types her notes and writes text in the afternoon.

1917 Matt Christopher is born, in Bath, Pennsylvania. He is the eldest of nine children. His mother is from Hungary and his father from Italy. Matt says he regrets being embarrassed by the way his parents talk and not learning either language. When he is fourteen, Matt begins writing poems and short stories. He writes detective stories during study hall in high school. After playing some semiprofessional and professional ball, Matt notices that there aren't any good baseball books for middle graders. So he writes one, *The Lucky Baseball,* in 1954. He expands his output with a series of nonfiction sports biographies of current stars.

▶ **WRITING TIP** Matt says first he picks the sport he's going to write about. Then he decides on the main character's problem. Then he chooses the story's scene. Next he picks characters' names. Then he outlines the plot. Matt says the first draft is the hardest.

▶ **READ MORE** Invite sports fans to take a look at Matt's books. Are they formula books or do different titles have individuality? How can a reader tell? Predictability isn't a bad quality: just ask all the (adult) mystery fans.

1942 Eileen Spinelli is born, in Philadelphia, Pennsylvania. When Jerry Spinelli is asked to name his favorite author, he answers, "My favorite author now is Eileen Spinelli, who happens to live in my house here. She's my wife. I'm lucky enough to be the first one to read her books. My favorite of her books is *Somebody Loves You, Mr. Hatch.*" Eileen also writes the Lizzie Logan series—and shares six children with Jerry.

AUGUST 17

misshapen
rough fellow. . . .

Myra Cohn Livingston,
"Douglas Fir," *Monkey Puzzle
and Other Poems*

BIRTHDAYS

1786 David "Davy" Crockett is born, in Hawkins County, Georgia. The subject of many tall tales, he himself tells plenty about his life as a frontiersman and adventurer.

▶ **READ MORE** Tall tales about Davy are included in a number of tall tale collections. Mary Pope Osborne offers a rousing tale in *American Tall Tales,* with wood engravings by Michael McCurdy:

An extraordinary event once occurred in the land of Tennessee. A comet shot out of the sky like a ball of fox fire. But when the comet hit the top of a Tennessee mountain, a baby boy tumbled off and landed upright on his feet. His name was Davy Crockett.

Steven Kellogg's exuberance is clear in a book featuring Davy's wife, *Sally Ann Thunder Ann Whirlwind Crockett.*

▶ **WRITING FUN** Invite students to write a tall tale anecdote about their own births.

1926 Myra Cohn Livingston is born, in Omaha, Nebraska. In a course in music theory the French composer Darius Milhaud advises Myra, a French horn player, to respect the rules of music before breaking them in the name of creativity. Myra says, "If I have remembered nothing else in my life, it was that principle that I have lived by it." A prolific poet and anthologizer, Myra has a personal book collection of more than 10,000 volumes of poetry.

▶ **WRITING TIP** Myra advises, "When you write a poem, either tell me something I have never heard before or tell me in a new way something I have heard before."

▶ **WORD FUN** Challenge students to describe a tree, plant, or flower using just three words—as Myra does in this day's quotation.

EVENT

1976 An eight-cent Canadian stamp is issued in honor of poet Robert Service. This Canadian poet is best known for his vivid ballads about life in the Yukon Territory during the gold rush of the late 1880s. Two of Robert's best-known poems, "The Shooting of Dan McGrew" and "The Cremation of Sam McGee," appear in *Songs of a Sourdough*.

▶ **OUT LOUD** For a rousing and unforgettable good time, read "The Cremation of Sam McGee" aloud.

AUGUST

18

Can You Sue Your Parents for Malpractice?

Paula Danziger

BIRTHDAYS

1926 Phil Hirsch is born, in New York City. Also known as Bob Vlasic and Norman Lemon Peel, Phil is the author of *One Hundred and One Pickle Jokes*.

▶ **ALL ABOUT NAMES** Invite students to speculate why the author of *One Hundred and One Pickle Jokes* might call himself Bob Vlasic. They can also suggest names he might use for some of his other books, *One Hundred and One Watch Jokes, Vampire Jokes and Cartoons, Gorilla Jokes, One Hundred and One Hamburger Jokes*.

▶ **WRITING FUN** Challenge students to write a pickle joke. For starters, they should make a list of all words having anything to do with pickles: types, sizes, colors, tastes.

1931 Seymour Chwast is born, in the Bronx, New York. A graphic designer, he has written several creative alphabet books, including *Still Another Alphabet Book* and *Alphabet Parade*. His *The Twelve Circus Rings* gives "The Twelve Days of Christmas" a new twist as a cumulative counting book, helping children identify mathematical patterns.

▶ **WORD FUN** Invite students to use the "Twelve Days" pattern to create a story of massive mayhem: "The Twelve Days of School" or "Twelve Days in the Cafeteria" might be a place to start. Or maybe students would like to consider "The Twelve Days of My Birthday."

1944 Paula Danziger is born, in Washington, D.C. Three books she remembers as all-time favorites from her childhood are *The Little Engine That Could, Catcher in the Rye,* and *Pride and Prejudice,* though Paula says the list could go on forever. She writes *The Cat Ate My Gymsuit* in longhand, and it takes her three years to finish it. Since then, Paula has written many wildly popular books for young adults and for middle graders, including such intriguing titles as *Can You Sue Your Parents for Malpractice?* and *There's a Bat in Bunk Five*. Paula, a former reading teacher and junior high English teacher, says that many of her books are autobiographical.

Paula says, yes, she did fail gym class, and yes, she does have a younger brother, and yes, she does have asthma, and yes, she still threatens to sue her parents. Paula points out that an anagram of *parents* is *entraps*.

▶ **WRITING TIP** Paula says, "Read as much as you can. Write and rewrite. Take acting lessons. You can learn a lot about characterization that way. Also, you should probably take typing lessons so that you can do this faster than I can."

Event

1938 The movie *The Wizard of Oz* is released. It stars Frances Ethel Gumm. The youngest of three sisters and called Baby Gumm by adults, she hates her name and changes it to Judy Garland.

AUGUST

A ball is thrown into the air and never returns to earth.

Would you believe your eyes?

Vicki Cobb,
Magic . . . Naturally!

Birthdays

1902 Ogden Nash is born, in Rye, New York. A distant ancestor gave his name to Nashville, Tennessee. Ogden has to drop out of Harvard after one year to make a living. In 1930, he sends a nonsense poem to *The New Yorker.* They buy it and ask for more. For the next forty years, Ogden makes a living off poems like "You shake and shake the ketchup bottle/nothing comes, and then a lot'll." Noted for his humorous verse for adults, he also writes for children. One of Ogden's daughters is named Isabel, which is also the name of the protagonist of one of his most famous poems. When that Isabel is threatened, she "didn't scream or scurry./She washed her hands and she straightened her hair up,/Then Isabel quietly ate the bear up."

▶ **ALL ABOUT NAMES** Invite students to consider what a city named for them might be called. *A Place Called Peculiar: Stories About Unusual American Place-Names,* by Frank Gallant, makes for irresistible browsing for all ages. There's everything here—from Two Egg, Florida, to Gnaw Bone, Indiana, to Waterproof, Louisiana, to Checkerboard, Montana, to Donnybrook, North Dakota, to Wagontire, Oregon, to, of course, the famous Intercourse, Pennsylvania.

▶ **READ MORE** *Riddle City: USA! A Book of Geography Riddles,* by Marco and Giulio Maestro, contains riddles featuring cities, lakes, rivers, and mountains. There's at least one riddle for every state in the country. Loreen Leedy's *Celebrate the 50 States!* salutes the natural wonders, remarkable people, historic events, and state bird and flower that make each state unique. Laurie Keller's *The Scrambled States of America* is a must-see volume. The states decide to swap spots so they can see another part of the country. This mixed-media, madcap volume has something for everyone—from the budding romance between Mississippi and Nevada to the subtlety of time-zone changes. The actual position and climate of the states has a lot to do with the plot, so those worrying about learning objectives should be satisfied.

1938 Vicki Cobb is born, in New York City. Vicki credits her outlook on education to her mother's forward-looking thinking. She sends Vicki to The Little Red School-house, in Greenwich Village, a joyful experience of hands-on activities. She says the most significant book of her childhood is *The Secret Garden.* "When I was about eight my father started reading it aloud to me. I became terrified that Mary would be discovered trespassing in the garden and I made him stop reading it. When I was ten, I decided that I should face my fears and I read the book myself. It came to represent a personal victory." Vicki earns her bachelor's degree from Barnard College with a degree in zoology and her master's degree from Columbia University's Teachers College. After teaching science, she turns her talents to writing on scientific topics, producing many award-winning books.

1857 To memorialize his wife, Sir Isaac Pitman writes her this phonetic epitaph:

> In memori ov
> Meri Pitman,
> Weif ov Mr. Eizak Pitman,
> Fonetic Printer, ov this Site.
> Deid 19 Agust 1857, edjed 64
> (Preper tu mit thei God)
> Emos 4, 12

Pitman, inventor of the stenographic Soundhand, devoted his life to spelling reform and phonetic shorthand.

1996 *Lilly's Purple Plastic Purse,* by Kevin Henkes, is published.

▶ **READING REFLECTION** Invite students to read the story and then to write a letter of advice to Lily.

AUGUST

20

Alison acquired an
Amaryllis for Beryl.

Anita Lobel,
Alison's Zinnia

EVENT

1811 Thomas Jefferson writes to Charles Willson Peale, "No occupation is so delightful to me as the culture of the earth, and no culture comparable to that of the garden. Such a variety of subjects, some one always coming to perfection, the failure of one thing repaired by the success of another, and instead of one harvest a continued one through the year. . . But though an old man, I am but a young gardener."

▶ **READING/WRITING CONNECTION** Invite students to find and share poems about gardens. Share a couple of alphabet books about gardens. *The Secret Garden,* by Frances Hodgson Burnett, is probably the most famous and beloved book about a garden in the library, but there are plenty of short books worth considering. *The Rose in My Garden,* by Arnold and Anita Lobel, and *Alison's Zinnia,* by Anita Lobel, are stunning structures with which to inspire children's creativity. *A Gardener's Alphabet,* by Mary Azarian, shows the down-to-earth components of gardens from manure and compost piles to Queen Anne's lace and also gives children a structure within which to organize information. *Gardens of the Imagination,* edited by Sophie Biriotti, is a literary anthology about gardens ranging from the Biblical Garden of Eden to "A Tale of Two Gardens," by Octavio Paz—with a whole lot in between.

AUGUST

21

If you were a shiny new
fishhook

And I were a bucket of
worms. . . .

X. J. Kennedy,
"What We Might Be,
What We Are"

BIRTHDAYS

1929 X. J. Kennedy is born, in Dover, New Jersey. At birth, he is named Joseph Charles Kennedy. He claims to be "one of an endangered species: people who still write in meter and rime." The man who grows up to be a respected poet is an avid fan of comics as a child. Then, at age thirteen he discovers science fiction. This paramount writer of nonsense verse sees these verses as fun and as a way to win readers over to deeper poetry later.

▶ **WRITING TIP 1** Kennedy says that for him poems seldom start from an idea. Rather, a poem "usually begins with a promising blob of language." Encourage students to keep a notebook of such promising blobs, bits of intriguing language that they may not "do anything" with but that they can come back to later and enjoy.

▶ **WRITING TIP 2** Kennedy writes his verse first in his head before he gets out of bed in the morning. "I can remember up to about twenty-four lines of verse before I write them down."

1953 Arthur Yorinks is born, in Roslyn, New York. When he is sixteen Arthur takes a deep interest in picture books, especially the work of Tomi Ungerer, William Steig, and Maurice Sendak. He is so fascinated by Sendak that Arthur knocks on the door of his idol and shows Maurice his own work. Later, Maurice introduces Arthur to Richard Egielski, which marks the beginning of a fruitful collaboration between the two artists. This award-winning author's language in award-winning picture books is quite unique. Sometimes strange, sometimes funny, it is always distinctive.

1954 Claudia Mills is born, in New York City. She grows up in New Jersey. In school, Claudia writes in every class, which, she says, is why she didn't learn much algebra. She writes poems on napkins and on the backs of church bulletins, as well as on math tests. Claudia says her first books are about girls, but since becoming the mother of two sons, she now writes about boys too.

▶ **THINK ABOUT IT** The day before Claudia is ten years old, she writes a poem that begins, "There is much magic in the age/Of ten, that year as rich as gold. . . ." She says the ages of ten, eleven, and twelve are magical for her as a writer. "I tell children that they could spend the rest of their lives just writing books about the things that happened to them in fifth grade."

EVENT

2000 Warner Brothers announces the major cast selections for the first Harry Potter movie, which is to be based on the first two Potter books.

▶ **THINK ABOUT IT** What do kids think? Is it a good idea or not a good idea to make a movie of a beloved book?

AUGUST 22

It was a small town by a small river and a small lake in a small northern part of a Midwest state.

Ray Bradbury,
The Halloween Tree

BIRTHDAYS

1920 Ray Bradbury is born, in Waukegan, Illinois. Ray is an imaginative child who suffers from nightmares. At age twelve, Ray gets serious about his writing and begins his habit of writing for at least four hours a day.

▶ **READ MORE** Ray's only picture book, *Switch on the Night*, is about a little boy who conquers his fear of the night. Ray writes the story when his wife is pregnant with their first child. Recalling his own fears of the dark as a child, he decides to write a story "to prepare my future children, in some small way, to meet the failure of the light and the rising of the moon." The book, first published in 1955, is reissued nearly fifty years later, illustrated by Leo and Diane Dillon.

1947 Will Hobbs is born, in Pittsburgh, Pennsylvania. He is one of five children. Will says reading helps him adjust to all the changes of schools caused by his Air Force family's moves. Growing up, his favorite books are *The Lord of the Rings* trilogy by J. R. R. Tolkien. Will teaches reading for seventeen years before becoming a full-time writer. His award-winning books, which frequently draw on Native American and wildlife themes, often reflect Will's own experiences: whitewater rafting down the Colorado, exploring countryside, and respecting and learning from the land of the west. Will currently lives in a house he built himself in the Colorado mountains.

▶ **WRITING TIP** To start writing a book, Will first reads for a couple of months, developing what he calls a "compost pile" of memories and information.

AUGUST 23

> Our ears were kept busy with the incessant chirp of grasshoppers. . . .
>
> Robert Louis Stevenson

BIRTHDAY

1927 Melvin Berger is born, in Brooklyn, New York. Melvin writes informational books for middle graders on topics ranging from comets to computers to mind control.

▶ **READING/WRITING CONNECTION** Ask students to choose a nonfiction book on a topic of their choice. They should describe how the author organizes information in this book. Then the class can choose a topic and plan together how they might find and organize information on this topic.

EVENT

1879 Robert Louis Stevenson, poet, travel writer, and author of popular children's books, rides a train across the North American continent, writing in his journal as he rides. On this day he is looking across the landscape of Nebraska, noting "the incessant chirp of grasshoppers; a noise like the winding up of countless clocks and watches, which began after a while to seem proper to that land."

▶ **WRITING TIP** Invite students to keep listening journals, where they describe what they hear on their way to and from school. Encourage them to turn a few of their impressions into similes.

▶ **WORD FUN** *Hotter Than a Hot Dog,* by Stephanie Calmenson, is about the warm relationship between the narrator and her granny. One of the games they play is deciding who's hotter: "I'm hotter than a hot dog in a campfire!" "I'm hotter than a salamander in the sun." "Hotter than a turkey in the oven!" This word fun might not get to the point of metaphoric sublimity, but it is a good start for children learning to think metaphorically. Ask student volunteers to offer entries from their listening journals for the class to play with in this metaphoric manner.

AUGUST 24

> The shadows are as important as the light.
>
> Charlotte Bronte,
> *Jane Eyre*

BIRTHDAYS

1894 Ellen Gwendolen Rees Williams is born, in Rouseau, Dominica, West Indies. At age sixteen she emigrates to England. Then, in 1929, she moves to Paris, where she begins to write under the name Jean Rhys. Jean's novel *Wide Sargasso Sea* reconstructs the early life of Antoinette Coswar, Mr. Rochester's insane first wife in Charlotte Bronte's *Jane Eyre,* thus making *Wide Sargasso Sea* a prequel to *Jane Eyre.*

▶ **THINK ABOUT IT** This possibility usually astounds students. Can they think of any beloved books for which it would be nice to have a prequel? Maybe they'd like to write favorite authors with suggestions.

1941 Merlin Tuttle is born, in Honolulu, Hawaii. Merlin's family moves to the mainland when he is five. After earning a Ph.D. in ecology and evolution, Merlin becomes curator of mammals at the Milwaukee Public Museum and does a lot of bat fieldwork. When he can't get major environmental groups interested in protecting endangered bats, Merlin forms Bat Conservation International, quits his job, and devotes his life to convincing the public about how useful and charming bats really are. He has written several books on the topic, for both adults and children, and he is the subject of a book by Laurence Pringle, *Batman: Exploring the World of Bats.* The book chronicles how a young boy turns his curiosity into a lifelong dream.

▶ **READ MORE** Invite students to find out more about bats (for starters, how many mosquitoes they eat). Ask if what they learn changes their opinions of these creatures.

EVENT

1847 Charlotte Bronte sends the manuscript of *Jane Eyre* to the publisher. She uses the pseudonym Currier Bell.

▶ **ALL ABOUT NAMES** Invite students to create pseudonyms and hand in a piece of writing using those pseudonyms. Then you can try to guess who is who.

▶ **READ MORE** *Author Unknown: On the Trail of Anonymous,* by Don Foster, Vassar English professor, is an adult book, but his findings are of interest to students: no two people use language in precisely the same way; our identities are encoded in the way we use language. Among other cases, Foster recounts how it took him less than a week to figure out the identity of the anonymous author of *Primary Colors.*

AUGUST

We has met the enemy, and it is us.

Walt Kelly,
Pogo

BIRTHDAYS

1913 Walt Kelly is born. He works as an animator at Walt Disney Studios, working on *Pinocchio, Dumbo,* and *Fantasia.* In 1941, Walt draws a character called Pogo in the *Albert the Alligator* comic strip, but within a few years *Pogo* is a separate strip.

1959 Lane Smith is born, in Tulsa, Oklahoma. He spends most of his childhood in the foothills of Corona, California, with his parents and his brother Shane. "Shane and Lane. My mom thought this was funny. Yeah, a real hoot. However, her brothers were named Dub, Cubby, Leo, and Billy-Joe! My dad's brothers were Tom and Jerry (this is the truth)!" Lane attributes his bizarre sense of design to long family car trips back to Oklahoma every summer. "Once you've seen a 100-foot cement buffalo on top of a doughnut stand in the middle of nowhere, you're never the same." While attending college Lane works at Disneyland as a janitor. "Only we weren't called janitors; we were called custodial hosts." One of Lane's first projects is a series of paintings depicting the letters of the alphabet, each inspired by his favorite holiday, Halloween. The publishers are so impressed that they hire Eve Merriam to write poems to accompany the illustrations. The resulting book is *Halloween ABC.* In the 1980s, Lane meets Jon Scieszka, and their *The True Story of the Three Little Pigs* explodes on the book scene. Lane explains, "I think Jon thought of the wolf as a con artist trying to talk his way out of a situation. But I really believed the wolf, so I portrayed him with glasses and a little bow tie and tried to make him a sympathetic victim of circumstance."

▶ **WORD FUN** Halloween in August? Why not! Invite students to create a list of Halloween words—and then compare their choices with Lane's and Eve's.

EVENTS

1852 Here is Henry David Thoreau's total journal entry for this day: "Rain. Rain."

▶ **WRITING TIP** Challenge students to come up with a repeated word or phrase that in describing a physical quality also creates a mood.

1902 *Al-Hoda,* the first Arabic daily newspaper in the United States, begins publication, in New York City.

▶ **FIND OUT** Invite someone from the community to tell the class about the Arabic language.

26

One day Morris the Moose saw a cow. "You are a funny-looking moose," he said.

Bernard Wiseman,
Morris the Moose

BIRTHDAYS

1922 Bernard Wiseman is born, in Brooklyn, New York. He is the author of the popular Morris the Moose series for young readers, in which Morris is always irritating Boris by misunderstanding things and asking too many questions. But in the end, friendship wins out.

1952 Will Shortz is born, in Crawfordsville, Indiana. Will is an enigmatologist, the only academically accredited one in the world, designing his own major at Indiana University, which has an independent study program. To pursue this degree, Will consults professors in English, philosophy, math, linguistics, journalism, and psychology. Will also has a law degree, but after graduating he skips the bar exam and begins creating puzzles. Former editor of *Games* magazine, Will is the crossword editor of the *New York Times*. The author or editor of twenty-three puzzle books, Will also creates a weekly puzzle segment for National Public Radio.

▶ **WORD FUN** Invite students to play word games: anagrams, palindromes, codes.

AUGUST

27

I know things about the family, and I'm the youngest. Maybe I know them because I'm the youngest. And they said things to me and thought I wouldn't understand.

Ann Rinaldi,
*The Coffin Quilt:
The Feud Between the Hatfields
and the McCoys*

BIRTHDAYS

1796 Sophia Smith is born, in Hatfield, Massachusetts, the daughter of a prosperous farmer. At her death, Sophia stipulates that her fortune be used to establish a woman's college in Northampton, Massachusetts. Smith College is chartered in 1871 and opens in 1875 with fourteen students.

▶ **READ MORE** Jane Yolen, a Smith alumnae, writes *Tea with an Old Dragon: A Story of Sophia Smith, Founder of Smith College.*

1934 Ann Rinaldi is born, in New York City. Ann's mother dies soon after she is born, and Ann goes to live with her aunt and uncle. When she returns to live with her father, a wicked stepmother enters the picture. By the time she is ten, books are Ann's friends and her way of escape from a lonely and miserable childhood. Ann says her husband, Ron, introduces sanity to her life. Their son, a high schooler, becomes involved in Revolutionary War reenactments, and Ann gets involved too. She starts doing research, and this research appears in her historical novels.

▶ **WRITING TIP** For Ann, writing is a job, and she writes every day from 9:00 A.M. to 2:00 or 3:00 P.M.

1943 Suzy Kline is born, in Berkeley, California. Suzy says her first serious writing begins when she is eight. She writes letters to her grandfather in Indiana, telling him what's happening at her house. Suzy has many books to her credit: characters in the popular Horrible Harry series keep getting their own series. But when Suzy visits schools, she brings her bag of rejections. She tells students they are her "no thank yous"—the stories no one wants. She tells students she saves them because ideas can be reworked—even the poem she wrote in third grade. Suzy is a longtime teacher and tells how her first book, *Shhhh!,* was inspired by her classroom. "I was in class . . . working with my second-grade students on a Beverly Cleary. . . . The children were thinking of favorite scenes to paint, and they were just bubbling with noise. So I walked around trying to show interest and 'shhhh'ed' them down. That night at dinner when my husband asked me to pass the salt, I looked at him and said, 'Shhhh!' He gave me a blank look, and so did my daughters. I realized I had so many shhhh's in my head they were erupting out of control, so I immediately went to my typewriter and put them in a story!"

1945 Suzanne Fisher Staples is born, in Philadelphia, Pennsylvania. Suzanne grows up loving books. "My grandmother read to us very day and bribed us with stories to help in her rock garden." A marketing director and foreign correspondent, Suzanne says she had never considered writing a novel—until she went to Pakistan. "There was something about the camels, the ancient stories and blue-tiled mosques, and people who build shrines where a beautiful poem was written, that set my heart to singing." Suzanne's first novel for young adults, *Shabanu: Daughter of the Wind*, is a Newbery Honor book.

EVENTS

1906 President Theodore Roosevelt sends the public printer a list of three hundred words that he thinks should be spelled according to the Simplified Spelling Board guidelines. This organization campaigns for deleting the *u* in *honour* and *parlour,* changes that eventually do come about. However, many of the proposed changes, such as *kissed* to *kist* and *though* to *tho,* create a public uproar. Congress questions the power of the president to change spelling and instructs the printing office that all materials sent to Congress must contain conventional spelling. Eventually, Roosevelt withdraws his order.

▶ **WRITING TIP** Invite students to come up with, say, ten words whose spelling they think should be revised. Then they should write a letter, making their case, sending copies to the local newspaper and to their Congressional representatives.

1912 Tarzan first appears—in a story by Chicago advertising writer Edgar Rice Burroughs—thus beginning the wildly popular saga of an English nobleman's son abandoned in the African jungle and brought up by apes.

1929 Popeye's life changes forever when Olive Oyle mistakenly plants a kiss on his cheek and they fall in love.

AUGUST

Our home was a corner grocery store and we were open for business every day of the year.

"In America, you can be anything you want to be," Dad told us.

That was good news because none of us wanted to be a grocer when we grew up.

Allen Say,
El Chino

BIRTHDAYS

1904 Roger Duvoisin is born, in Geneva, Switzerland. Roger begins studying music at age seven and later attends the Geneva Conservatory of Music. He also studies mural painting and stage scenery design at the Ecole des Arts Decoratifs. Roger's interest in ceramics and textiles leads to a job offer in New York to design textiles. He and his wife move to the United States in 1925. A two-time Caldecott Medal winner, Roger and his wife collaborate on *The Happy Lion*. They get the idea from an actual event: a lion's escape from a circus in a small French town causes much excitement among the populace, but the well-fed lion is calm and peaceful as it wanders the streets.

1908 Roger Tory Peterson is born, in Jamestown, New York. At age twenty-six, he writes *Field Guide to Birds*, which revolutionizes the field of guide books by grouping birds by their resemblance to one another.

▶ **READ MORE** Invite students to compile a list of books in which birds are important. Paul Fleischman's *Townsend's Warbler* and Barbara Brenner's *On the Frontier with Mr. Audubon* are a good place to start. Students may be inspired to begin bird-spotting logs, where they note date and time they spot different types of birds.

1915 Tasha Tudor is born, in Boston, Massachusetts. Her given name is Starling Burgess, but her father nicknames her Natasha after the heroine in Tolstoy's *War and Peace*. Tudor is Tasha's mother's maiden name. Tasha's parents divorce when she is nine, and she goes to live with family friends while her mother pursues a career in art. Believing she had a past life in the 1830s, Tasha creates surroundings in rural Vermont to correspond with that time period. Her books reflect this atmosphere.

1937 Allen Say is born, in Yokohama, Japan. Because of World War II, his family moves a lot, and Allen attends seven different grade schools. "I was terrified of schools and teachers," he remembers. When he is twelve, Allen apprentices himself to a renowned cartoonist, who introduces him to both Eastern and Western drawing styles. Allen describes this experience in *The Ink-Keeper's Apprentice,* which is an account of his own boyhood. Allen still sends his mentor every book he creates. When he is sixteen, Allen comes to the United States. He receives the Caldecott Medal for *Grandfather's Journey.*

▶ **READING REFLECTION** Allen says, "A good story should alter you in some way; it should change your thinking, your feeling, your psyche, or the way you look at things." Invite students to keep a "reading changes" journal for two weeks. They should write the title of books read and comment on a change in feeling or way of looking at things. Emphasize that such a change can be a very small twinge or a great big aha!

1959 Kevin Hawkes is born, in Virginia. When asked by third graders in Orono, Maine, how he learned to draw and where he gets his ideas, Kevin replies, "To learn how to draw you practice drawing. When you want to develop your imagination, read, read, read." Kevin and his family live on a small Maine island that is a twenty-minute ferry ride from the mainland. Kevin's home has three children and no television. Kevin says he's not anti-TV; he just knows that turning off the tube forces kids to create their own entertainment.

▶ **THINK ABOUT IT** Invite students to make a list of one hundred things they can do instead of watching television. The website <*www.tvturnoff.org*> offers lots of suggestions and information about what kids do during the annual weeklong event held each April.

1961 J. Brian Pinkney is born, in Boston, Massachusetts, the son of an artist and a writer. He graduates from the Philadelphia College of Art and receives an M.A. from the School of Visual Arts, in New York City. Brian starts playing drums when he is eight years old. He keeps a set of drumsticks in his studio.

EVENT

1963 Martin Luther King, Jr., leads a civil rights march on Washington, D.C. At the Lincoln Memorial he delivers his famous speech: "I have a dream that this nation will rise up and live out the true meaning of its creed 'We hold these truths to be self-evident, that all men are created equal.'" "We Shall Overcome" is the theme song on this march.

AUGUST

Nimmy, nimmy, not, my name's Tom Tit Tot.

Tom Tit Tot,
retold by Joseph Jacobs

BIRTHDAYS

1854 Joseph Jacobs is born in Sydney, Australia, and later emigrates to the U. S. An eminent folklorist, Joseph's retellings of folk and fairytales are illustrated by a host of artists. His *Tom Tit Tot* is a humorous version of *Rumpelstiltskin.*

1952 Karen Hesse is born, in Baltimore, Maryland. A sickly child, she finds comfort only in rides in the family car. She loves books, reading for hours in an apple tree in the back yard. When she's not in the tree, she's at the Enoch Pratt Free Library near her house. Karen reads her way through the picture books, the chapter books, and finally the novels. Karen says *Hiroshima,* by John Hersey, changes her life, helping her see the world in a way she hadn't known. The many fans of this Newbery Medal–winning author feel her work does the same for them.

1769 Edmond Hoyle dies. In 1742, Edmond writes *A Short Treatise on the Game of Whist* for students he is teaching how to play the game. He also organizes rules for playing backgammon and chess. His book on games is published in many editions, and the expression "according to Hoyle" becomes synonymous with the idea of playing according to the rules.

▶ **WRITE MORE** Invite students to write directions for playing a game.

1962 At age eighty-eight, Robert Frost leaves on a goodwill tour to the Soviet Union sponsored by the U. S. State Department.

▶ **THINK ABOUT IT** Ask students what poets they'd like to see go as goodwill ambassadors to foreign countries. Maybe students would like to write the President, suggesting the idea.

AUGUST

By the dim and yellow light of the moon, as it forced its way through the window shutters, I beheld the wretch—the miserable monster whom I had created. His eyes, if eyes they may be called, were fixed on me. His jaws opened, and he muttered some inarticulate sounds, while a grin wrinkled his cheeks.

Mary Wollstonecraft Shelley, *Frankenstein*

BIRTHDAYS

1797 Mary Wollstonecraft Shelley is born, in London, England. She writes *Frankenstein* when she is nineteen years old. She and her husband and two friends have a contest to see who can write the best ghost story. Mary is the only one who finishes a tale. Although she writes four other novels and numerous essays, nothing gets the attention that her first work does. The work has been adapted for movies, drama, and numerous illustrated editions, including one by Barry Moser.

1909 Virginia Lee Burton is born, in Newton Centre, Massachusetts. She spends her childhood in California. Instead of toys, her father gives her beautifully illustrated books for birthdays and Christmas. Virginia is sure her interest in picture books stems from this. Virginia goes to Boston intending to be a dancer, but she studies drawing with George Demetrios, a well-known sculptor, whom she marries. She is the author of perennially popular books for young readers, including *The Little House* and *Mike Mulligan and the Steam Shovel*. Virginia regards her sons as collaborators on the books. She shows them pictures and drafts, making changes until they like the results.

▶ **WRITING TIP** For Virginia, the pictures come first. She pins them on the walls of her studio so she can see the whole book. When the pictures are done, Virginia writes the text. "Whenever I can," says Virginia, "I substitute picture for word."

1925 Laurent de Brunhoff is born, in France. *Babar* is born in 1931 when Laurent's mother begins telling bedtime stories about a kind and noble elephant who lives in the jungle. Her husband Jean likes the stories and decides to illustrate them. When Laurent is twelve, his father dies of tuberculosis, leaving unfinished *Babar and Father Christmas*. Laurent helps his uncle fill in the colors for this book. When Laurent finishes high school, he goes to art school and one day decides to try creating a Babar book of his own. *Babar and That Rascal Arthur* is published in 1946, and there have been twenty-seven more since then. In 1989, Babar makes his television debut on HBO in a sixteen-part television series.

1938 Donald Crews is born, in Newark, New Jersey. A popular author/illustrator of concept books, Donald says of his autobiographical work, "*Bigmama's* has been in my head for a long time. Some of the story is in *Freight Train*. But as I chose not to draw people in my earlier books, I could not actually have created *Bigmama's* until now." Donald says he invited his editor, Susan Hirschman, to a Mother's Day dinner at his parents' house. "Family meals include my parents, my brother and sisters, my wife, Ann, my daughters, nieces, nephews, and special guests. After dinner the talk usually turns to the past, and that leads to the summers we spent in Florida at Bigmama's. That night, in order to give Ann and Susan and the younger family members an idea of how everything looked, I began sketching as we talked. And I saved the sketches." Those sketches become the core of a new picture book, a book in which Donald remembers his summers with a woman who told him, "Boy, you going to amount to something."

EVENT

1990 Felipe Carbonnel begins telling jokes at the Lima Sheraton Hotel, Lima, Peru. He does not stop for one hundred hours, setting a world joke-telling record.

▶ **READING TIP** Do your students want to hold a joke-reading/telling afternoon?

AUGUST

31

. . . very thick and sultry, dogdayish.

Henry David Thoreau, in his journal

BIRTHDAY

1908 William Saroyan is born. In the preface to his Pulitzer Prize–winning drama, *The Time of Your Life*, William writes, "In the time of your life, live—so that in that good time there shall be no ugliness or death for yourself or for any life your life touches. Seek goodness everywhere, and where it is found, bring it out of its hiding-place and let it be free and unashamed."

EVENTS

1853 Henry David Thoreau notes in his journal that the growth of plants commonly called weeds in a swamp where he walks "impresses me like a harvest of flowers. I am surprised at their luxuriance and profusion." Thoreau describes the August swamp as "very thick and sultry, dogdayish" and August as a month of "green corn and melons and plums and the earliest apples . . . and weeds."

▶ **WRITING TIP** Thoreau offers young writers a nice entree into word creation. Out of the familiar phrase "dog days of summer" he creates *dogdayish* to describe the August doldrums. Invite students to add a word to *dayish* trying to describe a quality of August—or any other month or season.

1995 Ruby Bridges Hall and Robert Coles receive honorary degrees from Connecticut College. Ruby tells her story of what it was like to be the six-year-old who integrated the New Orleans Public Schools—and Dr. Cole's involvement in her life—in a sophisticated picture book for all ages, *Through My Eyes.*

SEPTEMBER

Homework! Oh, homework!
I hate you! You stink!

Jack Prelutsky,
Homework! Oh, Homework!

SEPTEMBER

1

Tublat, Kalas's husband, was sorely vexed, and but for the female's careful watching would have put the child out of the way. "He will never be a great ape," he argued. "Always will you have to carry him and protect him. What good will he be to the tribe? None; only a burden."

Edgar Rice Burroughs,
Tarzan of the Apes

BIRTHDAYS

1875 Edgar Rice Burroughs is born, in Chicago. He is a soldier, business executive, gold miner, cowboy, storekeeper, and policeman before he takes up writing. *Tarzan of the Apes* is published in 1914, the first of twenty novels depicting the adventures of a boy stranded in Africa and raised by apes. Translated into more than fifty languages, the Tarzan books have inspired movies, radio serials, television shows, and a comic strip.

▶ **OUT LOUD** Betsy Byars's take on a female Tarzan in *Me Tarzan* is a winner.

1946 Jim Aronsky is born, in New York City. He has no formal art training but learns techniques from his father, a draftsman. Jim does illustrations for *Cricket, Jack & Jill,* and *Ranger Rick* for a number of years before he writes his own books. Now a resident of northern Vermont, Jim shares his love of nature with readers, providing detailed information about plants and animals. Jim says, "My books are personal. I write only of what I have seen."

▶ **WRITING/DRAWING CONNECTION** Jim's books don't provide how-to instructions but help young readers become more aware of their surroundings, to make personal discoveries, and above all, to notice details. In this spirit, invite students to take a walk in the area near the school—with the thought of finding details they don't think anyone else will notice. Back in the classroom they can write about or draw these details—or both.

EVENTS

1853 In his journal Henry David Thoreau describes the different hues of asters he and his sister collect on an afternoon walk: deep bluish-purple; bright lilac-purple; pale bluish-purple, turning white; purplish pink; pale pinkish purple; and violet.

▶ **CELEBRATE** Invite students to notice color variations on another walk near the school, finding words to distinguish variety in hue.

1968 The first school for circus clowns opens, in Venice, Florida. Many future performers with Ringling Brothers and Barnum & Bailey Circus learn their art here. Prospective students are asked a series of interesting questions on the college application form: "List five movies you'd like to see again; list five of your favorite books; name your favorite foods. What part of the world would you most like to visit? Why? Describe your first proud accomplishment; what is the most important life lesson you've learned to date? When was the last time you cried? For what reason?" Ask students to consider what the people reading these answers will learn about the applicants. How do these qualities differ from what people reading high-stakes test answers learn about students?

▶ **READ MORE** In *The Most Excellent Book of How to Be a Clown,* Catherine Perkins offers step-by-step instructions on clowning.

1979 *Amelia Bedelia Helps Out,* by Peggy Parish, is published.

▶ **READING/WRITING CONNECTION** The story structure makes it a natural for readers theatre, with students zeroing in on the dialogue. Invite students to plan a party for Amelia, inventing the funniest food ever (sponge cake, marble cake—reading cookbooks will show them lots of possibilities). They can add party hats decorated with funny idioms—such as "hold your horses," "frog in the throat," and so on.

► **READ MORE** Fred Gwynne titles such as *A Chocolate Moose for Dinner* and *The King Who Rained* provide another take on the same topic—and inspiration for students who want to draw pictures about homonym confusion.

SEPTEMBER

2

Why does a dog have a curl in its tail?

So fleas can loop the loop.

John Bierhorst,
*Lightning Inside You . . .
and Other Native American
Riddles*

BIRTHDAYS

1820 Lucretia Peabody Hale is born, in Boston, Massachusetts. She writes the first American nonsense classic, *The Peterkin Papers*, noodlehead tales with a New England flavor, about a problem-prone family.

► **READ MORE** Invite younger students to read Harry Allard and James Marshall's The Stupids series and older students to read Isaac Bashevis Singer's *Zlateh the Goat*, seven folktales from Chelm, a village of fools.

1936 John Bierhorst is born, in Boston. He grows up in Ohio. As a young boy, John loves classifying plants. After traveling to Peru and hearing the Quechua language, John becomes engrossed in American Indian life. He translates and adapts numerous collections of American Indian stories, poems, and songs.

► **READ MORE** Invite students to compare Doctor Coyote fables with Aesop fables. For starters, which animal is pictured as wise—and which as the dunce—in each?

1937 Bernard Most is born. Bernard credits his son Glenn with giving him the idea for his first published book. "When Glenn was in first grade, he wrote that he wished the dinosaurs would come back. That gave me the idea for *If the Dinosaurs Came Back*." When Bernard visits schools, he tells children, "Desire and believing in yourself is more important than 'natural' talent. You must love what you do and work very hard to make your own 'luck' happen. Too many children, as well as grown-ups, get discouraged easily and give up on their goals and dreams."

► **WRITING TIP** Invite students to create their own "if the dinosaurs came back" pictures and possibilities. Then show them Bernard's book—they will be amazed and delighted that some of their ideas are similar to this and some even better than his. If they have trouble getting started, you can give them this advice from Dougie, a third grader: "A Bridgasaurus could get people and cars across a big river." But hold off giving prompts; when divergent thinking erupts independently, it is magic.

1942 Demi is born, in Cambridge, Massachusetts. Her name at birth is Charlotte Dumaresq Hunt. She attends school in Guanajuato, Mexico, and Los Angeles, then travels to India on a Fulbright scholarship. Demi says the two strong influences on her art are *The Mustard Seed Garden Manual* of painting, written in 1679, and her husband, Tze-si Jesse Huang, who shares the traditional stories of his youth with her. Demi paints on silk, using traditional ingredients in her paint, adding powdered jade "for good fortune." Demi says, "Everything alive is magic. To capture life on paper is magic. To capture life on paper was the aim of Chinese painters. That is my aim too."

► **READ MORE** In her illustrations for *Grass Sandals: The Travels of Basho,* by Dawnine Spival, Demi creates remarkable artwork resembling porcelain paintings. Students will enjoy "reading" the illustrations as well as the verse.

EVENT

1893 Beatrix Potter writes what becomes one of the most famous letters in all literature—a "picture letter" to five-year-old Noel, who is sick in bed: "My dear Noel, I don't know what to write you, so I shall tell you a story about four little rabbits whose names were Flopsy, Mopsy, Cottontail, and Peter. . . ."

What to the American slave is your Fourth of July? I answer, a day that reveals to him, more than all other days of the year, the gross injustice and cruelty to which he is the constant victim.

Frederick Douglass:
In His Own Words,
edited by Milton Meltzer and
illustrated by Stephen Alcorn

BIRTHDAY

1929 Aliki Liacouras Brandenberg is born, in Wildwood Crest, New Jersey. Illustrator of over one hundred books, both her own and those of other writers, Aliki describes drawing in kindergarten: "I drew a portrait of two families—each with three girls and a boy named Peter—my family and Peter Rabbit's. My teacher told my parents, 'She's going to be an artist.'" Aliki says her two children appear in most of her books "even if they sometimes look like cats or mice." Alika says, "I love the privacy of books—both reading them and making them." Aliki writes both fiction books, in which she expresses her feelings, and nonfiction books, in which she researches subjects she is interested in and wants to know more about.

▶ **READ MORE** *Marianthe's Story: Painted Words, Spoken Memories* tells of a little girl who is new in the classroom and can't speak English, so she expresses her feelings by painting. The paintings appear on the verso pages; on the recto pages the girl narrates what is going on in the paintings and shares memories of her homeland in Greece.

EVENT

1838 Frederick Augustus Washington Bailey escapes from slavery in Baltimore and makes his way to New York City, where he is protected by the Underground Railroad. He changes his name to Frederick Douglass and becomes one of the great leaders of the antislavery movement.

▶ **READ MORE** *Frederick Douglass: In His Own Words*, edited by Milton Meltzer and illustrated by Stephen Alcorn is an informative and beautiful volume. Milton Meltzer provides notes to explain each of Frederick Douglass's writings. Stephen Alcorn explains that he has conceived his illustrations as a series of images kindred in spirit to a nineteenth-century crazy quilt rather than as literal illustrations of certain passages. "Like a medieval scribe gone mad with design, I commenced to work on this cycle of prints, in search of a visual equivalent to that elusive, indomitable spirit that could not be broken."

"Those are powerful books Richard," he said. "Those books will stay with you for the rest of your life. But for now," he said, looking around the office, "you should keep them to yourself."

William Miller,
Richard Wright
and the Library Card

BIRTHDAYS

1908 Richard Wright is born, near Natchez, Mississippi. After Richard's father leaves the family when he is young and his mother is stricken with a paralyzing illness, Richard is raised by relatives. Richard's novel *Native Son*, a searing indictment of racism, is a best seller and the first book by an African American chosen as a Book-of-the-Month Club selection.

▶ **READ MORE** *Richard Wright and the Library Card*, by William Miller, is a fictionalized account of a scene in Richard's autobiography *Black Boy*. It describes Richard's struggle to check out books from the whites-only library in Memphis.

1912 Syd Hoff is born, in New York City. One of his early memories is going on a subway ride with his family and then, when he gets home, drawing a picture of the subway conductor because he is fascinated by the shape of the conductor's cap. Syd knows he wants to grow up and draw like the cartoonists in the newspaper. At fifteen, he enters the National Academy of Design to study fine art, where he becomes convinced he wants to paint like Rembrandt, Monet, and DaVinci. After selling a cartoon to *The New Yorker* when he is eighteen, Syd decides he is a cartoonist. Drawings made to divert his daughter's attention from her illness become *Danny and the Dinosaur*.

1939 Joan Aiken is born, in Rye, Sussex, England, daughter of American poet Conrad Aiken and stepdaughter of English writer Martin Armstrong. Joan decides at age five that she, too, will be a writer. From age five, she starts keeping a diary, taking it with her wherever she goes. Joan fondly remembers *Peter Rabbit*, *The Just So Stories*, and *Pinocchio*, as well as Walter de la Mare's poems in *Peacock Pie*. "I still know many of his poems by heart," she says.

▶ **WRITING TIP** Joan advises students, "Try to write a few pages every day. Never write anything that bores you. Collect interesting stories from the newspapers."

SEPTEMBER 5

Were Rembrandt alive today, he'd likely be producing masterpieces on the copy machine.

Paul Fleischman,
Copier Creations

BIRTHDAYS

1945 Roxie Munro is born, in Mineral Wells, Texas. At age six, she wins first prize in a countrywide art contest. After college, Roxie works as a clothing designer and a courtroom artist for television and newspapers. She also paints fourteen covers for *The New Yorker*. Roxie says her art requires active seeing. "When I walk down the street, ride a bus, or go up an escalator, I feel the changing space and notice the flow of patterns. . . . My mind organizes reality. I'll notice two gray cars, a red car, a black car, and two more red cars—aha!—a pattern." Roxie says sometimes she imagines herself within such a scene. "Suddenly I am in the tiny car on the winding road or swinging down the big-city avenue."

▶ **ART TIP** Invite students to draw a picture of the classroom from their own vantage point from within the scene. For starters, they should look for patterns in this scene.

1952 Paul Fleischman is born, in Monterey, California, the son of well-known children's book author and fellow Newbery Medal–winner Sid Fleischman. Growing up, Paul has no intention of being a writer. He prefers riding his bike and looking for "found objects," which he uses in sculptures. But Sid regularly reads chapters of his work to the family, and they give suggestions about what should happen next in the story. Paul says, "We grew up knowing that words felt good in the ears and on the tongue, that they were as much fun to play with as toys." Music is important too. Paul and his mother play the piano, his sisters play the flute, and his father plays the guitar. Paul's writing reflects a wide-ranging curiosity in music, the natural world, history, string stories, and, as he demonstrates in *Copier Creations*, using copy machines to make decals, silhouettes, flip books, films, and much more.

▶ **WRITING TIP** Paul points to the opening sentence of *Saturnalia* to show how deliberate his writing is: "The weather vanes of Boston were pointed north—the frigates, the angels, the cocks, the cows—and so, below, was Mr. Baggot." Paul points out that this sentence has three parts, each of which contains four primary stresses. "I work out my books in detail before starting, so that most of my writing time is devoted not to sense but to sound: to rhythm, to the rhyme of *so* and *below*, then the pivot to the alliteration with *Baggot*." Paul refers to this process as "playing in the vast sandbox of the English Language." And that's just one sentence!

EVENTS

1963 *Clifford the Big Red Dog*, by Norman Bridwell, is published. Norman invents the dog he wanted as a young boy, one that he could ride around on and who would be a fun companion.

▶ **ALL ABOUT NAMES** Norman plans on calling the big red dog Tiny, but his wife thinks that name doesn't have enough pizzazz and suggests he call the dog Clifford after an imaginary friend from her childhood.

1989 *Madeline*, a Caldecott Honor book by Ludwig Bemelmans, celebrates its fiftieth birthday. Ludwig gets the idea for the book when a car-bicycle mishap puts him into the trees—and the hospital. "The sisters in that hospital wore large, starched white hats that looked like the wings of a giant butterfly. In the room next to mine was a little girl who had her appendix out. In the ceiling over my bed was a crack that had the habit of sometimes looking like a rabbit." Invite students to reread Madeline—and look for the rabbit.

SEPTEMBER 6

The sun is but a morning star.

Henry David Thoreau,
Walden

BIRTHDAY

1869 Siegmund Salzmann is born, in Budapest. He spends most of his life in Vienna, where he is a journalist using the pen name Felix Salten. In 1923, Felix's pleasure in the wildlife of the Alps gives him the idea for a book, and he writes *Bambi: A Life in the Woods.* Whittaker Chambers translates the American edition when he is eighteen years old; Barbara Cooney illustrates it.

EVENTS

1847 Henry David Thoreau leaves Walden Pond after a stay of more than two years.

1967 A teacher tells Harper & Row editor Ursula Nordstrom that according to her district curriculum mandates she is supposed to teach students Emerson's "Essay on Friendship." Instead, she reads *Charlotte's Web* aloud because "it does everything Emerson could have done."

SEPTEMBER 7

REVILE LIVER!

Jon Agee,
Sit on a Potato Pan, Otis!

BIRTHDAY

1860 Anna Mary Robertson is born, in Washington Country, New York. When she is seventeen, she marries Thomas Moses, a farmer. They have ten children, five of whom die in infancy. When she is seventy-eight years old Grandma Moses, who has never had an art lesson and whose fingers are too crippled by arthritis to continue embroidering pictures, starts painting. Her work is immediately popular. At age one hundred she illustrates Clement Moore's *'Twas the Night Before Christmas.*

▶ **READ MORE** *Grandma Moses: Twenty-five Masterworks,* by Jane Kallir and Grandma Moses, *The Year with Grandma Moses,* by W. Nikola-Lisa, and *Grandma Moses: Painter of Rural America,* by Zibby Oneal, give a good overview of Grandma Moses and her work.

EVENTS

1991 The Avon, Colorado, town council votes to name the town's new 150-foot bridge across the Eagle River *Bob.* The town spokesperson said, "I don't think people are going to forget Bob. You can spell it backwards or forwards and still get it right."

▶ **READ MORE** Challenge students to come up with more names that read the same forwards and backwards. Then they may want to read *Go Hang a Salami! I'm a Lasagna Hog!* and *So Many Dynamos! and Other Palindromes,* both by Jon Agee.

2000 The Seymour B. Durst Old York Library and Reading Room is dedicated, at the Graduate Center of the City University of New York. It contains three thousand of the rarest books from the late Seymour Durst's private collection, along with furnishings from his study. When Durst died, in 1995, books about New York fill every space of his five-story New York townhouse. The refrigerator is even stuffed with books (he ate out). Sixteen of the twenty rooms in his house, as well as the closets, are devoted to his book collection, with each room having a different theme. If a book fell into three different categories, then Durst would buy three copies, so each of the related rooms had its own copy. Durst's own favorite book about New York was E. B. White's *Here Is New York.* On-line access to much of the collection will be made available at *www.oldyorklibrary.org*

▶ **READ MORE** *The Library,* by Sarah Stewart, illustrated by David Small, is dedicated to and about the real life of spinster librarian Elizabeth Brown, who also finds a way to solve the problem of too many books.

SEPTEMBER

8

Your nose would be a source of dread

were it attached atop your head

Jack Prelutsky,
"Be Glad Your Nose Is on Your Face," *The New Kid on the Block*

BIRTHDAYS

1940 Jack Prelutsky is born, in Brooklyn, New York. His all-time favorite book is *The Wind in the Willows.* After Jack graduates from the High School of Music and Art, in New York City, where he studies voice, he works at a music store in Greenwich Village. Jack has also been a cab driver, a busboy, a photographer, a furniture mover, a potter, and a folksinger. In addition to writing poems children love, Jack also edits wonderful poetry anthologies. He says, "I think children need poetry the way children need bread and water and air. And art and architecture and everything else. It's just another piece of the puzzle."

▶ **WORD FUN 1** In *Ride a Purple Pelican,* Jack combines poetry with geography, with all the verses containing place names. Challenge students to get out a map and see what they can do: "Late one night in Kalamazoo,/the baboons had a barbecue...."

▶ **WORD FUN 2** Jack says that *Rolling Harvey Down the Hill* is about the kids he grew up with in the Bronx. "I simply talk about the things we did—pulling practical jokes on each other, wrestling, and playing games." Invite students to write about playing a game with (or a trick on) a friend.

1948 Michael Hague is born, in Los Angeles. Michael's mother encourages his talent for drawing. Michael recalls being greatly influenced by the comics, especially Prince Valiant. Michael says, "As an artist I have not only the pleasure but the duty to daydream. It is part of my work." Michael's work is also influenced by the classic illustrators Arthur Rackham, N. C. Wyeth, and Howard Pyle. Both Michael and his wife, Kathleen, graduate from the Los Angeles Art Center College of Design. After college he works for Hallmark Cards and Current, Inc., designing greeting cards and calendars. His first picture book illustrations are for Jane Yolen's *Dream Weaver.*

1954 Jon Scieszka is born, in Flint, Michigan. Jon notes that he is "second oldest and nicest of six brothers." When asked where he gets his ideas, Jon lists his elementary school principal dad, his registered nurse mom, *Mad* magazine, *The Rocky and Bullwinkle Show,* four years of premed education, an M.F.A. in fiction from Columbia University, Robert Benchley, *Green Eggs and Ham,* five years spent painting apartments in New York City, his lovely wife, his daughter and son, ten years as a teacher, living in Brooklyn. Jon gets the idea for *The True Story of the Three Little Pigs!* after rewriting fairy tales with his second-grade class. Jon sees his three Time Warp chapter books as a tribute and an offering to all of those kids who are looking for something entertaining and smart to read. Jon hopes the Time Warp books will help kids connect to lots more books.

▶ **READING TIP** Jon's favorite things to read are fairy tales, myths, legends, comic books, graphic novels, history, poems, novels, science books, picture books, short stories, newspapers, funny bits, codes, hieroglyphics, encyclopedias, dictionaries, subway ads, sides of cereal boxes, matchbook covers, mattress tags, and any little scraps of paper with writing on them.

► **READING TIP** In the spring 2001, Jon launches GUYS READ! a literacy initiative for boys. For more information see: *www.guysread.com*

► **WORD FUN** *Baloney (Henry P.)* shows the importance of imagination when you are in a tight spot. It also contains lots of weird words that seem to come from outer space (which literary sleuths will have fun figuring out). The book has its own website: *www.baloneyhenryp.com*

► **WORD FUN** Individual tales in *The Stinky Cheese Man and Other Fairly Stupid Tales*—"The Princess and The Bowling Ball," "Little Red Running Shorts," and "Cinderumpelstiltskin"—should get kids thinking about other nutty titles. Once a list of titles and characters is posted, let the writing begin.

EVENT

1962 When a young fan complains that the Narnia books have no maps, C. S. Lewis responds, "But why not do one yourself! And why not write stories for yourself to fill up the gaps in Narnian history? I've left you plenty of hints—especially where Lucy and the Unicorn are talking in *The Last Battle*. I feel I have done all I can!"

► **WRITING TIP** Invite students to create a map for a story they love.

SEPTEMBER

9

Nothing ever happens in Antler, Texas, but in fact a lot happened in the summer of 1971 to young Toby Wilson.

Kimberly Willis Holt,
When Zachary Beaver Came to Town

BIRTHDAYS

1906 Aileen Fisher is born, in Iron River, Michigan, near the Wisconsin border. Aileen and her brother have all kinds of pets—cows, horses, and chickens. Shortly after getting her degree from the School of Journalism at the University of Missouri, Aileen sells "Otherwise," a nine-line verse, to *Child Life* magazine. Eventually she decides to get out of the city and live on a two-hundred-acre ranch in Colorado. Aileen writes poems about small, everyday things.

► **WRITING TIP** Aileen advises, "Set up a regular schedule." Aileen sits at her desk four hours a day, from 8:00 A.M. to 12:00 noon. She does first drafts by hand, saying she can't imagine writing verse on a machine.

1922 Mildred Pitts Walter is born, in De Ridder, Louisiana. She is the seventh child in her family. Her father is a log cutter, her mother a midwife and beautician. Her parents give her a sense of pride in herself, a person who is loved and who is capable of loving others. Mildred works as a shipwright helper, an elementary school teacher, and a civil rights activist for CORE. Mildred didn't grow up planning to become a writer, but her work as a teacher shows her that students need books about and by African Americans.

1960 Kimberly Willis Holt is born, in Pensacola, Florida. When Kimberly is thirteen years old, she pays two dollars at the Louisiana State Fair to see the fattest boy in the world. She doesn't realize she will grow up to write a book about the incident, but she says all of her stories seem to be coming-of-age stories about outsiders. "I think it's because I've never gotten over being twelve years old." Kimberly says she gets lots of ideas, but she doesn't commit to an idea until "I really know the voice of that character." Kimberly never thought about being a writer until she read Carson McCullers's *The Heart Is a Lonely Hunter* when she was twelve. Then she knew that "more than anything I longed to write a story that caused a lump to form in someone's throat."

The dog ate my homework.

You've heard that before?

This one ate the table,

Then chewed through the door.

Sarah Holbrook,
The Dog Ate My Homework

1839 Isaac Kaufman Funk is born, in Clifton, Ohio. A Lutheran minister, he has a passion for language and starts a publishing firm with a partner, Adam Willis Wagnalls. Funk and Wagnalls encyclopedias are sold in supermarkets. Today, *Funkand Wagnalls.com* offers an online encyclopedia, dictionary, thesaurus, world atlas, and a media gallery, which includes a rich selection of historical/cultural speeches—ranging from Neil Armstrong's words when he set foot on the moon to Winston Churchill's Iron Curtain speech to remarks by Groucho Marx and Babe Ruth.

1947 Rebecca Jones is born, in Evergreen Park, Illinois. Rebecca's favorite book growing up is *Black Beauty*. She also loves the "orange biography books" that tell the stories of famous people's childhood. Among her books are *The Biggest, Meanest, Ugliest Dog in the Whole Wide World*.

▶ **READ MORE** In *My Dog, My Hero*, Betsy Byars and her two daughters, Betsy Duffey and Laurie Myers, collaborate to tell the stories of eight brave dogs. In *A Dog's Gotta Do What a Dog's Gotta Do*, Marilyn Singer tells true stories of dogs that have jobs to do. Sara Holbrook offers a collection of poems titled *The Dog Ate My Homework* that features her own dog on the cover.

There came a terrible roar from Kong as he strained with all his might against the chains.

Anthony Browne's *King Kong,*
from the story conceived
by Edgar Wallace
and Merian C. Cooper

1946 Anthony Browne is born, in Sheffield, England. His father is an art teacher, a professional boxer, and drummer in a jazz band who writes poetry for his two sons and urges them to do well in athletics. Anthony dedicates *King Kong* to the memory of his dad: "for me, the original Kong." Anthony discovers *Alice's Adventures in Wonderland* when he is nine years old. Thirty years later he reillustrates it. Anthony takes a course in graphic design at Leeds College of Art and becomes a medical artist at Manchester Royal Infirmary. Getting ready for an interview to get into a course to study medical illustration Anthony makes some detailed paintings of a dissected rat. Anthony says he likes drawing the insides of people's bodies as well as the outsides, but after three years he finds the work repetitive. "If you've seen one stomach operation, you've seen 'em all." Anthony leaves medical illustration and goes to work designing greeting cards. He draws a gorilla for a birthday card and, liking the opportunity for contrasts they provide, has been drawing them ever since. (He notes that a gorilla having nothing to do with the story crept into a double-page spread of *The Tunnel*.) Anthony says that planning a picture book is like planning a film, a combination of close-ups and long shots. Asked why there are so many zoos in his stories, Anthony replies, "I have very mixed feelings about zoos. I wish they weren't necessary. But I think that I'm interested in the ideas of cages and entrapment of all kinds and at all levels—even my pictures are usually trapped within boxes." Anthony's favorite contemporary book authors? "The great Maurice Sendak and Chris Van Allsburg."

▶ **READ MORE** Anthony dedicates *Willy's Pictures* to "all the great artists who have inspired me to paint." The reader gets a chimp rendition of paintings by everyone from Jean van Eyck to George Seurat to Vincent van Gogh to Henri Rousseau to Frida Kahlo. And lots lots more. Foldout pages at the end show the original paintings and tell the reader about the puzzle running throughout the book.

EVENT

1936 *The Story of Ferdinand,* by Munro Leaf, is published. This gentle bull is more interested in smelling flowers than bullfighting. The book is a tremendous hit with adults, who read it as a comment on the civil war in Spain; it's a hit with children too.

SEPTEMBER 12

July 30

Dear Bruce Springsteen,

I think I loused it up— the date with Kristy. I know I loused it up. Real sweet.

I don't think she'd ever go out with me again. I might as well face it— when it comes to girls, I'm sad, real sad.

Kevin Major,
Dear Bruce Springsteen

BIRTHDAY

1949 Kevin Major is born, in Stephenville, Newfoundland, the youngest of seven children. Although interested in journalism in high school, Kevin graduates from college with a bachelor of science degree. After teaching a few years, Kevin quits to concentrate on writing. Kevin's impact on Canadian children's literature has been compared to that of Judy Blume in the United States. When asked what his next book is about, Kevin says, "There is something unsettling about letting other people into the world you are writing. Before you know it they will be giving their opinions about the worth of it, or poking at the characters to see if they are real, or telling you it might be interesting to add this-or-that."

▶ **WRITING TIP** Kevin advises, "Keep [your writing] all to yourself until you get it just the way you want it."

EVENTS

1945 Mr. Stuart Little of 16th East 48th Street, New York City, writes to E. B. White's publisher, Harper & Row. Mr. Little doesn't want to make any trouble about E. B. White giving a mouse his name. He just asks if the publisher will send him a copy— signed by the author.

1954 *Lassie* premiers on television. Originally, Eric Knight writes a short story for the *Saturday Evening Post.* Two years later he expands this into a novel for adults, *Lassie Come Home.*

▶ **READ MORE** In 1999, award-winning author Rosemary Wells adapts *Lassie Come Home* as a chapter book with illustrations by Susan Jeffers, saying the book "is not a 'boy and his dog' story at all. It is about being forced to make a choice between having something to eat and keeping something you love."

1984 Rhoshandiatellyneshiaunneveshenk Koyaanfsquatsiuty Williams is born on this date to Mr. and Mrs. James L. Williams, in Beaumont, Texas. According to the *Guinness Book of World Records,* this is the longest name appearing on a birth certificate.

▶ **READING TIP** Invite students to collect interesting names they encounter in the books they read. Post them on a Names board. *What's in a Name?,* by Paul Dickson, contains lots of interesting names of real people. There are the aptronyms (James Bugg, exterminator; C. B. Footlick, podiatrist; M. Worms, parasitologist); interesting real names (Beatrix Meats Balls, Rosebud Custard, Georgiana Turnipseed, Serepta Worms); and lots, lots more.

▶ **ALL ABOUT NAMES** For those who can stand really bad puns and other verbal oddities, there's a very funny *Marriage Names* website (<*http://www.geocities.com/ Heartland/Hills/3456/hp_marriage.html*>) that explains what would result if, for example, Olivia Newton-John married Wayne Newton, then divorced him to marry Elton John: she'd be Olivia Newton-John Newton John.

So please, oh please, we beg, we pray,

Go throw your TV set away,

And in its place you can install

A lovely bookshelf on the wall.

Roald Dahl,
*Charlie and the
Chocolate Factory*

BIRTHDAYS

1857 Milton Hershey is born in Derry Church, Pennsylvania. Leaving school in the fourth grade, he becomes an apprentice first to a printer and then to a candy maker. At age 19, Milton opens his own candy shop. By 1911, Hershey's is selling $5 million worth of chocolates a year and Milton builds a town.

▶ **ALL ABOUT NAMES** The streets in Hershey are named to fit into a chocolate theme. Invite students to think of appropriate names for another candy town, a pasta town, a pizza town, a vegetable town, or whatever.

▶ **RESEARCH TIP** The Palo Alto Historical Association puts online the history of the street names in the city. Challenge students to do the same for your locale.

1916 Roald Dahl is born, in South Wales, to Norwegian parents. When he is fourteen, a teacher notes on his report card that he "seems incapable of marshalling thoughts on paper." Roald is badly injured in a plane crash in World War II, and while he is recovering he begins to write about his war experiences. He writes the movie script for the James Bond movie *You Only Live Twice.* Telling his children bedtime stories convinces Roald that maybe he can write children's books. Roald's *Charlie and the Chocolate Factory* is a perennial favorite. Roald says he writes very slowly, a book taking about six years. Roald says that for him two hours of fiction writing is the limit and he walks out of his workroom in a daze. He also points out that fiction writers live in a world of fear, with each day demanding new ideas.

▶ **WRITING TIP** Roald says keeping a notebook is essential. Plot ideas are hard to come by, and whenever a writer thinks of one he'd better write it down or he'll forget it. Roald says every story he's written has started out as a three-line idea in his notebook.

1943 Mildred D. Taylor is born, in Jackson, Mississippi. Mildred says, "From as far back as I can remember my father taught me a different history from the one I learned in school." Margaret says her father learned some stories from his parents and grandparents, as they had learned from theirs. Mildred is awarded the 1976 Newbery Medal for *Roll of Thunder, Hear My Cry.* She acknowledges that this book comes from the values by which she and so many other black children were raised. "I wanted to show a family united in love and self-respect, and parents, strong and sensitive, attempting to guide their children successfully, without harming their spirits, through the hazardous maze of living in a discriminatory society." Mildred says she hopes that the Logans in her books "will provide those heroes missing from the schoolbooks of my childhood, Black men, women, and children of whom they can be proud."

EVENT

1929 On his thirteenth birthday, Roald Dahl is sent off to boarding school at Repton. His school experiences prove to be a rich source of stories. In Roald's words, "Every now and again, a plain grey cardboard box was dished out to each boy in our House, and this, believe it or not, was a present from the great chocolate manufacturers, Cadbury. Inside the box there were twelve bars of chocolate, all of different shapes, all with different fillings and all with numbers from one to twelve stamped on the chocolate underneath. Eleven of these bars were new inventions from the factory. The twelfth was the 'control' bar. . . ." Roald and his schoolmates are asked to taste each bar carefully, give it a grade, and comment on why they did or didn't like it. Roald says this was an important experience for him because it made him realize that large chocolate companies actually do possess inventing rooms.

SEPTEMBER

If a flower blooms once, it goes on blooming somewhere forever. It blooms on for whomever has seen it blooming.

William H. Armstrong, *Sounder*

BIRTHDAYS

1914 William H. Armstrong is born, in Lexington, Virginia. As a child William is entertained with stories told by a neighbor. One of his favorites is the saga of a loyal "coon dog." When he writes *Sounder*, a Newbery Medal book, William remembers his neighbor's tales.

1949 Diane Goode is born, in Brooklyn, New York. As a child Diane loves books and art. She's been drawing ever since she can remember. Every summer she travels to Italy and France to visit relatives and museums. She studies art history at Queens College, getting her degree in fine arts. Although Appalachia is the setting for her Caldecott Honor illustrations for *When I Was Young in the Mountains*, much of Diane's art shows her love of Europe. Diane says she always begins by making a rough dummy of a work, then makes hundreds of sketches, moving things around, adding details, cutting parts. Over and over she tries out new versions—until she's satisfied. Then she does the final art, working with watercolors on opaline parchment. Diane is often drawn to illustrating the classics, but she brings her own unique vision to traditional tales. Her version of *The Emperor's New Clothes*, for one, is set in the Court of Louis XIV, with very ornate clothing and powdered wigs. And since all the characters are dinosaurs, it's Marie Antoinette meets stegosaurus.

▶ **READ MORE 1** Invite students to compare Diane's *Emperor* with the Naomi Lewis translation illustrated by Angela Barrett, where the scene is the belle époque—1913. Then they can take a look at Kathryn Lasky's *The Emperor's Old Clothes*, illustrated by David Catrow.

▶ **READ MORE 2** Diane says she's met many people who have a favorite poem in *A Child's Garden of Verses*, by Robert Louis Stevenson. Illustrating these poems causes her to fall in love with them again. Invite students to find one Stevenson poem that speaks to them.

1950 John Steptoe is born, in Brooklyn, New York. This Caldecott Medal–winning author-illustrator publishes his first book, *Stevie*, when he is eighteen. In accepting the Caldecott Honor award for *Mufaro's Beautiful Daughters*, John says, "The award gives me hope that children who are still caught in the frustration of being black and poor in America will be encouraged to love themselves enough to accomplish the dreams I know are in their hearts."

EVENT

1814 Detained on board a British ship, Baltimore lawyer Francis Scott Key is pleased to see that the American flag is still flying over Fort McHenry the morning after an overnight British naval bombardment. (Mary Pickersgell and her mother and daughter worked ten hours a day to finish the flag, made of four hundred yards of wool bunting, weighing two hundred pounds, and measuring forty-two feet by thirty feet.) Inspired by the sight, Francis Scott Key writes the words of "The Star Spangled Banner."

▶ **READ MORE** Two very good reads about Key and the flag are *The Star-Spangled Banner*, by Peter Spier, and *By the Dawn's Early Light*, by Steven Kroll.

I spent the next weeks on my hands and knees, armed with a box of Kleenex and a sketchbook, following the ducks around the studio and observing them in the bathtub.

Robert McCloskey,
Caldecott Medal acceptance
speech for *Make Way for
Ducklings*

BIRTHDAYS

1870 Watty Piper is born, in Milford, Massachusetts. Watty writes the ever-popular *The Little Engine That Could*. Platt and Munk, the publishers, own a trademark on the phrase "I think I can."

1914 Robert McCloskey is born, in Hamilton, Ohio. As a boy he likes drawing, dismantling clocks, and inventing things. Playing the harmonica is another of his talents. When he invents a machine for whipping cream, the only problem is that it sprays cream all around the kitchen. Readers may see some similarities between McCloskey's boyhood and that of one of his heroes named Homer. Robert wins a scholarship to study art in Boston. There, he enjoys sketching in the Boston Public Garden. He says to create a book like *Make Way for Ducklings*, "You have to rather think like a duck." He studies ducks in the Boston garden, and when he moves to New York he studies duck specimens at the American Museum of Natural History. In New York, he brings ducks to live in his apartment. Ducks make a lot of noise in a small apartment, and in his book, Robert names the ducklings Jack, Kack, Lack, Mack, Nack, Pack, and Quack.

1934 Tomie de Paola is born, in Meriden, Connecticut, into a mixed Irish and Italian family. Many of Tomie's books reflect his lifelong interest in folktales, but Tomie says he told the story of the early influences on his development as an artist so often that finally his editor suggested it would make a good book. *The Art Lesson* is the result. Tomie has created other autobiographical picture books, including *Watch Out for the Chicken Feet in Your Soup* and *Nana Upstairs and Nana Downstairs.* He has extended his autobiographical writing to chapter books.

1949 Sara Holbrook is born. Her favorite teacher is her seventh-grade English teacher, who asks students to make their own books. She is also a performance poet, galloping around the room while she reads "The Midnight Ride of Paul Revere." Sara begins writing poetry for her daughters when they are small. She puts the poems in a blank book and her daughters illustrate them.

▶ **WRITING TIP** Sara says that to become a poet you have to read a lot. "Not just poetry, but everything. . . . Do lots of writing. All kinds of writing helps—write poetry, articles for the school paper, e-mail to friends—all the practice will help you to find your voice."

EVENTS

1928 *The Weekly Reader* magazine first appears.

1973 *Cajun Night Before Christmas*, illustrated by James Rice, is published. James sets the familiar verse in Louisiana. He has also illustrated a Texas version, a Gullah version, and an Irish version. James says he researches the settings carefully to make them as accurate as he can. "I find that the contrast of reality and fantasy contributes to the humor and appeal." In *The Annotated Night Before Christmas*, editor Martin Gardner provides a whole volume of takeoffs on this verse—everything from *Mad* magazine parodies to punk rock.

▶ **WRITING FUN** Invite students to create a sequel to *Night Before Christmas* set in your school.

She was a perfect baby, and she had a perfect name. Chrysanthemum.

When she was old enough to appreciate it, Chrysanthemum loved her name.

And then she started school. "I'm named after my grandmother," said Victoria.

"You're named after a flower."

Kevin Henkes,
Chrysanthemum

BIRTHDAYS

1898 H(ans) A(ugusto) Rey is born, in Hamburg, Germany. He begins drawing when he is two. His favorite spot is the Hagenbeck Zoo, where he learns to imitate animals. Very proud of his lion's roar, he once roars for three thousand children gathered in an auditorium in Atlanta. Even as an adult, the first thing H. A. does when traveling is to visit the local zoo. H. A. and his wife Margret come to the United States in 1940. The manuscript for *Curious George* is one of the few things they carry with them when they flee the Nazi invasion of Paris on their bicycles. In creating books, H. A. mostly draws, and Margret mostly writes. H. A. says creating a book is hard work, taking more than a year. He and Margret argue over the beginning, the ending, the illustrations. They write and rewrite, draw and redraw.

1926 John Knowles is born, in Fairmont, West Virginia. His parents are from New England, so when he is fifteen, John leaves West Virginia for Phillips Exeter Academy, a prestigious boarding school in New Hampshire. The entrance exam asks him to write an essay about a novel of his choice. In John's words, "I knew better than to pick some commercial work like *Gone with the Wind*, opting instead for a novel I knew to be a classic, *Jane Eyre*." John's first report card, with a 28 in math and a 14 in physics, convinces him he'll flunk out. He teaches himself to study. But it's not all work and no play; John remembers "intense leg-wrestling matches under the table in Mr. Whitman's American history class." A picture of the first page of John's manuscript for *A Separate Peace* is available at *http://www.exeter.edu/library1/ separate_peace/manuscript.html*

1946 Joanne Ryder is born. Joanne, who specializes in books about nature, says that "writing picture books is a good life and a joyful way to make a living. It's a life I like very much." Joanne says there is plenty in the world to wonder and write about, and she's written about lots of wildlife—from snails to sharks. She's written about Hua Mei, the new panda at the San Diego zoo. When Joanne isn't writing books, she is a docent at the San Francisco Zoo. The subject of Laurence Yep's *Cockroach Cooties* suggests that Joanne's interests have rubbed off on her husband (she's married to Laurence).

EVENTS

1620 The *Mayflower* leaves Plymouth, England, for North America. There are thirty-two children on the boat, including fifteen Johns, eight Williams, six Edwards, five Marys, and three Elizabeths. The most unusual first names include Wrestling, Humility, Peregrine, Resolved, Love, and Remember. A baby born during the journey is named Oceanus Hopkins.

▶ **ALL ABOUT NAMES** It's not difficult to figure out why the baby is named Oceanus. Students can have a good time—and learn a lot about atlases—by coming up with names for babies born in other geographical locations or during unusual circumstances: on mountaintops, in deserts, during hurricanes, and so on. Ask students to analyze names in terms of syllables. Are kids' names today, on average, shorter or longer than those of Puritan kids?

1787 Printers prepare five hundred copies of the United States Constitution for the official signing ceremony. The document is read aloud, approved, and signed the next day, now known as Citizenship Day.

▶ **READ MORE** *Shh! We're Writing the Constitution,* by Jean Fritz, is a good, informative read.

1991 *Chrysanthemum,* by Kevin Henkes, is published. This is a perfect story.

▶ **READ MORE** Although the temptation will be fierce to do how-did-you-get-your-name projects, resist the urge. Some books should not be junked up by projects. Instead, encourage students to read more books by Kevin Henkes. Hold a Henkes read-fest. The world will be better for it.

1996 *The Abracadabra Kid,* by Sid Fleischman, is published. In this autobiography Sid reveals how surprised he is to find himself an author. Ever since fifth grade, when he saw his first magic act, he's wanted to be a magician. "I was dazzled. The moment he finished his act and ushered us gawkers back onto the sidewalk, I knew what I wanted to be. Someone else could be President of the United States. I wanted to be a magician."

SEPTEMBER

On a January night in 1945 we were walking to we didn't know where.

Anita Lobel,
*No Pretty Pictures:
A Child of War*

BIRTHDAYS

1883 William Carlos Williams is born, in Rutherford, New Jersey. His father is from Britain and his mother is a Puerto Rican–born woman of Basque and French descent. William grows up in a household speaking French, Spanish, and British English. In high school, William starts writing poems and decides he will be a poet and a physician. He studies at the University of Pennsylvania Medical School, becoming a pediatrician. He also wins the Pulitzer Prize for poetry. One of his famous poems is about eating plums, another features a red wheelbarrow. William reminds us to pay attention to the ordinary, to take another look.

▶ **WRITING TIP** Invite students to choose an object from their desks and to make a list of words describing that object: only descriptive words and phrases appealing to the five senses allowed.

1947 Gail Carson Levine is born, in New York City. Her father owns a commercial art studio and her mother is a teacher. Although Gail belongs to a writing club in elementary school and writes poems for a student anthology in high school, her real ambition is to be an actor or a painter. But after college she works in state government departments concerned with labor and welfare. She writes several unpublished children's books, and then a writing class assignment spurs Gail to start on *Ella Enchanted.* She can't think of a plot and so she decides to write a Cinderella story. Gail quickly realizes she doesn't want Cinderella to be a goody two-shoes character. The resulting novel is named a Newbery Honor book.

▶ **READ MORE** Cinderella variants offer lots of possibilities, from picture books to novels. Often overlooked are the male Cinderellas. Richard Chase's *Jack Tales* contains an Appalachian version; Roald Dahl's *James and the Giant Peach* is based on Cinderella elements, as is T. H. White's *The Sword in the Stone.* Arthur Yorinks offers a time-travel Cinderella in *Ugh.* Other popular picture-book male tales include Bernice Myers's *Sidney Rella and the Glass Sneaker,* Margaret Hodges's *The Kitchen Knight,* Shirley Climo's *The Irish Cinderlad,* and Babette Cole's *Prince Cinders.*

EVENTS

1939 N. C. Wyeth works on correcting plates for *The Yearling.* Earlier in the year Wyeth had gone to Florida to research the setting and to meet Marjorie Kinnan Rawlings. Marjorie is worried about having her Pulitzer Prize–winning novel illustrated, but legendary editor Maxwell Perkins reassures her, saying that most books in the Illustrated Classics Series are adult books. "Most of the best books in the world are read both by children and adults. This is a characteristic of a great book . . . and that is the thing that assures it a long life."

1998 *No Pretty Pictures*, by Anita Lobel, is published. It is an extraordinary account of her childhood: having the Nazis burst into her home in Poland when she is five years old, hiding out with her brother and nanny, being sent to a succession of concentration camps—and recovering. The reader looks on Anita's sunny art through new eyes after reading this moving autobiography, which gives us even more cause to celebrate the sunshine Anita offers.

1998 *A Creepy Countdown*, by Charlotte Huck, is published.

▶ **WORD FUN** It's not too early to get ready for Halloween. Young writers will enjoy using Charlotte's rhyming-couplet structure ("One tall scarecrow standing on a hill/Two lumpy toads sitting very still") as inspiration for their own Halloween counting books.

▶ **WRITING TIP** Challenge writers of all ages to try for more alliteration within the structure: where Huck has "furry bats" and "skinny witches," they can have "black bats" and "woeful witches." Even better, they can have "black bats blinking," and so on. Another possible structure for older children is "The Twelve Hours of Halloween."

BIRTHDAY

1709 Samuel Johnson is born, in Lichfield, England, the son of a bookseller. He gains fame as an essayist, dictionary maker, and conversationalist.

▶ **OUT LOUD** In honor of Samuel Johnson, who held literary conversations in his salon, help children understand the difference between talk and conversation. Hold a literary tea. Group students' chairs in clusters of four, five, or six. Then students can enjoy punch and cookies while they discuss books they have read. You can get things started by giving each group a few questions: *Why do you think the main character did what he or she did? Would you have done that? Have you ever known anyone with a problem like that? Did this book remind you of any others?*

EVENT

1980 Writer Katherine Ann Porter dies.

▶ **WRITING TIP** Katherine gave unconventional writing advice: "I always write my last line, my last paragraphs, my last page first." Edna Ferber also wrote the last line first. Teachers often advise students to look carefully at the opening sentences of stories. Ask students to compile a bulletin board of strong endings.

BIRTHDAYS

1867 Arthur Rackham is born, in London, England. He is one of twelve children. After seven years taking evening classes at the Lambeth School of Art while working fulltime in an insurance office, Arthur gains fame with the publication of an edition of *Grimm's Fairy Tales* featuring his illustrations. In her Caldecott Medal acceptance speech for *Saint George and the Dragon*, Trina Schart Hyman observes that in her nine months working on the illustrations, in addition to learning about ancient herb lore, wildflowers, the life of ancient Celts and Britons, and pre-Arthurian armor and weapons, "I learned that Arthur Rackham drew the best dragons in the world."

▶ **READ MORE** There aren't any dragons, but here are two of numerous Arthur Rackham sites online showing samples of his remarkable art: *http://www.datadesignsb.com/art/rackham/rackham.html* and *http://www.bpib.com/illustrat/rackham.htm*

1894 Wallace Wadsworth is born, in Indiana. He is the author of *Paul Bunyan and His Great Blue Ox*.

▶ **READ MORE** Invite young readers to read about Paul in any of many wonderful versions—from Dell McCormick's and Glen Rounds's classic versions to more modern updates by Beverly and Ed Emberley, Steve Shannon, Audrey Wood, and Steven Kellogg. Reading about Paul will give everybody a tall treat.

▶ **WRITING FUN** Challenge students to depict a good tall-tale villain by using the simile *he (she) was as mean/onery/sneaky as....*

1941 James Haskins is born, in Demopolis, Alabama, into a family with strong storytelling traditions. Jim says his Aunt Cindy was the greatest storyteller who ever lived. In her mixed-up versions of traditional folktales, Hansel and Gretel meet the Three Little Pigs. When James is growing up the Demopolis Public Library is off limits to African Americans, but his mother manages to buy him an encyclopedia, one volume at a time, from a supermarket. Jim feels that the fact that his early reading is based exclusively on the encyclopedia is probably a reason he prefers writing nonfiction. When he's a teenager, Jim and his mother move to Boston and he attends the Boston Latin School. Jim works as a stock trader, teacher, professor, and reporter as well as prolific author of nonfiction for children. Jim believes that the truth is not just "stranger than fiction," but also more interesting.

▶ **READING/WRITING CONNECTION** Jim writes in a wide variety of genres, and his *Count Your Way Through . . .* series provides a provocative framework for students' own creations. They choose a country (or a city or state) and use the numbers from one to ten to present historical/cultural information about that place. The result can be as simple or as sophisticated as the child doing it.

EVENTS

1920 Poet Robert Frost writes to his daughter Lesley, "I spent a good deal of my time as a teacher urging . . . that all our work in literature and composition fails if it doesn't put libraries large or small into homes."

1928 Mickey Mouse appears for the first time, in Walt Disney's cartoon *Steamboat Willie*. Disney first gives his little creature the name Mortimer Mouse, borrowed, he says, from that of a pet mouse he keeps in his studio. As the story goes, Mrs. Disney does not like the name Mortimer, saying it sounds too formal. She suggests Mickey. Maurice Sendak remembers loving Mickey as a boy and that Mickey "is the hero of my picture book *In the Night Kitchen*. It seemed natural and honest to reach out openly to that early best friend while eagerly exploring a very private, favorite childhood fantasy. *In the Night Kitchen* is a kind of homage to old times and places—to Laurel and Hardy comedies and King Kong, as well as to the art of Disney, comic books in general. . . ."

In October of the year,

he counts potatoes
dug from the brown
field. . . .

Donald Hall,
Ox-Cart Man

BIRTHDAYS

1928 Donald Hall is born, in New Haven, Connecticut. As he is growing up, Don's mother reads poems to him, and when he goes to the family farm in New Hampshire every summer, his grandfather recites poetry all day long. In the morning, Don writes poems; in the afternoon he hays with his grandfather, listening to his long, slow stories of old times. By age twelve Don is under the spell of Edgar Allan Poe. "I wanted to be mad, addicted, obsessed, haunted and cursed." Now, writing about family, baseball, a sense of place, a sense of knowing who you are, Don begins each day at 4:30, writing until 10 A.M. Readers of *Here at Eagle Pond* know that Don writes so many letters that his local post office assigned him his own personal zip code. In his words, "You could look it up; there's only one 03230-9599 in the universe. 'Don

Hall,' it says." Don calls this "postal knighthood." A noted poet for adults, Don also has a career writing children's books. Sometimes the two careers are combined. The poem "Ox-Cart Man" first appears in *The New Yorker* in 1977. Don later turns it into a picture book. Readers can see nineteen drafts of the poem in Don's handwriting at *http://www.izaak.unh.edu/specoll/exhibits/drafts.htm*

▶ **WRITING TIP** Don's "The Museum of Clear Ideas" is a poem for adults, but it is provocative to tell children about the structure. The poem is based on the nine innings of a baseball game: marked by nine stanzas, nine syllables per line, and so on. Just ask students to contemplate the possibilities of creating structures that mirror content.

1941 Arthur Geisert is born, in Dallas, Texas. Trained as a teacher, Arthur discovers that he would rather draw. While his wife teaches, Arthur tries to sell his artwork. After many rejection notices, Arthur finally gets published, and his second book, *Pigs from A to Z*, is named a *New York Times* best-illustrated picture book of 1986. Arthur draws several books with a biblical theme, but then he's back to pigs. *Oink* is followed by *Oink Oink* and then by two counting books, *Pigs from 1 to 10* and *Roman Numerals I to MM*. (Arthur points out that the total number of pigs in this book is MMMMDCCCLXIV, or 4,864.) In *Etcher's Studio*, Arthur shows how an etching is made and the studio equipment used in the etching process.

▶ **ART TIP** It is important to point out that Arthur, like most artists, doesn't sit and daydream about pigs and then draw them from those daydreams. Arthur uses his neighbor's pigs as models when he draws the pigs in *Oink* and *Oink Oink*.

EVENT

1999 *Time* magazine puts Harry Potter on its cover, a first for a children's book character in the seventy-five-year history of the magazine.

SEPTEMBER
21

The adverb is not your friend.

Stephen King,
On Writing:
A Memoir of the Craft

BIRTHDAYS

1908 Jun Atsushi Iwamatsu is born, in Kago-shima, Japan, the son of a country doctor. He says, "I was always a rascal in school." Jun's father is very pleased to learn his son wants to be an artist because he believes that art is for humanity. Jun and his wife move to the United States in 1939 so that he can study art. When war is declared against Japan, Jun becomes involved with the U. S. Office of Strategic Services. And he changes his name to Taro Yashima. "It was the symbol of homesickness to me. *Taro* means fat boy, healthy boy; *Yashima* means eight islands, old Japan, peaceful Japan."

▶ **OUT LOUD** Every school year should start with a read-aloud of *Crow Boy*, a powerful book for all ages.

1947 Stephen King is born, in Portland, Maine, the second son. When Stephen is two, his father abandons the family and his mother is forced to move the family frequently, working at low-paying jobs. But his mother reads to him and encourages him. She pays Stephen twenty-five cents each for stories he writes, sending them to her sisters. Later, she encourages him to send his manuscripts to publishers. At age thirteen, Stephen writes and sells his first horror stories—for a quarter—to friends at school. In 1965 Stephen publishes his first story, "I Was a Teenage Grave Robber," in *Comics Review*. Stephen says the one book he wishes he'd written is William Golding's *Lord of the Flies*.

▶ **WRITING TIP** In *On Writing: A Memoir of the Craft*, Stephen says story must take the front seat to research. "You may be entranced with what you're learning about flesh-eating bacteria, the sewer system of New York, or the I.Q. potential of collie pups, but your readers are probably going to care a lot more about your characters and your story."

EVENT

1814 Thomas Jefferson offers to sell his personal library of 6,487 books to Congress to replace the ones burned by the British on August 24. Congress accepts the offer, but as soon as the tenth and last wagonload of his books leaves for Washington, Jefferson writes to John Adams, "I cannot live without books," and he starts buying more. The Library of Congress is the largest library in the world, with nearly 119 million items on approximately 530 miles of bookshelves. The smallest book in the Library of Congress is *Old King*. At 1/25″ × 1/25″, the pages can only be turned with the use of a needle. The largest book is John James Audubon's *Birds of America*, containing many life-size illustrations of birds. Students can find out more fascinating facts about the Library of Congress, as well as visit virtual exhibits, at *http://lcweb.loc.gov*

SEPTEMBER

It was not until I was almost full-grown and left my village that I found our village was like no other.

Ann Grifalconi,
The Village of Round and Square Houses

BIRTHDAYS

1929 Ann Grifalconi is born, in New York City. Before a career as a freelance writer and illustrator of children's book, Ann is an artist and designer in advertising and display. Ann's books, including her Caldecott Honor book, *The Village of Round and Square Houses*, is credited with expanding the scope of children's literature by presenting realistic accounts of other cultures in both text and art.

1953 Clarence Miller, Jr. is born, in Virginia Beach, Virginia, the son of a baker. He changes his name to Olivier Jean-Paul Dominique Dunrea. Olivier says he was born on "the wrong side of the tracks" to a mother who married at fourteen. Nobody in the family reads but they do tell stories, and the bigger and better the story, the more attention a person gets. Olivier is very shy at school, but he likes the books there. "The first illustrated book I remember reading was Wanda Gag's *Millions of Cats*. To this day, I love that book with all my heart. *Charlotte's Web* is another favorite." Olivier works as a waiter, secretary, actor, and management consultant before becoming a writer and illustrator and teacher of children's art and theater.

SEPTEMBER

One evening a few weeks later, when the cygnets were asleep, the swan said to the cob, "Have you noticed anything different about one of our children, the one we call Louis?"

E. B. White,
The Trumpet of the Swan

BIRTHDAY

1950 Bruce Brooks is born, in Richmond, Virginia. When his parents divorce, Bruce splits his time between their homes in Washington, D.C., and North Carolina. Bruce says being a good talker and storyteller helps him when he has to change schools all the time. In school, Bruce invents different plots for the stories he reads in basal readers. He starts writing seriously in fifth grade. He writes comics, creating one issue a month.

▶ **WRITING TIP** Bruce says writing is his job and he does it eight hours a day—just as other people do their jobs.

1970 E. B. White writes a letter, replying to a disgruntled reader, "When I start a book, I never know what my characters are going to do, and I accept no responsibility for their eccentric behavior."

1981 The statue of a bear in honor of Winnie-the-Pooh is unveiled at the London Zoo. Pooh books have been translated into thirty-two languages, including the Yiddish "Vini-Der-Puh," translated by Leonard Wolf, a noted Dracula scholar. When Pooh climbs the tree in search of honey, it's "Krakh! 'Oy gevalt!'"

SEPTEMBER

24

I'm sure no one can understand a young boy like his grandfather can.

Wilson Rawls,
Where the Red Fern Grows

BIRTHDAY

1913 Wilson Rawls is born, in Scraper, Oklahoma. He is nicknamed Woody. There are no schools available, so Wilson's mother teaches her children as she can. And she reads aloud to them. Wilson thinks all books are "about 'Little Red Riding Hood' and 'Chicken Little'—GIRL stories" until his mother brings home a book that changes his life—Jack London's *Call of the Wild*. Wilson carries the book with him wherever he goes and reads it over and over. He dreams of writing such a book, but his family is too poor even to buy paper and pencils. In his teens Wilson becomes an itinerant carpenter, working in Mexico, in South America, in Alaska, and elsewhere. Because of his lack of education, Wilson is ashamed of his writing. He burns his first five book manuscripts instead of sending them to a publisher. "I was sure it was pure trash," Wilson admits. "I also knew my grammar was poor and my vocabulary was zero." His wife encourages him to rewrite *Where the Red Fern Grows*, one of the manuscripts he had burned. (Imagine burning a manuscript you have worked on for twenty years.) She edits the manuscript, correcting punctuation and spelling, and Doubleday publishes it in 1961. At first it doesn't sell, but then it catches fire. As Jim Trelease points out, *Red Fern* is one of the great American dog stories. "And like those other books, *Red Fern* is about far more than just a dog."

▶ **WRITING TIP** Wilson says children are always asking him for advice about being a writer. "And I always tell them to do a lot of reading. Read and write, and don't give up."

▶ **READING REFLECTION** Ask students at what age books start being divided into "girl books" and "boy books." Will ten-year-old girls read books about boys? And vice versa? Some books transcend such categories. Ask students, *What does it take to make a book universal?*

EVENT

1853 Charles Dickens writes an article for the journal *Household Words*, complaining that slang is ruining the language.

▶ **READ MORE** What would Charles make of Paul Dickson's *Slang: The Authoritative Topic-by-Topic Dictionary of American Lingoes from All Walks of Life?* or *The American Heritage Dictionary of Idioms*, with its entry on "eat": eat and run, eat crow, eat high off the hog, eat like a bird, eat one's hat, eat one's heart out, eat one's words, eat shit. Or Jerry Dunn's *Idiom Savant: Slang as It Is Slung,* which includes the colorful lingo of American subcultures from animators to zine readers. Robert L. Chapman's *Thesaurus of American Slang* includes over 17,000 zippy synonyms for thousands of slang words—the whole nine yards—from AC-DC to zombie. So if one looks up "monkey business," one gets funny business, hanky-panky, hocus-pocus, skullduggery.

25

Prune pits, peach pits, orange peel,

Gloppy glumps of cold oatmeal. . . .

Shel Silverstein,
"Sarah Cynthia Sylvia Stout
Would Not Take the Garbage
Out," *Where the Sidewalk Ends*

BIRTHDAYS

1897 William Faulkner is born, in New Albany, Mississippi, the oldest of four sons. He is raised in nearby Oxford. He hates high school and drops out to work in his grandfather's bank. William's books about the people, the land, and the ancestors he knows win him the Nobel Prize in literature. William has a unique cure for hiccups. Once, with his publisher along, he hires a biplane and pilot, telling the pilot to climb to three thousand feet and then turn the plane topsy-turvy. The publisher admits, "When we landed, Faulkner's hiccups were gone."

▶ **READING/WRITING/RESEARCH CONNECTION** Invite students to explore hiccup lore—in the community and also in folklore volumes. Alvin Schwartz is a good resource. In the community students can investigate whether different cultures employ different methods for curing hiccups. *Hickup Snickup,* by Melinda Long, will help younger researchers get started.

1930 Sheldon Allan Silverstein is born, in Chicago, Illinois. Shel says as a kid he really wants to be a good baseball player, but he isn't any good at it so he starts to draw and write. In the early sixties he composes folk music performed by leading singers. Shel's poems, collected in *Where the Sidewalk Ends* and *A Light in the Attic*, are beloved by children of all ages. They contain the fears and wishes of children, as well as plenty to make children laugh. Sometimes poignant, they are most times wonderfully silly.

▶ **READ MORE** Read Shel's poems for the sheer joy of it. Read them because they are clever and playful and wonderfully philosophical. Don't do crafts about them. Don't read "Boa Constrictor" as part of a study unit on the Amazon—even though the whole unit, aligned with the *Standards,* is available on the Internet, complete with rubrics.

1947 Jim Murphy is born, in Newark, New Jersey, the son of a certified public accountant and a bookkeeper. Jim says he didn't willingly read a book in his boyhood until a high school teacher announced that we "absolutely, positively must not read" Hemingway's *A Farewell to Arms.* "I promptly read it and every other book I could get a hold of that I felt would shock my teacher." Jim works at repairing boilers, tarring roofs, putting up chain-link fences, operating a mold injection machine, and doing maintenance for two apartment buildings before becoming a children's book editor. Later, as a writer, Jim realizes how valuable these early work experiences are. Jim's book *Weird and Wacky Inventions* challenges readers to try to guess the purpose of strange inventions. His other titles include *Two Hundred Years of Bicycles, The Indy 500, Tractors,* and *Baseball's All-Time Stars.*

1961 James Ransome is born, in Rich Square, North Carolina. James says his early drawings are of hot rods and images copied from comic books and the Bible. James's grandmother asks him to read the Bible to her, and the dramatic illustrations spark his imagination. His school offers no art classes, so James gets how-to-draw books from the library. Then in fifth or sixth grade he enrolls in a correspondence course that he finds in the back of a comic book, "How to Draw Gags and Cartoons and Get Rich!" While a student at Pratt Institute one of James's instructors is Jerry Pinkney.

EVENTS

1901 Beatrix Potter writes one of her famous picture letters to children. This one is about Squirrel Nutkin. Potter says this tale is one of "rudeness, disobedience, and retribution."

▶ **READING TIP** Ask students to consider whether they would rather read this tale or one of "obedience and good manners."

1986 Barbara Esbensen's *Words with Wrinkled Knees* is published.

▶ **WORD FUN** Barbara isolates particular animal qualities—from the waddling of the hippopotamus to the hissing of the snake—and creates poetic images about these qualities. Invite students to write an animal name on a slip of paper; then put all the slips into a box. Then challenge students to draw a name and research it, searching for words to create an image that refers to some factual information.

1998 As part of the New York Is Book Country fair, Yumi Heo conducts a book illustration workshop at the Queens Museum of Art. Early in her career, Yumi practices her art skills by going to Grand Central Station and sketching the people there.

▶ **READ MORE** Whether she is illustrating other writers' work, such as *A Is for Asia*, by Cynthia Chin-Lee, or her own work, such as *The Green Frogs: A Korean Folktale*, Yumi's brightly detailed pencil, oil, and collage illustrations are very distinctive and distinguished.

2000 *Gathering Blue,* by Lois Lowry, is published. Lois notes, "We who write tend to fall in love with our characters. We create impossible journeys—with extraordinary destinations—for them to take, and we place hideous obstacles in their way. But because we love them, we want them to get through safely, unscathed, and triumphant." Lois says that because creative artists have the capacity to triumph and to make a difference, she makes Kira an artist.

SEPTEMBER

26

Macavity, Macavity, there's no-one like Macavity,

There never was a Cat of such deceitfulness and suavity.

T. S. Eliot,
"Macavity: The Mystery Cat"

BIRTHDAYS

1774 John Chapman, better known as Johnny Appleseed, is believed to have been born, in Leominster, Massachusetts.

▶ **READ MORE** Johnny Appleseed is a popular subject. Students can read many different accounts of his life's work, from the poetry of Vachel Lindsay and Reeve Lindbergh to the tall tales of Steven Kellogg to the biographical accounts of Aliki, Margaret Hodges, Andrew Glass, Laurie Lawlor, and Meridel Le Suer. There is definitely an abundance of Appleseed. In *Johnny Appleseed,* S. D. Schindler's expressive artwork brings beautiful and droll detail to Stephen Vincent Benét's verse.

1888 T(homas) S(tearns) Eliot is born, in St. Louis, Missouri, the youngest of seven children. Their father entertains them by drawing faces on their boiled eggs. He also draws cats. Eliot inherits his father's love of cats as well as his messy penmanship. The long-running Broadway musical *Cats* is based on Eliot's poem collection *Old Possum's Book of Practical Cats.* Eliot says all cats have three names and that one of those names is secret, known only to the cat.

▶ **WHAT'S IN A NAME** Invite students to write and share paragraphs about their cats' names and how they got them.

▶ **WORD FUN** Celebrate "suavity." Whenever you can, let your students experience the power of making up words. When children see that a Nobel Prize–winning poet likes to play with words, even invent words, they are astounded and excited. New worlds of possibility explode before their eyes.

EVENT

1772 Benjamin Franklin writes a letter to Georgina Shipley including some lines about the death of her pet squirrel: "Here Skugg/Lies snug/As a bug/In a rug."

September

27

Strange sounds come from the house.

Can you hear them? Listen:

SWISH, SWASH, SPLASH, SWOOSH. . . .

Bernard Waber,
The House on East 88th Street

BIRTHDAYS

1924 Bernard Waber is born, in Philadelphia, Pennsylvania, the youngest of four children.

▶ **WRITING TIP** Bernard emphasizes the importance of revising, pointing out that revising means "to see again." Revising, says Bernard, gives an author another chance to look at the story. Usually, he says, he finds ways to improve it.

▶ **READ MORE** Bernard likes writing riddles with a difference. The ones in *Pets in Trumpets* are unique. To answer the riddles, kids need to look for pets in trumpets, weasels with easels, and an ill gorilla. ("What makes a city street more colorful? A tree.") In *ANTics!*, Cathi Hepworth offers a more sophisticated version of the same idea. In her alphabetic list of ants, Cathi points to such famous people as Rembrandt and Santa Claus and to admired characteristics such as brilliant and flamboyant. The book is a vocabulary lesson as well as a game with droll art to complement the text.

1933 Paul Goble is born, in Haslemere, England, the son of a harpsichord maker and a musician. One of Paul's earliest memories is walking around the neighborhood in American Indian regalia that his mother has made for him. In 1977, Paul moves to the United States, living first in South Dakota and later in Nebraska. In his Caldecott Medal acceptance speech for *The Girl Who Loved Wild Horses*, Paul says the question he is most often asked is "How is it that an Englishman comes to write books about American Indians?" Paul credits his mother, who read aloud the complete works of Grey Owl and Ernest Thompson Seton to him. For eighteen years Paul's love of Indians is a hobby while he pursues his career in industrial design, though he and his son spend summer vacations camping with Sioux friends in South Dakota and Crow friends in Montana.

EVENT

1961 Harper & Row editor Ursula Nordstrom writes to Fred Gipson about a manuscript he has submitted titled *King of the Wild Country*, "What a terrific story! I am sure you can expand it, and I certainly hope you will want to. It is practically perfect as it stands for an adult short story especially in a magazine called *Western Magazine*. . . ." Ursula then offers Fred some specific advice for revising the story, including the fact that it needs a better title. After Fred revises it, *Old Yeller* becomes a Newbery Honor book.

September

28

With coarse rice to eat, with water to drink, and my bended arm for a pillow, I still have joy in the midst of these things. Riches and honors acquired by unrighteousness are to me as a floating cloud.

Confucius

BIRTHDAYS

551 B.C. Confucius is born, in Shantung province. The Chinese philosopher's given name is Kung-Fu-Tzu, and Confucius is a translation. Himself a teacher, Confucius holds the revolutionary view that all people who have the desire to learn, not just the aristocracy, deserve the opportunity for education. In 213 B.C. , Chinese officials decide that books are a threat to their rule, and all Confucian books are burned except for one copy of each, which is kept in the Chinese State Library.

▶ **THINK ABOUT IT** Invite students to consider the impact of a national or local government's denying people access to certain books.

1909 Alfred Gerald Caplin is born, in New Haven, Connecticut. He studies at several art schools, including the Chicago Academy of Fine Arts, the Philadelphia Museum, and the Boston Museum of Fine Arts. As Al Capp, he begins to draw comic strips, creating *Li'l Abner*. He populates a mythical hillbilly land called Dogpatch and ridicules business tycoons, politicians, gangsters, experts, entertainers, and members of upper-class society.

EVENT

2000 Laurie Lawlor gives a talk at the Mitchell Museum of the American Indian, at Kendall College, in Evanston, Illinois. Laurie is discussing her book *Shadow Catcher: The Life and Work of Edward S. Curtis*. Curtis, an early twentieth-century photographer, spent thirty years in remote regions of the United States and Canada photographing and researching eighty American Indian tribes. Laurie's favorite books as a child are the Trixie Belden stories, Nancy Drew mysteries, and *The Secret Garden*. Her favorite author is E. B. White. Laurie grows up to be a prolific author of both fiction and nonfiction.

SEPTEMBER 29

Today is my birthday. I am now ten years old and Papshka gave me this journal to write in. All this paper just for me!

Marissa Moss,
Hannah's Journal

BIRTHDAYS

1941 Laurie Adams is born, in New York City. She is the coauthor of *Alice and the Boa Constrictor*, wherein a fourth grader is disappointed in her new pet boa constrictor.

▶ **READ MORE** Many children dream of owning unusual pets. Joyce Altman's *Lunch at the Zoo: What Zoo Animals Eat and Why* taps into this interest—and provides a fact-filled, behind-the-scenes account of what everything from boa constrictors to porcupines eat at some of the biggest zoos in the country.

1959 Marissa Moss is born, the daughter of an engineer. When Marissa is nine she sends her first illustrated children's book to a publisher, a story about an owl's tea party written in rhymed couplets. Later Marissa earns a degree in art history. The author and illustrator of the popular Amelia's Notebook series, Marissa gets the idea for these books when she opens a composition book with a mottled black-and-white cover and starts to write and draw. She tries to draw and write the way she remembers doing when she was nine. Marissa likes the freedom this genre gives her. She can have Amelia paste all sorts of items into her notebook, giving the artist Marissa all sorts of challenges.

EVENT

1892 Mark Twain notes in his journal that the main difficulty of having his head shaved bald is the flies. "They like it up there better than anywhere else; on account of the view, I suppose." Twain says for the flies his bald head is "their park, their club, their summer resort. They have garden parties there and conventions and all sorts of dissipation. . . . They come before daylight and stay till after dark."

SEPTEMBER 30

I am a city child
I live at The Plaza

Kay Thompson,
Eloise,
drawings by Hilary Knight

BIRTHDAYS

1898 Edgar Parin D'Aulaire is born, in Munich, Germany, to parents who are both artists. He makes his first picture book when he is twelve—describing the adventures of his grandmother as she drives a buggy across the prairie while pursued by Indians. Edgar explains that this is his idea of what America is like. Edgar meets his wife Ingri at art school in Paris. They come to the United States in 1929. Edgar and Ingri receive the Caldecott Medal for their biography *Abraham Lincoln*. To write this book, and to make Lincoln come alive for children, the pair follow Lincoln's path, pitching their tent wherever he stayed. They believe to write the book they have to "see it, smell it, hear it, really live it."

1929 Carol Fenner is born, in Almond, New York. She is the oldest of five children. She is grateful to her "magic" aunt, a librarian who tells unforgettable fairy tales and provides her nieces and nephews with wonderful books. Carol's mother reads poetry aloud at bedtime in a voice that "purred with wonder." At age eleven Carol writes plays that children perform in the basement. When she is high school she begins writing novels.

▶ **OUT LOUD** Carol says that it is important to read aloud—even when no one is around. Reading aloud lets the writer "hear the shape of the words."

EVENT

1994 A fortieth birthday party for *Eloise* is held at the Barnes and Noble superstore on 82nd and Broadway, in New York City.

▶ **THINK ABOUT IT** Ask students to plan a party for Eloise. What would the invitations look like? What games would they play? What presents would they give Eloise? What literary characters would they invite to the party? Invite students to consider celebrations for other literary favorites.

OCTOBER

October

When we can't get a single other coin into the jar, we are going to take out all the money and go and buy a chair . . . A wonderful, beautiful, fat, soft armchair.

Vera B. Williams,
A Chair for My Mother

Birthday

1956 Deborah Hautzig is born, in New York City, the daughter of a musician and a writer. Deborah says that "the one vital thing I tell myself about writing is: 'You're not out to teach; you're not out to preach. You're out to tell a story about real people, and anything anyone else derives from it is a fringe benefit.'" A prolific author, Deborah writes the Little Witch series.

Events

1851 Henry David Thoreau buys a railway ticket to Burlington, Vermont, for fugitive slave Henry Williams. Williams is so grateful that later, when he has managed to purchase his freedom for $600, he buys a china statue of Uncle Tom and Eva, protagonists in Harriet Beecher Stowe's antislavery novel *Uncle Tom's Cabin*, and walks from Boston to Concord to give it to Henry.

1982 Vera B. Williams's *A Chair for My Mother* is published. This story about Rosa and her mother and grandmother, a close-knit, working-class family, receives a Caldecott Honor award. It is hard to imagine a story more perfect.

1990 Ed Young receives the Boston Globe–Horn Book Award for *Lon Po Po: A Red-Riding Hood Story from China*. He advises the audience to "take time for eight matters of the heart":

Take time for repose
Take time to read
Take time to think
Take time to work
Take time to play
Take time to be cheerful
Take time to share
Take time to rejoice

▶ **READING TIP** Invite students to think about this list and to talk about which of these qualities they are and are not given time for in their school day. Solicit ideas for finding more time for "matters of the heart" during the school day.

October

The only emperor is the emperor of ice cream.

Wallace Stevens,
"The Emperor of Ice Cream"

Birthdays

1879 Wallace Stevens is born, in Reading, Pennsylvania. After graduating from Harvard, Wallace works as a journalist before entering New York Law School. After he comes a noted poet, Wallace continues to work at the Hartford Accident and Indemnity Company, walking two miles from his home to the office every day. Hartford residents place thirteen stone markers along his route, with a stanza from "Thirteen Ways of Looking at a Blackbird" on each marker.

▶ **WRITING TIP** Wallace says, "I write poetry when I feel like it. I write best when I can concentrate, and do that best while walking." He carries slips of papers in his pocket and puts down ideas and notes as they occur to him.

▶ **WORD FUN** Although "The Emperor of Ice Cream" is definitely a poem for adults, children can have fun examining possibilities the title suggests. What would they decree if they were Emperor of Ice Cream?

1941 Jennifer Owings Dewey is born, in Chicago, the daughter of an architect. She is raised in New Mexico. Jennifer writes her first book when she is ten. Because Jennifer likes writing about extreme environments, about the boundaries between one habitat and another, she travels to remote places to do research. *Antarctic Journal: Four Months at the Bottom of the World* is the result of four months she spends hiking, sailing, and filling her sketchbook in the Antarctic. Jennifer says, "Writing about the world we live in prevents running out of ideas."

▶ **WRITING TIP** "Write what you know," Jennifer advises. But notice that she spends a lot of time getting to know new things.

EVENTS

1950 Charles Schulz's "Peanuts" comic strip appears for the first time. Five decades later the strip appears in more than thirty languages in seventy countries. Charles Schulz, a shy man, reports that the cartoons he submitted for his high school yearbook were rejected.

1991 Binney & Smith Inc., the manufacturer of Crayola crayons, announces it is bringing back eight colors from retirement. When the company stopped putting maize, violet blue, raw umber, orange yellow, blue gray, green blue, orange red, and lemon yellow in the box of 64 colors a year ago, replacing them with neon colors, there was a public protest. The eight crayons are now called "classics." Kenneth E. Lang, the founder of RUMPS, the Raw Umber and Maize Preservation Society, says, "Raw umber and maize represent a bygone time in America. You can't draw a picture of Nebraska or Kansas or South Dakota without using these colors."

▶ **WRITING/READING CONNECTION** Invite students to conduct research on the class's favorite color in the Crayola box. When they have discovered the top colors, challenge them to come up with adjectives to go with the colors: *cozy peach, positively peach*, whatever. Then, they can ponder how feelings about a color change, depending on the context. How does *fire engine red* differ from *ruby red* and why? How does the effect on the reader differ if one says "as white as a lace gown" or "as white as a glob of Elmer's Glue"?

OCTOBER

3

Suzy tried to make peace. "He's a nice, friendly old tramp, Mama," she explained, "and he's going to live with us."

"I'm not a friendly old tramp," said Armand indignantly. "I'm a mean, cranky old tramp, and I hate children and dogs and women."

Natalie Savage Carlson,
The Family Under the Bridge

BIRTHDAYS

1906 Natalie Savage Carlson is born, in Kemstown, Virginia. Natalie's book *The Talking Cat and Other Stories of French Canada* has direct roots in the stories told by her French-Canadian mother. Natalie's husband's career with the U. S. Navy takes them to every state in the United States but Alaska and also to Paris, France. Natalie's work with French orphans leads to her Orpheline series and to *The Family Under the Bridge*, a Newbery Honor book. A prolific writer, Natalie is also the author of the Spooky books.

1948 Marilyn Singer is born, in New York City. Until she is five, Marilyn shares a bed with her grandmother in the living room, and she continues to share a room with her until she is twelve. Marilyn credits her writing career to her grandmother's stories. "Every night before I went to sleep, she would tell me a marvelous tale. . . . My grandmother made me feel that the world is magical, beautiful, always interesting, always unique." A former high school teacher and script writer for *The Electric Company*, Marilyn's writing spans a variety of genres, including picture books, poetry, mysteries, young adult fantasies, and nonfiction.

▶ **READ MORE** Marilyn's books about dogs include *Chester, the Out-of-Work Dog; It's Hard to Read a Map with a Beagle on Your Lap;* and *A Dog's Gotta Do What a Dog's Gotta Do: Dogs at Work.*

1936 J. R. R. Tolkien sends the completed typescript of *The Hobbit* to the Allen & Unwin publishing house. As the story goes, Professor Tolkien, tired of correcting student papers, starts doodling on scratch paper. He writes, "In a hole in the ground there lived a Hobbit," and thus is born the rich fantasy world of Bilbo Baggins and *The Lord of the Rings*.

▶ **READING/WRITING CONNECTON** Invite students to write a paragraph about what might happen when their teacher gets tired of correcting student papers. Some might like to write a letter of advice to the teacher-tired-of-correcting-papers.

OCTOBER

Each maxim read "As Poor Richard Says" or "Says Poor Richard." Now, there never was any REAL Poor Richard. Ben just made him up, and I always considered it downright dishonest. So wherever the name occurred, I removed it and substituted Amos. This was not vanity on my part, but merely a desire for honesty, for there really was an Amos. Besides, it was the only name I could spell.

Ben and Me,
discovered, edited, and
illustrated by Robert Lawson

BIRTHDAYS

1862 Edward Stratemeyer is born, in Elizabeth, New Jersey. A prolific writer, he creates the Nancy Drew, Bobbsey Twins, Tom Swift, and Hardy Boys series, among others. Edward writes 150 books himself and directs the writing of more than 600 other titles. Lilian Ross, a staff writer at *The New Yorker* for more than fifty years, recalls fondly her reading of dozens of the Bobbsey Twins books: *The Bobbsey Twins at the Seashore, The Bobbsey Twins in a Houseboat, The Bobbsey Twins in the Great West, The Bobbsey Twins at the Circus*, and so on. Says Ross, "For me, the two pairs of twins were the most enviable, the most fortunate children in the world."

▶ **READ MORE** A fun take-off on the Tom Swift books are Tom Swifties—such excruciatingly pun-filled stuff as "Yes, I have been reading Voltaire," Tom admitted candidly; "My parents are called Billy and Nanny," Tom kidded; "I see," said Tom icily. The key to the puzzle is always in the adverb. Here is one of more than 800 Swiftie sites listed in a Google search: *<http://thinks.com/words/tomswift.htm>*. For the punphobic: don't say you weren't warned.

1892 Robert Lawson is born, in New York City. He grows up in Montclair, New Jersey. After graduating from art school Robert works as a freelance artist for popular magazines. He and his wife design Christmas cards, creating one card a day for three years, to pay off the mortgage on their house at Rabbit Hill, in Westport, Connecticut. Winner of both the Caldecott and the Newbery Medals, Robert says he never thinks about whether he is drawing and writing for adults or children. "I have never changed one conception or line or detail to suit the supposed age of the reader. . . I have never, I hope, insulted the intelligence of any child."

1924 Donald Sobol is born, in New York City. Donald becomes interested in writing at Oberlin College. Although he writes a variety of books, he is best known for his stories about Leroy Brown, better known as Encyclopedia Brown, the boy detective who uses observation, deduction, and logic to solve mysteries.

▶ **ALL ABOUT NAMES** Leroy's nickname is an invitation to examine nicknames in general. For starters, students might investigate how many presidents have had nicknames. Carl Sifakis's *The Dictionary of Historic Nicknames* reveals that Dwight Eisenhower, for example, said that being known as Ugly Ike and Little Ike (his older brother was Big Ike) made him a scrapper and able to stand up to the harshness of military life. Invite discussion about "mean" nicknames.

1941 Karen Cushman is born, in a Chicago suburb. She moves to Los Angeles when she is ten. Things she loves to read as a child include *Uncle Wiggly's Storybook*, Little Lulu and Donald Duck comics, *The Story of Ferdinand, Homer Price, Caddie Woodlawn, Blue Willow, Strawberry Girl*, the Bobbsey Twins series, and *Mad* magazine. Karen says she found writing in school to be hard work. "Like many other students, I procrastinated, suffered, and counted words." At home, though, when she is thirteen, Karen writes an epic poem cycle based on the life of Elvis. Karen graduates from Stanford with a degree in English and Greek, and then she gets many jobs—

and quits them. Over the years Karen has lots of book ideas, but *Catherine, Called Birdy* is the first idea she turns into a book. It takes her three years to research and write. Karen points out that learning about the battles, kings, and cathedrals is easy. But she also has to learn about beekeeping, shearing sheep, ointments and remedies, superstitions and fears, clothing, food, language, table manners, bathing habits, privies. This first book wins a Newbery Honor; Karen's second book, *The Midwife's Apprentice*, earns the Medal.

▶ **READING/WRITING CONNECTION** Invite students to look closely at how a favorite author uses facts. Reading poems on a topic they have researched shows students that poets also "use" facts to inform their work.

1944 Susan Meddaugh is born, in Montclair, New Jersey. After studying French literature and fine arts in college, Susan works as a designer and art director at a publishing company. Susan is inspired to write a book about the family dog after her sons ask her, "If Martha-Dog ate alphabet soup, would she be able to talk?" The Martha Speaks series is born.

EVENT

1987 The mallard family of Robert McCloskey's *Make Way for Ducklings* is honored in the Boston Public Gardens with a larger-than-life bronze sculpture of the ducks. Robert recalls, "I first noticed the ducks when walking through the Boston Public Garden every morning on my way to art school." When he returns to Boston four years later, Robert notices the traffic problem caused by the ducks, and the "book just sort of developed from there." So that he can draw the ducks accurately, Robert buys four squawking mallards and keeps them in his apartment while he observes and draws them. *Make Way for Ducklings* receives the Caldecott Medal and sells more than two million copies.

OCTOBER

5

Camilla Cream loved lima beans. But she never ate them. All her friends hated lima beans, and she wanted to fit in. Camilla always worried about what other people thought about her.

David Shannon,
A Bad Case of Stripes

BIRTHDAYS

1928 Louise Fitzhugh is born, in Memphis, Tennessee, an only child of wealthy parents. Louise's parents divorce when she is young and her father obtains custody. She writes *Harriet the Spy* and *Nobody's Family Is Going to Change*.

1959 David Shannon is born, in Washington, D.C. He grows up in Spokane, Washington. After receiving a fine arts degree, David creates book jackets as well as illustrations for the *New York Times, Time* magazine, and *Rolling Stone*. David says, "As a kid, I loved *Oliver Twist*, but I liked the Artful Dodger more than Oliver. And I always thought the villains in Disney movies were really cool." David admires the great names Charles Dickens came up with, noting that "the right name can really help define a character." When David is five years old, he writes and illustrates his first book. On every page he puts two words he knows how to spell—*No* and *David*. On each page he draws a picture of something he isn't supposed to do. His adult revision of the story becomes a Caldecott Honor book. David says that months after finishing *How Georgie Radbourn Saved Baseball*, he realizes the villain, Boss Swaggert, is "the spittin' image" of his sixth-grade math teacher.

▶ **READING REFLECTION** Ask students to consider the way Camilla Cream's name might define her character.

EVENT

1903 At a time when the average worker in the United States is earning $400 annually, popular painter of western scenes Frederic Remington sells reproduction rights for twelve pictures a year for four years to *Collier's Weekly*—he will receive $1,000 a month.

OCTOBER

6

My great-great-great-grandmother did great things. Elizabeth lived during the Revolutionary War, but she did not fight in it.

Betsy Hearne,
Seven Brave Women

BIRTHDAY

1942 Betsy Hearne is born, in Wilsonville, Alabama. A noted librarian, researcher, and book reviewer, Betsy also writes children's books. In *Seven Brave Women*, Betsy tells the story of seven women in her own family who made history by not by fighting in wars. She speaks of the family values that descend through generations, and a few precious artifacts too—a spinning wheel, a quilt, pieces of hand-painted china, a brass teapot, a green Irish lap harp, and stories. "My great-great grandmother . . . worked on a farm all her life. Even when she was tired, or mad, or lonely, she had to work hard."

▶ **ORAL RESEARCH** Invite students to interview their parents about the work they do.

EVENTS

1876 The American Library Association is established, in Philadelphia, by a group of public librarians for the purpose of supplying "the best reading for the largest number at the least expense." Melvil Dewey, originator of the Dewey Decimal System, is one of the association's founders. The American Library Association presents the prestigious Newbery and Caldecott Medals each year.

1908 Rudyard Kipling writes to his son, "Dear old man, Your last letter was a beauty as far as its length but it was vilely spelt. I don't think I have ever seen quite so many mistakes in so few lines. . . . Howe wood yu lick it if I rote you a leter al ful of mis speld wurds? I no yu know kwite well howe to spel onli you waonte taik the trubble to thinck."

▶ **WRITING TIP** Invite students to write a letter of advice to either a poor speller or the parent or teacher of a poor speller. Ironically, young Kipling's phonetic spelling is quite similar to the reforms advocated by Isaac Pitman and others.

2000 With a headline of "Lawyer Writes an Udder Bestseller," the *American Lawyer Media* notes that legal associate Doreen Cronin has written a *New York Times* bestseller, *Click, Clack, Moo: Cows That Type.*

▶ **READING REFLECTION** Doreen Cronin and her fiancé, also an associate, have a running argument over the meaning of the story. She says, "It's about the power of education and writing." He says, "You're out of your mind. It's a book about unions." Ask young readers who gets to decide what a book means, the reader or the author?

▶ **WORD FUN** Invite students to list as many cow-related words as they can. Then they can try writing headlines in the vein of "Lawyer Writes an Udder Bestseller." ("Lawyer Milks Legal Background to Pen Bestseller" is another possibility. Once you get started, there are lots of moovelous possibilities.)

▶ **READ MORE** In a hysterical romp, *George Washington's Cows*, David Small shows the pampered lives of cows at Mount Vernon.

The ho! and hey! and
whoop-hooray!

Though winter clouds
be looming

Remember a November
day

Is merrier than mildest
May

With all her blossoms
blooming

James Whitcomb Riley,
"The Rapture of Our Year"

BIRTHDAYS

1819 James Whitcomb Riley is born, in Greenfield, Indiana, second son of a lawyer and politician and named for an Indiana governor. James's family worries that because he can't seem to learn history or mathematics, he'll never amount to anything. At sixteen, James quits school and joins a group of itinerant sign painters. Later he works for a newspaper. In his fifties, James contributes verse to the *Indianapolis Journal*. Every October a Riley Festival is held in Greenfield.

▶ **THINK ABOUT IT** Ask students what writer their state might honor. They can write a letter to legislators, making a case for their candidate.

1893 Alice Dalgliesh is born in Trinidad, in the West Indies, the daughter of an English mother and a Scottish father. Alice says in the dry season she plays outside; in the rainy season she reads. In her adult life, whenever she sees a copy of *Alice's Adventures in Wonderland* or *The Swiss Family Robinson* she remembers the patter of raindrops on a corrugated iron roof. Alice starts writing her own stories when she is six. When Alice is thirteen, the family moves to England, and she wins a five-pound box of chocolates for a story sent to the children's page of a magazine. When Alice is nineteen, she goes to America to train as a kindergarten teacher. Alice notes that *The Silver Pencil* and *Along Janet's Road* are both partly autobiographical, using the backgrounds of four countries.

EVENT

1783 An ad for Noah Webster's *Speller* prices the book at fourteen cents. It is selling at a rate of 500 to 1,000 copies a day.

It was a nice day until
Mrs. Hanson couldn't
find the Scholastic Book
Club money. She was
scrabbling around her
desk during reading. . . .
Finally she interrupted
the class. "Did anyone
see a large manila
envelope on my desk?"

Barthe DeClements,
Nothing's Fair in Fifth Grade

BIRTHDAYS

1920 Barthe DeClements is born, in Seattle, Washington. A long-time teacher, counselor, and psychologist, Barthe writes *Nothing's Fair in Fifth Grade* to convince children they should be kind to students who are regarded as class rejects. Barthe considers counseling and writing "parallel vocations" and hopes that in writing a story about a misfit whom readers can really hate at the beginning of the book but can come to understand and even root for, "I might change more heads than I could by just talking to kids."

▶ **READING/WRITING CONNECTION** Ask students what they think: is school fair in any grade? Invite them to write a letter to an imaginary member of next year's class, advising him or her of the fairness or unfairness of school. Students might also consider whether reading books about misfits changes their behavior in their own classroom.

1930 Faith Ringgold is born, in Harlem, New York, daughter of a sanitation worker and a dressmaker. Faith says, "I had a wonderful childhood growing up in Harlem with many wonderful role models as neighbors. . . . My mother taught me to sew and her mother taught her." A public school art teacher for eighteen years, Faith is best known for her painted story quilts—art that combines painting, quilted fabric, and storytelling. In 1996, two mosaic murals for the platforms of the West 125th Street IRT Subway in Harlem repeat designs from Faith's original paintings. Faith's original *Tar Beach* quilt is in the Solomon R. Guggenheim Museum, in New York City.

1943 R(obert) L(awrence) Stine is born, in Columbus, Ohio. One of Bob's earliest memories is when he is three—his mother reading a chapter from *Pinocchio* every day before naptime. Bob remarks, "The original is so gruesome; it has to be one of the most frightening books ever written. I remember, especially, one point in the story, where Pinocchio puts his feet on the stove and falls asleep, and his feet are burned off. That stayed with me a long time." Another early influence is *Mad* magazine and comic books, particularly the EC Horror comics, with titles like *Tales from the Crypt* and *The Vault of Horror.* Bob gets the writing urge at age nine and keeps at it through Ohio State University, where he majors in English and edits a college humor magazine. After college, he moves to New York City and edits *Bananas,* a humor magazine at Scholastic. Then Bob moves from humor to horror and starts writing the Goosebumps books. Bob says his own son has never read a single one of the more than 300 million R. L. Stine titles in print. "He won't read them. He never would. It was just a way to make me nuts. And now he's too old for them."

▶ **WRITING TIP** For Bob, writing is work: seven hours a day, six days a week. He says, "I love dreaming up titles and ideas, and I love the actual writing part. But it's hard to dredge up the energy to revise." Bob acknowledges that every book needs revising.

1945 Pamela Service is born, in Berkeley, California, the daughter of a dentist. Diagnosed as dsylexic, Pamela doesn't start reading on her own until third grade, and because reading is so difficult, she only reads stories that are very imaginative: fantasy and science fiction. She also likes historical fiction. In her popular *Stinker from Space,* an alien comes to Earth and inhabits the body of a skunk.

Event

1937 E. B. White writes to a friend that although he thinks piano lessons are a good idea, he doesn't think a child should have lessons on Saturdays. Saturdays, says White, are for playing outdoors.

▶ **WRITING TIP** Invite students to write a letter to their own parents, making a case for Saturdays being a day for play.

. . . one day when he was reading a book called The Arabian Nights, *he discovered a wonderful name: Ali Baba. There were no other Ali Babas in his class. . . . It was the perfect new name for a boy who wanted to be different.*

Johanna Hurwitz,
Hurray for Ali Baba Bernstein

Birthday

1937 Johanna Hurwitz is born, in New York City. While in high school, Johanna gets a job in the library and has been working in libraries ever since. Johanna says the characters of Nora and her brother Teddy in the Nora books are based on her own children but the mother in those books is more patient than she is.

▶ **READING/WRITING CONNECTION** As a librarian, Johanna tries to help kids find "breakthrough books," books they can see like a movie in their heads. Ask students which books they can "see" this way. Can they look carefully and figure out what elements in a story make scenes easy to "see"?

▶ **WRITING TIP** When Johanna sits down to write, she first writes a letter to a friend, as a warm-up exercise. Before the next writing assignment, invite students to try this technique.

Event

1899 Frank Baum writes the last word of his 40,000-word manuscript. He takes another piece of paper and writes, "With this pencil I wrote the manuscript of 'The Emerald City,'" and dates it. Then Frank attaches the stub of the pencil to the paper, frames it, and hangs it over his desk. He signs a contract for *From Kansas to Fairyland,* a title that changes to *The City of the Great Oz.* In January 1900, Frank registers *The Land of Oz* with the Copyright Office, but the title is soon changed again, to *The Wonderful Wizard of Oz.*

1959 Eudora Welty reviews *Charlotte's Web* in the *New York Times Book Review*, declaring that it is perfect for anyone over eight or under eighty.

George was painting in oils. "That ocean doesn't look right," said Martha. "Add some more blue. And that sand looks all wrong. Add a bit more yellow." "Please," said George. "Artists don't like interference."

James Marshall, "The Artist," *The Complete Stories of Two Best Friends*

BIRTHDAYS

1942 James Marshall is born, in San Antonio, Texas. He grows up on a farm near there. He is the author-illustrator of the widely acclaimed George and Martha series, the *Cut-Ups, Portly McSwine*, and *Carruthers*. And his zany illustrations to fairy tales turn the genre on its ear. With his fictitious collaborator Edward Marshall, James creates the Space Case series and the Fox series, among others. With his real collaborator Harry Allard, he creates the inimitable Miss Nelson books and the Stupids. James says Viola Swamp, Miss Nelson's mean alter ego, is based on his own second-grade teacher, who squashed his early artistic efforts.

▶ **READING/DRAWING CONNECTION** Invite students of any age to conduct an author/illustrator study of how James Marshall uses detail. For starters, what details does he put in his illustrations that are not in the text?

1946 Robert D. San Souci is born, in San Francisco. Robert's earliest memories are of being read to. He says, "I would listen carefully to stories that were read to me, then I would retell them to my younger sister and brothers. But I would add a new twist or leave out parts I didn't find interesting." In school, Robert writes for the school paper and the yearbook. Today, he is best known for his retellings of folktales drawn from a wide range of cultures, retellings undergirded by meticulous scholarship. He works with his brother, the illustrator Daniel San Souci, on a number of projects. Their first book, *The Legend of Scarface*, is based on a Blackfoot Indian folktale. Robert returns frequently to variations on the Cinderella theme: *The Talking Eggs: A Folktale from the American South*; *Sootface: An Ojibwa Cinderella Story*; *Cendrillon: A Caribbean Cinderella*; and *Little Gold Star: A Spanish American Cinderella Tale*.

▶ **READING TIP** Reading variants on the Cinderella theme helps students "see" what *theme* really means—and how different details, stories set in entirely different settings and time periods, can support the same theme.

1953 Nancy Carlson is born, in Minneapolis, Minnesota. She is the author-illustrator of the Harriet series, the Louanne Pig series, and the Loudmouth George series. Nancy says, "Everything that happens in the Harriet books happened to me when I was growing up." Similarly, the other main characters are based on children she knew in school. The drawings for Harriet are inspired by Nancy's golden retriever, Dame. When she walks Dame around a lake near her house, children come up and say, "Hi, Harriet," because they recognize her from the books.

EVENT

1968 E. B. White writes a friend in Philadelphia, asking him to do some research at the Philadelphia Zoo. "How would you like to do some sleuthing for an aging fiction writer? . . . One of my fictional characters has had the rotten nerve to take me to Philadelphia. . . . Are there any Trumpeter Swans in residence today? How many?" White goes on to ask a lot of detailed questions about the bird lake, the swans, and other birds. Readers of *The Trumpet of the Swan* will understand why White also asks his friend about nightclubs in Philadelphia. After the book is published, officials at the Philadelphia Zoo put up a sign marking the spot where Louis and Serena courted.

OCTOBER **11**

No one had ever seen what Amos Root saw on that September afternoon in 1904. Standing in a cow pasture near Dayton, Ohio, he looked up and watched a flying machine circle in the sky above him.

Russell Freedman,
The Wright Brothers: How They Invented the Airplane

BIRTHDAYS

1929 Russell Freedman is born, in San Francisco. The boy whose parents met in a bookstore grows up to win the Newbery Medal for *Lincoln: A Photobiography* and a Newbery Honor for *Eleanor Roosevelt: A Life of Discovery*. In his acceptance speech for *Lincoln*, Russell recounts the pleasures of eyewitness research: "I visited Lincoln's log-cabin birthplace in Kentucky, his boyhood home in Indiana, and the reconstructed village of New Salem, Illinois, where he lived as a young man. I went to Springfield, with its wealth of Lincoln historical sites, and to Washington, D.C., for a firsthand look at Ford's Theatre and the rooming house across the street where the assassinated president died." Russell believes "there's something magic about being able to lay your eyes on the real thing—something you can't get from your reading alone."

1958 Bill Farnsworth is born, in Norwalk, Connecticut. Bill knows from an early age that he wants to be an artist. After graduating from art school, Bill starts illustrating children's books. Bill spends a lot of time doing research for a book, going to the location where the story is set to take photos and make sketches. He wants his realistic oil paintings to give the reader the sense of being where the main character in the story is.

▶ **WRITING/DRAWING CONNECTION** Ask students to write and illustrate a paragraph about the front of the school. Then take a field trip outside, asking them to take notes and make sketches. Then they can come back to class and rewrite and redraw.

OCTOBER **12**

The women work because the white folks give them jobs— washing dishes and clothes and floors and windows.

Ann Petry,
The Street

BIRTHDAY

1908 Ann Lane Petry is born, in Old Saybrook, Connecticut, the daughter of a pharmacist and a chiropodist. She is proud to be in a family of four generations of African-American New Englanders born in Connecticut. With a Ph.D. in pharmacy, Ann marries a mystery writer, moves to New York, and writes for newspapers.

EVENT

1961 An angry letter appears in the *New York Times*, accusing *Webster's Third International Dictionary*, popularly abbreviated as W3, of surrendering to the "permissive school." Critics accuse the dictionary of abandoning its role as the guardian of linguistic purity, citing one example: the dictionary has included the word *ain't*, noting that it is "used orally in most parts of the U. S. by many cultivated speakers."

▶ **TALK ABOUT IT** Ask kids: should *ain't*—and everything else—be in the dictionary?

OCTOBER **13**

I scattered seed enough to plant the land

In rows from Canada to Mexico

Arna Bontemps,
"A Black Man Talks of Reaping"

BIRTHDAY

1902 Arna Bontemps is born, in Alexandria, Louisiana. He moves to Los Angeles when he is three. Arna receives strict religious training at boarding school and after college goes to Harlem to teach in a Seventh-Day Adventist academy. In 1924, he publishes his first poem in *The Crisis*, the magazine of the National Association for the Advancement of Colored People. After receiving a degree in library science, Arna builds Fisk University into a center for African American research.

EVENTS

1958 Michael Bond's *A Bear Called Paddington* is published. The book begins, "Mr. and Mrs. Brown first met Paddington on a railway platform. In fact, that was how he came to have such an unusual name for a bear, for Paddington was the name of the station." In illustrating the book, Peggy Fortnum visits the London Zoo and uses a Malayan sun bear as her model for about fifty drawings, thirty of which she ends up using in the book.

1995 In Portland, Oregon's Grant Park, four blocks from the *real* Klickitat Street, the Beverly Cleary Sculpture Garden is dedicated, unveiling three sculptures: Ramona Quimby; Henry Huggins; and Henry's dog, Ribsy.

OCTOBER

14

At first, it was fun to pick the berries. The children enjoyed being out in the sun all day and running barefoot and having a good time while they worked.

Lois Lenski,
Strawberry Girl

BIRTHDAYS

1893 Lois Lenski is born, in Springfield, Ohio. She is the fourth of five children and grows up in a nearby farming community. Her parents' belief in the goodness of work is revealed in the fact that Lois is a prolific author. In her words, "I have a strong urge to work; I am not happy unless I am at work." After writing highly regarded historical novels, Lois decides to write books that "illumine the whole adventure of living." She goes out and lives among ordinary people, writing a series of regional novels that present people formerly invisible in children's books. *Strawberry Girl* wins a Newbery Medal.

1894 e(dward) e(stlin) cummings is born, in Cambridge, Massachusetts. Growing up, his favorite comic strip is *Krazy Kat.* When he is eight years old, e. e. starts writing a poem every day. He continues this habit until he is twenty-two. As an adult, he writes his name in small letters, trying to divorce himself from vanity. Similarly, he doesn't use the uppercase first person I, but always the lowercase i. He enjoys using unusual punctuation and creating new words. In 1935, Cummings borrows money from his mother to self-publish a book of poetry that many publishers have rejected. Here's the dedication page: "No Thanks to: Farrar & Reinhart, Simon & Schuster, Coward-McCann, Harcourt Brace, Random House," and so on. He lists all the publishers who rejected the manuscript.

1926 Miriam Cohen is born, in Brooklyn, New York. Miriam is a strong advocate of the emotional rights of young children. Many of her popular books feature the same cast of children and their school anxieties and triumphs.

1928 Polly McQuiston Cameron is born, in Walnut Creek, California. She writes *I Can't, Said the Ant: A Child's Book of Nonsense.*

▶ **WRITING FUN** Challenge students to follow Polly's lead and create a list of rhyming animal remarks: "Scat!" said the cat; "I will," said the shrill; and so on.

EVENT

1926 *Winnie-the-Pooh,* by A. A. Milne, is published, in London. One week later it appears in New York. The book has been translated into thirty-two languages, including Latin and Yiddish.

OCTOBER

15

A shout runs

From tower to tower,
the whole wall's length;
they stretch

Their eager bows, and
whirl the javelin-thong.

Virgil,
The Aeneid

BIRTHDAYS

70 B.C. Virgil is born. The author of the *Aeneid*, the first great literary epic (the *Iliad* being an epic based in oral tradition), his birthday is now celebrated as World Poetry Day.

▶ **OUT LOUD** Ask each child to prepare a poem to recite to the class on this day.

1940 Barry Moser is born, in Chattanooga, Tennessee. This award-winning illustrator comments, "I came to books later in life than most of the people in my field. I did not read books as a kid. I read *Alice in Wonderland* when I was 41." Barry notes that his love of printmaking is what brings him to books. He has his own Pennyroyal Press, for which he produces editions of such books as *Moby-Dick* and *The Scarlet Letter* with black-and-white, wood-engraved illustrations. Barry insists, "Doing books for children is no less an art than doing books for adults, no less sophisticated," and he thinks it is too bad that the picture-book format is "reserved almost exclusively for children. There should be picture books for adults (other than magazines)."

▶ **ART TIP** Barry points out that he concentrates on a central subject in his illustrations, and "that is why it is the exception rather than the rule to find a recognizable background in a Moser illustration."

EVENT

1860 Eleven-year-old Grace Bedell, of Westfield, New York, writes a letter to presidential candidate Abraham Lincoln, advising him that if he wants to be elected president he should let his whiskers grow: "you would look a great deal better for your face is so thin." He follows her advice!

▶ **READ MORE** *Lincoln's Little Girl,* by Fred Trump, gives an account of the correspondence between Grace and Abe, Grace's adult life, and what happened to their letters.

▶ **WRITING TIP** Invite students to talk with buddy writers about advice they can offer the mayor, the governor, the President, or some other leader. It can be in reference to a big world problem or a not-so-big problem. After all, Grace's advice is not on a big world problem, but more than one hundred years later, she's still famous for it.

OCTOBER

16

Every afternoon, as they
were coming from
school, the children
used to go and play in
the Giant's garden.

Oscar Wilde,
"The Selfish Giant,"
The Fairy Tales of Oscar Wilde

BIRTHDAYS

1758 Noah Webster is born, in West Hartford, Connecticut. He is one of five children. Noah's *Spelling Book* teaches frontier children to read. By 1869, it has sold more than sixty-two million copies, outsold only by the Bible. Noah's monumental work, *An American Dictionary of the English Language,* contains twelve thousand more words and forty thousand more definitions than any earlier dictionary. Revised editions are still in print. In both his speller and his dictionary, Noah emphasizes American spelling, grammar, and pronunciation, as distinguished from the British, changing *plough* to *plow* and so on.

▶ **WORD FUN** Invite students to create a bulletin board of "weird" words, words whose idiosyncratic spelling does not make sense and should be reformed. You may want to share parts of "English Is Tough Stuff," a verse created to help teach English to multinational personnel at the North Atlantic Treaty Organization headquarters, near Paris (for a copy, see <*http://www.milk.com/random-humor/english_poem.html*>).

1854 Oscar Fingal O'Flahertie Wills Wilde is born, in Dublin, Ireland. Known for his comic plays for adults, Oscar also writes fairy tales. Acknowledging the influence of Hans Christian Andersen, Oscar says these tales are "meant partly for children, and partly for those who have kept the childlike faculties of wonder and joy." Oscar's son remembers, "When he grew tired of playing he would keep us quiet by telling us fairy stories, or tales of adventure, of which he had a never-ending supply."

1888 Eugene O'Neill is born, in a New York City hotel. He spends his boyhood traveling with the theater troupe in which his father is an actor. An avid reader as a teenager, he especially likes the plays of George Bernard Shaw and the political writings of Emma Goldman. After he is kicked out of college, Eugene prospects for gold in Honduras, ships to South America and South Africa as a seaman, tours as an actor, and works as a newspaper reporter. After Eugene has gained some fame as a playwright, a movie executive telegraphs, asking him to come to Hollywood and write a screenplay, instructing Eugene to reply in a collect telegraph of no more than 20 words. Eugene answers: No No No No No No No No No No No No No No No No No No No O'Neill.

1900 Edward Ardizzone is born, in Haiphong, French Indochina (now Vietnam). He moves to England at age five. While working as a statistical clerk, Edward, at his mother's urging, attends art classes three nights a week. Growing up in a busy seaport town gives him material for the Little Tim and the Brave Sea Captain series, which begins as tales he tells his own children.

1942 Joseph Bruchac, III, is born, in Saratoga Springs, New York. Joseph is raised by his grandparents, who run a small general store. Kids call him Four-Eyes because of his glasses; his grandparents call him Sonny. At college he's known as The Owl, because he's always up late at night, reading. His grandmother, a law school graduate who never practices law, keeps the house filled with books. His grandfather, of Abenaki Indian descent, teaches Joseph to walk quietly in the woods and to fish. In second grade, Joseph begins writing poems to his teacher. Today, Joseph lives in the same house in which he was raised by his grandparents. Among some Abenaki friends, he is known as Sozap, the Abenaki way of pronouncing Joseph.

▶ **WRITING TIP** Joseph says writing is like climbing a mountain: you have to do it one step at a time, one page at a time.

EVENT

1999 Wendelwin Van Draanen's *Sammy Keyes and the Runaway Elf* is published, number four in the ongoing series starring the intrepid sleuth who lives with her grandmother in a seniors-only building and leads an action-packed life. Wendelwin is a high school computer science teacher; she also coordinates the yearbook and manages the school newspaper. She is also a part-time singer in a rock band. She finds time to write by getting an early start—at five A.M. She says this early start on writing charges her up for the whole day. Wendelwin says that she is inspired to write her first book, *How I Survived Being a Girl*, by Ray Bradbury's *Dandelion Wine*. Not surprising, growing up she enjoys *Mad Scientist Club*, *Encyclopedia Brown*, Nancy Drew, and the Hardy Boys. "I couldn't read enough of them, which I guess is why I can't seem to stop writing Sammy Keyes mysteries!"

OCTOBER

17

When he said, "Zebras, disembark!" he saw, to his dismay,

that there were many animals still waiting in the ark.

Ann Jonas,
Aardvarks, Disembark!

BIRTHDAY

1711 Jupiter Hammon is born. The first African American to publish his own poetry, his birthday is commemorated as Black Poetry Day.

▶ **READ MORE** *I, Too, Sing America: Three Centuries of African American Poetry* is a sumptuous volume with brief biographical sketches of the poets. *Ashley Bryan's ABC of African American Poetry* presents an A-to-Z look at twenty-five poems and one spiritual, plus Ashley's powerful visual images. These books are a wonderful introduction to the rich heritage of African American poetry.

▶ **OUT LOUD** Ask small groups of students to prepare choral readings/recitations of poems written by African American poets.

EVENTS

1937 Huey, Dewey, and Louie, Donald Duck's nephews, appear for the first time in the cartoon strip. Their movie debut comes a year later. In Danish, the triplets are known as Rip, Rap, and Rup; in Dutch, Kwik, Kewek, and Kwak; in Spanish, Jorgito, Juanito, and Jaimito; in French, Riri, Fifi, and LouLou.

▶ **WORD FUN** Encourage students to find out how their names are rendered in other languages.

1990 *Aardvarks, Disembark!,* by Ann Jonas, is published. Ann offers an innovative alphabet book—and awareness of endangered animals—from zerens to aoudads. There's lots of information—and inspiration.

OCTOBER

18

What is all that stuff on the $1 bill? Why are those tree leaves encircling the portrait on the $50 bill?

Nancy Winslow Parker,
Money, Money, Money:
The Meaning of the Art and
Symbols on United States
Paper Currency

BIRTHDAYS

1930 Nancy Winslow Parker is born, in Maplewood, New Jersey. Although hers is not a literary family, Nancy knows from an early age that she wants to be an artist. She remembers reading *National Geographic,* but mostly she is outside swimming, sailing, and climbing trees. After twenty years working in public relations, Nancy begins writing and illustrating children's books, fulfilling a lifelong ambition. Although one of Nancy's stories is about a boy named Charlie who receives a three-thousand-pound hippopotamus from his Uncle Clyde, many of her books are factual and she spends a lot of time doing research.

▶ **RESEARCH TIP** Invite students to read one of Nancy's factual books. Then they should find two more sources to see if they can find facts she omitted.

1930 Esther Hautzig is born, in Vilna, Poland. When Esther is ten, she and her family are sent to Siberia in a cattle car. While working for a children's book publisher, Esther writes children's cookbooks and other how-to books. Then she writes *The Endless Steppe,* a book about her family's experience as prisoners in Siberia during World War II.

▶ **WRITING TIP 1** Esther says that when writing becomes "too much" for her, she stops and sews or embroiders to relieve the tension.

▶ **WRITING TIP 2** Esther advises keeping a journal every day. "Everyone is unique. Write down your story."

1942 Colin Willment is born, in London, England. He takes his stepfather's name, Thompson, when his mother remarries. After many adventures in different parts of the world, Colin starts writing and illustrating children's books in 1990 and reports that since then he has "never looked back or even sideways." Colin says Bellingen, where he lives (about eight hours north of Sydney, Australia), is probably the most beautiful place on earth. Colin says, "My favourite children's book is the same one now I'm fifty-seven as it was when I was a child—*The Wind in The Willows*. I now have it on cassette read by Alan Bennett, which I play at least once a year. Close runner up and almost equal would be the Winnie-the-Pooh books."

▶ **READING TIP** Colin says, "If a children's book cannot be enjoyed properly by adults there is something wrong with either the book or the adult reading it."

▶ **WRITING TIP** Once he has the idea for a picture book, Colin writes at the computer, finishing the story before he starts the pictures. As he makes the pictures, the story may change. "Sometimes a picture might contradict the writing. Other times the picture may repeat the writing."

OCTOBER

19

General Border
gave the order. . . .

Sergeant Chowder
brought the powder.

Barbara and Ed Emberley,
Drummer Hoff

BIRTHDAYS

1931 Ed Emberley is born, in Maiden, Massachusetts. Ed starts drawing when he is three years old and begins drawing for a living when he is thirty. Asked which he enjoys more, writing or drawing, Ed replies, "Drawing. Drawing. Drawing. Drawing." In his 1968 Caldecott Medal acceptance speech Ed explains the woodcut technique he uses. Working on pine boards with just three inks—red, yellow, and blue—he and his wife, Barbara, are able to create the impression of thirteen distinct colors. Ed explains that the creative process is not easy. "When I am looking for an idea or trying to tie down a concept for a new book, I am restless, tired, fearful, superstitious, withdrawn, and just about the crabbiest person you would ever want to meet. When I settle down to an idea and get a few pages, I feel like a happy, powerful, creative genius destined for greatness!"

▶ **ART TIP** Ed creates his illustrations on the computer and says the best computer program for first or second graders is Kid Pix; for second grade and above, it's Superpaint.

1946 Philip Pullman is born, in Norwich, England. Philip spends part of his childhood in Australia at a time when TV is unavailable, so a lot of his early experience of stories comes from the radio. He remembers loving "Faster than a speeding a bullet—more powerful than a locomotive—able to leap tall buildings in a single bound. Is it a bird? Is it a plane? No! It's SUPERMAN!" That is exciting, but seeing a Superman comic changes Philip's life. And then he loves Batman comics even more.

▶ **WRITING TIP** Philip doesn't say "I am a writer" but rather "I write stories." He says the emphasis must not be on yourself but on the story. Philip emphasizes that you must write even when you don't want to. Sometimes it's very hard to stare at an empty page and try to think of what to put next. "Tough. Your job is to sit there and make things up, so do it."

1955 Dan Gutman is born, in New York City. He grows up in Newark, New Jersey. In graduate school Dan decides he'd rather be a writer than continue his psychology studies. The first check Dan receives for his writing—for fifteen dollars, from a Staten Island newspaper—hangs framed over his desk. In 1992, when Dan's son is two years old, he decides to write for children. He loves visiting schools. "When I visit a school I inspire the kids, the kids inspire me, and I even get paid for it!"

▶ **WRITING TIP** On his Internet site, Dan posts seven of the rejection letters he received for *Honus & Me* before Avon Books accepted the manuscript, showing children that even published authors get rejected a lot. Dan says here's what he learned in the three years it took him to get the book published: life is tough. Other people don't always recognize good things. If you truly believe in something, don't ever give up, no matter how many times you are rejected.

EVENT

1902 Three days before his twentieth birthday, N. C. Wyeth arrives at Howard Pyle's school of illustration, in Wilmington, Delaware. Pyle is known as running the best illustration school in the country and limits enrollment to twenty students. Eight years later on this date, Charles Scribners publishers invite N. C. to illustrate *Treasure Island*, the first of twenty-six classics he illustrates in their series. Although N. C.'s paintings are reduced to eight inches by ten inches for the books, he likes to paint the original oils on larger surfaces—thirty-two inches by forty inches.

OCTOBER

One night, after thinking it over for some time, Harold decided to go for a walk in the moonlight.

Crockett Johnson,
Harold and the Purple Crayon

BIRTHDAYS

1906 David Johnson Leisk is born, in New York City. He grows up on Long Island. After college he works in an ice plant, in advertising, as a professional football player. David says he writes under the name Crockett Johnson because Leisk is too hard to pronounce and Crockett is his childhood nickname. The creator of famous comic strips with wide syndication, Crockett also creates the Harold series, stories about the boy with the purple crayon. In 1971, a parent writes the publisher of *Harold and the Purple Crayon*, saying her son liked the book so much when he was little that in honor of his high school graduation they are giving him a new copy.

▶ **READING REFLECTION** Invite students to think of a favorite book they'd like to receive when they graduate from high school.

1940 Robert Pinsky is born, in Long Branch, New Jersey. In 1997, he is named U. S. poet laureate.

▶ **WRITING TIP** Robert says, "If thinking about the way certain words sound alike and different is pleasurable for you, then enjoy it. If not, don't worry about it. The poem I write, for me, is more like giving a party for readers than like giving an exam. . . ."

1950 Nikki Grimes is born, in Harlem, New York. As a "black foster child from a dysfunctional and badly broken home," Nikki loves books and she vows, "When I grow up I'll write books about children who look and feel like me."

▶ **WRITING TIP** In *C Is for City*, Nikki uses the alphabet, as well as alliteration, rhythm, and rhyme, to portray an urban setting. Challenge students to come up with an ABC description of the place where they live.

EVENT

1986 *Cherries and Cherry Pits,* by Vera B. Williams, is published. In the book, every time the main character, Bidemmi, visits her upstairs neighbor, she gets a new magic marker—because Bidemmi likes to draw pictures of stories as she tells them. The reader gets the four stories about cherries and cherry pits that Bidemmi tells within the story that Vera is telling.

▶ **CELEBRATE** Invite students to share stories of favorite foods and use magic markers. For a fun way to launch these stories, invite children to list the foods on a strip of adding machine tape that stretches down the hallway.

21

Mrs. Jane Tabby could not explain why all four of her children had wings.

Ursula K. LeGuin,
Catwings

BIRTHDAYS

1929 Ursula K. Le Guin is born, in Berkeley, California. She is best known for her Earthsea cycle, in which she develops a fantasy world that is very complete in its details of geography, language, traditions. Ursula explains the origin of the Catwing books: "I drew a picture of a cat with wings on my shopping list. The cat kept flying around in my head until I sat down and wrote the story."

1943 Ann Cameron is born, in Rice Lake, Wisconsin, the daughter of a lawyer and an English teacher. Her favorite person is her grandfather, who tells her stories and teaches her Swedish. Ann says from age seven to ten her best friend is a boy named Bradley, and memories of their time together inform her Julian stories, although the inspiration for the first Julian book comes from a friend's childhood in South Africa. Ann is the unpaid supervisor of a municipal library in Guatemala. With donations, she manages to keep the library open six days a week. Ann says living in two countries makes her life bigger.

EVENT

1971 In the fall semester at Yale, Maurice Sendak is teaching a course on bookmaking. Among his students are Paul Zelinsky, Eve Rice, and Sandra Boynton.

▶ **THINK ABOUT IT** Invite students to consider: If Maurice Sendak were your teacher, what would you ask him? What would you want him to teach you?

22

For the past fifty years we have been planting trees. And every year to celebrate a holiday called Tu b'Shvat, children from all over the world send us thousands of seedlings to plant.

Neil Waldman,
The Never-Ending Greenness

BIRTHDAYS

1882 N(ewell) C(onvers) Wyeth is born, in Needham, Massachusetts. He illustrates many children's books, including *Treasure Island* and *Kidnapped*. He teaches painting to his son, Andrew Wyeth, who teaches it to his son, Jamie Wyeth.

1947 Neil Waldman is born, in the Bronx, New York. Neil says that even as a young child he realized that finger painting and coloring books are more than just fun. "They were important tools that led to a road of joy, discovery, and fulfillment." He resents going to school and finding out that art is not considered as important as reading, math, and science. For twelve years, Neil does the least amount of work possible to get by in school—and works on his art at home. As a young boy Neil sees a book of Vincent Van Gogh's paintings. "I was awestruck. I remember thinking that until I saw those amazing pictures, I'd never really seen the sky. I began looking up every day, and today the skies are a central element in my own landscapes."

▶ **READ MORE** In *The Starry Night*, Neil creates a spectacular book depicting New York City in the style of Vincent Van Gogh.

EVENT

1837 Henry David Thoreau begins the journal that he will keep for the next twenty-five years. Some days he writes only a few words, but in twenty-five years he writes more than two million words and fills fourteen published volumes. Earlier, Thoreau had started a journal a few times but never stuck with it. After Ralph Waldo Emerson asks him, "Do you keep a journal?" he starts in earnest—and sticks to it.

▶ **WRITING TIP** Invite students to keep a journal—outside of class—for two weeks. They should write down what time it is when they make their entry each day. Do they discover anything about their habits? Are they morning writers or evening writers? Do they write about the same topics? How many words do they think they'll write if they keep going for the next twenty-five years? What's the best part about keeping a journal? What is the worst part? Do they want to keep going? Or stop?

OCTOBER 23

Ping lived with his mother and his father and two sisters and three brothers and eleven aunts and seven uncles and forty-two cousins.

Marjorie Flack,
The Story About Pac

BIRTHDAYS

1897 Marjorie Flack is born, in Greenport, Long Island, New York. She writes a series of primary-grade books featuring Angus, a Scotch terrier, which she says is partially based on real-life pets and their adventures.

▶ **WRITING TIP** Marjorie says much of her inspiration comes from the places where she lives. Invite students to describe something about their city or town that probably not many people have noticed.

1963 Gordon Korman is born, in Cote St. Luk, Montreal. At age twelve, Gordon writes his first book, *This Can't Be Happening at Macdonald Hall!* for a seventh-grade English project. He mails the manuscript to the address on the bottom of an Arrow Book Club order form, and the book is published. By the time Gordon graduates from high school he has written five books for Scholastic.

EVENTS

1991 Donald Crews's *Bigmama's* is published. See August 31, Donald's birthday, for the story of how Donald decided to write this book.

▶ **WRITING TIP** Invite students to write about a visit with relatives. They might write about a meal, a game they play, a story they hear. They might describe the trip there, the house itself, or any number of other things. They should make a list of specific possibilities and then select just one to develop.

1999 Virginia Hamilton celebrates national Make a Difference Day by speaking to second and third graders at Wilkie's Bookstore, in Dayton, Ohio. She tells the children, "I want you all to become smart readers. As a writer, I want you to read, not only my books, but *all* books you see. Read everything. Never stop reading. . . ."

▶ **READ MORE** Virginia points out that animal folktales help children understand that all manner of life is worthy and valuable.

OCTOBER 24

Slake sat, his back against the wall, his heart a racing machine, his spirit a frightened cat, his limbs a weak and uncoordinated collection of gears.

Felice Holman,
Slake's Limbo

BIRTHDAYS

1788 Sarah Josepha Hale is born, in Newport, New Hampshire. She writes "Mary Had a Little Lamb," which is based on an actual event.

▶ **WRITING FUN** Invite students to create a sequel to "Mary Had a Little Lamb." Another popular device is to challenge students to rewrite the verse without using any *As*, then without *Es*, or some other letter of their choice. Ask students which letters are easier and which harder to omit.

1919 Felice Holman is born. Felice writes her first book, a volume of poetry, when she is eight years old. When writing *Slake's Limbo*, the story of a boy who runs away from a bad home and lives in the New York subway, Felice does a lot of research on the subway system. She learns its history, the layout of the entire system, and how a boy might get water, food, and a place to sleep while managing to stay hidden.

▶ **RESEARCH TIP** Invite students to investigate the history of a building in town—such as the school, city hall, or a business.

25

[A bed] lumpy and knobby with half-finished books.

Anne Tyler,
Tumble Tower

BIRTHDAY

1941 Anne Tyler is born, in Minneapolis, Minnesota. She attends high school in Raleigh, North Carolina. Her favorite writer is Eudora Welty; Welty shows her that "very small things are often really larger than the large things." In addition to numerous novels for adults, Anne writes *Tumble Tower*, featuring Princess Molly the Messy and her royal family of neatniks. Anne's daughter Mitra Modarressi illustrates the book.

▶ **WRITING TIP 1** Anne puts unlined index cards all around the house—with ballpoint pens nearby. So when she gets an idea there's a card handy for jotting it down. The pen in the bedroom has a light on it. Another aide in her writing is a collection of almanacs dating back to 1948. Invite students to browse in almanacs and try to figure out why they might be of help to a novelist.

▶ **WRITIING TIP 2** Anne says she doesn't write about people she knows. "That would be no fun. . . . I want to live other lives."

EVENT

1870 The first postcard is mailed, in the United States.

▶ **READING/WRITING CONNECTION** Invite students to ask relatives and friends to send picture postcards to the class when they travel. Students can use a wall map to keep track of where these postcards originate. The cards can be the source of a lot of information and fun.

26

Every new puppy has to learn to behave.

Steven Kellogg,
Pinkerton, Behave!

BIRTHDAY

1941 Steven Kellogg is born, in Norwalk, Connecticut. Steven says he grows up with a crayon in his hand, drawing and telling stories to his younger sisters. He covers his bedroom walls with drawings and thinks about joining a *National Geographic* expedition so he can draw animals in Africa. Steven's grandmother is a great influence, telling him stories of her childhood. The celebrated author-illustrator loves ice cream, chocolate, and the color green, as well as opera and long hikes. Pinkerton is a Harlequin Great Dane who weighs 35 pounds when he joins the Kellogg family and tips the scales at 105 pounds three months later. Steven says Pinkerton thrives on a diet of erasers he finds in Steven's studio; outdoors Pinkerton enjoys chewing down trees. At one year old, Pinkerton is still growing, and it's obvious that he's becoming "a GREAT DANEOSAURUS." Steven quotes a passage in Thoreau's *Walden* to explain the unique personality of this dog, whom he features in several books: "If a man does not keep pace with his companions, perhaps it is because he hears a different drummer. Let him step to the music which he hears, however measured or far away."

▶ **READ MORE** Invite students to hold a Steven Kellogg day, reading their favorite books and finding new ones to enjoy.

EVENTS

1822 At age seventeen, Hans Christian Andersen belatedly enrolls in grammar school. He towers over his eleven-year-old classmates. Hans has endured a very unhappy childhood. His father dies when he is eleven, his mother is illiterate and very superstitious, his grandfather is insane.

▶ **READING TIP** Ask students to consider Hans's very unhappy circumstances as they read one of his tales of their choice.

1965 E. L. Konigsburg recalls the announcement in the *New York Times* on this date regarding the bargain acquired by the Metropolitan Museum of Art: "It had obtained at auction a statue for $225, and the statue was possibly the work of Leonardo da Vinci or of his teacher, Andrea del Verrocchio. When I used that piece of information as well as the experience of waiting in line to see a famous work of art in my book *From the Mixed-Up Files of Mrs. Basil E. Frankweiler*, I changed the possible sculptor of the mystery statue from Leonardo to Michelangelo. Because I liked Michelangelo better; I didn't resent [Leonardo] at all." Then Konigsburg studies Leonardo, and the result is *The Second Mrs. Giaconda*.

OCTOBER

He slapped me because I am a pig. . . . If I were a boy or a man he wouldn't have done it."

Walter R. Brooks, *Freddy and the Bean Home News*

BIRTHDAYS

1889 Enid Bagnold is born, in Rochester, Kent, England. When Enid is nine, her family moves to Jamaica, and she is transformed by the experience. She begins writing stories and poems. During World War I, Enid works as a nurse at British hospitals and as an ambulance driver in France. In 1935 *National Velvet* is published, with illustrations by Enid's daughter.

1924 Constance C. Greene is born, in New York City. Both of Constance's parents work for the New York *Daily News*, so she is born into a writing household. Constance leaves college after two years because she is eager to get a job in newspapers. Her first job is working nights in the mailroom. Constance says reading *Harriet the Spy* gives her the inspiration to write her own series about Al. "Al was thirteen when I started out and after six books, I've reluctantly made her fourteen."

▶ **THINK ABOUT IT** Another series star, Harry Potter, is getting older and, according to plan, will be seventeen in the final volume. Do Harry fans think this is a good idea—or not? What about Nate the Great, Junie B. Jones, and Henry and Mudge? Max and Ruby? Why don't they age? (It's kind of hard to tell with George and Martha.)

▶ **WRITING TIP** Constance says that polite eavesdropping can be very productive. While window shopping she hears one child say to another "Have a weird day." And she uses it in *I Know You, Al*. Now she receives mail from fans who close their letters with "Have a weird day." Invite students to "eavesdrop" for interesting turns of phrases—and to start a list.

EVENT

2000 The Friends of Freddy National Convention meets, in Windham, New York, a biannual weekend of book trading, talk, and pork-free dinners celebrating the twenty-six-volume Freddy the Pig series, the creation of Walter R. Brooks, a New York advertising man and staff writer for *The New Yorker*. An essayist in the *New York Times Book Review* says that the books "evoke the most subversive politics of all: a child's instinctive desire for fair play. Brooks speaks powerfully to his young readers' moral sense without ever overtly moralizing."

OCTOBER

28

Knock knock.

Who's there?

Wooden shoe.

Wooden shoe who?

Wooden shoe like to know?

Leonard Kessler,
*Old Turtle's 90 Knock-Knocks,
Jokes, and Riddles*

BIRTHDAYS

1921 Leonard Kessler is born, in Akron, Ohio. He writes the Old Turtle series, including *Old Turtle's 90 Knock-Knocks, Jokes, and Riddles.* Leonard remembers that when he was a little boy his grandmother lived with his family. Every night she told him a story. She also told funny jokes and riddles.

1951 Gwendolyn Battle-Lavert is born, in Paris, Texas. A longtime teacher and principal, Gwendolyn says, "Every family has a recorder. I happen to be the one for my family." Gwendolyn says she gets her inspiration from her mother. She takes stories her mother told and reworks them.

EVENT

1859 Henry David Thoreau writes in his journal: "I heard one boy say to another in the street today, 'You don't know much more than a piece of putty.' "

▶ **READING TIP** Alvin Schwartz's volumes on folklore contain a number of colorful insults. Words do hurt, but by turning insults into a study of language, students can learn to diffuse the emotional impact of the language. Here are a couple from *And the Green Grass Grew All Around*: "Cowardy, cowardy custard/ Eat your father's mustard" and "I'm the boss, Applesauce."

OCTOBER

29

Raw carrots taste
Cool and hard
Like some crisp metal.

Valerie Worth, "Raw Carrots,"
*All the Small Poems and
Fourteen More*

BIRTHDAY

1933 Valerie Worth is born, in Philadelphia, Pennsylvania. Valerie says she writes her small poems about things that strike a chord in her, which can be a coat hanger, a lawn mower, turtles, or hollyhocks.

▶ **WRITING TIP** Valerie says students should write poems for the fun of it, for the joy they find in a love of words and the things those words describe. Invite students to make a list of things they love. They might make a list, too, of words they love—and then see if they can make any connections.

EVENTS

1945 Ballpoint pens go on sale at Gimbel's department store, in New York City. These novelty items cost $12.50.

1986 A letter written by Thomas Jefferson sells at auction in New York City for $360,000, the most ever paid for a letter.

OCTOBER

30

The monster rose into the air like a great cloud. Its scales melted into raindrops that fell like a summer shower, cleansing the sea.

Eric Kimmel,
Gershon's Monster

BIRTHDAY

1946 Eric Kimmel is born, in Brooklyn, New York. A noted storyteller and authority on children's literature, Eric's earliest memories are of his grandmother, who lives with his family, telling him stories from her own childhood in Europe. Eric says, "The best present I ever received was a volume of *Grimm's Fairy Tales*, which I loved so much that I literally read it to pieces." His all-time favorite, as child and grown-up, is Mark Twain. Eric loves old things—old books, old pictures, old tools, old songs, and especially old stories. His hobby is playing the banjo. Eric enjoys writing in the folktale genre because characters can do things ordinary people wouldn't be able to do.

▶ **WRITING TIP** Eric says the rhythm of language is crucial. "If a story reads aloud well, there's a good chance it'll be a winner."

► **READING TIP** Invite students to share with the class a folktale in which the main character accomplishes something ordinary people wouldn't be able to do.

1950 Stephen Trimble is born, in Denver, Colorado, the son of a geologist. A ranger and naturalist, Stephen is an acclaimed photographer and writer on the landscape of the American West.

► **WRITING TIP** Stephen talks of the importance of the on-the-spot journal. When writing natural history, he needs to jot down impressions of the landscape as he sees it; it's not good enough to rely on memory later. Stephen also uses an on-the-spot journal when interviewing Indian people in the Southwest, saying, "Using a journal is a very different kind of invasion of space than switching on a tape recorder."

EVENTS

1892 Beatrix Potter observes in her journal that Benjamin Bouncer "is an abject coward, but believes in bluster." The rabbit "once fell into an aquarium head first, and sat in the water which he could not get out of, pretending to eat a piece of string. Nothing like putting a face upon circumstances." Beatrix uses her pet Benjamin Bouncer as the model for Benjamin Bunny, who appears with Peter Rabbit in *The Tale of Benjamin Bunny* in 1904. Benjamin Bouncer travels with Beatrix on the train, walking on a leather strap.

1984 The annual Christmas postage stamp goes on sale. This year it is designed by Danny LeBoccetta, a fourth grader in Jamaica, New York.

OCTOBER

31

To fear is one thing. To let fear grab you by the tail and swing you around is another.

Katherine Paterson,
Jacob Have I Loved

BIRTHDAYS

1924 Arthur Stephen Dunning is born, in Duluth, Minnesota. With Edward Lueders and Hugh Smith, he edits *Reflections on a Gift of Watermelon Pickle*, an anthology of 114 poems by modern poets. First published in 1966, it is the Scholastic Tab Book Club choice in January 2001.

► **READING/WRITING TIP** Stephen recommends copying good poems. Copying teaches one to slow down as a reader, to pay close attention.

1932 Katherine Paterson is born, in Quing Jiang, China, the daughter of missionaries. She is awarded the Newbery Medal for *Bridge to Terabithia* and *Jacob Have I Loved*, the Newbery Honor for *The Great Gilly Hopkins*. Katherine confesses that her own "fourth grade was a time of almost unmitigated terror and humiliation for me. I recognize now that some of my best writing had its seeds in that awful year." She remembers two people with great fondness from that horrible time. One is a librarian and the other is Eugene Hammett, "the other weird kid in the fourth grade." Treated as outcasts by the other children, Katherine and Eugene become friends. Katherine says she has had different favorite books at different times in her life, but she remembers loving the stories her mother read by A. A. Milne, Beatrix Potter, Kenneth Grahame, Kipling, Stevenson. "They have all stood the test of time and I'm still rereading all of them." Katherine adds, "All of my work is an attempt to write something that will touch a reader the way *The Secret Garden* affected me at eight."

1934 Helen V. Griffith is born, in Wilmington, Delaware. Helen works in her family business. She says distributing roofing and siding materials has never given her a story idea. She gets most of her ideas from dogs she has known. "I can imagine what my dog is dreaming about or what she and my cat discuss when I'm not around. I can design a time machine or make up a tall tale, and nobody says, 'Grow up, Helen'—because I'm a children's book writer."

1991 At Chicago's O'Hare Airport an announcement over the loudspeaker requests, "Will passenger Dracula please pick up a white courtesy telephone." Later over the loudspeaker, a message is broadcast, "A Chicago ordinance prohibits black cats from entering the terminal area."

▶ **WRITING TIP** Invite students to create official-sounding Halloween announcements.

▶ **READING/WRITING CONNECTION 1** Challenge students to read these spooky tongue twisters three times fast to a friend. Then they should write some twisters of their own.

Big black bug's blood.

Seven spooks scoop celery soup.

Rich witches wear ruby-red witchwatches.

▶ **READING/WRITING CONNECTION 2** Invite students to turn familiar Mother Goose rhymes and other verse into Halloween rhymes. For example: Mary had a little bat, Its wings as black as night.

NOVEMBER

Knock knock.
Who's there?
Annie.
Annie who?
Annie body seen the turkey?

NOVEMBER

What, me worry?

Alfred E. Newman,
mascot of *Mad* magazine

BIRTHDAYS

1871 Stephen Crane is born, in Newark, New Jersey. Drawing on his work as a freelance reporter in New York city slums, he publishes *Maggie, a Girl of the Streets* at his own expense, using the pseudonym Johnston Smith, the two most frequently listed names in the New York telephone book. Stephen's second book, *The Red Badge of Courage*, the psychological study of a young soldier in the Civil War, gains him international acclaim. Today, Stephen's experimental free verse is frequently anthologized.

1926 Hilary Knight is born, in New York, the son of artist-writers. Hilary says Maurice Boutet de Monvel's 1887 book showing drawings of "naughty children using damask curtains for handkerchiefs and forks as combs planted the seed that became Eloise."

1938 Nicholasa Mohr is born, in New York City. Nicholasa grows up speaking English with her brother and the "sweet sounds" of Puerto Rican Spanish with her mother. She remembers, at age four, her brother helping her learn to read—by using such comic books as Dick Tracy and Popeye. Nicholasa remembers the first book she checks out of the library. "It was *Pinocchio*. I took it out seven times. Finally, the librarian said to me, 'You know, it will *always* be here.'"

EVENT

1952 *Mad* magazine, the creation of Harvey Kurtzman and William Gaines, goes on sale. The motto of the magazine's mascot, Alfred E. Newman, is, "What, me worry?" Although the magazine, which pokes fun at culture, is immediately popular with children and adults, *Time* magazine refers to it as a fad that will soon disappear. In 2000, it celebrates its 400th issue. Many credit *Mad* with inspiring *National Lampoon*, Second City, *Saturday Night Live*, and David Letterman.

NOVEMBER

Give me your tired, your poor, your huddled masses yearning to breathe free.

Emma Lazarus,
"The New Colossus"

EVENTS

1883 At the request of the committee raising funds for a pedestal for the Statue of liberty, poet Emma Lazarus writes a sonnet titled "The New Colossus," which is inscribed on the pedestal.

▶ **READ MORE** Students can learn more about Emma Lazarus in *I Lift My Lamp: Emma Lazarus and the Statue of Liberty*, by Nancy Smiler Levinson.

1944 Harper & Row editor Ursula Nordstrom writes to Crockett Johnson, "We loved the pictures for *The Carrot Seed*. Thanks a lot for a beautiful job. It's going to be a beautiful book."

3

Crickwing despised his nickname, and he avoided hearing it by staying away from the other creatures.

Jannell Cannon,
Crickwing

BIRTHDAYS

1938 Betty Bao Lord is born, in Shanghai, China. At age twelve, she takes a job typing envelopes for an insurance company to help pay for her education. As a young reader Betty is very moved by *The Diary of Anne Frank*. It later inspires her to write the story of her sister, from whom she was separated for seventeen years. The book is called *Eighth Moon: The True Story of a Young Girl's Life in Communist China*. Betty says *In the Year of the Boar and Jackie Robinson* started out as a book for adults. The book is largely based on her own Americanization, growing up in Brooklyn, and after struggling to find a "voice" for the manuscript, she finally realizes she should tell the story in a child's voice.

1957 Janell Cannon is born, in Minnesota, where she is also raised. A self-taught artist and writer, Janell loves animals, especially creatures that are misunderstood. Working at a public library developing a summer reading program, Janell discovers that the only two books about bats are out of print, so she creates her own story, *Stellaluna*. Hoping to convince young readers that bats are more deserving of affection than fear, Janell observes, "Fruit bats don't drink blood and won't get caught in your hair. I hope to show them in a positive light so they might be given more respect." In *Crickwing* Janell writes a story about "how easy it is to become a bully if one is bullied . . . but it's possible to change one's path and find creative, constructive ways to deal with life's injustices." Jane notes that Crickwing's scientific name is *Blaberus giganea*. "Which sounds like he is a big blabbermouth!"

▶ **RESEARCH TIP** Invite students to find out more about either bats, pythons, or cockroaches—and to figure out a way to report their findings to the class.

▶ **READ MORE** In Laurence Yep's *Cockroach Cooties*, when someone expresses alarm that Bobby is touching a dirty bug, Bobby replies, "He's not dirty. Cockroaches are as fussy as cats. They're always grooming themselves." Laurence explains that because of his wife, author and bug lover Joanne Ryder, he knows a lot about bugs.

EVENTS

1991 With *Where I'm Coming From* debuting in twenty newspapers, Barbara Brandon becomes the first nationally syndicated African-American cartoonist.

2000 An exhibit of J. Otto Seibold's handmade collages opens at the Yerba Buena Center for the Arts, in San Francisco. Otto, a self-taught artist, has done the illustrations for *Olive Reindeer* and *Pig in the Spigot*.

▶ **READ MORE** In *Pig in the Spigot*, Richard Wilbur writes short poems to encourage children to enjoy the fun of words within words, such as the pig in the spigot, the ant in the pantry, and the bug in the bugle. Invite students to compile their own lists of words that contain a smaller word.

4

I'm a believer.

Gail Haley

BIRTHDAYS

1897 Sterling North is born, in Edgerton, Wisconsin. Growing up, his favorite companions are his pets, which include a crow named Edgar Allan Poe, baby skunks, and a raccoon named Rascal. Rascal eats at the family dinner table, occupying Sterling's old high chair and drinking warm milk from a bowl. A literary editor and essayist, Sterling begins writing books to amuse his own son and daughter. *Rascal*, which draws on Sterling's adventures with his own raccoon, is a classic tale of an eleven-year-old and his pet raccoon.

1939 Gail Haley is born, in Charlotte, North Carolina. Her Caldecott Medal book, *A Story, A Story*, the retelling of the African spider tale, is inspired by a year she spends living in the Caribbean. Haley says, "I'm a believer. I was born that way. I believe in children, stories, and magic. I believe that crystals sing, that animals have souls, and that the moon follows me. I cry at movies; I am enraptured by puppets; I deliberately take part in rituals. I believe that it really matters to the rest of the world when we follow our dreams. And every summer I build a sand castle with my son."

▶ **WRITE MORE** Invite students to create their own *I am enraptured by . . .* statements.

EVENTS

1922 Howard Carter, famed British Egyptologist, uncovers the steps leading down to the entrance gallery of the tomb of mid-fourteenth-century B.C. pharaoh Tutankhamen.

▶ **READ MORE** Invite students to find out more about King Tut. Good places to start are *Mummies Made in Egypt,* by Aliki; *Tutankhamen's Gift,* by Robert Sabuda; and *Tut's Mummy Lost—and Found,* by Judy Donnelly. John Frank provides a poetic account of Carter's discovery in *The Tomb of the Boy King.*

1974 Encouraged by an elderly beekeeper, Jim Aronksy begins his first journal, recording daily encounters with wildlife. Fifteen years later he comments, "My books are personal. I write only of what I have seen. . . . I try to expand my readers' background to include the bogs, fields, woods, streams, ponds, hillsides, and mountaintops that surround the towns and cities where most people live. I want to let people know that there are many wild places still left in the country and millions of wild animals roaming freely. . . ."

▶ **WRITING TIP** Jim says he is a regular guy who values his own experiences and observation. "You don't have to be an expert to have valid observations and experiences." Jim reminds students that having an experience with real wildlife overshadows thousands of images on a computer screen. Invite students to write about some wild thing they have observed—and to explore what their relationship to that thing might be.

NOVEMBER

5

Strange white folk one day shall come across the Great Sea and crowd red men off the earth—so an old sachem warned our people many, many winters ago.

Marcia Sewall,
Thunder from the Clear Sky

BIRTHDAYS

1935 Marcia Sewall is born, in Providence, Rhode Island. She spends her summers in rural Maine. Marcia says these summers in Maine give her an appreciation of people who live close to the earth and an appreciation for landscape. Marcia says her sense of who the character in a story is inspires the way she illustrates a story. Her companion pieces *The Pilgrims of Plimoth* and *The People of the Breaking Day* describe the lives of the first European settlers in Plymouth Colony and the people of the Wampanoag tribe that inhabited the area, their differing relationships with the land providing narrative tension.

▶ **READ MORE** *The Times of Their Lives: Life, Love, and Death in Plymouth Colony,* by James and Patricia Deetz, a book for adults, gives down-to-earth realistic information about the Pilgrims, starting out with a description of the first Thanksgiving that draws from the only primary document from the period.

1935 Paula Feder is born, in New York City, the daughter of a school principal. Perhaps it is not surprising that Paula, who is an elementary teacher, writes a book entitled *Where Does the Teacher Live?*

▶ **WRITING TIP** *Where Does the Teacher Live?* can provoke funny responses. Students enjoy the pattern, "The teacher must live at _____ because _____."

1938 Nancy Smiler Levinson is born, in Minneapolis, Minnesota. After working as a reporter, *Time* magazine researcher, book editor, and Head Start teacher, she becomes a freelance writer. Nancy's book *Clara and the Bookwagon* tells the real-life story of a young girl who wants to read. Nancy says she likes to write nonfiction so that it "reads like a story."

NOVEMBER

We had sand in the eyes and the ears and the nose,

And sand in the hair, and sand-between-the-toes.

A. A. Milne,
When We Were Very Young

BIRTHDAYS

1814 Adolphe Sax, inventor of the saxophone, is born.

1854 John Philip Sousa is born. Composer and bandmaster known as the March King, he also designs the sousaphone.

▶ **WORD FUN** Invite students to invent musical instruments that could be named after them. They can draw a picture of and write a dictionary definition of these instruments.

EVENTS

1924 *When We Were Very Young* by A. A. Milne is published in England.

1996 Nikki Giovanni gets her audience's attention at the Countee Cullen Community Center, in Harlem, New York, when she remarks that she misses the outhouses of her childhood growing up in Tennessee. She points out that outhouses were solitary and gave her the chance to read in silence.

▶ **THINK ABOUT IT** Ask students to reflect on solitary places where they like to read. Create a special, solitary reading place in the classroom.

NOVEMBER

It is the story of Mafatu, the Boy Who Was Afraid.

Armstrong Sperry,
Call It Courage

BIRTHDAY

1897 Armstrong Sperry is born, in New Haven, Connecticut. Armstrong grows up listening to his great-grandfather tell stories about his life as a sailor in the South Pacific. He enjoys drawing and even illustrates his homework. After serving in World War I, Armstrong attends the Yale School of Fine Arts; the Art Students League, in New York; and Colorassi's Academy, in Paris. *Call It Courage*, a Newbery Medal winner, is about a Polynesian boy shunned by his people because he fears the sea.

EVENTS

1874 In a cartoon in *Harper's Weekly* magazine, the elephant makes its first appearance as a symbol for the Republican Party.

▶ **THINK ABOUT IT** Invite students to discuss what qualities might make the elephant a good symbol. Divide the class into teams and ask them to choose symbols for their groups.

1955 In an interview in the *New York Times*, poet Robert Frost says, "I have never started a poem yet whose end I knew. Writing a poem is discovering." Years before, another poet, Ezra Pound, wanting to show off his jujitsu skills, throws Robert over his shoulder. They are in a restaurant at the time.

Having had some time at my disposal when in London, I had visited the British Museum, and made some search among the books and maps in the library regarding Transylvania. . . .

Bram Stoker,
Dracula

BIRTHDAY

1847 Bram Stoker is born, in Dublin, Ireland. He works for ten years as a civil servant and then leaves Ireland to become secretary and business manager for the famous English actor Sir Henry Irving. He writes many books, but the one for which he is remembered is the classic horror novel *Dracula*. The character of the vampire Count Dracula, of Transylvania, has inspired many movies and sequels.

EVENTS

1731 Benjamin Franklin opens the first subscription library, in Philadelphia. This is the first attempt to make books available to anyone who wants them. Members donate money to buy the books, and then use the books free of charge. According to researchers at Indiana University, the average woman reads for 164 minutes a day and the average man, 150 minutes.

▶ **THINK ABOUT IT** Invite students to keep track of how much time they spend reading each day. Who do they think reads more: Boys or girls?

1836 Mt. Holyoke Seminary opens for classes. It is the first college in the United States intended specifically for women. Eighty students attend the first year. The second year, four hundred are turned away for lack of room. Its three-year curriculum covers many of the subjects studied in men's colleges: grammar, geography, ancient and modern history, algebra, human physiology, botany, natural and intellectual philosophy, calisthenics, music, and French. A typical day starts at 5:30 with a half-hour study period before breakfast. Calisthenics are at 7:30, followed by classes. After a full day and evening of classes and study, students go to bed at 9:15 P.M.

▶ **THINK ABOUT IT** Invite students to design an ideal school curriculum.

1897 A reading room for the blind is opened at the Library of Congress.

▶ **FIND OUT MORE** Invite student researchers to find out about Braille and report back to the class, teaching their classmates to write a word in Braille.

1981 Writing in *Book World*, Maurice Sendak says his favorite Babar book is *The Travels of Babar*—a book "full of alarming and very amusing twists of fate." Maurice appreciates the fact that "for the one and only time in all the books, Babar loses his fine balance and has a good old temper tantrum. He is brought out of it by Celeste. The two alternately comfort each other in times of stress."

Pull up some carrots.
Shake off the dirt.
Pack the tomatoes.
Tuck in your shirt.

Lois Ehlert,
Market Day

BIRTHDAYS

1912 Kay Thompson is born, in St. Louis, Missouri. Her famous Eloise is born during Kay's nightclub act. In apologizing for being late for a rehearsal, Kay explains in a high, childish voice that her name is Eloise and she is six. The other performers in the skit join the game, each inventing a juvenile identity on the spot. Kay chooses the Plaza Hotel in New York City for the location of the story because she stays there often and also performs there. Kay's portrait hangs in a place of honor in the hotel, and a room is named after her. The furnishings and décor are taken from the book illustrations.

▶ **LITERARY LICENSE** Invite children to form groups, with one person assuming the identity of a favorite literary character. Then others in the group can respond as other characters in the story—or as characters in other stories.

1935 Lois Ehlert is born, in Beaver Dam, Wisconsin. Lois enjoys doing the research for her books—visiting museums and aquariums and talking to experts. She likes to use real objects as models and may make three or four book dummies for one idea, usually changing the text a dozen times or more. Lois says that early in her education at art school she discovers she likes cutting and pasting—creating collage—more than drawing. Lois says collage gives her greater freedom to experiment with different arrangements on the page. Lois saves things—buttons, scraps of material, telephone wire—until it finds a place in her art.

▶ **FIND OUT MORE** Invite students to try making a collage of "found" objects. They can do the same thing with "found" words, cutting words out of magazines and newspapers and finding interesting ways to arrange them on the page.

1937 Lynn Hall is born, in Chicago. She grows up in Des Moines, Iowa. Not surprisingly, dog and horse stories are her favorite books. Author of the Dagmar Schultz series and many other books, Lynn says she didn't write as a child. She adds, "My childhood did prepare me in one important way for a writing career in that it fostered my love for solitude. From a very early age I knew, without understanding, that I was the square peg in the family, and in my circle of friends."

NOVEMBER

10

The Moon's the North Wind's cookie

He bites it, day by day. . . .

Vachel Lindsay,
"What the Little Girl Said"

BIRTHDAY

1879 Vachel Lindsay is born, in Springfield, Illinois. Believing in a close connection between poets and the public, in 1906 Vachel goes on a walking tour through the southern United States. He earns his room and board by reciting poems. Later, he makes similar trips in other areas of the country.

▶ **OUT LOUD** Invite students to explore the possibilities of earning money to buy books for the library by becoming a strolling poet in the community. For a contribution, they can recite a poem to whoever wants to hear it.

EVENTS

1855 Henry Wadsworth Longfellow's poem "The Song of Hiawatha" is published, celebrating a Native American legend. Henry becomes the first American to earn his living by writing poetry. To this day, not many poets are able to do this.

1969 *Sesame Street* debuts on 170 Public Broadcasting stations. Jim Henson wants to create a Muppet character a child can live through. And so Big Bird—all eight feet two inches of him—is born. Carroll Spinney, the puppeteer who performs Big Bird, is actually inside him. The costume gets so hot that Big Bird has to be built with his own fan inside. Jim plays Kermit, his favorite Muppet. About a year after Sesame Street goes on the air, Big Bird appears on the cover of *Time* magazine.

1999 Korean book illustrator and author Yumi Heo speaks at the Elvehjem Museum, in Madison, Wisconsin, sharing her unique experiences in America. She says while growing up in Korea her mother always encouraged her to draw. "She knew I had talent and I liked to draw." Yumi is disappointed not to get into the college of her choice, a fine arts college. Instead, she studies graphic design. She finds graphic design, which includes drawing a stamp, a calendar, and posters, too confining, so she

Tell me one good thing
you ever did in your
life—what you can
remember of it.

Kurt Vonnegut,
The Sirens of Titan

travels to New York to earn her master's degree at the School of Visual Arts. Yumi's artwork for *A Is for Asia* experiments in both traditional and tradition-breaking styles. *The Green Frogs: A Korean Folktale* is a *pour quoi* tale explaining why green frogs sing when it rains.

BIRTHDAYS

1922 Kurt Vonnegut is born, in Indianapolis, Indiana. In high school Kurt writes for the daily school paper. "Rather than writing for a teacher, which is what most people do, writing for an audience of one—for Miss Green or Mr. Watson—I started out writing for a large audience." Kurt says, "Each person has something he can do easily and can't imagine why everybody else is having so much trouble doing it. In my case, it was writing. In my brother's case, it was mathematics and physics. In my sister's case, it was drawing and sculpting."

1942 Diane Wolkstein is born, in New York City. Diane has loved stories as long as she can remember, and for thirty years she has been telling stories to large audiences at the statue of Hans Christian Andersen, in New York's Central Park. Diane says, "Stories let us explore the farthest place in the universe and the deepest recesses of the human heart. They present possibilities. They let us try out different emotions and characters. Stories are treasures which last forever."

1947 Bob Barner is born, in Tuckerman, Arkansas. Bob earns a college degree in fine arts and works as an art therapist at a hospital. Bob says that *The Elephants' Visit* is inspired by doodles. But then he decides to find out about real elephants, and the result is *Elephant Facts*.

▶ **READING TIP** Invite students to look at a fanciful and a factual book on the same topic. They should compile two lists, facts and fancies, finding examples of each in the books. Then they can talk about how they figure out what goes in which list.

12

Then I, Nate the Great,
know what to do. I will
draw a map of every
street between your
house and the grocery
store and we will follow
the map.

Marjorie Sharmat,
Nate the Great and the Lost List

EVENT

1647 Massachusetts passes America's first compulsory school law.

▶ **THINK ABOUT IT** Invite students to consider what life might be like without school.

BIRTHDAYS

1815 Elizabeth Cady Stanton is born, in Johnstown, New York. At the first Women's Rights Convention, in 1848, Elizabeth declares, "We hold these truths to be self-evident, that all men and women are created equal."

▶ **READ MORE** Jean Fritz says she doesn't normally choose to "spend months with an aggressive person single-mindedly devoted to a cause. But Elizabeth Cady Stanton was a joy to be with. Besides, for every freedom I have, I owe her a debt of gratitude." The result of Jean's work is *You Want Women to Vote, Lizzie Stanton?*

1928 Marjorie Weinman Sharmat is born, in Portland, Maine. Nate the Great fans won't be surprised to learn that when Marjorie is eight she wants to be a detective. She and a friend publish a newspaper they name "The Snooper's Gazette." Marjorie first book, *Rex,* is about a little boy who runs away from home to live with an elderly neighborhood man, pretending to be his dog. But it's Nate who wins her heart. Marjorie says she loves Nate from the beginning and knows she wants to write more books about him. Marjorie lets readers in on a writing secret. After writing Nate stories for more than twenty years, she works hard at making each story different. One device she uses is to work backward—starting with the ending and then creating the case and the clues leading up to it.

▶ **WRITING TIP** Marjorie employs the same technique as the novelists Edna Ferber and Katherine Anne Porter, who wrote the last line of their novels first—and then went to the beginning and worked at figuring out how to get there. Remind students to pay close attention to good endings.

NOVEMBER

13

Green leaves a-floating,
Castles of the foam. . . .

Robert Louis Stevenson,
"Where Go the Boats?,"
A Child's Garden of Verses

EVENT

1859 A flying trapeze act is performed for the first time, by Jules Leotard, in Paris.

▶ **ALL ABOUT NAMES** Invite students to investigate other apparel named for people: Levis, the Stetson hat, the Eisenhower and Nehru jackets, and so on. Laurie Carlson's *Boss of the Plains: The Hat That Won the West* provides a fascinating and fun account of John Stetson's creation.

BIRTHDAYS

1850 Robert Louis Stevenson is born, in Scotland. Sickly as a young child, Robert studies engineering and law. Everyone thinks that, following family tradition, he will design lighthouses. Robert is admitted to the bar, but he never practices, preferring to write. And he lives the stories he writes. Although still suffering from poor health, he travels to the gold fields in California and to islands in the South Seas. *Treasure Island* begins as a detailed map of an island Robert and his stepson draw. His *A Child's Garden of Verses*, regarded as one of the finest poetry collections for children ever published, is still popular.

1945 Paul Cohen is born, in Brooklyn, New York. A high school chemistry teacher and athletic coach, he writes riddle books with Joanne E. Bernstein. Paul says in writing riddle books, he includes a few that children might not understand but their parents will. "Children especially enjoy evoking laughter from their parents and may gain a little knowledge from the explanation of the joke." ("Why does the moon go to the bank? To change its quarters.")

NOVEMBER

14

His mother was ugly
and his father was ugly,
but Shrek was uglier
than the two of them
put together. . . . Any
snake dumb enough to
bite him instantly got
convulsions and died.

William Steig,
Shrek!

EVENTS

1862 Lewis Carroll notes in his diary, "Began writing the fairytale of Alice—I hope to finish it by Christmas." When noted writer George Macdonald reads *Alice's Adventures* to his son, the little boy says, "There ought to be sixty thousand volumes of it."

2000 Elementary students from Boston and Waltham, Massachusetts, board the USS *Constitution* to launch Reading Is Fundamental's eleventh annual read-aloud program. Old Ironside's commander, William Foster, reads to them.

▶ **OUT LOUD** Invite students to choose a book to read aloud to someone younger—or older. People in Senior Citizens centers enjoy being read to as much as kindergartners do.

BIRTHDAYS

1840 Claude Oscar Monet is born, in LeHavre, France. Known to his family as Oscar, he regards school as a prison, preferring to spend time in the water near his home. Oscar doodles in his notebooks and by the time he is fifteen he is well known and sought after as a caricaturist. At age eighteen, Oscar goes to Paris to become a painter, becoming the founder of Impressionism and one of the foremost landscape painters of all time.

▶ **READ MORE** *Once Upon a Lily Pad: Froggy Love in Monet's Garden,* by Joan Sweeney, is a charming introduction to Monet's most famous series of paintings, *Nympheas* (*Water Lilies*)—from the point of view of frogs who are convinced he is painting them. A foldout reproduction of one of the paintings now hanging in the Carnegie Museum of Art, in Pittsburgh, Pennsylvania, is included.

1899 Patricia Miles Martin, also known as Miska Miles, is born, in Cherokee, Kansas. A teacher and prolific author, Miska writes about a variety of cultures and animals. She says that most of her inspiration comes from the things that are most important to her: children, animals, and birds. *Annie and the Old One*, a Newbery Honor book, reflects Miska's interest in the Navajo culture. Miska says that although she writes fiction, accuracy is crucial.

1907 William Steig is born, in Brooklyn, New York. As a child, William's favorite book is *Pinocchio*, though *Robinson Crusoe* also rates high. After drawing cartoons for *The New Yorker* for many years, William follows a publisher's suggestion that he write a children's book. At age sixty, he creates *Roland the Minstrel Pig* and *C D B!* William makes up for his late start by winning both the Caldecott Medal (*Sylvester and the Magic Pebble*) and the Newbery Medal (*Abel's Island*). As William's many fans know, he likes to use interesting words and to make up his own.

▶ **READ MORE** William Steig's *Grown-ups Get to Do All the Driving* provides some views of adults that will send youngsters into gales of laugher as well as inspire them to write a sequel.

1907 Astrid Lindgren is born, in Vimmerby, Sweden. She grows up on a farm near the village. Although they are expected to help with the farm work, Astrid and her three brothers and sisters spend a lot of time playing. Astrid does not plan to become an author. *Pippi Longstocking* grows out of stories she tells her own daughter. Later, Astrid writes these stories down as a gift for her daughter and then, when she enters the manuscript in a contest, it wins first prize. This book is followed by over one hundred more.

1946 Nancy Tafuri is born, in Brooklyn, New York, the daughter of a graphic designer mother who encourages her drawing. Her mother thinks she would make a great interior decorator, but Nancy decides she doesn't want to fix up other people's houses. She emphasizes that even though her picture books for young children are fiction, accuracy is important. "I research all my animals and plants, and I then reduce them to their basic, fundamental shapes. I often use four-by-five snapshots as reference for my drawing."

EVENTS

1851 "Call me Ishmael. Some years ago—never mind how long precisely—having little or no money in my purse, and nothing particular to interest me on shore, I thought I would sail about a little and see the watery part of the world. . . ." The novel with arguably the most famous opening in American literature, Herman Melville's *Moby-Dick* is published on this day. Ishmael narrates the story of a sea captain's search for Moby-Dick, the great whale that had once crippled him.

1960 Ruby Bridges, age six, integrates William Frantz Public School, in New Orleans. Federal marshals who escort Ruby advise, "Just walk straight ahead and don't look

"I just happen to like three-letter words today. There are a lot of big topics with only three letters—God, for example, and Art, and bugs."

"Bugs has four letters."

"Bug then. . . . There are more kinds of bugs than anything you know," he said, "except stars in the three-letter sky."

Daniel Pinkwater,
Borgel

back," as angry crowds outside the school chant, "Two-four-six-eight, we don't want to integrate." Norman Rockwell paints a magazine cover picture about the event.

▶ **READ MORE** Nearly forty years later, Ruby writes her touching memoir of this experience in *Through My Eyes*, which wins the 2000 NCTE Orbis Pictus award for nonfiction. Ruby tells of being the only student in the classroom with one wonderful teacher who teaches her to read and write.

2000 In its forty-eighth year of publication, *Mad* magazine publishes its four-hundredth issue. The issue includes a parody of the popular children's book *Good-night Moon*.

BIRTHDAYS

1897 David McCord, an only child, is born, in New York City. He graduates from high school in Portland, Oregon. Although he hasn't taken any science in high school, David majors in physics at Harvard. Ranked as one of the top twentieth-century poets for children, David receives the first award for excellence in poetry for children given by the National Council of Teachers of English. Readers of David's poetry soon see how much pleasure he takes in the sounds of words.

▶ **WORD FUN** In "Glowworm," David plays on the creature's name, coining words and phrases: *knowworm, down belowworm,* and *slowworm.* Then he ends the poem with "*Helloworm!*" Invite students to search for other compound creature names for which they can coin other compound words.

1941 Daniel Manus Pinkwater is born, in Memphis Tennessee. He grows up in Chicago and Los Angeles and studies sculpture at Bard College. "Weird" is one way to describe Daniel's stories, which include a 266-pound chicken on the loose and a blue moose helping out in the kitchen. Another way to describe them is "fun!"

EVENTS

2000 In Tift County High School football stadium, in rural South Georgia, seven thousand schoolchildren and adults vying for a place in the *Guinness Book of World Records* as the "Reading Capital of the World" recite a passage from Dr. Seuss's *The Cat in the Hat.*

2000 *Kidspeak,* a dictionary of children's words, expressions, and games by Dr. June Facto, is launched at the Melbourne [Australia] Museum. The author points out that Australian English is a mix of regional English, Scottish, Irish, and Welsh dialects; Aboriginal languages; and a hundred European and Asian tongues. "You can't do a dictionary like this without standing in delighted awe at the linguistic creativity of the very young," says Dr. Factor. The dictionary contains more than 350 insults, but there are also plenty of entries for the language of friendship.

▶ **RESEARCH** Encourage students to start a word wall on which they post new and interesting words they hear or read.

BIRTHDAYS

1915 Jean Fritz is born, in Hankow, China. As a child she dislikes her name. "The name Jean was so short, there didn't seem to be enough room in it for all the things I wanted to be." Known for her unconventional histories, Jean says she writes these books not as a curriculum aide, but as a journalist covering a beat, admitting that ever since her childhood she has wanted to be "right in the middle of what's happening."

She could not remember a time when she had not known the story; she had grown up knowing it.

Robin McKinley,
The Hero and the Crown

▶ **READ MORE** Ask students to read a Jean Fritz book carefully, looking for the writing techniques she uses to place the reader "right in the middle of what's happening."

▶ **WRITING TIP** Jean advises children who like to write to keep a diary. "Write down what happens."

▶ **WHAT'S IN A NAME** Invite students to find out how they were named; the meaning of their names; the average name length in your class. Students may enjoy creating an alphabetic list of names. Point out that in some cultures a person's real given name is a secret known only to that person and sometimes one other person such as a godparent, grandparent, or priest. In other cultures, students are allowed to choose new names when they are twelve. Invite students to consider this possibility. Is it something they would like to do? An online resource (<*http://www.behindthename.com*>) gives lots of information about given names.

1939 Victoria Chess is born, in Chicago. She is raised in Connecticut. As a young student, Victoria is asked to leave the Boston Museum School because her work habits are considered "lax." This person who was judged to have poor work habits has produced more than thirty popular books.

▶ **READ MORE** In *Speak! Children's Book Illustrators Brag About Their Dog*, edited by Michael J. Rosen, Victoria brags about Bruno, who always brings home a present from his neighborhood walks: a bunch of bananas, a dead woodchuck, a chicken (not dead), a very large zucchini squash, and so on.

▶ **WRITE ABOUT IT** Invite students to write about a funny incident with their pets.

1952 Robin McKinley is born, in Warren, Ohio. Her father's job as a naval officer takes the family around the world. As a child her favorite authors are Andrew Lang, Rudyard Kipling, L. Frank Baum, and J. R. R. Tolkien. In her Newbery Medal acceptance speech for *The Hero and the Crown*, Robin notes that she was clumsy as a child and remains clumsy as an adult. "I can't remember a time when the stories I told myself weren't about shy, bumbling girls who turned out to be heroes. They were usually misfits, often orphans, and invariably misunderstood by those around them. . . . I'm glad for my stubbornness and awkwardness now—and for the fact that my family moved around so much, which also protected me a little from peer pressure. . . . Being a self-proclaimed obstinate misfit meant I could hold on to my growing obsession with girls who do things."

▶ **READING REFLECTION** Invite students to list fictional heroes and heroines who are misfits and those who aren't. Which list is longer: books with main characters who are misfits or with those who fit in with the crowd?

NOVEMBER

17

. . . his heart was two sizes too small.

Dr. Seuss,
How the Grinch Stole Christmas

EVENT

1879 Joel Chandler Harris publishes "Brer Rabbit, Brer Fox, and the Tar Baby," in *The Atlanta Constitution*, the first of many Uncle Remus tales (Harris's retellings of African-American tales that he researches and collects).

▶ **READ MORE** Julius Lester and Jerry Pinkney have collaborated on three volumes of Uncle Remus tales.

BIRTHDAY

1904 Theodore Bernstein is born, in New York City. After college, he joins the *New York Times* as a copy editor, later becoming suburban editor, foreign editor, and founding editor of the international edition. *Newsweek* calls him the "linguistic policeman" of the *New York Times*. His "Winners and Sinners" in-house bulletin calls staff attention to examples of good and bad usage in the newspaper. It becomes the basis for a number of well-regarded books on language usage. He also writes *Bernstein's Reverse Dictionary*.

▶ **WORD FUN** Students can try a "reverse dictionary" game. Someone comes up with the definition; others try to guess the word.

EVENTS

1734 Colonial journalist and printer Peter Zenger is arrested for libeling the government. His acquittal is a landmark in freedom of the press.

▶ **READ MORE** Discuss newspaper editorial and op-ed (*opposite-the-ed*itorial) pages, illustrating how important Zenger's acquittal is to our right to disagree with government leaders. Bringing in opposing views on the same topic from different papers helps children see this point.

1805 Guided by Sacajawea, a woman of the Shoshoni people who carries a baby on her back, Meriwether Lewis and William Clark reach the Pacific Ocean. When President Jefferson sends Meriwether Lewis and William Clark on this journey of exploration, he asks them to keep careful notes. Scholars have been studying their notebooks ever since. Among other things, they make detailed notes on 122 different animals they see along the way.

▶ **WRITING TIP** Ask students to keep a journal of exploration for one week. In it they should make notes and drawings of every animal they see during this time. At the end of a week, they can compare notes. Who saw the most animals? Which type of animal was seen most? Who has notes on the most unusual animal? And so on.

2000 The movie version of Dr. Seuss's *How the Grinch Stole Christmas* opens.

BIRTHDAYS

1939 Nancy Van Laan is born, in Baton Rouge, Louisiana. Nancy says listening to stories is the best part of growing up in her grandparents' home, in Alabama. By kindergarten Nancy knows that what she wants to do is "paint pictures, make up stories, and dance on my toes." And by the age of seventeen, she has her own dance company. Nancy says she spends many months thinking about a story before she writes it down. "I listen to my thoughts, play around with them inside my head, and wait until they become a rhythm, like a song rising up inside me." Nancy writes in longhand before revising on the computer. She writes on anything that's handy, once writing a story on a tablecloth in a restaurant. After eating she asks for permission to take the tablecloth home.

▶ **WRITING TIP** Nancy says she doesn't know how a story will end when she starts, but the last line is very important. "If the last line isn't written satisfactorily, whatever happens beforehand will turn out to be a disappointment."

1939 Margaret Atwood is born, in Ottawa, Canada, the daughter of an entomologist. Margaret acknowledges that as a child she is not happy to have a November birth month. "November was a drab, dark, and wet month, lacking even snow." As an adult she discovers that November is very good, astrologically speaking, for poets.

▶ **READ MORE** *Princess Prunella and the Purple Peanut* is an alliterative romp. ("Princess Prunella lived in a pink palace with her pinheaded parents, Princess Patty and Prince Peter, her three plump pussycats, Patience, Prue and Pringle, and her puppy dog.") Margaret's dedication reads, "For my mother, who read to me/And my daughter who got read to." For kids craving more consonants, Pamela Duncan

NOVEMBER

18

Shout, Jabba Jabba,
Munch, Jabba Jabba,

Swing, Jabba Jabba,
Sing, Jabba Jabba

Nancy Van Laan,
So Say the Little Monkeys

Edwards and Henry Cole join forces in *Dinorella: A Prehistoric Fairy Tale,* which is devoted to *ds.* ("Dinorella is dying to go to the dance, but her dreadful stepsisters, Doris and Dora, declare she's too dowdy and dull. Dinorella is stuck in the den until Fairy-dactyl arrives and bedecks Dinorella with dazzling diamonds.") Many adults can't stand this kind of daffyness; many kids love it.

EVENTS

1895 Beatrix Potter notes in her journal that her pet rabbit Peter likes to jump on the tea table.

▶ **WRITING TIP** Invite students to write about something funny an animal they know has done. This can be a real pet or an animal they've read about.

1960 The *New York Times* reports that Ruby Bridges's father has been fired. Mr. Bridges's employer admits that he has been a good worker in his four years of employment, but he said whites in the area are making threats. Ruby tells child psychiatrist Robert Coles, "I knew I was just Ruby, just Ruby trying to go to school. . . . I guess I also knew I was the Ruby who had to do it." Forty years later, Ruby says she likes being invited to schools to talk about that year. "I find that Ruby's story so inspires children. They feel they finally have a hero who is like them."

▶ **THINK ABOUT IT** Ask children how they'd feel if they were the only student in the whole school, if all the other children had been taken out because their parents did not want them going to school with children of a different race. After reading Ruby's story, students might want to write her a letter:

Ruby Bridges Hall
The Ruby Bridges Educational Foundation
P.O. Box 870248
New Orleans, LA 70187

NOVEMBER

19

. . . a nation of the people, by the people, and for the people. . . .

Abraham Lincoln

BIRTHDAY

1943 Margaret Musgrove is born, in New Britain, Connecticut. A high school English teacher, she writes *Ashanti to Zulu: African Traditions,* with rich illustrations by Leo and Diane Dillon.

▶ **RESEARCH AND WRITE** Invite student teams to create their own alphabetic culture books. They can write about the history of their town or state; they can write about the country their parents or ancestors came from. Individual students might want to write their own autobiographies, using the alphabet as a framing structure.

▶ **READ MORE** Another good model for a geographic presentation is *A Is for Asia,* by Cynthia Chin-Lee, illustrated by Yumi Heo.

EVENTS

1863 Edward Everett, the keynote speaker at the dedication of a national cemetery in Gettysburg, Pennsylvania, delivers a two-hour speech honoring those who died in the July battle. Then President Abraham Lincoln speaks for less than two minutes. Some newspapers criticize Lincoln's speech for being so short and "undistinguished." Years later people recognize Lincoln's Gettysburg Address as a masterpiece.

1956 The Ford Motor Company announces the name of its revolutionary new automobile. Ford has considered more than six thousand possibilities, including

I'm Sneaky Bill, I'm terrible mean and vicious.

I steal all the cashews from the mixed-nuts dishes.

William Cole,
"Sneaky Bill"

Zip and Drof (Ford spelled backwards). The previous October, Ford officials had asked Marianne Moore, the distinguished poet, to invent a name for them. They tell her they want a name that will give customers the idea of elegance and fleetness. Ms. Moore's suggestions include the Ford Silver Sword, the Pastelogram, Mangoose Civique, Anticipator, Intelligent Whale, and the Utopian Turtle Top. Ford officials reject Ms. Moore's suggestions and decide to name their new car Edsel, in honor of one of Henry Ford's sons. The Edsel is the most spectacular flop in automotive industry.

▶ **WHAT'S IN A NAME** Invite students to list car names they like. Then they can try to figure out why the car manufacturers give cars the names they do. They can also write and ask.

BIRTHDAYS

1620 Peregrine White is born, on board the Mayflower just off Cape Cod, and becomes the first child born to English parents in New England. Another child born during the voyage is named Oceanus.

▶ **ALL ABOUT NAMES** Invite students to think of other names that would have special meaning for a child born on the Mayflower.

1919 William Cole is born, in Staten Island, New York. He works as a clerk in a deli and in a bookstore. Then he becomes publicity director and editor at publishing firms. In 1955, his first edited poetry collection, *Humorous Poetry for Children*, is published. William, the editor of more than fifty poetry anthologies, says that an anthology should lead young readers to more books. William says, "Why do I write poems? Because it's fun; writing a poem for kids is something like working out a puzzle, testing my wit." William Cole's advice to children writing poetry is "Have fun first!"

▶ **WRITING TIP** Since his teenage days, William has clipped and filed away "anything from a newspaper or magazine that struck my fancy." He gets ideas for poems from these clippings.

EVENTS

1877 Thomas Edison speaks famous words into a recording device he has invented: "Mary had a little lamb,/Its fleece was white as snow;/And everywhere that Mary went/The lamb was sure to go." These well-known words are the first acoustically recorded human speech. The verse, which recounts an actual event, a pet lamb following eleven-year-old Mary Stewart to school in Boston, was written in 1830, by Sarah Josepha Hale.

▶ **WRITE ABOUT IT** The poem inspires parodies. Invite students to try their hand at a parody or a sequel.

21

By the next morning the tight place in his stomach was gone. By the morning after that Matt decided that it was mighty pleasant living alone.

Elizabeth George Speare,
The Sign of the Beaver

1993 When asked what book he wishes he had written, Tedd Arnold replies, "Mother Goose! Mother Goose is the Queen-mother of children's literature. . . . I collect Mother Goose editions and enjoy reading about the history of the rhymes."

▶ **READ MORE** Children (and adults) enjoy rereading childhood favorites. Invite students to read Mother Goose rhymes to each other.

2000 After fifteen years and with over 180 million books in print, Scholastic publishes the last title in the Baby-Sitters Club series, by Ann Martin. *Graduation Day*, released on this day, includes a letter from Ann and a timeline offering highlights from the girls' years together. The books have been translated into more than nineteen languages and have inspired an HBO television series, a feature film, videos, trading cards, and other merchandise.

▶ **THINK ABOUT IT** Invite students to make a list of key elements in their favorite series books. Are there certain features they expect to be there? Every time?

BIRTHDAYS

1908 Elizabeth George Speare is born, in Melrose, Massachusetts. A high school English teacher, she is awarded the Newbery Medal for *The Witch of Blackbird Pond* and *The Bronze Bow* and the Newbery Honor for *The Sign of the Beaver*. Elizabeth loves doing the research to find out the kinds of houses her imaginary people lived in, the clothing they wore, the food they ate, and so on. Gathering this material for a book takes a year or more.

1908 Leo Politi is born, in Fresno, California. When he is seven, he returns to his mother's hometown, near Milan, in northern Italy. He studies art and becomes an art teacher. After returning to the United States, he lives and works on Olvera Street, in Los Angeles, sketching tourists. *Pedro, the Angel of Olvera Street*, about a famous Mexican celebration on the street, is named a Caldecott Honor book. Drawing on his boyhood interest in two swallows that came to nest every spring under the roof beams of his grandfather's house, Leo writes *Song of the Swallows*, about the Mission of Capistrano, a Caldecott Medal book. Leo finds writing more difficult than illustrating. "I work and rework my material up to the very last day of my deadline."

EVENTS

1787 Eight-year-old Peter Mark Roget makes the first entry in his notebook. He writes, "Peter, Mark, Roget. His Book." He fills many notebooks with his passion for collecting words. Years later, Peter Mark gives this same notebook, in which he has made voluminous notes on astronomy and meanings of Latin words, to his son. Peter Mark's passion for collecting and categorizing words lives today in the popular reference work *Roget's Thesaurus*, a book he starts and his son and grandson continue.

▶ **READING/WRITING CONNECTION** A *New Yorker* cartoon by M. Stevens shows a dinosaur with a thought balloon: ". . . large, great, huge, considerable, bulky, voluminous. . ." The caption reads "Roget's Brontosaurus." Invite students to create another Roget creature. Then they can pair up, choosing two animals and showing in thought balloons how each animal sees the other Roget-style.

1820 At age thirteen, Henry Wadsworth Longfellow publishes his first poem, "The Battle of Lovell's Pond," in the Portland, Maine *Gazette*.

▶ **WRITING TIP** There is nothing like seeing one's words in print. Newspapers don't print much poetry any more, but they do print letters to the editor. Encourage students to write a letter. They can also look for publications that publish student work.

1828 The first issue of the *Cherokee Phoenix* is printed, both in English and in the newly invented Cherokee alphabet. The alphabet is the creation of Sequoya, known to most Americans as George Gist (sometimes recorded as Guest) and to the Cherokee as Sikwayi. He is given the name Sequoya by missionaries. Fascinated by books, he dreams of creating a written version of his native Cherokee language. He divides all Cherokee sounds into eighty-six characters, making a symbol to represent each one. It takes him twelve years, but the result is so logical and so simple that people can learn the language in a few days. Sequoya's five-year-old daughter is the first one to read the new language. Sequoya teaches thousands of Cherokee to read and write. The giant redwood tree in California is named for him in honor of his remarkable achievement.

▶ **WHAT'S IN A NAME** Invite students to explore words of Native American origin in your locale.

▶ **READ MORE** Other stories about the Cherokee are not so sunny. A number of books about the tragic Trail of Tears are accessible to students. For starters, try *Only the Names Remain: The Cherokee and the Trail of Tears,* by Alex W. Bealer.

1969 Audrey and Don Wood are married. When Audrey, the eldest of three daughters, is a baby, her father, an art student, earns extra money painting murals for the Ringling Brothers' Circus, in Florida. So Audrey grows up with circus entertainers as friends. As a child Audrey loves to create stories. Inspired by Dr. Seuss, she even crosses out his name in one of her books so it reads: "*Horton Hatches an Egg,* by Audrey." These days, Audrey hopes she does her work well enough to lead readers into new worlds, "worlds of delight and truth, humor and magic."

BIRTHDAYS

1914 Charles Berlitz is born, in New York City. The grandson of Maximilian Berlitz, founder of the Berlitz Language Schools, Charles is also a gifted linguist, speaking twenty-five languages.

▶ **WORD FUN** Invite students to create multilanguage picture books. For example, "Favorite Pets" can have the names of animals in, say, four languages. "Favorite Foods" can do the same for foods. Encourage students to come up with other ideas.

1958 Jamie Lee Curtis is born, in Los Angeles. Following in the footsteps of her parents, Jamie is a noted actress. She is also the author of best-selling picture books. Jamie draws on her own experiences to inspire her stories. While attending an outdoor birthday party with her son, Jamie sees guests rush for shelter when a thunderstorm threatens. But one child unties all the birthday balloons, and they float into the stormy gray sky. A little girl asks, "Where do balloons go?" which becomes the title of one of Jamie's books.

▶ **WRITE ABOUT IT** Invite students to explore this question—and then compare their stories with Jamie's.

▶ **READ MORE** After more than thirty years, the winsome tale of a balloon with a mind of its own, *The Red Balloon,* by Albert Lamorisse, has not lost its charm.

EVENT

1908 SOS is adopted as the international distress signal. Contrary to popular opinion, the letters don't stand for anything—they are simply the easiest to send.

▶ **READING/WRITING TIP** Invite students to investigate the Morse Code. Perhaps some students will want to create their own code—for writing secret messages. They will be interested to know that Thomas Jefferson created a secret code machine.

NOVEMBER **22**

Today I feel silly. Mom says it's the heat.

I put rouge on the cat and gloves on my feet.

I ate noodles for breakfast and pancakes at night.

Jamie Lee Curtis,
Today I Feel Silly

NOVEMBER **23**

"Koly, you are thirteen and growing every day," Maa said to me. "It's time for you to have a husband."

Gloria Whelan,
Homeless Bird

BIRTHDAY

1923 Gloria Whelan is born, in Detroit, Michigan. A social worker, Gloria draws inspiration from the woods and water near her home, in Oxbow Lake in northern Kalkaska County, for her writing. She points out that "life in a remote setting is always an inward journey." *Homeless Bird*, the 2000 winner of a National Book Award, is a nicely detailed account of how a young Indian girl's life goes terribly wrong and how she thinks up a better future all by herself.

EVENTS

1897 J. L. Love patents the pencil sharpener. Many years later, in Betsy Byars's *The Burning Questions of Bingo Brown*, Bingo devises a special route from his desk to the pencil sharpener that takes him by the desk of every student—so that he can check up on what everybody is doing.

▶ **WRITING TIP** Invite students to create a list of ways they "take a break" from work in the classroom and/or ways they check up on what everybody is doing. (Maybe they won't want to let their teacher read their lists.)

1939 The Montgomery Ward Company decides it wants to have something special for Santa Claus to give to children when they visit him in the store. They ask Robert May, an advertising copywriter, to write a poem that can be printed up in booklets to hand out in the stores. May comes up with the idea of a reindeer with a shiny nose who helps Santa deliver his gifts. He suggests possible names of Rollo, Reginald, and Rudolph. The company gives out 1.4 million copies of "Rudolph, the Red-Nosed Reindeer." In 1946, Johnny Marks decides to write a song about the reindeer. Gene Autry records it, and it goes to the top of the Hit Parade. Total record sales have passed a hundred million dollars.

▶ **READ MORE** *Olive the Other Reindeer,* by Vivian Walsh and J. Otto Seibold, has a slim premise but one young readers enjoy. Olive mishears the line in the "Rudolph" song "All of the other reindeer/used to laugh and call him names" as "Olive, the other reindeer." Olive suddenly has an identity crisis: Olive is a dog, but she heads for the North Pole to join Santa's reindeer team.

BIRTHDAYS

1826 Carlo Lorenzini is born, in Florence, Italy. Carlo admits to being a real terror in school. In later life he becomes interested in reform to make schools a better place for kids to be. He writes several books about education. In 1881, he writes a book about a puppet. He takes the name of his mother's village as his pen name, Collodi. *The Adventures of Pinocchio* has been translated into more than a hundred languages. Popular children's author and New Yorker cartoonist William Steig says, "Often at work or in everyday living I do things or have experiences for which I find symbols that somehow derive from Collodi's great book."

1849 Frances Hodgson Burnett is born, in Manchester, England. She moves to Knoxville, Tennessee, as a teenager. In 1909, she writes *The Secret Garden*, which begins: "When Mary Lennox was sent to Misselthwaite Manor to live with her uncle, everybody said she was the most disagreeable-looking child ever seen. It was true, too." One thinks of William Steig's opening to *Shrek!* (see November 14). Unheralded when it first appears, today *The Secret Garden* is by far Frances's most popular book and is remembered with fondness by such contemporary writers as Katherine Paterson.

NOVEMBER

24

. . . the most disagreeable-looking child ever seen.

Frances Hodgson Burnett,
The Secret Garden

▶ **READING REFLECTION** Ask students which book they are more likely to read, one that begins "He was the nastiest, rudest boy in town" or one that begins "He was the nicest, most polite boy in town." Why?

1921 Yoshika Uchida is born, in Alameda, California. During her senior year at college, following the bombing of Pearl Harbor, Yoshika and her family are sent to a Japanese internment camp, along with 120,000 Japanese Americans. Yoshida provides a moving account of her childhood, including this experience, in *The Invisible Thread*. She also writes historical novels about Japanese Americans.

19-- Gloria Houston is born, in Marion, North Carolina. When she is seven, her aunt gives her *Little Women*, and Gloria knows she wants to become a writer like Jo. Growing up, she hears her mother and father tell stories about the family and about local history, and she publishes poetry in teen magazines. Gloria describes herself as a rebellious, problem student who loves school but easily gets bored and escapes into fantasy. Gloria's eighth-grade teacher encourages her to write a saga based on local history, and a romance between an Indian princess and a British soldier is the result. Her teacher saves this work, and when Gloria's first book is published he sends her a copy of that eighth-grade manuscript. Gloria's books are based not on historical figures, but on characters and incidents from her North Carolina youth. She writes about her fourth-grade teacher in *My Great-Aunt Arizona*, and, reports Gloria, "It's all true." *The Year of the Perfect Christmas Tree* is fiction but based on real people. Gloria writes it as a Christmas gift to her mother.

▶ **WRITING TIP** Gloria says one way to get family stories is to ask questions. Tell students to go to the oldest relative or family friend they know. Then ask them about their parents. Where were they from? What did they do for a living? What kind of food did they prepare for special meals? And so on. Invite students to take some of this information and write a special family story as a holiday gift for the coming season.

Long ago, when Persia was a land of princes and poets, there lived a maiden named Settareh. Her name meant "Star," and it was given her on the day she was born. . . .

Shirley Climo,
The Persian Cinderella

BIRTHDAYS

1909 P. D. Eastman is born, in Amherst, Massachusetts. Before becoming a best-selling author of children's books, he works for Disney Studios. He also works for United Productions of America, where he helps develop the cartoon character Mister Magoo. P. D.'s classic *Are You My Mother?* has sold more than one million copies. Another million-seller is his collaboration with Dr. Seuss, *The Cat in the Hat Dictionary*.

1928 Shirley Climo is born, in Cleveland, Ohio. Shirley says her earliest memory is "rocking in a creaky wicker porch swing while my mother, a children's author, recited her stories. Long before I could read, I'd begun telling my own tales to anyone willing to listen." When Shirley is sixteen, her first magazine story is published. Although Shirley has written numerous types of books, folklore remains her favorite genre. Shirley points out that folklorist Andrew Lang once said, "Nobody can write a new fairy tale; you can only mix up and dress the old stories and put characters into new dresses." Shirley adds, "For me, playing dress-up is fun at any age." Shirley's most successful books draw on the more than seven hundred versions, worldwide, of the Cinderella tale. Among her various retellings are Egyptian, Korean, Persian, and Irish versions.

▶ **THINK ABOUT IT** Challenge students to update the Cinderella motif. Who might serve as a fairy godmother figure in modern times? What other devices in the ancient tale need to be updated? For example, where might Cinderella and the prince meet? Invite students to list key elements in the Grimm or Perrault tale and then provide modern updates.

1935 Mordicai Gerstein is born, in Los Angeles, California. He attends the Chouinard Institute of Art, moves to New York City, and works as a designer and director of animated films for television. For his first book, *Arnold of the Ducks*, about a boy raised by ducks, Mordicai draws on memories of favorite childhood reading: *Tarzan* and Kipling's *The Jungle Book*. His *Mountains of Tibet* and *The Wild Boy* are both on the *New York Times* annual best-illustrated books list. Mordicai's *The Absolutely Awful Alphabet* introduces the letters in an unusual way: A is for "arrogant," C is for "cantankerous," and so on. Mordicai says, "I make my books for everyone, not just children. All of us either are children or have been children, so that childhood is an experience we all have in common."

▶ **WRITING TIP** Alphabet books usually deal with "nice" words. Invite students to follow Mordecai's lead and create ABCs of nasty words: including the "awfully arrogant Amphibian" and the "impossible Ignoramus." For an added challenge, students can try to create an alphabetic sentence for each word, such as *Stubborn Sarah shrieks shrilly*. This is a great way to emphasize parts of speech.

1946 Marc Brown is born, in Erie, Pennsylvania. He receives a degree in painting from the Cleveland Institute of Art. Marc is born Mark, but after seeing the work of Marc Chagall, he changes his name to Marc. He credits his high school art teacher with encouraging him to work with watercolors and for devoting a lot of time to his success. Marc has worked as a truck driver, short-order cook, soda jerk, college professor, gentleman farmer, television art director, actor, and costume and set designer. His popular character Arthur begins as a bedtime story to his son, and the first Arthur story is published in 1976 (*Arthur's Nose*). Marc hides his children's names in most of his books. Marc says he envies kids because, growing up, they are right in the middle of their own exciting stories. "I have to try to remember," he laments. When Marc visits schools, he's on the lookout for stories, because he knows that's where great story material exists. "After all, practically all of my characters come from third grade."

▶ **READING/WRITING CONNECTION** Invite students to make a list of things that happen to Arthur in several stories. Then they can make a list of things that have happened in school that could become part of another Arthur plot.

1952 Ellen Zolotow is born, in New York City. When she's sixteen she decides she doesn't like her birth name Ellen because it means Queen, and she is antiauthoritarian. She creates a new name for herself, Crescent, meaning "the growing" and adds Dragonwagon. Crescent says, "If I had any idea how many countless thousands of times I would have to explain this ridiculous name [Dragonwagon], I would have chosen something a lot less flashy. But by the time I realized how long the rest of my life would be, I already had a couple of books out and the start of a professional reputation. Besides, I love the letters I get from American Express beginning, 'Dear Mr. Wagon. . . .'"

▶ **WHAT'S IN A NAME** Invite students to invent names whose meanings would describe their characters, either their physique or their personality. For example, a professional basketball player might be called Henry Longfellow.

NOVEMBER
26

Perhaps they wouldn't have to move on after a month or so! Perhaps Dad was going to stay put and she and Lupe could become real friends.

Doris Gates,
Blue Willow

BIRTHDAYS

1901 Doris Gates is born, in Mountain View, California. Doris doesn't learn to read until she starts attending school when she is eight, but she already loves stories because her mother reads aloud every night. A librarian when the Depression forces a cutback in her job, Doris decides to use her extra day off to write books for children. *Blue Willow*, a Newbery Honor book, is about the ten-year-old daughter of migrant workers who have a tough time finding work during the Depression.

1922 Charles Schulz is born, in Minneapolis, Minnesota. In eighth grade, Sparky, as he is known to family and friends, fails every subject. He is cheered up when his family acquires a mixed-breed black-and-white dog, the inspiration for Snoopy. Sparky flunks physics in high school, with a grade of zero. He also flunks Latin, algebra, and English. The one subject Sparky likes is drawing, but his cartoons are rejected by the school paper. One day he is sitting in his dad's barbershop reading about Frank King (who drew *Gasoline Alley*). When Sparky reads that Frank makes $1,000 a week, he turns to his dad and says, "That's what I'm going to do. I'm going to draw a comic strip and I'm going to earn $1,000 a week." One of Sparky's friends at the Bureau of Engraving in Minneapolis is named Charlie Brown. Brown dies in 1983, never having married or had children. But a child with his name lives on.

1935 Laurence Pringle is born, in Rochester, New York. Feeling neglected and ignored as a child, he explores the forests, springs, and ponds in the rural area near Rochester. After he receives a camera for Christmas, he photographs birds' nests and wildflowers. He keeps a nature journal, and at sixteen he sells an article on crow behavior to *Open Road* magazine. Laurence believes that science is a great interest for children because "science, at its best, stands for hope, curiosity, truthfulness, and the joy of discovery." Laurence's more than seventy nature books range in subject from dinosaurs to vampire bats to killer bees to global warming to the monarch butterfly.

1954 Roz Chast is born, in Brooklyn, New York, the daughter of a teacher and an assistant principal. Roz says her parents would let her read classic comics but she had to sneak to friends' homes to read *Mad* magazine and Archie comic books. While in high school, Roz attends the Manhattan Art Students League. She earns a bachelor's degree in fine arts from the Rhode Island School of Design. Roz has worked as cartoonist for *The New Yorker* since 1979; she is one of the magazine's most popular staff cartoonists. A *Publishers Weekly* profile hails her as "probably the funniest woman in the world." Roz has collaborated with Jane Read Martin and Patricia Marx on *Now Everybody Really Hates Me* and *Now I'll Never Leave the Dinner Table*.

▶ **READ MORE** Roz's *Childproof: Cartoons About Parents and Children* will provoke much laughter as well as send shivers of recognition in the faculty room.

EVENTS

1789 By proclamation of President George Washington, Americans celebrate the first national Thanksgiving Day, offering thanks for the Constitution.

▶ **READ MORE** *Turkeys, Pilgrims, and Indian Corn: The Story of Thanksgiving Symbols,* by Edna Barth, is filled with provocative Thanksgiving lore and activities. For example, although there was no room aboard the Mayflower for cattle or other livestock, at least two dogs sailed with the Pilgrims, a mastiff and a spaniel. For adults, *The Times of Their Lives: Life, Love and Death in Plymouth Colony,* by James and Patricia Scott Deetz, provides the only "eyewitness description of the events that were to become the basis of a uniquely American holiday." They point out that the standard view of the origins of Thanksgiving is essentially mythical. For starters, there were twice as many Indians as settlers present, and participants drank plenty of beer.

BIRTHDAY

1950 Kevin Henkes is born, in Racine, Wisconsin. He is one of five children. His favorite book as a child is *Is This You?*, by Ruth Krauss, illustrated by Crockett Johnson—and he still has it. He recalls, "I remember drawing at a very early age. I loved

NOVEMBER 27

Wemberly worried about everything.

Big things, little things, and things in between.

Kevin Henkes,
Wemberly Worried

it. And my parents and teachers told me I was good at it—that made me love it all the more." Kevin remembers liking Garth Williams's art so much that he looked for novels he had illustrated. At age nineteen Kevin takes a plane from his home in Racine to New York City, hoping to find a publisher. And he does—Greenwillow Books. Henkes names his cat E. B., in honor of a writer he admires a lot.

▶ **WRITE ABOUT IT** Invite students to make "worry lists." Then they can choose to write about a worry or do as Kevin does and poke fun at their own worries. Students can also reflect on whether or not worries change over time. Did they worry about different things two years ago?

A successful life and a happy life is one measured by how much you have accomplished for others and not one measured by how much you have done for yourself.

From a letter Ed Young receives from his father

EVENT

2000 The *New York Law Journal* prints an item about a New York lawyer who collects antique typewriters and has become a children's book author. Drawing both on her profession and her hobby, Doreen Cronin has penned *Click, Clack, Moo: Cows That Type*. In the book some cows find an old typewriter and start sending in demands to Farmer Brown.

▶ **READ MORE** Don Marquis, who wrote a column for the New York *Evening Sun*, created Archy, a cockroach with the soul of a poet, who came in after office hours and left messages on his typewriter. Archy's work is collected in *Archy and Mehitabel*.

▶ **WRITE ABOUT IT** Students might enjoy updating Marquis's and Cronin's stories by inventing an animal or insect who takes over a computer.

BIRTHDAYS

1931 Ed Young is born, in Tientsin, China, near Peking, the son of a structural engineer. He is one of five children. Ed says he remembers his mother looking at his "uncomely report cards" year after year, saying, "Eddy, I wonder what is to become of you." His mother's glance has warmth as well as concern, and Ed knows that she realizes formal schooling comes second to his dreams. As a child growing up in China, the illustrations of N. C. Wyeth capture Ed's imagination; he wants to grow up and be an illustrator like Wyeth. In 1951, Ed comes to the United States to begin architectural studies, abandoning this plan in 1954 to study art. While working in advertising in New York City, Ed spends his lunchtime sketching animals in the Central Park Zoo. When Ed receives the Boston Globe–Horn Book Award for best book illustration for *Lon Po Po: A Red-Riding Hood Story from China* (which also wins the Caldecott Medal), he tells the audience he has a sign over his desk reminding himself to "take time for matters of the heart."

▶ **READING TIP** Invite readers to compare some of the many other versions of *Little Red Riding Hood* with *Lon Po Po*.

▶ **WRITING TIP** Most versions show the reader that Little Red Riding Hood has a problem—how to get that basket of food to her sick grandmother. Challenge students to offer alternative transportation for a modern-day Little Red Riding Hood:

> She could ask her mother to do it.
> She could call a taxi.
> She could send the basket with the Meals-on-Wheels van.

1952 Stephanie Calmenson is born, in Brooklyn. She also writes under the name of Lyn Calder. A prolific author, she has also been a teacher and an editor. Stephanie says she didn't ever dream of being a writer when she was growing up but now she realizes that from the day she learned to read she has always read every word on a copyright page. "No matter how tiny the notice, or how long the roman numeral copyright date, I read it."

▶ **WRITING TIP** Stephanie believes that an important influence on her career as a writer is that growing up she developed the habit that continues to this day: She writes letters. As a child she wrote to pen pals; she wrote to friends and family when she went to summer camp; she wrote to companies and magazines, letting them know what she thought of their product. Stephanie hated writing school compositions but she loved writing letters. Encourage students to find people to whom they can write letters every day this week. Make it a goal: a letter a week.

NOVEMBER

29

If you had the brain of a brachiosaurus . . . your brain would be smaller than a pea!

David M. Schwartz,
If You Hopped Like a Frog

EVENT

1783 While he is away from home attending meetings of Congress, Thomas Jefferson writes a letter to his eleven-year-old daughter Patsy, advising her, "Take care you never spell a word wrong. Always before you write a word consider how it is spelt, and if you do not remember it, turn to a dictionary. It produces great praise to a lady to spell well."

▶ **WRITING TIP** What do students think of Jefferson's advice? Invite students to write a letter to him, offering their opinions.

BIRTHDAYS

1832 Louisa May Alcott is born, in Concord, Massachusetts. She is one of four girls. One million copies of her books are sold during her lifetime. Best-selling adult-nonfiction writer Tracy Kidder recalls, "One of the books I really loved, at the fairly advanced age of eleven, was Louisa May Alcott's *Little Women*." Tracy didn't want anybody to know what he was reading, but admits he found it "absolutely captivating."

1898 C(live) S(taples) Lewis is born, in Northern Ireland. He starts writing his first book when he is eight years old, a fantasy novel called *Boxen*. He grows up to be a professor of Medieval and Renaissance English at Cambridge University and the author of many scholarly works as well as the Chronicles of Narnia series.

1918 Madeleine L'Engle, an only child, is born, in New York City. She is named for her great-grandmother Madeleine, but known as Mado in the stories young Madeleine's mother (also named Madeleine) tells her. She recalls her experience at boarding school in England as "absolutely splendidly horrible," adding, "I still get books out of it." Madeleine notes, "It took two years of rejection slips from twenty or thirty publishers before I found a grown-up editor who could understand *A Wrinkle in Time*." Once published, the book wins the Newbery Medal—and immediate popularity with children. The question Madeleine is asked most often is, "Why haven't we ever seen Charles Wallace as an adult in any of the books? Is he dead?" Madeleine replies, "Charles Wallace is alive and well until I hear otherwise." She adds that when she learns about Charles, she will write about him.

▶ **WRITING TIP 1** Madeleine L'Engle advises young writers, "Keep a journal that you don't show anybody."

▶ **WRITING TIP 2** Asked to name the ten top things that have made her a writer, Madeline replies:

Growing up in a New York apartment full of books.

Having parents who read aloud to each other every night.

Being an only child with my own room.

Having godparents who gave me books.

Knowing that truth is stranger than fact.

Reading George MacDonald's books at a young age.

Greek and Roman myths

The Bible

Fairy tales

Shakespeare

NOVEMBER

30

One summer day, Henry and his friend decided to go to Fitchburg to see the country. "I'll walk," said Henry. "It's the fastest way to travel."

D. B. Johnson,
Henry Hikes to Fitchburg

1951 David Schwartz is born, on Long Island, New York. David says he has wondered about big numbers since he was a small child. This curiosity results in the popular *How Much Is a Million?* As a child, David is fascinated by both microscopes and telescopes because they transport him on imaginary journeys into outer space and into hidden worlds. "I could be both a giant and a dwarf at the same time!" While riding his bike he calculates how long it would take to ride a magical bike all the way around the earth—or to the moon or Jupiter. David estimates how many books are in his town's public library, and then he tells himself, "With so many books, surely I could write just one!" In college, David studies biology and then becomes an elementary school teacher. He has published more than thirty books since *How Much Is a Million* appeared in 1985.

▶ **READ MORE** Students who read *G Is for Googol, On Beyond a Million,* and *If You Hopped Like a Frog* will find lots of amazing information with which to astound everyone they know. Besides that, they'll learn something about numerical relationships.

BIRTHDAYS

1667 Jonathan Swift is born. The author of *Gulliver's Travels,* Swift is a famous essayist and very concerned that the English language is being corrupted. He writes a letter to a magazine, protesting the use of such abbreviations as *couldn't.* He proposes forming an Academy that will "expunge all words and phrases that are offensive to good sense."

▶ **THINK ABOUT IT** Challenge students to think of some ways language use might change. For example, what would happen if the apostrophe were eliminated from contractions? Emily Dickinson, for one, didn't use it, writing *doesnt* instead of *doesn't.* Do we really need it?

1835 Samuel Clemens is born, in Florida, Missouri. He takes his pen name Mark Twain from his early experiences as a riverboat pilot on the Mississippi River. *Mark twain* is a river term meaning a depth of two fathoms (twelve feet), a depth considered just barely safe for navigation. On the occasion of winning the National Book Award for poetry, Richard Wilbur comments, "When I was young, our family spent every Christmas season with my maternal grandparents, and every year I reread the same three books—Lewis Carroll's two stories about Alice, and Mark Twain's *Huckleberry Finn.* From the last I learned, over and over, that plain colloquial language is capable of subtlety and can lift into the lyrical." Ernest Hemingway said, "All modern literature comes from one book by Mark Twain called *Huckleberry Finn....* It's the best book we've had."

▶ **WHAT'S IN A NAME** Invite students to consider occupations and hobbies that interest them. Can they invent pen names from some terminology connected with these concerns?

▶ **WRITING TIP** On page 400 of writing *Tom Sawyer*, Mark gets stuck, saying, "the story made a sudden and determined halt and refused to proceed another step." Two years later, Mark rereads the last chapter he'd written and discovers that "when the tank runs dry you've only to leave it alone and it will fill up again in time, while you are asleep, also while you are at work on other things. . . ." He starts writing again and finishes the book "without any trouble."

1931 Margot Zemach is born, in Los Angeles, California. She remembers that she was very good at roller-skating because "it is something a loner can do." She studies at the Los Angeles County Art Institute and the Vienna Academy of Fine Arts, where she meets Harve Fischstrom, who becomes her husband and collaborator, using the name Harve Zemach. Margot says, "Children are fascinated by detail. . . . Children need detail, color, excellence—the best a person can do. I always think, when I'm drawing the view of a town or the inside of a hut: 'Would I have liked to live there?' One doesn't need meticulous authenticity of costume or architecture; to a certain extent, one can invent one's own styles of dress and house shapes. But things have to be made real. The food has to be what you'd want to eat, the bed has to be what you'd want to get into right away. But, all in all, I'm not sure that one should consciously bear in mind that the drawings are meant for the gaze of children. If I make a book for children, I draw it the same as I'd draw for grown-ups."

1944 D. B. Johnson is born, in East Derry, New Hampshire. A former newspaper artist and comic strip artist, D. B.'s freelance illustrations appear in major periodicals. His first picture book, the prize-winning *Henry Hikes to Fitchburg*, is inspired by a passage in Henry Thoreau's *Walden*: "I have learned that that swiftest traveler is he that goes afoot."

▶ **READING/WRITING CONNECTION** Invite students to write a fable that has "the swiftest traveler is he that goes afoot" as its moral.

Dᴇᴄᴇᴍʙᴇʀ

Dᴇᴄᴇᴍʙᴇʀ

Once there was a speckled hen who laid an egg every day,

only to have it taken by a little Tomten every morning.

Jan Brett,
Hedgie's Surprise

Bɪʀᴛʜᴅᴀʏs

1916 Adrien Pearl Stoutenburg is born, in Darfur, Minnesota. Adrien works as a librarian, political reporter, and freelance writer. The author of more than forty books, she is best known for her *American Tall Tales*, which retells the stories of Paul Bunyan, Pecos Bill, Mike Fink, Davy Crockett, Johnny Appleseed, and John Henry in a way that emphasizes tall-tale elements they all have in common.

▶ **READ MORE** In *The Bunyans*, by Audrey Wood, illustrated by David Shannon, we learn that Paul has a wife and two children. Wedding invitations "were so large, only one needed to be sent to each state. Everyone could read them for miles!" *The Saginaw Paul Bunyan*, by James Stevens, explains how Paul caused the absence of whales in the Great Lakes. According to Mary Pope Osborne's *American Tall Tales*, illustrated by Michael McCurdy, after Paul and Babe the Blue Ox had logged all the trees in Minnesota, Washington, Oregon, and Alaska, they moved on to the Arctic Circle.

▶ **WRITING FUN** Invite students to take one of these ideas—or make up one of their own—to write a tall-tale incident.

▶ **ALL ABOUT NAMES** In a project called Yukon Tall Tall Tales, children at the Selkirk Elementary School in Whitehorse, capital of the Yukon, give themselves tall-tale names and then write tall tales about these new personas. Some of the names are Borealis Bruce, Gold Nugget Gerald, Klondike Katherine, Midnight Sun Meghan, Sourdough Sam, and Snow Pile Sara. You can read the tales at *http://www.yesnet.yk.ca/schools/selkirk/gallery/tttales/content.html*

1949 Jan Brett is born, in Hingham, Massachusetts. Growing up, Jan's favorite book is *Millions of Cats*, by Wanda Gag. Jan decides early on that she is going to be an illustrator, and while she is a student at the Boston Museum School, she spends hours in the Museum of Fine Arts. Jan travels frequently with her husband, a member of the Boston Symphony Orchestra, and her research on these travels appears in her work.

1952 Scott Barry is born, in Flushing, New York. He writes the *Kingdom of Wolves*, a book about the lives and habits of wolves, which he illustrates with his own photographs taken during his study of thirty-five wolves over seven years. Barry says, "I am doing exactly what I would like to do most: teaching the public about the things that are closest to my heart—wildlife, wilderness, a healthy natural world, and a healthy human society."

▶ **READ MORE** Other good wolf reads include *Wolf Christmas*, by Daniel and Jill Pinkwater; *White Fang*, by Jack London, illustrated by Ed Young; *Julie's Wolf Pack*, by Jean Craighead George; and *Never Cry Wolf*, by Farley Mowat.

Eᴠᴇɴᴛ

1955 A bus driver in Montgomery, Alabama, asks Rosa Parks to give up her seat on the bus to a white man. When Rosa refuses, she is arrested and jailed. Dr. Martin Luther King leads the Montgomery Bus Boycott, which lasts 381 days.

▶ **READ MORE** *Rosa Parks: My Story*, by Rosa Parks with Jim Haskins, shows that there is even more to Rosa's story than this courageous act of defiance. *If a Bus Could Talk*, by Faith Ringgold, offers an offbeat picture-book account.

One day a chicken ran across a road. This startled some cows, who stampeded over an ancient bridge.

David Macaulay,
Why the Chicken Crossed the Road

BIRTHDAYS

1943 William Wegman is born, in Holyoke, Massachusetts, son of a factory worker. William earns a degree in fine arts from the Massachusetts College of Art. By dressing his weimaraners in costumes and photographing them as Cinderella, Little Red Riding Hood, and so on, William takes picture books into new territory.

1946 David Macaulay is born, in Burton-on-Trent, England. David's childhood is filled with play and invention. He likes buildings things using spools and thread and cigar boxes. David's family moves to the United States in 1957, and he studies architecture at the Rhode Island School of Design. David says architecture showed him how things work and how to deal with problems of any scale.

▶ **WORD FUN** Why the chicken crossed the road is the theme of a lot of jokes. Challenge students to answer the question from the point of view of various literary characters. For example, the Three Little Pigs might say the chicken crossed the road because it wanted to get away from the big bad wolf.

EVENT

1819 Widower Thomas Lincoln marries widow Sarah Bush Johnston. Ten-year-old Abraham is pleased that Sarah brings three books to this marriage: Noah Webster's *The American Spelling Book*, Daniel Defoe's *Robinson Crusoe*, and *The Arabian Nights*. Abraham's cousin Dennis Hanks recalls that "Abe'd lay on his stummick by the fire and read [*The Arabian Nights*] out loud to me 'n' Aunt Sairy. . . ." When Hanks calls the book "a pack of lies," Abraham replies, "Mighty fine lies." Hanks says Abraham reads the book a dozen times "an' knowed them yarns by heart."

▶ **READING/RESEARCH TIP** Invite students to interview three adults they know, asking each to name three favorite books they remember from their childhood. Then students can compile the results, perhaps producing a poster for the classroom or library, or a newsletter. Encourage students to search out the well-remembered books.

But I am who I am
And that's even better.

Sheree Fitch,
If I Were the Moon

BIRTHDAY

1956 Sheree Fitch is born, in Ottawa, Ontario, Canada. Sheree credits her teacher Mrs. Goodwin with showing her that she might be a poet one day. When Sheree writes a silly poem about her last name, Mrs. Goodwin puts it on the board so other students can enjoy it, observing that this is in a genre called nonsense poems. "A lightbulb went off in my life," recalls Sheree. "I told Mrs. Goodwin, 'Maybe I'll be a writer,' and she said, 'Maybe you will.'" Years later at a book-signing for *Toes in My Nose*, someone standing in line says, "Don't sign the book; sign my forehead." It is Mrs. Goodwin.

▶ **OUT LOUD** Sheree loves tongue twisters because "the more mistakes you make, the more fun it is—and where else in life is it really fun to make mistakes?"

▶ **READ MORE** Tongue twisters are irresistible. Here are a few volumes: *Oh Say Can You Say?*, by Dr. Seuss; *World's Toughest Tongue Twisters*, by Joseph Rosenbloom; *Six Sick Sheep: One Hundred Tongue Twisters*, by Joanna Cole; *Mexican Tongue Twisters: Trabalenguas Mexicanos*, by Robert J. Haddad.

4

Once upon a time in Spain there was a little bull and his name was Ferdinand.

Munro Leaf,
The Story of Ferdinand

BIRTHDAYS

1835 Samuel Butler is born, in Britain. He writes a popular book, *Erewhon.* That's *nowhere* spelled backward (with two letters reversed to make it easier to pronounce).

▶ **WORD FUN** Invite students to explore what happens when they spell words backward. Joel Agee's *Go Hang a Salami! I'm a Lasagna Hog!* and *So Many Dynamos!* show students the fun involved in creating palindromes, phrases that read the same forward and backward.

1905 Munro Leaf is born, in Hamilton, Maryland. He works as a manuscript reader for several publishers. Munro writes *The Story of Ferdinand*, about a peaceful bull, to protest the brutality of the Spanish Civil War. Although it is a picture book for children, it is a bestseller with adults too. Munro says he wrote the story in forty minutes—as a gift for Robert Lawson, who didn't like the conformity required in illustrations for children's books. Munro tells him, "Rob, cut loose and have fun with this in your own way."

1940 Bruce Hiscock is born, in San Diego. Growing up, Bruce is a good reader but isn't much interested in fiction; he's mainly interested in reading to find out how to do things: build boats, find out what plants he can eat if he ever has to survive in the woods, fish. He becomes a research chemist and equine drug tester at Saratoga Harness Track, as well as a substitute schoolteacher. And a writer.

▶ **READ MORE** Invite everyone to bring a good nonfiction book to read today.

EVENT

1983 A new Jewish Theological Seminary library is dedicated, in New York City. Of the library's 250,000 books, many ancient and irreplaceable, 85,000 are lost on April 18, 1966, in a fire that destroys the original library. The rest of the books are saved by the people in the neighborhood. Hundreds of volunteers, from kindergarten children to the officers of a large corporation, form a human chain and pass the books out of the building and into hands of people who know how to dry those that are water soaked. These books include the most complete collection of Judaica in the world.

▶ **READ MORE** The inspiring story of a community rallying to help a neighbor is told in *Fire! The Library Is Burning,* by Barry D. Cytron.

5

The wind has such a rainy sound

Moaning through the town. . . .

Christina Rossetti,
"The Wind Has Such
a Rainy Sound"

BIRTHDAYS

1753 Phillis Wheatley is born, in Senegal, West Africa. She is brought to the United States in 1761 and bought as a slave by a Boston tailor named John Wheatley. Given special privileges not accorded most slaves, Phillis learns to read and write, writing her first poetry when she is fourteen. After General George Washington reads a poem she writes about him in 1776, he invites Phillis to visit his headquarters.

1830 Christina Rossetti is born, in London, England. Her two older brothers are writers, as is her older sister. Their mother, a teacher, teaches the children at home. Christina enjoys sketching exotic animals at the London Zoological Gardens. In 1850, seven of Christina's poems are published.

1910 Jim Kjelgaard is born, in New York City. He spends his childhood on farms in the Allegheny mountain range running through Pennsylvania. He is a trapper, laborer, and surveyor's assistant before deciding to write stories for children. Jim loves dogs, and he writes about them. In his own home, Jim always has at least one dog and sometimes as many as seven.

▶ **READ MORE** Compile a class list of good dog stories and poems. For younger readers, the Henry and Mudge series is a good place to start. There's also *Stone Fox,* by John Reynolds Gardiner. For older readers, *Where the Red Fern Grows,* by Wilson Rawls, is a must read. (Calling any of these a dog story is a gross injustice.)

1933 Harve Fishtrom is born, in Newark, New Jersey. An instructor in history and social science, he takes his wife's surname, Zemach, to write picture books. His variant of *Rumpelstiltskin* with his wife Margot's illustrations wins the Caldecott Medal.

▶ **READ MORE** In *The Girl Who Spun Gold*, illustrated by Leo and Diane Dillon, Virginia Hamilton offers a West Indian variant of the little-man tale. The stunning illustrations are created with four-color metallic paint with gold as a fifth color. In *The Rumpelstiltskin Problem*, Vivian Vande Velde points out to YA readers that the Rumpelstiltskin tale is full of holes. She offers six alternative versions to explain what really happened.

DECEMBER

6

. . . those who want to bad enough will . . . .

John Reynolds Gardiner,
Stone Fox

BIRTHDAYS

1905 Elizabeth Yates is born, in Buffalo. She is awarded the Newbery Medal for *Amos Fortune, Free Man.* After reading inscriptions on grave markers in a cemetery near her home, in Petersborough, New Hampshire, for Amos Fortune and his wife, Violet, Elizabeth wants to know more. She spends a year researching this African prince who becomes a slave in Boston and then, at age sixty, buys his freedom, helping others to do the same.

1944 John Reynolds Gardiner is born, in Los Angeles, the son of two teachers. John says, "As a boy I was a rebel. Whatever my parents wanted me to do, I did the opposite. My mother wanted me to read. So I didn't read." John says his mother should have locked up books in a case and ordered him not to touch them. Then he would have found a way to get to them. John's mother reads aloud to him every night, and he now knows this had a good effect. John doesn't read a novel (the first one he reads is *Exodus*) until he is nineteen years old. In high school, John's teachers warn him he will never succeed in college because his grammar and spelling are so poor. In college he's put in remedial English classes with foreign students who don't speak English. "And," says John, "they got better grades on their compositions than I did." John admits that the manuscript he sends to a publisher has misspelled words and bad grammar. Why did the publisher buy it? Because, says John, the publisher knew that "someone who may not have a good command of spelling or grammar may still be able to write a good story." That story is the phenomenally popular *Stone Fox.*

EVENTS

1902 An eight-cent stamp honoring Martha Washington is issued, making her the first American woman to appear on a U. S. stamp.

▶ **WRITING/RESEARCH TIP** Postage stamps are a fascinating, inexpensive source of interesting research topics for children. Buy a bag or two at a hobby store. Students can sort them into categories and then select a stamp subject about which they will find three facts to report back to the class.

▶ **CELEBRATE** Honor favorite books or characters by inviting students to paint large stamp posters for their choices. *Go to Your Studio and Make Stuff: The Fred Babb Poster Book* has a great stamp poster to use as a model, along with dozens of other inspiring ideas that can be adapted for classroom use.

1983 A twelfth-century illuminated manuscript by a monk at the Heimarshausen Abbey, in Germany, sells for $11.9 million at Sotheby's in London.

DECEMBER 7

Over the years she'd done everything to try and improve his school record. Threats. Bribes. Even punishments.

Anne Fine,
Flour Babies

BIRTHDAYS

1897 John Robert Tunis is born, in Boston. After graduating from Harvard and serving in the army, John tries to sell articles as a freelance writer. He compares sending manuscripts to publishers to being a door-to-door salesman, saying "I must have been no more welcome." John works as a sports writer for the *New York Evening Post* and writes articles for the leading magazines of the day. At the age of forty-nine, John writes his first novel, *Iron Duke.* He then writes twenty more juvenile sports novels, featuring commitment to the team, hard work, and sacrifice.

1947 Anne Fine is born, in Leicester, England, daughter of a scientific experimental officer. When Anne's mother has triplets, Anne is sent off to boarding school. Anne can't remember a time when she wasn't reading. At age eight, her favorite book is *The Boy Next Door,* by Enid Blyton. Anne's favorite subject in school is English but she confesses she isn't so sure she'd like it today, not with all that "drafting and re-drafting." Anne says, "We were allowed just to write and we never had to go back to anything a second time except to correct spellings." Now that she's a professional writer of more than twenty-five titles, Anne doesn't mind redrafting, but she works in "absolute silence" and hides her work from anyone who comes in the room.

▶ **WRITING TIP** Anne's advice for anyone who wants to be a writer is "Read, read, read. The practice for writing is not writing, but reading."

EVENT

1968 Richard Dodd returns a book on febrile diseases checked out by his great-grandfather from the University of Cincinnati Medical Library in 1823. The fine, $2,254, is waived.

▶ **READ MORE** In contrast, the library mishaps of the hero of Barbara Ann Porte's *Harry in Trouble* don't seem nearly so dramatic. Harry doesn't forget to bring books back; he keeps losing his library cards.

▶ **READING TIP** Invite the librarian to visit and enlist students' help in locating missing books. She may want to tell students which categories of books come up missing the most. (In many schools joke books and cookbooks are high on the "lost" list.)

DECEMBER 8

Once upon a time, in a kingdom by the sea, there lived a little Princess named Lenore. She was ten years old, going on eleven. One day, Lenore fell ill on a surfeit of raspberry tarts and took to her bed.

James Thurber,
Many Moons

BIRTHDAYS

1894 James Thurber is born, in Columbus, Ohio. He loses an eye while playing William Tell with his brother. E. B. White introduces James to the editor of *The New Yorker* and James is a regular contributor of stories, essays, and cartoons for more than thirty years. James doodles cartoons all the time, even drawing on the walls of the *New Yorker* offices. David McCord says James's books for children are filled with "impossible tasks, indomitable courage, improbable solutions, appropriate wizardry, and nothing so serious or warped as not to be funny."

▶ **READING REFLECTION** Invite students to construct a plot outline of the basic fairy tale. What elements are common in most tales? How does one of Jon Scieszka's tales, for example, turn this structure on its ear?

1894 E. C. Segar is born, in Chester, Illinois. He creates the *Popeye* comic strip.

▶ **READ MORE** Encourage students to share a favorite cartoon strip with the class, explaining what they like about it.

1940 Mary Azarian is born, in Washington, D.C. A teacher in a one-room school, Mary is a prize-winning freelance printmaker and illustrator. The Vermont Board of Education commissions her alphabet posters, originally designed for her own class-room, for use in primary grades throughout the state. The collected posters are published as *The Farmer's Alphabet*. Mary dedicates *A Symphony for the Sheep* to "the memory of our first sheep, two Columbia yearling lambs purchased from a farm several miles across the valley from our farm. We brought them home in the back seat of our 1955 Chevy, and when we opened the door, they sprang from the car and bolted down an abandoned road. They were young and frisky and we weren't able to catch them. We never saw them again."

DECEMBER 9

In the great forest a little elephant is born. His name is Babar.

Jean de Brunhoff,
The Story of Babar

BIRTHDAYS

1899 Jean de Brunhoff is born, in Paris. He studies art at the Ecole Alsacienne. His wife invents a character she calls Babar the Elephant King, and when Jean sees how much his children love Babar, he begins drawing the characters—and writing the stories. Barbar may be little in *The Story of Babar, the Little Elephant*, but the book is not. It is three times as large as most children's books.

1928 Joan Blos is born, in New York City, the only child of a teacher. Majoring in physiology in college, Joan does graduate work in psychology. Her interest in children's literature comes later. Joan's books are research-intensive. To get the language right for a book like *A Gathering of Days*, which is set in the 1830s, Joan researches the clothing, household furnishings, tools, and other parts of the lives of people living then.

▶ **WRITING TIP** What Joan enjoys most of all about creating a book of historical fiction is doing the research. She calls it a treasure hunt.

1937 Mary Downing Hahn is born, in College Park, Maryland. In school, Mary is known as the class artist. She hates writing reports. At age thirteen, she writes her first book, *Small Town Life*, about a girl named Susan. But then there is a long gap. Mary doesn't publish *The Sara Summer,* her first book, until she is forty-one. Since then, she has averaged a book a year.

▶ **WRITING CHALLENGE** Keeping readers on the edge of their seat isn't easy. Mary usually types four to six versions of every book, working to get the suspense just right. Offer a challenge to students. Ask them to finish this simile for a mystery, a scary story, a funny story, and a sad story: *a piece of chalk as white as . . .* or *a sky as dark as. . . .*

DECEMBER 10

. . . you must believe without seeing.

George MacDonald,
The Princess and the Goblin

BIRTHDAYS

1787 Thomas Hopkins Gallaudet is born, in Philadelphia, Pennsylvania, and edu-cated at Yale College. Thomas becomes interested in the education of the deaf and goes to Europe to learn methods. He establishes the first school for the deaf, now Gallaudet University. According to a 1999 survey by the Modern Language Association, American Sign Language is the fastest-growing language offered at U. S. colleges. A number of high schools offer it as an alternative to traditional foreign language classes. ASL professionals point out that ASL is a different language, with its own syntax and grammar.

▶ **FIND OUT MORE** Invite volunteers to learn some ASL phrases and teach the rest of the class.

1824 George MacDonald is born, in Huntley, Scotland. His mother dies when he is eight. At sixteen, George enters the University of Aberdeen, majoring in chemistry and physics. Later he earns another degree, in theology. An arithmetic teacher, MacDonald writes fairy stories for children that have a strong influence on such writers as C. S. Lewis and J. R. R. Tolkien. Robin McKinley has adapted one of MacDonald's stories, *The Light Princess*, for today's readers.

1830 Emily Dickinson is born, in Amherst, Massachusetts. Emily spends almost all her life close to her home in Amherst, Massachusetts. After going off to Mount Holyoke Seminary for one year, she begins to withdraw from social activity; by the time she is thirty, Emily stops leaving the house altogether. Although she continues to write letters to friends, she stops seeing them. During her lifetime she publishes seven poems. After death, her sister discovers a thousand more in a bureau drawer. Knowing this, one is very touched by her poem that begins "This is my letter to the world,/That never wrote to me. . . ."

▶ **READ MORE** Young readers can find touching portraits of Emily in *The Mouse of Amherst,* by award-winning poet Elizabeth Spires, and in *Emily,* by Michael Bedard, illustrated by Barbara Cooney. Their teachers can find inspiration in *Visiting Emily,* edited by Sheila Coghill and Thom Tammaro. Presenting poems inspired by the life and work of Emily—from Maxine Kunin picturing Emily mastering Microsoft to X. J. Kennedy commenting on the answering machine at her Homestead to William Stafford pointing out that Emily "was the stillest one"—this is a volume to savor.

1851 Melvil Dewey is born, in Adams Center, New York. While a student working in the Amherst College library, he becomes frustrated by the way books are organized and invents a new system, now known as the Dewey decimal book classification system.

▶ **READ MORE** Take students on a Dewey Decimal tour of the library, asking them to guess which are the most popular library numbers, which books are checked out most often. Then they can confirm their guesses with the librarian.

1903 Mary Norton is born, in London, England, the daughter of a physician. Very nearsighted, she writes the Borrowers series, about people six inches tall or less. Their miniature world shows ingenuity. Since they own nothing and must "borrow," the family uses champagne corks as kitchen stools, blotting paper as carpet, a thimble as a bucket, and so on. Writer Lawrence Weschler's seven-year-old daughter, Sara, leaves notes behind the refrigerator to one of the Borrowers, whom she believes live in their home. Her father secretly takes the letters and writes responses.

▶ **READ MORE** Two irresistible books about small, everyday items being transformed to other uses (a Ferris wheel made of scissors, skyscraper walls of saltines, pretzel chairs, and much much more) are Joan Steiner's *Look-Alikes* and *Look-Alikes Jr.* The books are a visual delight for readers of all ages, from 6 to 106, and one doesn't even care that the text doesn't come close to measuring up. The constructions are a delightful puzzle—and a Borrowers' paradise.

1945 Ann Turner is born, in Northhampton, Massachusetts, the daughter of an artist mother. Ann says growing up in a family that is interested in different peoples and cultures influences her writing. Ann says writers write for the same reason readers read—to find out what happens, to learn how the story ends. Ann says she has to keep writing to find these answers for herself.

EVENT

1903 Just one week before the Wright brothers make their first successful flight, at Kitty Hawk, a *New York Times* editorialist writes of the futility of trying to fly. The paper calls experiments on a flying machine a "waste of time and money."

▶ **READ MORE** *The Wright Brothers: How They Invented the Airplane,* by Russell Freeman, contains original photographs by Wilbur and Orville Wright.

DECEMBER

11

While they were on safari in Africa, young Scotty Lazardo wandered away from camp and returned with a dinosaur.

William Joyce,
*Dinosaur Bob
and His Adventures
with the Family Lazardo*

BIRTHDAYS

1910 Willard Espy is born, in Olympia, Washington. After working for *Reader's Digest* for fifteen years, Espy begins inventing word games, writing nearly a book a year, including *An Almanac of Words at Play, Have a Word on Me,* and *A Children's Almanac of Words at Play.* His highly acclaimed *Rhyming Dictionary* contains 80,000 rhyming words.

▶ **WORD FUN** Invite students to create rhyming lists—of words that are not spelled alike.

▶ **WORD FUN** Here's a homonym puzzle invented by Willard. The idea is to find homonyms that will fit in the blanks. Willard gives a hint: This is a rhyming homonym puzzle.

I met a wise antelope, born in a zoo;
And I wish that I knew what that *** *** ****.

(new gnu knew)

▶ **READ MORE** Introduce students to a rhyming dictionary.

1957 William Joyce is born, in Shreveport, Louisiana, a child who always loves drawing. "My dad says I was born with a pencil in my hand." William says, "In school I could draw 'Dinosaurs Eating Teachers' better than anyone else. . . ." William admits that his early pictures have "horrible things going on, you know, arms and legs and guts and heads just flinging about all over the place—it was great." His parents provide art lessons and William has his first solo show at age fourteen. William's seventh book, *Dinosaur Bob and His Adventures with the Family Lazardo,* is a smash hit. When a writer for *The Oxford American* picks up the book, immediately flipping to the first page of text, William takes the book from him, saying, "Just like an adult! You skipped over the map!" William turns to the frontispiece, where the reader can trace the route of Bob and the Family Lazardo from the Belgian Congo to their arrival in New York. William says he writes the book to "get revenge for *Old Yeller* and *King Kong,*" to have a creature come into a regular neighborhood and survive. If Maurice Sendak hadn't created *Where the Wild Things Are,* William says, he wouldn't be doing what he does now.

▶ **THINK ABOUT IT** Maurice Sendak, Anthony Browne, and William Joyce all acknowledge the huge influence of the movie *King Kong.* Ask students to figure out why. If they haven't seen the movie, ask them to find "similarities" among the three author/artists.

EVENT

1999 Rafe Martin conducts a storytelling workshop at Cobblestone School, in Rochester, New York. Rafe says that growing up, family stories are important. His grandmothers each tell of leaving home at sixteen to come alone to America. His father tells about flying rescue missions in the Himalayas during World War II, stories filled with jungles, rogue elephants, cobras, headhunters, and holy men. His mother reads fairy tales and tells him Aesop's fables. "One of our favorites was *The Tortoise and the Hare.* 'Slow and steady wins the race.' As I didn't write my first book until I was thirty-five, I clearly took that story's theme to heart."

▶ **READ MORE** Rafe says folktales gives us a way to experience justice, to see good rewarded and evil punished, something we all long for, especially since our daily news is built on tales of injustice. "Traditional tales keep the flames of such possibility alive." Invite students to read some of Rafe's retellings of old tales, finding examples of justice to share with the class.

▶ **READING REFLECTION** Invite students to give examples of "justice achieved" in fairy tales they know.

I've been told that when the twelve storks brought baby Paul to his mother in Kennebunkport, Maine, he didn't weigh more than 104 or 105 pounds—and 46 pounds of that was his black, curly beard.

Barbara Emberley,
Paul Bunyan

BIRTHDAYS

1821 Gustave Flaubert is born, in Rouen, France. He is the son and brother of doctors. Considered the family dunce, Gustave fails his law exams and decides to devote his time to writing. He writes very slowly, reading each sentence out loud so he can get the cadence right. He writes and rewrites *Madame Bovary* for six years before he feels it's right.

1932 Barbara Emberley is born, in Chicago, Illinois. Barbara meets her husband, Ed, while attending the Massachusetts College of Art, where she is studying fashion design and illustrating. While in college neither has any interest in creating children's books. But before long they are working together on books.

▶ **READING/WRITING CONNECTION** Barbara's *The Story of Paul Bunyan*, illustrated by Ed Emberley, discusses Paul's size with classic understatement—and interjects a surprise detail at the end (see quote above). Invite students to write their own *I've been told . . .* sentences using this structure. The content can be totally different, but tell them to watch—and follow—the language pattern.

EVENTS

1851 Joel Roberts Poinsett dies. The American diplomat introduced the popular Central American plant that bears his name into the United States. It becomes associated with Christmas.

▶ **ALL ABOUT NAMES** Challenge students to find other plants, flowers, or foods named for people. Invite them to invent a flower based on their own first or last name. Examining gardening books for flower names and characteristics will help get them started. They should give their invented plants botanical descriptions and provide information about planting season, needs, hardiness, and so on. They can also make careful botanical drawings.

1955 *Life* magazine comments on the heroine of the new book by the same name who is very popular across the nation. "Eloise is likely to be the most controversial literary heroine of the year. She charms and terrifies like a snake!"

▶ **READ MORE** Invite students to take a look at Kay Thompson's *Eloise* and see whether they can find what might terrify adults. Can students think of other books that might terrify adults?

DECEMBER

Ernest Henry
Shackleton knew all
about the weather in
the Antarctic.

Jennifer Armstrong,
*Shipwreck at the Bottom
of the World*

BIRTHDAY

1935 Judi Friedman is born, in Milwaukee. She is the author of *The ABC of a Summer Pond.*

▶ **WRITING TIP** The ABC format provides an excellent organizing device for students to present research findings.

EVENT

1902 Antarctic explorers Ernest Shackleton and Robert Scott try to take their minds off the cold and hunger by reading Darwin's *The Origin of Species* aloud to each other. In his journal Ernest briefly notes their chronic hunger: "Could do [with a] good feed. Anything would do."

▶ **READING TIP** Invite small student groups to choose a book or poem collection to read aloud to one another over the course of a week or two.

▶ **READ MORE** Shackleton goes back to Antarctica in 1914, and several riveting books chronicle this journey: *Shipwreck at the Bottom of the World: The Extraordinary True Story of Shackleton and the Endurance*, by Jennifer Armstrong (illustrated with more than forty photographs taken by a member of the expedition); *Spirit of Endurance: The True Story of the Shackleton Expedition to the Antarctic*, by Jennifer Armstrong, illustrated by William Maughan; and *Trial by Ice*, by K. M. Kostyal and Alexandra Shackleton.

DECEMBER

[Spending the] winter
among the Mandans
enabled Lewis and Clark
to watch many unique
ceremonies. Their
journals provided the
first written descriptions
of various Indian rites.

Rhoda Blumberg,
*The Incredible Journal of Lewis
and Clark*

BIRTHDAY

1917 Rhoda Blumberg is born, in New York City. She is a radio scriptwriter and journalist before becoming a children's writer. Rhoda says in working as a researcher for CBS radio she develops a passion for information. She discovers that nonfiction is "as gripping as fiction—a fantastic discovery." A nonfiction buff, Rhoda collects American history books.

EVENTS

1862 Louisa May Alcott reports to the Union Hotel Hospital in Washington, D.C., as a volunteer nurse in the Civil War. Later, when she publishes *Hospital Sketches*, based on a journal she has kept, each copy sells at fifty cents; Louisa May receives four cents, and ten cents goes to the support of orphans made fatherless or homeless by the war.

1965 Harper & Row editor Ursula Nordstrom launches a series of short notes to author Crosby Bonsall, who is late in delivering the manuscript. "Where is the book?"

DECEMBER

Breathe-in experience,
breathe-out poetry

Muriel Rukeyser,
"Poem Out of Childhood"

BIRTHDAYS

1859 Dr. L. L. Zamenhof is born, in Poland. He develops the international language Esperanto, which is named after his pseudonym, which means "one who hopes." The spelling of words in Esperanto is phonetic. The vocabulary is created from root words taken from Latin, the Romance languages, and German. The number of basic roots is reduced through extensive use of affixes. For example, *granda* means "great" and *mal* indicates "the opposite. So *malgranda* means "small."

▶ **WORD FUN** Invite students to choose ten English words that people use every day. Then they can take the words into the community and find translations in as many languages as possible. Once the class has assembled a list of the words in many languages, talk about the similarities and differences.

1913 Muriel Rukeyser is born, in New York City, in, she says, "the house where a famous gangster lived, beside Grant's Tomb. . . ." Muriel says sets of books were in her house, bought like pieces of furniture: Dickens, Dumas, Victor Hugo, *Britannica*, the *Book of Knowledge*, and so on. Muriel says that, for her as a child, these books have "nothing to do with the poetry of books." Poetry becomes important to Muriel, and it transforms her life. She says, "I thought that real men went to the office every day. The joy of learning that people wrote poems and that was what they could do with their lives was very great." By high school, Muriel is writing poetry seriously, and when she is twenty-one, her volume *Theory of Flight* receives the Yale Younger Poets Prize.

EVENT

1965 Harper & Row editor Ursula Nordstrom writes author note to Crosby Bonsall, asking, "Ou est le livre?"

DECEMBER

. . . I'd rather tell my story and leave the teaching to others. Let's just say they all paid a high price indeed for having their wishes come true.

Bill Brittain,
The Wish Giver

BIRTHDAYS

1917 Arthur C. Clarke is born, in Minehead, Somerset, England. Arthur's interest in science starts very early in life. As a child he draws maps of the moon using a homemade telescope. At nineteen, Arthur moves to London and joins the British Interplanetary Society. After serving as a radar instructor during World War II, Arthur studies physics and mathematics at King's College. He writes science-fiction short stories and novels. He is best known for the story on which the movie *2001* is based.

1930 William Brittain is born, in Rochester, New York. He grows up in Spencerport. He credits the librarian with introducing him to King Arthur and his knights, Tom and Huck, and "above all, Sherlock Holmes and Doctor Watson." William Brittain, a junior high teacher for more than twenty-nine years, becomes Bill Brittain in 1978, when *All the Money in the World* is published. The book is inspired by a real conversation Bill overhears between two students making incredible wishes. Each is trying to outdo the other, and finally one says, "I wish I had all the money in the world!" Bill says his hometown of Spencerport, a small town in upstate New York, is the village pictured in such novels as *Devil's Donkey* and *The Wish Giver*. Bill confesses that he is Tom in *Who Knew There'd Be Ghosts?*

▶ **OUT LOUD** Teachers and students agree that Bill's books are great read-alouds.

1932 Quentin Blake is born, in Britain. Quentin says Honore Daumier, the French illustrator, is one of his early heroes. As a teenager Quentin starts drawing for *British* magazine. A prolific illustrator of children's books, Quentin is widely recognized for his long-term collaboration with Roald Dahl. Quentin says children often ask him where he gets his ideas. He replies that the real answer is a mystery but the immediate answer is that ideas for art come from authors. Quentin enjoys working with other people's words and ideas as much as his own. "It's like being given a ticket to visit someone else's imagination, and you never quite know what you will find there."

▶ **WRITING/DRAWING CONNECTION** Invite students to pair up, one writing a personal narrative story and the other illustrating it. Once they've finished, they should talk about how the artist chose what to illustrate—and how the writer feels about the interpretation. Children are usually surprised to learn that most often publishers choose who will illustrate an author's manuscript and author and illustrator don't communicate about the work.

1965 Still trying to get Crosby Bonsall to send her the manuscript he has promised to deliver, Harper & Row Editor Ursula Nordstrom writes, "Donde esta el libro?"

▶ **THINK ABOUT IT** Invite students to make lists of reasons they don't do homework. Maybe they can team up to create a book of good excuses.

DECEMBER

She leaned far out on the window-sill,

And shook it forth with a royal will.

"Shoot, if you must, this old gray head,

But spare your country's flag," she said.

John Greenleaf Whittier, *Barbara Frietchie*

BIRTHDAYS

1807 John Greenleaf Whittier is born, near Haverhill, Massachusetts. A Quaker, John devotes himself to the abolition of slavery. His popular poem "Barbara Frietchie" is based on the probably apocryphal but legendary American heroine who defied Confederate troops led by Stonewall Jackson as they advanced through Frederick, Maryland. According to legend, Barbara stood at the upper window of her home waving the Stars and Stripes.

1931 David Kherdian is born, in Racine, Wisconsin. He grows up in a close-knit Armenian community. A lackluster student, David drops out of high school. After obtaining a GED certificate, he later earns a degree in philosophy from the University of Wisconsin and begins a career as a poet. David marries children's book author and illustrator Nonny Hogrorian, and they collaborate on a number of children's books. David's award-winning *The Road from Home: The Story of an Armenian Girl*, is a fictionalized biography of his mother, written in the first person. The sequels *Finding Home* and *Root River Run* continue her story.

1952 Raúl Colón is born, in New York City. His family moves to Puerto Rico when he is ten. Raúl says he has wanted to draw for as long as he can remember. One of his first pictures is a huge trailer truck. He loves comic books and often draws from them. At age twelve, Raúl sends a letter to the Famous Artists' School that advertises in comic books. They send a local newspaper cartoonist to Raúl's house—to tell his parents he has talent. Raúl studies commercial art in high school—three or four hours a day—learning everything from photography to silkscreening to advertising. A children's book editor notices Raúl's work in the *New York Times* and asks him to try a picture book. The result is *Always My Dad*, by Sharon Dennis Wyeth.

▶ **DRAWING TIP** Raúl's father shows him a technique for drawing faces by making a grid on a photograph. Then Raúl copies the image onto grid paper, one square at a time.

EVENTS

1865 Charles Dickens' *A Christmas Carol* is published. In the Preface, Charles writes, "I have endeavoured in this Ghostly little book, to raise the Ghost of an Idea, which shall not put my readers out of humour with themselves, with each other, with the season, or with me. May it haunt their houses pleasantly. . . ." A perennial favorite, the book has been made into countless movies and television shows, including a version by the Muppets. The story has a dramatic opening: "Marley was dead to begin with. There is no doubt whatever about that."

▶ **WRITING TIP** Invite students to create their own "There is no doubt whatever about that" openers.

1965 Harper & Row editor Ursula Nordstrom doesn't give up. She writes author Crosby Bonsall, "Achtung! Wo ist der buch?"

18

Veronica exploded. "You're such a spineless little coward," she screamed at him. "That's why they're always hitting you, and pushing you, and biting you. You're the biggest kid in your class, and everybody picks on you, and you never lift a finger. Why didn't you hit him back?"

Marilyn Sachs,
Veronica Ganz

BIRTHDAYS

1916 Carla Greene is born, in Minneapolis, Minnesota. She writes simple books providing introductions to various occupations—with such titles as *Truck Drivers: What Do They Do?*

▶ **WRITE ABOUT IT** Ask students to interview a parent or other adult about what he or she does at work. Then they can write an informational text. An alternative is for the class to invite someone from the community who does an interesting job to visit; they can conduct a whole-class interview.

1927 Marilyn Sachs is born, in the Bronx, New York. Marilyn says she is born into a family of storytellers. Marilyn, who loves books, knows from an early age that she will become a writer. Marilyn's mother dies when she is twelve. After arguing with her father over her desire to go to college, Marilyn leaves home at seventeen. She becomes a librarian in Brooklyn and continues this work after moving to San Francisco. Marilyn says that Veronica of *Veronica Ganz* is a composite of all the bullies she suffered in school.

▶ **WRITE ABOUT IT** Invite students to write a letter of advice to a bully or to a person being bullied.

▶ **READ MORE** Ask students to compile a bibliography of books featuring bullies.

EVENT

1999 Here are the top books in the first annual Bookworm Awards, posted on *kidsreads.com*, the first book and author site created especially for kids 6–12:

Over the Moon, by Rachel Vail, illustrated by Scott Nash

This Land Is Your Land, by Woody Guthrie, illustrated by Kathy Jakobsen

To Everything There Is a Season, by Leo and Diane Dillon

Lottie's New Beach Towel, by Petra Mathers

Insectlopedia, by Douglas Florian

10 Minutes Till Bedtime, by Peggy Rathman

Squids Will Be Squids: Fresh Moral, Beastly Fables, by Jon Scieszka and Lane Smith

Beyond the Mango Tree, by Amy Bronwen Zemser

Badger's Bad Moon, by Hiawyn Oram, illustrated by Susan Varley

▶ **THINK ABOUT IT** Invite students to create their own book awards and send a list of the winning books to the local newspaper and TV station.

19

I read the story as I ate my chicken a la king. The king who would voluntarily eat this stuff should have his taste buds examined.

Eve Bunting,
Face at the Edge of the World

BIRTHDAY

1928 Eve Bunting is born, in Maghera, Northern Ireland, a small town with no library. Eve's parents surround her with books, and her father often reads aloud. Eve's favorite book growing up is *Anne of Green Gables*. When she attends boarding school, Eve loves writing, and she often does other kids' writing homework for them. Eve gives up the idea of becoming an English teacher when she fails an English class in college. Eve emigrates to the United States with her husband and children in 1958. When she notices a listing for a writing class at a community college, Eve remembers she once loved writing and decides to try it. Now Eve is an acclaimed and prolific author and the new library in Maghera has an Eve Bunting shelf, with a banner above reading LOCAL AUTHOR.

▶ **WRITING TIP 1** Eve says ninety percent of the ideas for stories come from what she reads in the newspaper and weekly periodicals. The other ten percent come from what she sees happening around her.

▶ **WRITING TIP 2** Eve writes with pencil and paper so that she can write wherever she is, on whatever is available, including airline barf bags.

EVENTS

1732 *Poor Richard's Almanac* is published, written by twenty-six-year-old Benjamin Franklin, who assumes a pen name: Richard Saunders, Philomath. Almanacs are very popular at that time, and they are all written by *philomaths*—lovers of learning. Benjamin writes this almanac for twenty-five years. Some of his famous aphorisms include:

Early to bed and early to rise/Makes a man healthy, wealthy and wise.

When you are good to others, you are best to yourself.

A mob's a monster; heads enough, but no brains.

Haste makes waste.

Do not do that which you would not have known.

Don't throw stones at your neighbors if your own windows are glass.

▶ **READING/WRITING TIP** Present the first half of some aphorisms to students, inviting them to invent the second half of this cause-effect structure. A word magnet game called A Rolling Stone Killed the Cat provides seventy-five proverbs cut in half—for people to rearrange. So all kinds of things are possible:

Laughter . . . killed the cat.

Curiosity . . . is a man's best friend.

A friend in need . . . should not throw stones.

▶ **READ MORE** *The Amazing Life of Benjamin Franklin,* by James Cross Giblin, is a riveting and sophisticated picture-book biography.

1854 Louisa May Alcott gives her mother a copy of her first published book, a collection of fables, along with this note: "Dear Mother, Into your Christmas stocking I have put my 'first-born,' knowing that you will accept it with all its faults. . . . Whatever beauty or poetry is to be found in my little book is owing to your interest in and encouragement of all my efforts from the first to the last. . . ." Although the Alcott family is very poor, Louisa's mother manages to find enough money to buy Louisa a good desk because she believes a professional writer needs a good desk.

1895 Aspiring poet Robert Frost marries Elinor White, a student at St. Lawrence University. They marry in one of two schoolrooms Rob's mother rents for tutoring students. Since Elinor's father disapproves of this match, he won't give permission for her to get married at home. Rob helps his mother teach school while Elinor finishes college. Years later, Rob dedicates a book of poems to his mother: "To Belle Moodie Frost Who Knew As A Teacher That No Poetry Was Good For Children That Wasn't Equally Good For Their Elders."

▶ **READ MORE** Invite students to choose a poem—any poem—they believe would be very good for their parents—and then go home and read it to them!

20

I want to go to the School of Names. I would like to know everybody . . . on this globe.

M. B. Goffstein,
School of Names

BIRTHDAY

1940 M(arilyn) B(rooke) Goffstein is born, in St. Paul, Minnesota, the daughter of an electrical engineer. M. B. says that growing up she learns that "work was the only real dignity, the only real happiness, and that people were nothing if their lives were not dedicated." M. B. attends Bennington College, in Vermont, choosing art as her work. There, she develops skills in writing, art, and printmaking. M. B. says she creates in her head, making few, if any, sketches.

EVENTS

1492 Christopher Columbus, aboard his ship in the Caribbean, writes in his log: "Today at sunset I anchored at Cape Caribata [now known as Pointe Saint Honore]. This harbor is very beautiful. . . . Once in, there is no fear from any storm in the world."

▶ **READ MORE** Here are a few good books about Columbus: *The Log of Christopher Columbus' First Voyage to America in the Year 1492*, abridged, by John O'Hara Cosgrave II; *Pedro's Journal: A Voyage with Christopher Columbus*, by Pam Conrad; *Where Do You Think You're Going, Christopher Columbus?*, by Jean Fritz; *Encounter*, by Jane Yolen; and *Follow the Dream*, by Peter Sis.

1900 Arctic explorer Admiral Robert Peary settles into his winter Arctic quarters, prior to a spring attempt to reach the North Pole. He writes in his diary that he enjoys "this freedom from care or annoyance, this freedom to do as I please." Peary notes that he gets up around five-thirty and makes himself a quart of coffee, then writes and arranges equipment. After lunch, he gets in his "twenty-four hours' supply of wood, ice, biscuits, etc." Later, using his diary as a resource, he writes a book about his experiences, *The North Pole*.

▶ **WRITING TIP** Invite students to fill out a Daily Appointments or To Do form, showing what they will do for a day of "freedom to do as I please." They may want to create such an imaginary day for themselves or for a favorite literary character.

▶ **READ MORE** *Call Me Ahnighito*, by Pam Conrad, illustrated by Richard Egielski, is the fact-based story of the car-size meteorite the 1894 Peary expedition dug out of the ground and sent to the American Museum of Natural History in New York. Pam chooses the unusual device of making the meteorite the narrator of the tale. Richard's interpretations of the Arctic get high praise.

21

. . . a thoroughbred in spirit as well as in blood.

Albert Payson Terhune,
Lad: A Dog

BIRTHDAY

1872 Albert Payson Terhune is born, in Newark, New Jersey. A newspaper reporter and editor, he dislikes the work and hopes to have a literary career. After writing several novels, two plays, a travel volume, and a number of short stories, Albert's short story about his pet collies is published in *Redbook* magazine. The story is so popular that Albert decides to write more. *Lad*, one of the best-loved dog stories of all times, is a continuation of the short story about his own collie. Noted writer Tobias Wolff remembers how much he loved Albert's books as a boy. Jane Yolen is another Terhune fan.

▶ **READING TIP** Hold a dog story read-aloud festival. Student teams can choose stories to share with the class. In *Speak!*, edited by Michael J. Rosen, forty-three children's book illustrators—from Douglas Florian to William Joyce to Alice Provensen to Elizabeth Sayles to Lane Smith to Arthur Yorinks, and lots more—brag about their dogs.

▶ **WRITE ABOUT IT** Suggest to students the possibility of writing to a favorite author who writes about dogs.

EVENTS

1937 Walt Disney's *Snow White* premiers, in Los Angeles.

▶ **READ MORE** "Mirror, mirror on the wall,/Who is the fairest of us all?" There are many beautifully illustrated traditional versions of Grimm's *Snow White and the Seven Dwarfs*, ranging from Wanda Gag's to Charles Santore's. Angela Barrett offers a sophisticated, mysterious rendition, depicting the seven dwarfs as small, kind men rather than the freakish figures of Disney. Fiona French provides an interesting update in *Snow White in New York*, a story set in the jazz age of the 1920s. *Stockings of Buttermilk*, edited Neil Philip, brings us a Kentucky Snow White tale, "A Stepchild That Was Treated Mighty Bad": "When Snow White got to be of an age to be noticed for being pretty in a way to make womenfolks jealous of her, her stepmother turned poison mean."

1965 Indefatigable, and ever-inventive, Harper & Row editor Ursula Nordstrom writes author Crosby Bonsall, "Hereway isay hetay ookbay? Ovelay."

▶ **WORD FUN** Here's the chance to encourage students to try out Pig Latin!

DECEMBER

22

. . . the sound
Of a diving frog

Bashō,
One Hundred Frogs, translated
by Kenneth Rexroth and edited
by Hiroaki Sato

BIRTHDAYS

1905 Kenneth Rexroth is born, in South Bend, Indiana. When he is ten, his mother is diagnosed with tuberculosis; with just two months left to live, she takes Kenneth with her to buy a coffin. Three years later, his father dies. In his late teens, Kenneth teaches himself Greek and, with a Japanese primer, begins to translate Oriental poetry, an endeavor that becomes his life's work.

▶ **READ MORE** Dawnine Spival's *Grass Sandals: The Travels of Bashō* draws on Bashō's journal and poetry about a journey across Japan. Illustrated by Demi, the artwork is exquisite, with each double-page spread including a segment of the story, a painting of Bashō on his journey, a haiku, and a word that appears in three forms: a painted Japanese character, its transliteration, and its translation into English. *Cool Melons—Turn to Frogs!,* by Matthew Gollub, with illustrations by Kazuko Stone, offers the life and poems of Issa, rendering the poems in Japanese in the outer page margins and the English translations as part of the story.

1935 James Newton is born, in Yakima, Washington. He writes *Forest Log,* a narrative explaining how a dead tree continues to support life.

▶ **WRITING TIP** The structural device of presenting nonfiction material in the form of a diary or log permits young writers at all levels to participate.

▶ **READ MORE** *The Tree,* by Judy Hindley, presents twelve different types of trees: their lore, their places in history, their uses.

1939 Jerry Pinkney is born, in Philadelphia, Pennsylvania. Encouraged by his parents, Jerry draws constantly as a child and his talent is recognized. He wins a scholarship to the Philadelphia Museum College of Art. Influenced by the art of Thomas Eakins, Charles White, Arthur Rackham, and Alan E. Cober, Jerry feels at odds with the abstract expressionism his teachers admire. Among Jerry's various projects, he designs twelve postage stamps for the U. S. Postal Service Black Heritage series. Jerry says his favorite illustration from *Turtle in July* is that of the Canadian goose. Jerry points out that Brer Rabbit, in the Uncle Remus tales, is the first African American folk hero, the cunning trickster who uses his wits.

1946 Trudy Krisher is born, in Macon, Georgia. She grows up in South Florida. She remembers her mother steering her away from a drinking fountain in a store without explaining why, merely pointing out that it was not the right one for her to drink from. *Spite Fences*, in which Maggie Pugh learns the importance of speaking truth out loud, tackles the issue of discrimination in a society that espouses equality. Trudy's favorite books by other authors are *Sylvester and the Magic Pebble*, by William Steig, *Tuck Everlasting*, by Natalie Babbitt, and *To Kill a Mockingbird*, by Harper Lee.

▶ **WRITING TIP** Trudy says, "An author gets her education everywhere—reading, traveling, talking to people, reading cereal box labels, listening to the news, paying attention to the way people talk, keeping her eyes open in the grocery store, at the bus stop, on a walk with the dog."

DECEMBER

23

Ma, a mouse has to do what a mouse has to do.

Avi,
Ragweed

BIRTHDAY

1937 Avi is born, in New York City. His twin sister gives him the name Avi when they are a year old, and he's used it ever since. Avi reads a lot; he also listens to the radio a lot. This prolific author and Newbery Award recipient is a poor writer in elementary school, and in high school he fails all his courses. As an adult he says, "No one book did it all," but he remembers *Pokey Little Puppy, Simpson and Samson*, the tales of Thornton W. Burgess, and the Freddy the Pig series with particular fondness. A former librarian, Avi spends eight to ten hours a day on his writing—and he does most of his research in libraries. Avi does all his writing on computer, and he rewrites his books between forty and fifty times before he's satisfied that they are finished. Avi says if he could meet an author from another era, he'd choose Robert Louis Stevenson, though he admires Dickens, Kipling, Hemingway, Shakespeare—and a host of others—too.

▶ **WRITING TIP 1** Avi says, "I think you become a writer when you stop writing for yourself or your teachers and start thinking about readers."

▶ **WRITING TIP 2** "Reading is the key to writing. The more you read, the better your writing can be."

EVENTS

1823 A stolen copy of Clement Moore's "An Account of a Visit from St. Nicholas," written as a Christmas present for his three daughters, is printed in the Troy, New York, *Sentinel*. Clement, a professor of Oriental and Greek literature at the General Theological Seminary of New York City, does not acknowledge that he is the author of popular verse we know as "'Twas the Night Before Christmas" until 1844. In 1999, the great-great-great-great-great granddaughter of Major Henry Livingston Jr. alerts Vassar College English professor and literary sleuth Don Foster that her ancestor is probably the author, not Moore. In *Author Unknown: On the Trail of Anonymous*, Don provides the careful textual analysis of this and other manuscripts he has investigated.

▶ **WORD FUN** This poem has inspired many parodies. In *'Twas the Night B'fore Christmas*, Melodye Rosales offers an African American version. Children are snug in their bed, "Dreamin' of candy an' sweet short'nin' bread."

1847 In a letter to her stepmother, Elizabeth Shaw Melville writes of her son Herman, "We breakfast at 8 o'clock, then Herman goes to walk and I fly up to put his room to rights, so that he can sit down to his desk immediately upon his return. Then I bid him good-bye, with many charges to be an industrious boy and not upset the inkstand. . . . At four we dine, and after dinner is over, Herman and I come up to our room and enjoy a cosy chat for an hour or so—and he reads me some of the chapters he has been writing in the day."

1867 Tickets for a lecture by Charles Dickens go on sale at 9 A.M. at the Tickner and Fields Old Corner Bookstore, in Boston. Crowds have been lining up since 10 o'clock the night before. In eleven hours, $14,000 worth of two-dollar tickets are sold.

DECEMBER 24

What adventures you must have had, Raggedy!

What joy and happiness you have brought into this world!

Johnny Gruelle,
Raggedy Ann Stories

BIRTHDAYS

1880 Johnny Gruelle is born, in Arcola, Illinois, son of a landscape painter. Johnny gets a job as a cartoonist for the *Indianapolis Star* when he is still a teenager. He works for various newspapers as cartoonist as well as essayist and columnist. Johnny paints a face on an old faceless rag doll his daughter Marcella finds, and Raggedy Ann is born. Then, at age fourteen, Marcella dies. In her memory, Johnny creates a series of Raggedy Ann adventures set in her nursery.

1951 Lynn Munsinger is born, in Greenfield, Massachusetts. While studying at the Rhode Island School of Design, Lynn knows she wants to do something with art, but she doesn't know what. Then, she loves a seminar on children's books so much she switches into the illustration department and focuses on children's books. Her favorite illustrators are Maurice Sendak and David McPhail. She also admires Wallace Tripp, Jim Marshall, Garth Williams, Tasha Tudor, and Rosemary Wells—in her words, "Anybody who creates good characters." Lynn loves *Martha Speaks,* by Susan Meddaugh, saying, "It's one of those books where you read it and slap yourself, and say, 'Why didn't I think of that?'" Lynn illustrates three books a year, saying it's not a good idea to try to do more.

EVENTS

1804 William Clark, on the trail in the Lewis and Clark Expedition, notes in his journal that the day is "Showery wet and disagreeable." Their dinner is spoiled elk and spoiled fish and a few roots. Clark also notes his Christmas gifts in his journal: two dozen white weasel tails from Sacajawea, the fifteen-year-old wife of the trader Toussaint Charbonneau and the expedition's interpreter. Her name is spelled several ways. When spelled with a *g* or *k* and accented on the second syllable, it is a Hidatsa term meaning "Bird Woman." A soft *j* makes it Shoshoni for "Boat Launcher."

▶ **READ MORE** Sacajawea usually plays a small role in accounts of the expedition. Students can learn more in *Sacajawea: The Story of Bird Woman and the Lewis and Clark Expedition,* by Joseph Bruchac.

1925 The headline in the *Evening News* stretches across the entire front page: "A CHILDREN'S STORY BY A. A. MILNE, on p. 7." On page 7 there's an excerpt from *Winnie-the-Pooh.* The book containing this story was published October 14, 1926, in London, October 21 in New York. Here's some advice from Pooh on what it takes to make him happy:

> "Well," said Pooh, "what I like best—" and then he had to stop and think. . . . "What I like best in the whole world is Me and Piglet going to see You, and You saying 'What about a little something?' and Me saying, 'Well, I shouldn't mind a little something, should you, Piglet?' and it being a hummy sort of day outside, and birds singing."

▶ **WRITING TIP** Asking students to make a list of what makes them happy provokes quite wonderful results. They may choose to write more about some items on their lists, but the lists themselves make a provocative exploration, one that might well become a delightful poster. Students may try their hands and hearts at coming up with a new word and list of attributes to describe what Pooh calls "a hummy sort of day."

1956 Michael Bond, a television cameraman, misses his bus and, because it is raining, wanders into the toy department of a large store in London. He notices a small bear on the shelf—the last one left. Michael leaves the store. He doesn't need any more Christmas presents and doesn't have much money with him, anyway. But he gets to thinking about that bear sitting there all by itself and goes back. He discovers he has just enough money to buy the bear for his wife. Five months later, Michael writes an editor, "I have just completed the rough draft of a book-length children's story. It is about the adventures of a bear called Paddington and I think it has possibilities."

DECEMBER

25

. . . shirtless and barefoot . . .

Private James Martin, diary entry

BIRTHDAYS

1920 Noël Streatfield is born, in England. Using her own experiences as the daughter of a country vicar and a professional actress, Noël creates a new genre, the "career novel." In the first book in her "shoes" series, Noël writes about the rigorous training of professional ballet performers. *Ballet Shoes* is so popular that it is followed by *Circus Shoes, Tennis Shoes, Skating Shoes,* and *Theater Shoes.* The books continue to be popular.

▶ **THINK ABOUT IT** Ask students whose professional shoes they'd like to know about. Once they decide, they can check the library and *Books in Print* to see if a book on that topic exists. Speaking of shoes, the Nashville-based shoemaker Johnston and Murphy has provided a pair of complimentary, custom-made shoes to every president since Millard Fillmore in 1850. President Clinton received two pairs of shoes. In addition to the Ambassador-style shoe he selected, the company also presented him with a pair of blue suede penny loafers because of his fondness for Elvis Presley.

1937 Mary Eleanor Jessie Shepard is born, the daughter of famed illustrator E. H. Shepard. When her father is unavailable to illustrate the *Mary Poppins* series, P. L. Travers decides she wants his twenty-three-year-old daughter to do it. Mary uses a wooden peg Dutch doll as a model for the British nanny.

EVENTS

(Christmas is a time of joy for many students. The following journal entries remind us all of some harsh realities people have faced on this day in U. S. history.)

1776 Col. John Fitzgerald, one of General Washington's aides, writes just before the Battle of Trenton: "It is fearfully cold and raw, and a snowstorm setting in. The wind is northeast and beats in the face of the men. It will be a terrible night for the soldiers who have no shoes. Some of them have tied old rags around their feet; others are barefoot, but I have not heard a man complain. They are ready to suffer any hardship and die rather than give up this liberty. I have just copied the order for marching."

1777 In Valley Forge, Pennsylvania, Private James Martin writes in his diary that the soldiers are "shirtless and barefoot" and without blankets. Surgeon Albigence Waldo notes in his diary that all they have for breakfast is "fire cake and water"; all they have for dinner is "fire cake and water." Fire cake is bread toasted over an open fire; the water comes from breaking through the ice in the creek.

▶ **READ MORE** The Scholastic Dear America diary series includes *The Winter of Red Snow: The Revolutionary War Diary of Abigail Jane Stewart,* by Kristiana Gregory.

1846 Mrs. Reed, a member of the Donner Party, which is prevented by waist-high snow from continuing their journey across the Sierra Nevada mountains, cooks a special Christmas treat for her children, who range in age from three to twelve: dried apples, beans, tripe, and a small piece of bacon. After this feast, there is no food left. Reed traps mice. They eat boiled hides. By the time the rescue party arrives seven weeks later, on February 19, from Sutter's Fort in Sacramento, forty members of the eighty-seven-member Donner Party have died.

▶ **READ MORE** Riveting accounts of the Donner tragedy include *Snowbound: The Tragic Story of the Donner Party*, by David Lavender, and *The Perilous Journey of the Donner Party*, by Marian Calabro.

DECEMBER 26

I have been waiting my whole life to go to school.

Jean Van Leeuwen,
Amanda Pig, Schoolgirl

BIRTHDAYS

1890 LeRoy Ripley is born. He claims he was born on Christmas day. He also says his name is Robert. Working as a sports writer in 1918, he compiles a book of sketches of people accomplishing odd sports feats. Later, he creates a cartoon, includes non-sports topics, and names the cartoon *Believe It or Not*. The cartoon develops a newspaper readership of eighty million.

▶ **READING TIP** Invite students to create a bulletin board of the most amazing facts they discover in their nonfiction reading.

1937 Jean Van Leeuwen is born, in Glen Ridge, New Jersey. Jean says she has always liked learning how people lived a long time ago. Jean says one reason she sets her historical Hanna trilogy in Fairfield, Connecticut, is because she thinks it will be helpful to choose a town that's near where she lives, making it easier to do research. She also wants a town where something dramatic happened during the American Revolution. Jean says, "As soon as I read that Fairfield had been burned in 1779, I knew this was the perfect setting." Jean is also the author of the celebrated Amanda and Oliver Pig series.

▶ **WRITE ABOUT IT** Ask students to think back to their first day of school and to describe a part of that day.

DECEMBER 27

"Well, sweet child," I says to her, "I knows I's a rough character, but if you was to agree to it, I could adopt you." "Pa!" says she, and she fell on me like Grandma on a chicken snake.

Diane Stanley,
Saving Sweetness

BIRTHDAYS

1904 Ingri Parin D'Aulaire is born, in Konigsberg, Norway. At age fifteen Ingri begins to study art seriously, in Oslo, Munich, and Paris, where she meets Edgar. After they move to the United States, Ingri refers to their partnership as Edgar and Ingri Incorporated! Their first book, *The Magic Ray*, grows out of an illustrated letter to their niece. In creating *Abraham Lincoln*, the D'Aulaires follow Lincoln's trail, pitching a tent wherever he once stayed. As Ingri says, we wanted to "smell the same flowers, be bitten by the same bugs, and have the same thunderstorms burst over our heads."

1915 Ted Rand is born, in Mercer Island, Washington. A noted illustrator of more than fifty books, Ted and his wife Gloria often collaborate; their work includes the Salty Dog series. In *Baby in a Basket* they tell the true story of what happens when, in 1917, Marie Boyer, Fairbanks's first kindergarten teacher, takes her three-year-old and four-month-old daughters 385 miles across the frozen wilds of Alaska in an open sleigh. A horse spooks and plunges off a ridge, throwing the children into the icy river. Ted says when he heard the story, he knew instantly how he would illustrate the Alaska setting and the storm—"every element in it made wonderful pictures in my head before I ever got it on paper. It's such an extraordinary story." In planning the illustrations, Ted researches old photos in Seattle and Juneau, looking for visual details of the early roadhouses and the frozen landscape. The sisters, who are still alive, are able to supply an early portrait of their mother and a picture of the type of sleigh they traveled in.

1943 Diane Stanley is born, in Abilene, Texas. She grows up in Texas, New York, and California. Diane studies to be a medical illustrator, taking two years of postgraduate art and premedical courses and spending another year studying art at the College of Art in Edinburgh, Scotland. She graduates from the Johns Hopkins University School of Medicine with an M.A. in medical and biological illustration. Once Diane starts reading to her own children she decides to change her career path and illustrate children's books. When preparing one of her highly acclaimed biographies, Diane has to do much more than find out about the person's life. She has to know about the clothes they wore, the food they ate, the landscape in which they lived, and so on.

EVENT

1904 James M. Barrie's play *Peter Pan* receives a rousing reception at its first performance, in London. Adults and children alike are enthusiastic, and the annual performance of the play at Christmas becomes an established custom. Peter says, "I don't want to go to school and learn solemn things. No one is going to catch me, lady, and make me a man. I want always to be a little boy and to have fun."

DECEMBER

28

You talk like your dad is a real pain, and that's the way I always felt about mine. But your dad looks like a great guy to me, so—well, maybe mine could be too, if I gave him a chance.

Emily Cheney Neville,
It's Like This, Cat

BIRTHDAYS

1895 Carol Ryrie Brink is born, in Moscow, Idaho. When Carol is orphaned at the age of eight, Carol's aunt and grandmother, both excellent storytellers, foster her interest in stories. Her Newbery Medal–winning *Caddie Woodlawn* is based on a story she hears often as she is growing up. It is the story of the Wisconsin childhood of her own grandmother, Caddie Woodhouse.

1919 Emily Cheney Neville is born, in South Manchester, Connecticut, the daughter of an economist. She is the youngest of seven children. Her mother dies when she is twelve. The "Cheney place" has a dozen or more houses inhabited by Cheneys, including those of her father's seven brothers, four sisters, and eleven first cousins. In high school Emily publishes two stories in the school magazine, one a fable about a camel and the other about a girl who visits her strange old uncle. At sixteen, Emily enters Bryn Mawr College, where she majors in economics and history. After college, she gets a job as a newspaper copy girl and later writes a daily column. When the youngest of her five children starts school, Emily starts writing again. She's never written in the first person before but finds writing in the voice of a fourteen-year-old boy arguing with his father to be fun. Emily says the Newbery Medal–winning *It's Like This, Cat* describes a childhood different from hers. Then Emily earns her law degree, becomes a lawyer, and stops writing.

1951 Cynthia DeFelice is born, in Philadelphia, Pennsylvania. She is one of four children. As a child Cynthia reads a lot but she doesn't write much and certainly never dreams of becoming a writer. Summer vacations begin with Cynthia, her sister, and her brothers being taken to a bookstore to pick out books for their summer reading. Cynthia reads classics as well as comic books; *Mad* magazine is her favorite thing to read. Cynthia's work as a librarian leads her to the oral tradition of storytelling. Then she realizes she wants to write stories as well as tell them.

▶ **WRITING TIP** When Cynthia writes *Weasel* she begins with the idea of two kids alone in a cabin. The story begins to emerge as she starts asking questions about these kids: Where are their parents? Who is the guy at the door? Give students a situation, asking them to ask questions about it. They can first try role-playing and then actually writing a scene about what happens. Here are a couple of possible opening scenes:

Two kids alone in the mall at midnight.

A classroom where the teacher doesn't show up—and the students don't tell anyone.

Two kids whose parents drive off from a gas station, not realizing the kids aren't in the car.

1954 Nancy Luenn is born, in Pasadena, California. She is inspired to start writing books one summer while working for the U. S. Forest Service. Going to the library, she discovers she's already read all the fantasy novels in the collection. She thinks, "Somebody should write some more." And she decides that she'll do it. At that time Nancy doesn't realize that after writing five or seven or nine drafts of a novel she won't want to read it. Nancy says she starts with picture books because she makes a common mistake of thinking that a shorter book will be easier to write. While working on *Nessa's Fish*, Nancy learns that writing a picture book is like writing a poem. The placement of every word is crucial.

DECEMBER

The penguins were now so well trained that Mr. Popper decided that it was not necessary to keep them on leashes. Indeed, they walked to the bus very nicely in the following line of march: Mr. Popper, Greta, Captain Cook, Columbus, Victoria, Mrs. Popper, Nelson, Jenny, Magellan, Adelina, Bill Popper, Janie Popper, Scott, Isabella, Ferdinand, Louisa.

Richard and Florence Atwater,
Mr. Popper's Penguins

BIRTHDAYS

1892 Richard Atwater is born Frederick Mund Atwater, in Chicago. He changes his name legally. After he, his wife, and two daughters see a film about the first Byrd Antarctic expedition, Richard gets the idea for *Mr. Popper's Penguins*, the story of a house painter who receives penguins as a gift and keeps them in the family refrigerator. Richard is working on the manuscript when he suffers a debilitating stroke. His wife revises the first and last chapters, leaving the middle as is. The book is a Newbery Honor title.

1943 Molly Bang is born, in Princeton, New Jersey. Molly says her parents give each other books illustrated by Arthur Rackham for birthdays and wedding anniversaries. Molly likes looking at the illustrations but decides she will become a doctor. But the only science course she passes in college is biology—and that's because her professor accepts a set of illustrations of starfish as a term paper. Molly switches her major to French, and after college goes to Japan, where she learns Japanese, calligraphy, and judo. After a brief stint at the *Baltimore Sun*, Molly works at illustrating folktales. This versatile artist is quick to acknowledge the help her editors give her. She recalls that the editors were not enthusiastic about her first three attempts to illustrate *The Paper Crane*. Each version she shows them is an entirely different style. Molly's attitude is, "Oh well, try again." Her fourth version, produced through a technique using cut paper dipped in glue, is greeted with enthusiasm and takes her a year to complete.

DECEMBER

30

The camel's hump is an ugly lump

Which well you may see at the zoo;

But uglier yet is the hump we get

From having too little to do.

Rudyard Kipling,
Just So Stories

BIRTHDAYS

1865 Rudyard Kipling is born, in Bombay, India. Called Ruddy as a young child, he suffers terrible treatment and lonesomeness when his parents send him back to England to go to school. (Students will be relieved to know that his mother, hearing of his misery, comes back from India to take care of him.) But Rudyard brings humor to this school experience in *Stalky & Co.* Rudyard's famous *Just So Stories*, written while he is living in Vermont, begin as stories he tells to his children. He explains how the camel got its hump, the elephant its trunk, and more. Rudyard Kipling receives the Nobel Prize for literature in 1907. He also invents winter golf, painting his golf balls red so he can play in the snow.

▶ **READING/WRITING CONNECTION** *Pour quoi* stories are a great format to encourage divergent thinking. Invite students to read some *Just So Stories* and then invent a cause and effect of their own. They may, like Kipling, want to write about animals. They may choose some other topic. For example, some people write about why the moon has phases, why it snows, and so on.

▶ **READ MORE** Once, when Ruddy throws away a bad report card rather than bring it home, his guardian beats him and makes him walk to school wearing a sign that says *Liar* pinned on his back.

▶ **WRITE ABOUT IT** Invite students to write a letter of advice to young Rudyard or to his parents about his school misery.

1922 Jane Langton is born, in Boston, Massachusetts. As a young child, Jane loves to read. She adores books by Arthur Ransome. Now, when Jane's not reading, she's listening to books on tape—while she's gardening or cooking or taking a bath. Jane's own novels begin with a sense of place. When she is writing *The Fragile Flag*, the story of a girl who tries to walk from Boston to Washington, D.C., to attend an antinuclear rally, Jane and her son drive the route, along Route 1. As they drive, Jane writes down everything she sees along the way. Jane also walks along Route 128 outside Boston, a very busy road, to see what it feels like.

▶ **WRITING TIP** Invite students to take notes of everything they see on the route between home and school.

1942 Mercer Mayer is born, in Little Rock, Arkansas. Because his father is in the Navy, the family moves often. In 1956, they settle in Honolulu. After studying at the Honolulu Academy of Arts, Mercer moves to New York City and studies at the Art Students League. He works for an advertising agency as he tries to create a portfolio that will interest publishers. His first book is *A Boy, a Dog, and a Frog.* Mercer says, "Children's books are a good place to call home."

DECEMBER

31

Ideas rise with the morning but never die. . . . Only names, places, people change.

Frank Marshall Davis

BIRTHDAY

1905 Frank Marshall Davis is born, in Arkansas City, Kansas. Frank discovers books and reading at the local public library. He studies journalism at Kansas State University, publishing his first poems while still in school. Journalist, editor, and poet, Frank's collection of poems *I Am the American Negro* is inspired by jazz rhythms.

EVENTS

1793 Fourteen-year-old Peter Mark Roget, the boy who grows up to make his life's work the categorization of language (*The Thesaurus of English Words and Phrases* is an enormously popular book that has twenty-five editions in his lifetime), writes to his uncle, "I am learning to write shorthand, which I find very useful for taking notes." He complains about his homework on Greek verbs. "I find it very tedious, and it takes up so much of my time that I have hardly any holidays at all." He also comments on the offensive smell of anatomy class "when the dead body has been kept too long, as was the case yesterday."

1913 The first crossword puzzle appears, created by journalist Arthur Wynne, who works on entertainment features for the *New York World.* By 1924, crossword puzzle books hold the top four positions on the best-seller list, causing dictionary sales to increase. The crossword puzzle remains the most popular indoor game in the United States.

▶ **WORD FUN** Encourage students to play a word game.

1991 According to a survey announced on National Public Radio, the top five girls' names for 1991 are Emily, Courtney, Chelsea, Kimberly, and Renee. The top five boys' names are David, Michael, Christopher, Kevin, and Zachary.

▶ **WRITING/RESEARCH TIP** Invite students to conduct research to discover the popular names in your school.

ⓈUBJECT INDEX

Animals, 1, 2, 3, 4, 5, 6, 7, 8, 11, 12, 13, 15, 16, 17, 18, 19, 20, 23, 24, 25, 27, 28, 30, 31, 33, 34, 35, 36, 38, 39, 40, 41, 42, 43, 46, 47, 48, 49, 51, 54, 55, 56, 57, 58, 59, 60, 62, 63, 64, 65, 67, 71, 72, 73, 74, 76, 77, 78, 79, 80, 82, 85, 86, 87, 88, 91, 93, 94, 95, 97, 98, 99, 100, 102, 103, 104, 105, 106, 108, 109, 110, 111, 112, 113, 114, 115, 118, 119, 124, 125, 126, 127, 128, 129, 131, 132, 135, 136, 137, 138, 139, 142, 147, 149, 152, 153, 154, 155, 157, 158, 159, 160, 165, 166, 172, 173, 174, 175, 177, 179, 180, 181, 182, 183, 185, 186, 187, 189, 190, 191, 192, 193, 194, 195, 196, 197, 198, 199, 200, 201, 204, 205, 206, 207, 210, 212, 215, 218, 219, 220, 221, 222, 223, 224, 226, 227, 229, 230, 231, 233, 234, 235, 236, 237, 241, 242, 243, 244, 245, 249, 250, 251, 252, 254, 256, 257, 263, 264, 265, 266, 267, 268, 269, 270, 271

Art tips, 1, 2, 5, 6, 12, 13, 19, 21, 58, 65, 71, 72, 97, 99, 100, 101, 107, 109, 114, 119, 121, 124, 127, 129, 130, 131, 132, 135, 136, 137, 138, 139, 142, 143, 145, 148, 152, 153, 159, 176, 177, 179, 180, 181, 182, 184, 186, 190, 195, 199, 206, 210, 211, 212, 213, 216, 224, 230, 247, 241, 259, 260, 264, 270

Cinderella stories, 7, 15, 17, 33, 47, 69, 109, 138, 143, 146, 148, 185, 189, 192, 210, 236, 242

Codes, 1, 2, 19, 20, 38, 42, 43, 71, 86, 184, 185, 229, 239, 240, 254, 271

Comics and cartoons, 1, 2, 4, 7, 8, 9, 12, 13, 14, 17, 22, 23, 25, 27, 30, 34, 36, 38, 51, 57, 58, 61, 62, 71, 75, 80, 93, 96, 107, 109, 111, 116, 121, 122, 125, 126, 127, 128, 129, 145, 146, 160, 161, 164, 166, 173, 175, 176, 179, 181, 184, 194, 196, 198, 200, 204, 205, 208, 212, 215, 216, 225, 226, 233, 239, 242, 243, 244, 248, 253, 260, 266, 268, 269

Creative process, 1, 2, 5, 6, 7, 20, 22, 24, 25, 26, 28, 29, 30, 31, 33, 37, 39, 40, 41, 45, 46, 47, 48, 50, 51, 53, 54, 56, 57, 58, 62, 63, 65, 68, 69, 71, 72, 73, 75, 79, 80, 83, 87, 90, 92, 93, 94, 95, 96, 97, 98, 99, 101, 102, 103, 106, 107, 108, 110, 116, 119, 120, 121, 122, 123, 126, 127, 129, 130, 131, 132, 133, 134, 135, 136, 137, 139, 141, 142, 145, 148, 152, 153, 156, 158, 159, 161, 164, 165, 166, 169, 170, 171, 173, 174, 177, 178, 180, 184, 185, 186, 188, 189, 190, 191, 201, 205, 206, 209, 210, 211, 216, 218, 221, 230, 236, 247, 248, 253, 257, 259, 263, 264, 268, 270

Dictionaries and other reference books, 2, 6, 11, 14, 21, 26, 27, 35, 38, 41, 44, 49, 52, 57, 71, 74, 75, 77, 78, 84, 91, 107, 120, 123, 126, 130, 131, 159, 176, 186, 193, 194, 197, 205, 208, 211, 213, 220, 234, 235, 239, 242, 256, 259, 271

Fables, 15, 38, 39, 110, 128, 134, 139, 140, 144, 180, 262, 269

Fairy and folk tales, 1, 2, 3, 4, 6, 7, 14, 15, 17, 18, 20, 21, 28, 29, 32, 33, 37, 38, 43, 45, 46, 47, 48, 51, 55, 63, 65, 67, 68, 69, 77, 94, 97, 109, 114, 115, 118, 119, 121, 122, 128, 136, 138, 141, 143, 145, 146, 148, 149, 150, 152, 153, 156, 163, 173, 180, 184, 185, 189, 190, 192, 193, 194, 197, 199, 201, 203, 209, 210, 213, 219, 220, 222, 223, 226, 230, 231, 232, 235, 245, 246, 250, 252, 253, 255, 256, 264, 270

Food, 4, 5, 9, 11, 17, 18, 25, 28, 29, 30, 34, 48, 49, 50, 53, 58, 59, 61, 63, 65, 67, 74, 75, 77, 86, 87, 93, 94, 117, 123, 124, 128, 136, 137, 138, 145, 151, 155, 156, 159, 178, 179, 180, 187, 188, 192, 194, 197, 198, 200, 201, 206, 212, 215, 220, 221, 222, 229, 248, 253, 257, 261, 263, 267, 268

Handwriting, 15, 46, 162

Journal- and notebook-keeping, 1, 5, 12, 16, 24, 28, 29, 30, 35, 36, 38, 40, 44, 48, 53, 56, 57, 58, 63, 64, 65, 72, 74, 76, 77, 81, 86, 88, 89, 91, 92, 93, 96, 98, 101, 107, 112, 114, 120, 123, 127, 129, 131, 133, 135, 136, 137, 149, 153, 154, 158, 160, 162, 163, 165, 166, 172, 173, 176, 178, 179, 182, 188, 201, 203, 204, 215, 218, 219, 222, 223, 226, 227, 232, 234, 236, 239, 244, 246, 258, 263, 264, 266, 267

Letters and postal service, 2, 3, 4, 5, 6, 7, 8, 10, 11, 12, 14, 18, 20, 21, 22, 29, 30, 31, 32, 34, 40, 41, 46, 47, 48, 52, 54, 56, 58, 60, 61, 63, 70, 71, 75, 82, 83, 84, 88, 92, 93, 96, 102, 105, 108, 110, 112, 113, 116, 118, 120, 121, 123, 126, 127, 129, 149, 152, 153, 154, 156, 157, 158, 162, 168, 170, 174, 180, 187, 194, 196, 198, 199, 207, 208, 209, 213, 216, 220, 221, 222, 223, 225, 245, 246, 247, 252, 255, 258, 259, 260, 261, 264, 265, 271

Libraries and librarians, 7, 9, 12, 18, 20, 21, 23, 24, 32, 36, 35, 39, 40, 50, 52, 54, 58, 59, 60, 66, 67, 68, 69, 70, 73, 75, 78, 82, 83, 85, 87, 88, 93, 96, 97, 99, 101, 103, 106, 114, 115, 126, 129, 136, 137, 138, 143, 147, 152, 154, 156, 164, 166, 167, 176, 181, 183, 184, 194, 196, 200, 201, 207, 209, 218, 223, 225, 226, 229, 243, 249, 251, 253, 255, 261, 270, 271

Metaphor and simile, 3, 4, 5, 18, 22, 35, 36, 48, 54, 73, 77, 78, 82, 84, 92, 95, 107, 115, 117, 120, 128, 129, 140, 147, 151, 172, 194, 203, 219, 230, 232, 251

Names, 2, 4, 6, 7, 8, 9, 10, 13, 15, 20, 21, 23, 28, 30, 33, 35, 36, 37, 42, 43, 46, 47, 49, 50, 52, 53, 56, 61, 62, 63, 69, 71, 72, 73, 75, 77, 78, 79, 87, 88, 92, 94, 97, 99, 100, 102, 104, 107, 108, 109, 113, 116, 117, 118, 119, 121, 122, 125, 127, 126, 128, 129, 130, 131, 133, 134, 138, 139, 142, 150, 159, 161, 165, 166, 168, 169, 170, 173, 175, 180, 182, 183, 187, 188, 190, 191, 194, 195, 196, 199, 200, 205, 206, 209, 212, 214, 215, 217, 228, 232, 234, 237, 238, 239, 243, 244, 246, 247, 249, 252, 257, 262, 265, 270, 271, 272

Newspapers, 2, 6, 8, 9, 10, 12, 13, 14, 17, 23, 29, 37, 40, 49, 52, 53, 54, 55, 63, 68, 74, 75, 77, 78, 80, 83, 84, 85, 97, 100, 103, 104, 114, 115, 119, 127, 128, 129, 148, 162, 163, 166, 175, 182, 211, 214, 221, 226, 228, 231, 235, 236, 237, 238, 239, 248, 249, 255, 262, 263, 265, 269, 270

Nonfiction, 3, 4, 5, 6, 10, 12, 16, 18, 23, 24, 25, 27, 33, 35, 39, 43, 44, 49, 52, 55, 59, 60, 61, 65, 67, 70, 71, 76, 77, 78, 81, 84, 87, 89, 90, 91, 95, 96, 98, 99, 101, 104, 105, 106, 107, 109, 111, 112, 113, 115, 116, 117, 119, 122, 123, 124, 126, 127, 129, 130, 131, 132, 139, 140, 141, 143, 144, 146, 148, 150, 152, 153, 154, 156, 157, 161, 163, 164, 165, 166, 167, 169, 172, 173, 175, 177, 178, 179, 180, 181, 183, 184, 186, 189, 191, 192, 193, 194, 196, 198, 199, 201, 204, 211, 213, 215, 223, 225, 227, 228, 231, 233, 234, 237, 240, 244, 246, 247, 249, 251, 252, 256, 258, 260, 261, 262, 263, 264, 266, 268, 269

Out loud, 2, 9, 11, 15, 19, 27, 29, 30, 32, 33, 34, 36, 38, 39, 40, 43, 44, 47, 49, 50, 51, 52, 55, 56, 58, 62, 63, 64, 65, 68, 69, 77, 79, 82, 85, 86, 91, 92, 99, 100, 102, 104, 106, 109, 114, 115, 116, 117, 118, 119, 122, 127, 128, 130, 137, 140, 142, 145, 147, 153, 154, 155, 157, 159, 161, 164, 165, 168, 174, 179, 182, 188, 189, 190, 193, 194, 195, 196, 200, 202, 204, 207, 208, 210, 213, 215, 220, 222, 228, 230, 231, 232, 234, 236, 242, 243, 250, 252, 256, 257, 258, 259, 261, 262, 271

Poets and poetry, 3, 4, 5, 6, 9, 11, 13, 14, 15, 16, 17, 18, 19, 20, 22, 25, 30, 31, 33, 35, 36, 37, 39, 40, 42, 43, 44, 46, 47, 48, 49, 50, 53, 54, 56, 57, 59, 60, 61, 62, 67, 68, 72, 73, 74, 76, 77, 78, 79, 80, 81, 84, 85, 86, 87, 88, 91, 92, 93, 94, 95, 96, 99, 100, 103, 105, 107, 112, 113, 115, 116, 119, 120, 121, 122, 123, 125, 128, 130, 132, 133, 143, 145, 147, 148, 149, 150, 151, 152, 157, 158, 159, 160, 161, 163, 164, 165, 166, 167, 168, 169, 170, 171, 172, 173, 174, 175, 177, 179, 180, 182, 184, 185, 186, 189, 190, 192, 193, 194, 195, 198, 199, 203, 206, 208, 211, 212, 213, 215, 216, 217, 219, 222, 223, 225, 226, 228, 230, 232, 234, 237, 238, 239, 243, 247, 250, 251, 255, 258, 259, 260, 261, 262, 264, 265, 270, 271

Proverbs, 14, 15, 23, 79, 139, 262

Reading reflection, 2, 5, 7, 24, 25, 26, 27, 33, 50, 67, 74, 84, 85, 87, 92, 94, 97, 100, 110, 112, 130, 133, 148, 170, 176, 189, 197, 206, 207, 210, 217, 222, 223, 235, 238, 241, 248, 253, 257

Reading/writing connection, 1, 3, 4, 5, 6, 9, 10, 13, 14, 16, 17, 23, 24, 30, 32, 33, 38, 39, 40, 41, 42, 47, 48, 50, 51, 52, 59, 61, 67, 70, 72, 75, 82, 88, 89, 90, 93, 96, 104, 111, 112, 116, 122, 131, 139, 140, 142, 145, 149, 151, 153, 154, 161, 162, 163, 170, 172, 179, 194, 198, 204, 205, 206, 208, 209, 210, 220, 223, 224, 239, 242, 243, 248, 257, 262, 271

Research tips, 13, 14, 23, 28, 32, 35, 57, 65, 71, 75, 76, 78, 80, 87, 101, 109, 113, 115, 116, 122, 124, 126, 132, 136, 138, 142, 143, 161, 165, 167, 174, 188, 190, 198, 199, 206, 207, 211, 212, 215, 219, 226, 229, 231, 233, 234, 237, 239, 250, 252, 254, 258, 267, 268, 271, 272

Schools and teachers, 7, 9, 25, 30, 31, 32, 33, 34, 35, 36, 38, 39, 40, 41, 43, 44, 45, 46, 47, 48, 52, 53, 55, 56, 57, 58, 60, 61, 62, 63, 68, 69, 70, 71, 72, 73, 74, 76, 78, 79, 82, 83, 87, 89, 91, 93, 100, 102, 103, 105, 112, 114, 115, 117, 118, 121, 123, 124, 125, 127, 128, 129, 130, 131, 133, 135, 136, 138, 142, 143, 144, 145, 146, 147, 148, 149, 151, 153, 155, 156, 159, 160, 161, 162, 164, 167, 168, 169, 171, 174, 175, 176, 177, 179, 180, 183, 184, 186, 187, 188, 189, 191, 192, 194, 195, 196, 198, 201, 205, 206, 208, 211, 214, 218, 222, 223, 227, 228, 229, 230, 231, 232, 233, 235, 236, 237, 239, 241, 242, 243, 244, 245, 249, 252, 254, 257, 259, 260, 261, 262, 263, 265, 266, 268, 269, 270, 271, 271

Science fiction and fantasy, 1, 5, 7, 8, 9, 10, 13, 18, 20, 27, 31, 41, 43, 52, 57, 60, 71, 79, 89, 97, 101, 102, 103, 109, 111, 120, 124, 126, 135, 140, 153, 156, 164, 171, 185, 205, 208, 209, 213, 216, 218, 223, 232, 234, 246, 247, 255, 259, 269, 270

Series books, 5, 8, 10, 12, 13, 16, 18, 19, 21, 24, 28, 29, 33, 34, 36, 38, 39, 42, 52, 56, 59, 60, 66, 70, 74, 76, 77, 78, 80, 86, 89, 93, 95, 97, 98, 100, 101, 102, 104, 106, 108, 109, 110, 112, 114, 115, 118, 119, 124, 128, 129, 130, 132, 136, 137, 144, 145, 150, 151, 152, 154, 158, 164, 167, 174, 175, 177, 184, 201, 203, 204, 205, 206, 208, 210, 212, 214, 219, 221, 222, 231, 233, 238, 265, 266, 267, 268

Spelling, 2, 55, 71, 72, 73, 94, 107, 108, 121, 126, 134, 170, 175, 205, 206, 207, 213, 246, 250, 252

Sports, 5, 9, 16, 21, 23, 44, 49, 61, 62, 63, 73, 93, 94, 95, 107, 113, 126, 131, 139, 143, 155, 160, 161, 162, 165, 167, 186, 194, 195, 206, 226, 234, 247, 253

Word fun, 1, 2, 3, 6, 8, 9, 10, 15, 18, 19, 22, 28, 30, 32, 42, 43, 44, 45, 46, 47, 54, 56, 57, 59, 62, 64, 67, 69, 73, 74, 76, 77, 81, 82, 84, 85, 86, 87, 88, 90, 91, 93, 94, 95, 98, 104, 105, 106, 108, 111, 113, 115, 116, 117, 124, 126, 127, 132, 133, 134, 138, 141, 144, 149, 151, 152, 156, 157, 166, 168, 169, 172, 173, 174, 176, 178, 180, 183, 184, 185, 190, 193, 194, 199, 200, 203, 205, 207, 212, 213, 215, 219, 220, 222, 226, 228, 232, 235, 240, 249, 250, 251, 256, 258, 264, 265, 272

Writing tips, 1, 5, 6, 7, 9, 11, 12, 15, 16, 17, 18, 19, 20, 22, 25, 28, 30, 31, 32, 34, 37, 39, 42, 44, 48, 50, 53, 54, 59, 60, 62, 63, 68, 72, 73, 74, 79, 84, 86, 88, 89, 92, 94, 99, 100, 102, 103, 104, 110, 111, 112, 114, 115, 118, 120, 121, 122, 123, 124, 126, 127, 130, 134, 135, 137, 138, 140, 142, 145, 146, 147, 148, 150, 151, 152, 153, 154, 155, 157, 158, 159, 160, 161, 162, 163, 164, 165, 166, 167, 168, 169, 170, 171, 172, 173, 174, 175, 177, 178, 180, 182, 185, 187, 188, 190, 192, 193, 195, 196, 197, 200, 203, 204, 207, 209, 212, 213, 214, 215, 216, 217, 218, 219, 220, 221, 222, 223, 224, 227, 231, 234, 236, 237, 238, 239, 240, 241, 242, 243, 244, 245, 246, 247, 249, 253, 254, 257, 260, 261, 262, 264, 265, 266, 269, 271

ⒶUTHOR INDEX

Aardema, Verna 6/6
Acuff, Selma Boyd 4/10
Ada, Ama Flor 1/3
Adams, John, 85, 128, 196
Adams, Laurie 9/29
Adamson, Joy 1/20
Addams, Charles 1/7
Adler, C. S. 2/23
Adler, David 4/10; 5, 116
Adler, Irving 4/27
Adoff, Arnold 7/16; 107
Aesop, 38, 256
Agee, Jon, 15, 57, 183, 251
Aiken, Conrad 8/5; 181
Aiken, Joan 9/4; 158
Alarcón, Francisco 2/21
Albee, Edward, 16
Albert, Burton Jr. 9/25
Alcorn, Stephen, 181
Alcott, Louisa May 11/29; 3, 5, 29, 86,
    144, 145, 166, 246, 258, 262
Aleichem, Sholom 2/18; 102, 145
Alexander, Lloyd 1/30; 116
Aliki 9/3; 164, 199, 227
Allard, Harry 1/27; 32, 162, 180
Allen, Jonathan 2/17
Almond, David 5/15
Altman, Joyce, 201
Alvarez, Julia 3/27; 62
Ames, Lee 1/8
Andersen, Hans Christian 4/2; 29, 77,
    119, 150, 214, 220, 231
Anderson, Dave 5/6
Anderson, Mary 1/20
Andriola, Alfred 5/24
Anholt, Laurence, 36, 65, 91
Anno, Mitsumasa 3/20
Anton, Jim, 14
Ardizzone, Edward 10/16; 114
Armstrong, Jennifer 5/12; 258
Armstrong, Louis, 139
Armstrong, William H. 9/14
Arnold, Caroline 5/16; 65
Arnold, Ted, 76, 238
Arnosky, Jim 9/1; 52, 227
Asimov, Isaac 1/2; 26, 75
Atwater, Richard 12/29
Atwater-Rhodes, Amelia 4/16
Atwood, Margaret 11/18
Auden, W. H., 120
Audubon, John James, 196
Avi 12/23; 54
Aylesworth, Jim 2/21
Azarian, Mary 12/8; 5, 10, 23, 65, 170

Babbitt, Natalie 7/28; 29, 265
Bacon, Francis 1/22
Bagnold, Enid 10/27
Bailey, John, 161
Baldwin, James, 30, 78
Balgassi, Haemi, 64
Bang, Molly 12/29
Banks, Lynne Reid 7/31
Banyai, Istvan, 4
Barner, Bob 11/11
Barks, Carl 3/27
Barrett, Angela, 189, 264
Barrett, Ron and Judi 7/25
Barrie, Sir James M. 5/9; 99, 130, 269
Barry, Dave, 1
Barry, Scott 12/1
Barth, Edna, 244
Bartlett, John 6/13
Barton, Clara, 22, 109
Base, Graeme 4/6; 68
Bashō, 264
Baskin, Leonard 8/15
Bate, Lucy 3/19
Bates, Katherine Lee 8/12; 149
Baum, L. Frank 5/15; 28, 78, 103, 109,
    130, 156, 209, 235
Baylor, Byrd 3/28; 111

Bealer, Alex, 240
Bedard, Michael, 81, 255
Beeler, Selby, 55
Begay, Shonto 2/7
Bellairs, John 1/17
Belloc, Hilaire 7/27
Bemelmans, Ludwig 4/27; 16, 29, 182
Bender, Robert, 5
Bendick, Jeanne 2/25
Benet, Stephen Vincent, 199
Bentley, Wilson Alwyn, 10
Berger, Barbara Helen 3/1
Berger, Melvin 8/23
Berger, Terry 8/11
Berlitz, Charles, 240
Bernstein, Joanne 4/21; 232
Bernstein, Theodore 11/17
Bierhorst, John 9/2
Bing, Christopher, 165
Biriotti, Sophie, 170
Bishop, Ann 3/3
Bjork, Christine, 129
Blair, Walter 4/21
Blake, Quentin 12/16
Blake, Robert 5/10
Bloom, Lloyd 1/10
Blos, Joan 12/9
Blount, Mary Christian 2/20
Blumberg, Rhoda 12/14
Blume, Judy 2/12; 87, 187
Bober, Natalie, 124
Bolognese, Don, 224
Bond, Michael 1/13; 92, 212, 267
Bond, Nancy 1/8
Bonham, Frank 2/25
Bonsall, Crosby, 258, 259, 260, 264
Bontemps, Arna 10/13
Boone, Daniel, 120
Borglum, John Gutzon 3/25
Boswell, James, 105, 125
Bowditch, Nathaniel, 81
Boynton, Sandra 4/3; 218
Bradbury, Ray 8/22; 57, 101, 103, 124,
    214
Braille, Louis 1/4
Brandenberg, Aliki. See Aliki
Brandon, Barbara, 226
Breathed, Berkeley 6/21
Brenner, Barbara, 175
Brett, Jan 12/1
Bridges, Ruby, 59, 60, 178, 233, 237
Bridwell, Norman 2/15; 182
Briggs, Raymond 1/18
Brillat-Savarin, Anthelme 4/1
Brink, Carol Ryrie 12/28
Brittain, Bill 12/16
Brock, Cole 5/29
Brontë, Charlotte, 122, 154, 162, 172, 173
Brontë, Emily 7/30; 162
Brooks, Bruce 9/23
Brooks, Gwendolyn 6/7; 78, 91, 145
Brooks, Walter 1/9; 5, 221
Brown, Marc 11/25; 112, 243
Brown, Marcia 7/13; 17, 138, 143
Brown, Margaret Wise 5/23; 7, 233
Browne, Anthony 9/11; 256
Browning, Robert, 132
Bruchac, Joseph III 10/16; 67, 99
Brunhoff, Jean de 12/9
Brunhoff, Laurent de 8/30; 229
Bryan, Ashley 7/13; 59, 133, 215
Buehner, Caralyn and Mark 5/20; 148
Buhler, Cynthia von, 84
Bulfinch, Thomas 7/15
Bunting, Eve 12/19; 69
Burch, Robert 6/26
Burgess, Gelett 1/30
Burgess, Jonathan 2/17
Burgess, Thornton 1/14; 265
Burkhert, Nancy Ekholm, 80
Burnett, Frances Hodgson 11/24; 86,
    95, 99, 130, 169, 170, 223

Burns, Robert 1/25
Burroughs, Edgar Rice 9/1; 95, 118,
    124, 175, 242
Burton, Sir Richard 3/19
Burton, Virginia Lee 8/30
Bush, Barbara, 155
Butler, Samuel 12/4
Butterworth, Oliver 5/23; 110
Butts, Alfred 4/13
Byars, Betsy 8/7; 32, 179, 186, 241
Byron, George Gordon Noel, 3, 49

Calabro, Marian, 268
Caldecott. Randolph 3/22; 95
Caldone, Paul, 97
Calhoun, Mary 8/3
Calmenson, Stephanie 11/28; 68, 172,
    245
Cameron, Ann 10/21
Cameron, Eleanor 3/23
Cameron, Polly 10/14
Campbell, Joseph 5/26
Campbell, Simms 1/2
Cannon, Janell 11/3
Capp, Al 9/28
Carle, Eric 6/25; 61
Carlson, Nancy 10/10
Carlson, Natalie Savage 10/3
Carlstrom, Nancy White 8/4
Carnegie, Andrew, 50
Carrick, Carol 5/20; 72
Carrick, Donald 4/7; 108
Carroll, Lewis 1/27; 16, 37, 41, 42, 64,
    94, 104, 109, 121, 126, 148, 159,
    186, 208, 232
Carter, David 3/4
Carter, Howard, 227
Caseley, Judith, 77
Cassedy, Sylvia 1/29
Catalanotto, Peter 3/21
Catlin, George 7/26
Caxton, William 8/13
Cazet, Denys 3/22; 32
Chapman, John, 199
Chapman, Robert, 197
Charlip, Remy 1/10; 85
Chase, Richard, 192
Chast, Roz 11/26; 20
Chaucer, Geoffry, 118, 167
Cherry, Lynne 1/5
Chess, Victoria 11/16
Chew, Ruth 4/8
Chin-Lee, Cynthia, 199, 237
Christelow, Eileen 4/22; 58
Christian, Mary Blount 2/20
Christopher, Matt 8/16
Chute, Marchette 8/16
Chwast, Seymour 8/18
Ciardi, John 6/24; 37, 39
Clarke, Arthur C. 12/16; 103
Cleary, Beverly 4/12; 174, 212
Clemens, Samuel. See Mark Twain
Clements, Andrew, 91
Clifton. Lucille 6/27
Climo, Shirley 11/25; 192
Coatsworth, Elizabeth 5/31
Cobb, Vicki 8/19
Coerr, Eleanor 5/29
Coghill, Sheila, 255
Cohen, Barbara 3/15
Cohen, Miriam 10/14; 129
Cohen, Paul 11/13; 82
Cole, Babette, 192
Cole, Brock 5/29
Cole, Henry, 65, 91, 236
Cole, Joanna 8/11; 59, 250
Cole, William 11/20; 67, 86
Collier, Christopher 1/29
Collier, James, 190
Collodi, Carlo 11/24; 139, 233
Colón, Rául 12/17
Colum, Padraic, 125

Comenius, Johann Amos, 63
Confucius, 200
Conly, Jane Leslie, 7
Conly, Robert Leslie 1/11
Conover, Chris 2/12
Conrad, Pam 6/18; 263
Cooney, Barbara 8/6; 81, 89, 124, 255
Cooney, Caroline 5/10
Corbett, Scott 7/27
Cormier, Robert 1/17
Coville, Bruce 5/16; 32, 162
Cox, Clinton 6/10; 101
Crane, Stephen 11/1
Creech, Sharon 7/29; 26
Crews, Donald 8/30; 19, 219
Crilley, Mark 5/21
Crockett, Davy, 167
Cronin, Doreen 3/28; 4, 207, 245
Crutcher, Chris 7/17
Cullen, Countee 5/30
cummings, e. e. 10/14; 28, 145
Cummins, Julie, 60
Curley, Lynn, 61, 127, 163
Curtis, Jamie Lee, 240
Curtis, Paul Christopher 5/10
Cushman, Doug 5/4
Cushman, Karen 10/4; 140
Cytron, Barry, 251

D'Aulaire, Edgar and Ingri 9/30 and
    12/27; 164
Dahl, Roald 9/13; 109, 192, 259
Dakos, Kalli, 32
Dalgliesh, Alice 10/7; 208
Danziger, Paula 8/18; 59
Daugherty, James 6/1
Davis, Frank Marshall 12/31
Davis, Hubert 4/30
Davis, Jim, 127
Day, Alexandra, 4
DeAngeli, Marguerite 3/14
de Brunhoff, Jean 12/9
de Brunhoff, Laurent 8/30; 229
DeClements, Barthe 10/8
Deetz, James and Patricia, 227, 244
DeFelice, Cynthia 12/28
Defoe, Daniel, 22, 155, 233, 250
Degas, Edgar, 91, 142
Degen, Bruce 6/14; 158
Deimini, Lisa 3/21
DeJong, Meindert 3/4
De La Mare, Walter 4/25; 94, 182
Demarest, Chris 4/18
Demi 9/2; 264
de Paola, Tomie 9/15
de Regniers, Beatrice Schenk, 37, 65
Dewey, Jennifer Owings 10/2
Dewey, Melvil 12/10; 207
Diaz, David, 59, 131
Dickens, Charles 2/7; 2, 69, 73, 79, 83,
    95, 109, 116, 117, 197, 206, 260,
    265, 266
Dickinson, Emily 12/10; 46, 60, 81,
    105, 113
Dickson, Paul, 187, 197
Dillon, Diane and Leo 3/3 and 3/13;
    53, 149, 171, 237, 252, 261
Disney, Walt, 17, 19, 124, 194, 264
Doctorow, E. L., 56
Dodge, Mary Mapes 1/26
Dodgson, Charles. See Lewis Carroll
Doherty, Craig, 91
Donne, John, 29
Donnelly, Judy, 227
Dooling, Michael 7/13; 10
Dostoyevski, Fyodor, 56
Douglass, Frederick, 181
Doyle, Arthur Conan 5/22; 14, 16, 42,
    66, 124
Doyle, Marty, 147
Dragonwagon, Crescent 11/25; 59
DuBois, William Pene, 32

Duck, Donald, 27, 62, 121, 215
Duffey, Betsy, 186
Dunbar, Paul Laurence 6/27; 22, 161
Duncan, Lois 4/28
Dunn, Jerry, 197
Dunning, Arthur Stephen 10/31
Dunrea, Olivier 9/22
Durst, Seymour, 183
Duvoisin, Roger 8/28
Dygard, Thomas J. 8/10
Dyer, Jane 3/7

Eastman, P. D. 11/25
Eaton, Tom 3/2
Eckert, Allen 1/30
Edens, Cooper, 97
Edison, Thomas, 238
Edwards, Pamela Duncan, 91, 236
Egielski, Richard 7/16; 61, 171
Ehlert, Lois 11/9
Ehrlich, Amy 7/24
Eisenberg, Lisa 4/19; 10, 32, 89
Eliot, T. S. 9/26; 100, 121, 122, 199
Emberley, Barbara 12/12; 194, 216
Emberley, Ed 10/19; 5, 194, 224, 257
Emerson, Ralph Waldo, 96, 108, 115, 149, 150, 218
Ernst, Lisa Campbell 3/13
Esbensen, Barbara Juster 4/28; 199
Espy, Willard 12/11
Estes, Eleanor 5/9; 35

Farber, Norma 8/9
Farjeon, Eleanor 2/13
Farley, Walter 6/26; 59
Farmer, Fanny, 4
Farmer, Nancy 7/9
Farnsworth, Bill 10/11
Faulkner, William 9/25
Fearnley, Jan, 61
Feder, Paula 11/5
Feelings, Tom 5/19; 107
Feiffer, Jules 1/26
Fenner, Carol 9/30
Ferber, Edna, 72, 193, 231
Ferlinghetti, Lawrence, 76
Fields, W. C., 30
Fine, Anne 12/7
Fisher, Aileen 9/9
Fisher, Dorothy Canfield 2/17
Fisher, Leonard Everett 6/24; 89, 127
Fisher, M. F. K. 7/3
Fitch, Sheree 12/3
Fitzgerald, F. Scott, 103
Fitzgerald, Gerald, 165
Fitzhugh, Louise 10/5; 88, 206, 221
Flack, Marjorie 10/23
Flaubert, Gustave 12/12
Fleischman, Paul 9/5; 77, 112, 126, 134, 175
Fleischman, Sid 3/16; 182, 192
Fleming, Candace, 90
Fleming, Denise 1/31
Fleming, Ian 5/28
Fletcher, Ralph 3/17
Florian, Douglas 3/18; 43, 65, 261, 263
Foltz, Charlotte, 4
Fontaine, Jean de la 7/8
Fonteyn, Margot, 13
Ford, Harrison, 68
Foster, Don, 144, 173, 265
Foster, Stephen 7/4
Fox, Mem 3/5
Fox, Paula 4/22; 8
Frank, Anne 6/12; 158
Frank, John, 227
Franklin, Benjamin 1/17; 18, 65, 90, 108, 128, 139, 199, 229, 262
Fraser, Betty, 14
Fraser, Mary Ann, 98
Frasier, Deborah 4/3
Freedman, Russell 10/11; 95, 157, 256
Freeman, Don 8/11
French, Fiona, 264
Friedman, Judi 12/13
Friedman, Kinky, 56
Fritz, Jean 11/16; 81, 157, 165, 191, 231, 263
Frost, Robert 3/26; 17, 47, 107, 123, 124, 177, 194, 228, 262
Fulghum, Robert 6/4
Funk, Charles Earle, 131

Funk, Isaac Kaufman 9/10

Gackenbach, Dick 2/9
Gag, Wanda 3/11; 142, 196, 249, 264
Gallant, Frank, 169
Gallaudet, Thomas Hopkins 12/10
Gammell, Stephen 2/10
Gandhi, Mahatma, 150
Gannett, Ruth Chrisman, 164
Gannett, Ruth Stiles 8/12
Gantos, Jack 7/2; 89, 137
Gardella, Tricia, 59, 67, 138
Garden, Nancy 5/15
Gardiner, John Reynolds 12/6; 252
Gardner, Erle Stanley 7/17
Gardner, Martin, 190
Garfield, Leon 7/14
Garland, Judy, 169
Garland, Michael, 112
Garrett, Thomas, 60
Garrison, Webb, 131
Gates, Doris 11/26
Geisel, Theodor. See Dr. Seuss
Geisert, Arthur 9/20
George, Jean Craighead 7/2; 61, 249
George, Kristine O'Connell 5/6; 95
Geringer, Laura 2/23
Gerrard, Roy 1/25
Gerstein, Mordicai 11/25
Gibbons, Gail 8/1; 6, 65
Giblin, James-Cross 7/8; 10, 262
Gibson, Althea, 139
Giff, Patricia Reilly 4/26
Gilson, Jamie 7/4
Ginsberg, Allen, 76
Giovanni, Nikki 6/7; 228
Gipson, Fred 2/7; 200
Gist, George, 239
Glass, Andrew, 120, 199
Goble, Paul 9/27; 131
Goffstein, M. B. 12/20; 263
Golding, William, 195
Goldman, Emma, 214
Gollub, Matthew, 264
Goode, Diane 9/14
Gorey, Edward 2/22; 97, 158
Gorman, Carl, 19
Graham-Barber, Lynda, 32, 129
Grahame, Kenneth 3/8; 71, 124, 216, 223
Gramatky, Hardie 4/12
Graves, Donald, 161
Gray, Kes, 49
Greeley, Horace, 162
Greenberg, David, 14
Greene, Bette 6/28
Greene, Carla 12/18
Greene, Constance C. 10/27
Greenfield, Eloise 5/17; 141
Greenwald, Sheila 5/26
Gregory, Kristiana, 267
Grey, Zane 1/31
Grifalconi, Ann 9/22
Griffith, Helen V. 10/31
Grimes, Nikki 10/20
Grimm, Jacob and Wilhelm 1/4 and 2/24; 7, 38, 222, 264
Groening, Matt, 8
Gruelle, Johnny 12/24
Gutenberg, Johannes, 69
Guthrie, Woody 7/14; 261
Gutman, Dan 10/19
Gwynne, Fred 7/10; 180

Haddad, Robert, 250
Hafner, Marilyn, 28, 93
Hague, Michael 9/8; 4, 156
Hahn, Mary Downing 12/9
Hale, Lucretia Peabody 9/2
Hale, Sarah Josepha 10/24
Haley, Alex, 107
Haley, Gail 11/4
Hall, Donald 9/20; 42, 119
Hall, Fitzedward 3/21
Hall, Katy McMullen 1/16; 32, 81, 89
Hall, Lynn 11/9
Hamilton, Edith 8/12
Hamilton, Virginia 3/12; 51, 117, 219, 252
Hammon, Jupiter 10/17
Hancock, John 1/23
Hansberry, Lorraine 5/19; 78, 107
Harris, Joel Chandler, 235

Harris, Ted, 9
Haskins, Jim 9/19; 249
Hautzig, Deborah 10/1
Hautzig, Esther 10/18
Hawkes, Kevin 8/28
Hawthorne, Nathaniel, 24, 53, 141, 162
Hayes, Daniel 4/17
Hearn, Michael Patrick, 103
Hearne, Betsy 10/6; 148
Heide, Florence Parry, 37
Heinlein, Robert, 9, 57
Heller, Joseph 5/1
Heller, Nicholas, 117
Hemingway, Ernest 7/21; 118, 265
Henkes, Kevin 11/27; 4, 32, 131, 170, 191
Henry, Greg, 106
Henry, Marguerite 4/13; 164
Henson, Jim, 230
Hentoff, Nat, 54
Heo, Yumi, 199, 230, 237
Hepworth, Cathi, 200
Herman, Charlotte 6/10
Hersey, John, 176
Hershey, Milton 9/13
Hesse, Karen 8/29; 134
Hest, Amy 4/28
Hindley, Judy, 264
Hinton, S. E. 7/22
Hirsch, Phil 8/18
Hirschi, Ron 5/18
Hiscock, Bruce 12/4
Hoban, Lillian 5/18
Hoban, Russell 2/4; 39
Hoban, Tanya 5/8
Hobbs, Will 8/22
Hoberman, Mary Ann 8/12; 35
Hodges, Margaret 7/26; 73, 192, 199
Hoff, Syd 9/4; 7
Hoffman, Mary 4/20
Hogrogian, Nonny 5/7
Holabird, Katherine 1/23
Holbrook, Sara 9/15; 165
Holland, Isabelle 6/16
Holman, Felice 10/24
Holmes, Sherlock 1/6; 3, 5, 42, 66
Holt, Kimberly Willis 9/9
Hopkins, Lee Bennett 4/26; 67, 142
Hopkinson, Deborah, 4
Horvath, Polly 1/30
Houston, Gloria 11/24
Howe, James 8/2; 32
Howe, Julia Ward, 31
Hoyle, Edmond, 177
Huck, Charlotte, 193
Hughes, Langston 2/1; 78, 96, 107, 119
Hughes, Ted, 96
Hunter, Mollie 6/30
Hurd, Clement 1/12; 46
Hurd, Edith Thacher, 7, 46
Hurd, Thacher 3/6
Hurwitz, Johanna 10/9
Hutchins, Hazel 8/9
Hutchins, Pat, 101
Hyman, Trina Schart 4/8; 4, 68, 152, 193

Innocenti, Roberto, 47
Irvine, Joan 6/22; 32, 45
Irving, Washington, 4
Isaacs, Ann, 4
Issa, 264

Jacobs, Joseph 8/29
Jacobsen, Kathy, 144, 261
Jacques, Brian 6/15
Janeczko, Paul 7/25
Jarrell, Randall 5/6
Jeffers, Susan, 47, 64
Jefferson, Thomas, 10, 21, 29, 48, 61, 65, 71, 74, 85, 89, 93, 96, 98, 128, 148, 170, 196, 222, 246
Jenkins, Steve, 55, 126
Jenner, Barbara 6/26
Johnson, Angela 6/18
Johnson, Crockett 10/20; 26, 151, 225, 244
Johnson, D. B. 11/30; 58, 141
Johnson, James Weldon 6/17
Johnson, Samuel 9/18; 78, 105, 125, 193
Jonas, Ann 1/28; 215
Jones, Charlotte Foltz, 123

Jones, James Earl, 119
Jones, Mother, 91
Jones, Rebecca 9/10
Joosse, Barbara 2/18
Jordan, June 7/9
Joyce, William 12/11; 68, 263
Jukes, Mavis 5/3
Juster, Norton 6/2

Kane, Gail 4/6
Karr, Kathleen 4/21
Katz, Bobbi 5/1; 92
Keats, Ezra Jack 3/13; 42, 44
Keats, John, 44
Keillor, Garrison 8/7; 105
Keith, Harold 4/8
Keller, Charles 3/30
Keller, Helen, 43, 71
Keller, Laurie, 169
Kellogg, Steven 10/26; 66, 162, 167, 194, 199
Kelly, Walt 8/25
Kennedy, Dorothy 3/8
Kennedy, John F., 89, 224
Kennedy, X. J. 8/21; 39, 48, 255
Kent, Jack 3/10
Kerr, M. E. 5/27
Kessler, Leonard 10/28
Ketcham, Henry 3/14
Ketchum, Liza 6/17
Key, Francis Scott, 189
Kherdian, David 12/17; 6
Kidd, Ronald 4/29
Kimmel, Eric 10/30
King, Martin Luther Jr. 1/15; 176
King, Stephen 9/21; 140
Kingel, Dorothy 7/26
King-Smith, Dick 3/27
Kipfer, Barbara Ann, 11
Kipling, Rudyard 12/30; 15, 16, 29, 71, 88, 103, 133, 207, 223, 235, 242, 265
Kjelgaard, Jim 12/5
Kline, Suzy 8/27
Knight, Eric Mowbray 4/10; 187
Knight, Hilary 11/1
Koch, Mary, 59
Knowles, John 9/16
Koch, Kenneth 2/27
Konigsburg, E. L 2/10; 221
Korman, Gordon 10/23; 79
Kraus, Robert 6/21
Krauss, Ruth 7/25; 244
Krisher, Trudy 12/22
Kroll, Steven, 189
Krull, Kathleen 7/29
Krumgold, Joseph 4/9; 109
Kunin, Maxine, 255
Kurtz, Jane 4/17
Kurtzman, Harvey, 225
Kuskin, Karla 7/17

L'Engle, Madeleine 11/29
Lamorisse, Albert, 240
Landon, Lucinda 8/15; 66
Lang, Andrew 3/31; 235
Langton, Jane 12/30
Larson, Gary 8/14
Lasky, Kathryn 6/24; 189
Lauber, Patricia 2/5
Lavender, David, 268
Lawlor, Laurie, 43, 71, 199, 201
Lawson, Robert 10/4; 32
Lazarus, Emma 7/22; 225
Leaf, Munro 12/4; 187
Lear, Edward 5/12; 16, 37, 77, 79, 80, 94, 104
Lee, Harper 4/28; 265
Lee, Laura, 159
Leedy, Loreen, 169
LeGuin, Ursula K. 10/21
L'Engle, Madeleine 11/29; 9
Lenski, Lois 10/14
Lent, Blair 1/22
Lessac, Frane 6/18
Lesser, Rika 7/21
Lester, Helen 6/12
Lester, Julius 1/27; 128, 235
LeSuer, Meridel, 199
LeTord, Bijou, 129
Letterman, David, 225
Levine, Gail Carson 9/17
Levinson, Nancy Smiler 11/5

Levy, Elizabeth 4/4
Lewin, Betsy 5/12
Lewin, Ted 5/6; 100
Lewis, C. S. 11/29; 7, 61, 89, 185, 246, 255
Lewis, E. B., 80
Lewis, Patrick J. 5/5; 93, 136
Lexau, Joan 3/9
Lincoln, Abraham 2/12; 3, 77, 108, 125, 201, 211, 213, 237, 250, 268
Lindgren, Astrid 11/14
Lindsay, Vachel 11/10; 199
Lionni, Leo 5/5
Lipsyte, Robert 1/16
Lisle, Janet Taylor 2/13
Little, Jean 1/2
Little, Mr. Stuart, 187
Livingston, Myra Cohn 8/17
Lobel, Anita 6/3; 68, 131, 170, 193
Lobel, Arnold 5/22; 68, 128, 170
Lofting, Hugh 1/14; 99
London, Jack 1/12; 249
London, Jonathan, 65
Longfellow, Henry Wadsworth 2/27; 14, 80, 81, 230, 239
Lord, Betty Bao 11/3
Loredo, Elizabeth, 59
Lorenzini, Carlo. See Carlo Collodi
Louie, Ai-Ling 7/18
Love, J. L., 241
Lovelace, Maud Hart, 29
Lowry, Lois 3/20; 133, 199
Luenn, Nancy 12/28
Luttrell, Ida 4/18
Lynch, Christopher 7/2
Lyon, George Ellen 4/25
Lyon, Mary 2/28

Macaulay, David 12/2; 60, 91, 250
MacDonald, George 12/10; 97, 232
MacDonald, Suse 3/4
MacLachlan, Patricia 3/3; 29, 30, 134
Madonna, 119
Maestro, Betsy 1/5; 95 , 169
Maestro, Giulio 5/6; 3, 169
Mahy, Margaret 3/21
Major, Kevin 9/12
Malcolm X, 107
Manes, Stephen 1/8
Marcus, Leonard, 58
Mark, Patricia, 20
Marquis, Don, 245
Marshak, Samuel, 6
Marshall, James 10/10; 16, 17, 18, 32, 97, 180
Martin, Ann M. 8/12; 238
Martin, Jacqueline Briggs 4/15; 5, 10
Martin, Rafe 1/22; 256
Marzollo, Jean 6/24
Masefield, John 6/1
Mathers, Petra 261
Mathis, Sharon Bell 2/26
Matisse, Henri, 129
Mayer, Mercer 12/30
Mayne, William 3/16
Mazer, Norma Fox 5/15
McAllister, Angela, 61
McClintock, Barbara 5/6
McCloskey, Robert 9/15; 70, 155, 206
McCord, David 11/15; 253
McCormick, Dell, 194
McCourt, Frank, 21
McCullers, Carson 2/19; 118, 185
McCully, Emily Arnold 7/1; 135
McCurdy, Michael 2/17; 108, 156, 167, 249
McDermott, Gerald 1/31; 28, 136
McDonald, Joyce 8/4
McDonnell, Christine 7/3
McKinley, Robin 11/16; 255
McKissack, Patricia 8/9; 116, 141
McMillan, Bruce, 120
McMullen, Katy Hall. See Katy Hall
McPhail, David 6/30
Meaker, Mary Jane. See M. E. Kerr
Meddaugh, Susan 10/4; 266
Mehta, Ved, 2
Meltzer, Milton 5/8; 141, 181
Melville, Herman 8/1; 233, 265
Merriam, Eve 7/19
Messick, Dale, 127
Michaelson, Richard, 166
Mikolaycak, Charles 1/26

Miles, Betty 5/16; 54
Miles, Miska 11/14
Millay, Edna St. Vincent 2/22
Miller, William, 181
Mills, Claudia 8/21
Milne, A. A. 1/18; 197, 212, 223, 228, 266
Mistral, Gabriela 4/7
Mohr, Nicholasa 11/1
Monet, Claude Oscar 11/14; 129
Montagu, John, 159
Montgomery, Sy, 87
Moore, Clement 7/15; 183, 265
Moore, Lilian, 53
Moore, Marianne, 145
Mooser, Stephen 7/4
Mora, Pat, 66
Morey, Shaun, 161
Morey, Walter 2/3
Morris, Judy 8/2
Morrison, Toni 2/18; 30
Moser, Barry 10/15; 42, 125, 177
Moses, Anna Mary Robertson 9/7; 7, 104
Moss, Marissa 9/29
Most, Bernard 9/2; 32, 249
Mouse, Mickey, 194
Mowat, Farley 5/12; 249
Muir, John, 131
Mullens, Edward Swift 2/25
Munro, Roxie 9/5; 60
Munsch. Robert 6/11
Munsinger, Lynn 12/24
Murphy, Jim 9/25; 98
Murray, James 2/7; 52
Musgrove, Margaret 11/19
Myers, Bernice, 192
Myers, Christopher, 112
Myers, Walter Dean 8/12; 107

Narahashi, Keiko 1/20
Nash, Ogden 8/19; 10, 169
Naylor, Phyllis Reynolds 1/4; 30
Neeson, Liam, 68
Nelson, Theresa 8/15
Nerlove, Miriam 7/24
Ness, Evaline 4/24; 89, 129
Neville, Emily Cheney 12/28
Newbery, John 7/19
Newman, Alfred E., 225
Newsome, Effie Lee 1/19
Newton, James 12/22
Nicholson, Nicholas B. A., 84
Nikola, Lisa W., 104
Nixon, Joan Lowery 2/3
Nordstrom, Ursula 2/1; 183, 200, 225, 237, 258, 259, 260, 264
North, Sterling 11/4
Norton, Mary 12/10; 9
Numeroff, Laura Joffe 7/14; 4
Nye, Naomi Shihab 3/12; 157

Oates, Joyce Carol, 18
O'Brien, Robert C. See Robert Leslie Conly
O'Connor, Flannery 3/25; 56, 58, 79, 113
O'Dell, Scott 5/23
Oneal, Zibby 3/17; 104, 183
O'Neill, Eugene 10/16
O'Neill, Mary LeDuc 2/16
Oram, Hiawyn 261
Osborne, Mary Pope 5/20; 167, 249
Oxenbury, Helen 6/2

Packard, Edward 2/16
Paley, Grace, 94
Parish, Peggy 7/14; 179
Park, Barbara 4/27; 32, 87
Parker, Nancy Winslow 10/18; 81, 105
Parker, Robert Andrew 5/14; 90
Parks, Rosa, 249
Parnall, Peter 5/23
Partridge, Eric 2/6
Pascal, Francine 5/13
Patent, Dorothy Hinshaw 4/30
Paterson, Katherine 10/31
Paulsen, Gary 5/17
Paz, Octavio, 170
Pearson, Gayle 7/12
Peary, Robert, 263
Peck, Richard 4/5; 111
Peck, Robert Newton 2/17

Peet, Bill 1/29
Pellowski, Michael 1/24
Pepys, Samuel 2/23; 1, 162
Perrault, Charles 1/12
Peterson, Roger Tory 8/28
Petry, Ann Lane 10/12
Pfeffer, Susan Beth 2/17
Phelps, Ethel Johnston 3/8
Phillips, Ammi 4/24
Phillips, Louis, 63, 166
Picasso, Pablo, 93
Pienkowski, Jan 8/8
Pike, Christopher, 79
Pilkey, Dav 3/4; 58, 98
Pinkney, Andrea, 133
Pinkney, J. Brian 8/28; 133
Pinkney, Jerry 12/22; 38, 133, 198, 235
Pinkwater, Daniel 11/15; 249
Pinsky, Robert 10/20; 99
Piper, Watty 9/15
Pitman, Sir Isaac 1/4; 170
Poe, Edgar Allan 1/19; 3, 116, 162, 194
Poinsett, Joel Roberts, 257
Polacco, Patricia 7/11; 49, 104, 165
Politi, Leo 11/21
Pollard, Penny, 15
Pomerantz, Charlotte 6/24
Pope, Alexander, 125
Porte, Barbara Ann 5/18; 253
Porter, Katherine Anne, 72, 193, 231
Porter, William Sydney Porter, 73
Potter, Harry, 43, 53, 140, 171, 195, 221
Potter, Helen Beatrix 7/28; 11, 14, 28, 36, 38, 114, 118, 180, 181, 198, 223
Prelutsky, Jack 9/8; 43, 67, 82, 87, 122
Primavera, Elise 5/19
Pringle, Laurence 11/26; 172
Prose, Francine 4/1
Provensen, Alice 8/14; 141, 263
Provensen, Martin 7/10
Pullman, Philip 10/19
Pyle, Howard 3/5; 184

Quackenbush, Robert 7/23; 78

Rackham, Arthur 9/19; 73, 184, 264, 270
Radley, Gail 5/21
Rand, Ted 12/27; 81
Ransome, Arthur 1/18
Ransome, James 9/25
Raskin, Ellen 3/13
Rathmann, Peggy 3/4; 139, 261
Rawlings, Marjorie Kinnan 8/8; 56, 192
Rawls, Wilson 9/24; 252
Reiss, Johanna 4/4
Remington, Frederick, 129, 207
Rexroth, Kenneth 12/22
Rey, A. and Margret 5/16 and 9/16; 61
Rhys, Jean 8/24
Rice, Eve, 218
Rice, James 2/10; 190
Riley, James Whitcomb 10/7; 40, 208
Rinaldi, Ann 8/27
Ringgold, Faith 10/8; 65, 133, 249
Ripley, LeRoy 12/26
Rivera, Diego, 30
Roberts, Willo Davis 5/29
Robertson, Keith 5/9
Rockwell, Anne 2/8; 116
Rockwell, Norman, 51, 60, 109, 116, 233
Rockwell, Thomas 3/13
Rockwood, Joyce 6/1
Rodgers, Mary, 7, 68
Roethke, Theodore 5/25
Roget, Peter Mark 1/18; 131, 239, 271
Roop, Connie and Peter 3/3
Roos, Stephen 2/9
Roosevelt, Franklin Delano, 84, 96
Roosevelt, Theodore, 4, 24, 160, 175
Rosen, Michael, 42, 235, 263
Rosenberry, Vera, 158
Rosenbloom, Joseph, 250
Rosenthal, Harold 3/11
Ross, Lilian, 205
Rossetti, Christina 12/5
Rosten, Leo 4/11
Rothman, Joel 4/6
Rounds, Glen 4/4; 194
Rowling, J. K., 53, 126, 140
Rubel, Nicole 4/29; 129
Rukeyser, Muriel 12/15

Russo, Marisabina 5/1
Ryder, Joanne 9/16; 226
Rylant, Cynthia 6/6; 252

Sabuda, Robert 3/8; 227
Sachar, Louis 3/20; 32, 133
Sachs, Marilyn 12/18
Saint-Exupery, Antoine de 6/29
Salinger, J. D. 1/1; 10, 56, 145
Salisbury, Graham 4/11
Salten, Felix 9/6; 124, 136
Sandberg, Carl 1/6; 22, 84
San Souci, Robert 10/10; 47, 146
Santayana, George, 48
Sarnoff, Jane 6/25
Saroyan, William 8/31; 56, 148
Saunders, Susan 4/14
Sax, Adolphe 11/6; 129
Say, Allen 8/28; 153
Scarry, Richard 6/5
Scarry, Richard Jr. (Huck) 1/21; 119
Schertle, Alice 4/7
Schindler, S. D., 199
Schnur, Steven 4/8
Schoenherr, John 7/5
Schoonmaker, Frances, 37
Schulz, Charles 11/26; 204
Schnur, Steven 4/8
Schwartz, Alvin 4/25; 2, 17, 126, 198, 222
Schwartz, Amy 4/2
Schwartz, David 11/29
Schwartzkopf, General Norman, 68
Scieszka, Jon 9/8; 28, 127, 128, 173, 261
Scott, Captain Robert F., 12, 16, 64, 84, 258
Scott, Sir Walter 8/15; 77, 110
Scruggs, Alfi, 59
Seabrooke, Brenda 5/23
Sebestyen, Ouida 2/13
Seeger, Pete, 144
Segar, E. C. 12/8
Seibold J. Otto, 226
Selden, George 5/14
Selkirk, Alexander, 22
Selsam, Millicent 5/30
Sendak, Maurice 6/10; 32, 56, 58, 68, 84, 85, 93, 94, 95, 98, 99, 135, 139, 145, 148, 171, 186, 194, 218, 229, 256
Service, Pamela 10/8
Service, Robert 1/16; 168
Seton, Ernest Thompson, 200
Seuss, Dr. 3/2; 29, 36, 56, 82, 110, 122, 126, 234, 240, 242, 250
Sewell, Anna 3/30; 103, 114, 186
Sewell, Marcia 11/5
Shackleton, Ernest, 258
Shakespeare, William 4/23; 116, 265
Shannon, David 10/5; 249
Shannon, George 2/14
Sharmat, Marjory Weinman 11/12
Shaw, George Bernard, 76, 214
Shelley, Mary Wollstonecraft 8/30; 49, 102
Shelley, Percy Bysshe, 49
Shepard, Ernest Howard, 11, 100, 114
Shepard, Mary Eleanor Jessie 12/25
Shephard, Esther 7/29; 267
Shortz, Will 8/26
Showers, Paul 4/12
Shulevitz, Uri 2/27
Sierra, Judy 6/8
Silverberg, Robert 1/15
Silverman, Erica, 47
Silverstein, Shel 9/25; 6, 28, 99
Simon, Seymour 8/9
Singer, Isaac Bashevis, 180
Singer, Marilyn 10/3; 186
Sis, Peter 5/11; 263
Sleator, William 2/13
Slobodkin, Louis 2/19
Small, David 2/12; 25, 184, 207
Smith, Betsy 7/29
Smith, Doris Buchanan 6/1
Smith, Janice Lee 5/12
Smith, Jos. A., 117
Smith, Lane 8/25; 43, 82, 127, 261, 263
Smith, Robert Kimmel 7/31
Snyder, Zilpha Keatley 5/11
Sobol, Donald 10/4
Soto, Gary 4/12
Sousa, John Philip 11/6

Speare, Elizabeth George   11/21
Sperry, Armstrong   11/7
Spier, Peter   6/6; 189
Spinelli, Eileen   8/16
Spinelli, Jerry   2/1; 167
Spires, Elizabeth   5/28; 255
Spival, Dawnine, 180, 264
Spooner, William Archibold   7/22
Spyri, Johanna   7/12; 136
Stafford, William, 255
Stanley, Diane   12/27
Stanley, Jerry   7/18
Stanton, Elizabeth Cady   11/12
Staples, Suzanne Fisher   8/27
Steger, Will, 157
Steig, William   11/14; 139, 241, 265
Steinbeck, John   2/27
Steiner, Joan, 255
Steptoe, John   9/14; 138, 189
Stevens, James, 249
Stevens, Janet   1/17
Stevens, Wallace   10/2
Stevenson, James   7/11; 67, 96
Stevenson, Robert Louis   11/13; 29, 74,
    98, 121, 124, 128, 130, 137, 172,
    189, 223, 265
Stewart, Sarah, 30, 68, 184
Still, William, 60
Stine, R. L.   10/8; 13
Stockton, Frank   4/5
Stoker, Bram   11/8
Stolz, Mary   3/24
Stone, Lucy   8/13
Stout, Rex, 56
Stoutenburg, Adrien Pearl   12/1
Stowe, Harriet Beecher, 203
Strasser, Todd   5/5
Stratemeyer, Edward   10/4
Streatfield, Noel   12/25
Sullivan, Anne, 43, 71
Sullivan, George, 81, 165
Sutcliff, Rosemary, 125
Sweeney, Joan, 129, 232
Swift, Jonathan   11/30
Swift, Tom, 201

Taback, Simms   2/13
Tafuri, Nancy   11/14
Talbott, Hudson, 70
Tammaro, Thom, 255
Tan, Amy   2/19
Tarcov, Edith, 37
Tate, Eleanora   4/16; 79

Taylor, Mildred D.   9/13; 30
Taylor, Theodore   6/23
Teague, Mark, 67, 68
Tenniel, Sir John   2/28; 18, 126
Terban, Marvin   4/28; 95
Terhune, Albert Payson   12/21
Thaler, Mike, 32
Thayer, Ernest Lawrence   8/14
Thomas, Dylan, 145
Thomas, Robert Bailey   4/24
Thompson, Colin   10/18
Thompson, Kay   11/9; 201, 202, 257
Thoreau, Henry David   7/12; 3, 35, 36,
    46, 47, 48, 58, 96, 108, 110, 131,
    137, 141, 150, 154, 173, 178, 179,
    183, 203, 218, 222
Thurber, James   12/8; 5, 29, 34, 35, 43,
    103, 104
Tolkien, J. R. R.   1/3; 57, 71, 89, 102,
    120, 171, 205, 235, 255
Tolstoi, Leo, 56, 150
Toscanini, Arturo, 38
Travers, P. L., 267
Trimble, Stephen, 223
Tripp, Wallace   6/26; 165
Truman, Margaret, 66
Trump, Fred, 213
Truth, Sojourner, 116
Tucker, Tom, 65
Tudor, Tasha   8/28; 87
Tunis, Edward   12/7
Tunis, John Robert   12/7
Turner, Ann   12/10
Tuttle, Merlin   8/24
Twain, Mark   11/30; 10, 23, 42, 54, 55,
    73, 75, 79, 80, 96, 97, 112, 118, 121,
    134, 136, 201, 222
Tyler, Anne   10/25

Uchida, Yoshika   11/24
Updike, John   3/18; 68, 103

Vail, Rachel   7/25; 261
Valenta, Barbara, 45
Van Allsburg, Chris   6/18; 65, 142, 186
Van Draanen, Wendelwin, 214
Van Gogh, Vincent, 36, 46, 54, 55, 65,
    83, 102, 218
Van Laan, Nancy   11/18
Van Leeuwen, Jean   12/26
Velde, Vivian Vande, 252
Vermeer, Jan, 142
Verne, Jules   2/8; 60

Vidal, Gore, 103
Viorst, Judith   2/2
Virgil   10/15
Voigt, Cynthia   2/25
Vonnegut, Kurt   11/11; 56
Vuong, Lynette   6/20

Waber, Bernard   9/27; 200
Wadsworth, Wallace   9/19
Wahl, Jan   4/1
Waldman, Neil   10/22
Walsh, Jill Paton   4/29
Walter, Mildred Pitts   9/9
Walton, Izaak   8/9
Walton, Rick   2/12
Ward, Helen, 24
Ward, Lynd   6/26
Warner, Gertrude Chandler, 66, 78,
    109
Washington, George, 69, 123, 207, 244,
    251, 267
Washington, Martha, 252
Watson, Clyde   7/25; 139
Watson, Wendy   7/7; 151
Wattenberg, Jane, 121
Weber, Bob Jr.   1/21
Webster, Noah   10/16; 14, 77, 107, 208,
    250
Wegman, William   12/2; 250
Weiss, Nicki   1/25
Wells, Rosemary   1/29; 89, 105, 187
Welty, Eudora, 103, 210, 220
Wheatley, Phillis   12/5
Whelan, Grace   11/23
White, E. B.   7/11; 4, 5, 28, 34, 55, 56,
    64, 79, 81, 135, 139, 141, 184, 187,
    196, 197, 209, 210, 237, 244, 253
White, T. H.   5/29; 29, 192
Whitman, Walt   5/31; 40, 92, 103
Whittier, John Greenleaf   12/17
Wiesner, David   2/5
Wiggins, Kate Douglas, 83
Wilbur, Richard   3/1; 18, 226, 247
Wilde, Oscar   10/16; 29, 150, 213
Wilder, Laura Ingalls   2/7; 78, 93, 237
Wildsmith, Brian   1/22
Willard, Nancy   6/26; 54
Williams, Garth   4/16; 87, 244
Williams, Jay   5/31
Williams, Margery   7/22
Williams,
    Roshandiatellyneshiaunneveshenk
    Koyaanfsquatsiuty, 187

Williams, Suzanne, 66
Williams, Tennessee   3/26
Williams, Vera   1/28; 69, 85, 121, 203,
    217
Williams, William Carlos   9/17
Wise, William   7/21; 61, 67
Wiseman, Bernard   8/26
Wisniewski, David   3/21; 10
Withers, Carl   3/20
Wodehouse, P. G., 104, 109
Wojciechowska, Maia   8/7
Wolfe, Tom   3/2
Wolff, Ashley   1/26
Wolfson, Evelyn   4/24
Wolkstein, Diane   11/11; 119
Wood, Audrey and Don, 240, 249
Woodson, Jacqueline   2/12
Woolf, Virginia   1/25
Worth, Valerie   10/29
Wright, Betty Ren   6/15
Wright, Richard   9/4; 40
Wrightson, Patrice   6/21
Wulffson, Don, 65
Wyeth, Jamie   7/6
Wyeth, N. C.   10/22; 137, 152, 184,
    192, 217, 245
Wyeth, Sharon Dennis   4/19; 260
Wynne, Arthur, 272

Yashima, Taro   9/21
Yates, Elizabeth   12/6
Yep, Laurence   6/14, 191, 226
Yolen, Jane   2/11; 33, 42, 138, 146, 174,
    224
Yorinks, Arthur   8/21; 145, 192, 263
Young, Ed   11/28; 7, 15, 124, 203, 245,
    249
Young, Karen Romano, 77
Younger, Barbara, 150

Zamenhof, L. L.   12/15
Zelinsky, Paul   2/14; 148, 218
Zemach, Harve   12/5
Zemach, Margot   11/30; 121, 141,
    247
Zemser, Amy Bronwen, 261
Zenger, Peter, 235
Zindel, Paul   5/15
Zion, Gene   10/5
Zolotow, Charlotte   6/26; 103